From the foreword

'In *Leadership Unplugged* Jacqueline Moore and Steven Sonsino have dedicated themselves to exploring how and why conversations are a foundation of great leadership. They zero in on leadership communications through two-way conversations and their direct impact on organizational strategy. They emphasize the importance of *uncomfortable* conversations and offer readers a thoughtful framework linking debate, discussions, and dialogues together so that managers can understand the complete lifecycle of leadership communications.'

Jay A. Conger, *Professor of Organizational Behaviour,*
London Business School

'There are many reasons for 3M's hundred years of progress. But the primary reason for 3M's success is the people of 3M. This company has been blessed with generations of imaginative, industrious employees in all parts of the enterprise, all around the world. It's an unshakeable belief in encouraging experiments and discovery that has fostered the innovative products and technologies for which 3M is known. Also, we listen carefully to our customers – commercial partners and consumers – then work hard to develop products that satisfy their needs. Helping customers find solutions is a strong part of our culture. In *Leadership Unplugged*, Jacqueline Moore and Steven Sonsino have bottled the spirit of innovation and defined an innovative way of leading that is breathtakingly simple. From their detailed knowledge of the way communication works at every level – between people and between organizations – they have analysed for us and defined ways of communicating that executives around the world can benefit from. We especially urge men and women from the world's most complex industries to read this book, to take the risks it proposes and to try new ideas. There should be no boundaries to the imagination and no barriers to cooperation where leadership is concerned.'

Kay Grenz, *Vice President for Human Resource, 3M, St Paul*

'*Leadership Unplugged* is shedding the amplifiers, the one-way wall of sound, the light show, and the special effects, to get to the essence of leadership as the acoustics of managing. It will challenge your beliefs about powerful management, because it makes the persuasive case that leadership is by conversations that establish values, meaning and direction. Communication skills, both listening and using compelling language, are underrated or ignored in most explications of leadership. Moore and Sonsino blend actual experience, academic research, and case studies to show how effective leaders use debate and discourse to influence change in their organizations.'

Thomas A. Pugel, *New York University*

'With this book Jacqueline Moore and Steven Sonsino support the view that leadership is theatre and that effective leaders are scriptwriters and editors, theatre stars, producers and directors who change discourse and model the discourse they want repeated and realized in the daily actions of others. From the idea of the new renaissance of value propositions we can see how we might experience the ethics of a leader through their performative theatre. This is Moore and Sonsino's move from the performance of monologues to the performance of dialogue and the importance of what they call listening furiously.'

David M. Boje, *Professor of Management, New Mexico State University*

Leadership Unplugged

The New Renaissance
of Value Propositions

Jacqueline Moore

and

Steven Sonsino

First published 2003 by
PALGRAVE MACMILLAN
Houndmills, Basingstoke, Hampshire RG21 6XS and
175 Fifth Avenue, New York, N.Y. 10010
Companies and representatives throughout the world

PALGRAVE MACMILLAN is the global academic imprint of the Palgrave Macmillan division of St. Martin's Press, LLC and of Palgrave Macmillan Ltd. Macmillan® is a registered trademark in the United States, United Kingdom and other countries. Palgrave is a registered trademark in the European Union and other countries.

ISBN 1–4039–0381–6 hardback

This book is printed on paper suitable for recycling and made from fully managed and sustained forest sources.

A catalogue record for this book is available from the British Library.

A catalog record for this book is available from the Library of Congress.

Editing and origination by
Curran Publishing Services, Norwich

10 9   8   7   6   5   4   3   2   1
12 11 10 09 08 07 06 05 04 03

Printed and bound in Great Britain by
Creative Print & Design (Wales), Ebbw Vale

For our children - Christopher, Amelia and Michael

In reality, does dialogue exist, ever? Or is the contrary the case – that what we think is dialogue never actually goes beyond parallel or overlapping monologues? Monologues between countries, social classes, races, multiple monologues in the home or in school, conjugal monologues, sexual monologues, all the possible forms of interpersonal monologue – how often do they attain the supreme status of genuine dialogue? Could it be that we merely speak and cease speaking, intermittently, rather than speaking and listening?

Augusto Boal, 1998. *Legislative Theatre*. London: Routledge, p. 4.

CONTENTS

LIST OF FIGURES

LIST OF TABLES

Having studied leadership for two decades, I have developed a deep appreciation for language skills as one of the essential dimensions of effective leaders. The phrase 'the limits on our words are the limits on our influence' captures the criticality of language if one wishes to lead. On the other hand, the image of leaders as great orators – individuals whose words and emotions powerfully stir us to action – reflects only a small portion of the job. Much of the influence of a leader is exercised in the form of daily conversations rather than speeches upon a platform. While these conversations have many aims – to discern reality, to give feedback, to encourage change – they are all dialogues with the leader's constituents. They are dialogues in the spirit of the ancient Greek meaning of the term – 'the truth' (*logue*) is 'between us' (*dia*). While leadership researchers have emphasized personal qualities such as vision, role modeling and values, few have examined this dimension of language and conversation. One unfortunate by-product of this is that managers and executives rarely pay attention to how they lead through language. As a result, they pay a high price when they fail to understand the power of language and communications – initiatives are misdirected, resistance forms, the wrong problems are tackled, strategies derail. Fortunately, however, help has arrived.

Five years of research into and study of the application and implementation of strategic conversations by leaders has produced *Leadership Unplugged*. The authors, Jacqueline Moore and Steven Sonsino, have dedicated themselves to exploring how and why conversations are a foundation of great leadership. They zero in on leadership communications through two-way conversations and their direct impact on organizational strategy. They emphasize the *un*comfortable conversations, knowing that leaders grasp a fundamental reality – no one really wants to change when they are feeling comfortable. It is therefore critical to engage people around the uncomfortable. That said, this must be done in a way that engages rather than dis-engages them. More often than not, however, conversations around the uncomfortable result in colleagues turning a deaf ear. In contrast, Moore and Sonsino explore how managers can create leadership conversations that bring others along, rather than pushing them away. In the process, they remind us that persuasion and influence are actually more about listening than telling. They offer readers a thoughtful framework linking debate, discussions and dialogues so that managers can understand the lifecycle of leadership communications. In addition, they explore the price that leaders pay when they don't listen, when conversations become confrontational debates and sets of arguments rather than true dialogues.

One of the most important aspects of the book is its focus on values. In the post-Enron, post-Marconi era, *Leadership Unplugged* brings us back to the critical importance of values-based leadership. Authors Jacqueline and Steven remind us as leaders that authenticity and sincerity must underpin all our communications. After all, authenticity is the foundation on which leaders base their credibility. It was Aristotle who said that those who persuaded could draw upon three dimensions, *logos*, *pathos* and *ethos*. Logos was a compelling rational set of arguments – a dimension that most managers today well understand. Pathos involved the emotions. With our growing interest in emotional intelligence and its links to leadership, we are just now coming to appreciate the significance of Aristotle's second element, pathos, in leading others. It was ethos (an ethical foundation), however, that Aristotle saw as most fundamental to persuasion, giving the speaker the strongest base from which to influence others. Given the times, managers must increasingly address this element of ethos in how they communicate. In other words, a manager's ethical stance is critical to their influence in a leadership role.

What is particularly refreshing about *Leadership Unplugged* is its detailed exploration of the language of leadership in extremely complex and turbulent times through the eyes of a new writing team. They are a husband and wife who were originally involved in training journalists before moving into the field of management and leadership development. Jacqueline is a *Financial Times* journalist and Steven is a researcher and tutor at the London Business School. It is a winning combination for a book on this topic. In closing, let me welcome you as a reader to a deeply engaging conversation about leadership and language. It is an experience well worth listening to. I believe you will find yourself becoming a much more effective leader along the way.

Jay A. Conger
Professor, London Business School
Author, *Winning 'Em Over* (Conger, 1998);
co-author, *Building Leaders* (Conger and Benjamin, 1998)

The New Renaissance of Value Propositions: The *Leadership Unplugged* Agenda

One day it occurred to a certain emperor that if he only knew the answers to three questions, he would never stray in any matter. What is the best time to do each thing? Who are the most important people to work with? What is the most important thing to do at all times? The emperor issued a decree throughout his kingdom announcing that whoever could answer the questions would receive a great reward. Many who read the decree made their way to the palace at once, each person with a different answer ...

Leo Tolstoy[1]

What is *Leadership Unplugged*? Who could benefit from exploring the methods and tools of *Leadership Unplugged*? And how do you 'do' *Leadership Unplugged*? Everyone we have met or interviewed in the course of writing this book has asked us these questions. They are important questions and ones that this whole book, as well as our teaching and consulting, sets out to answer. Here is a working definition.

Leadership Unplugged is a practical guide to the art and science of strategic conversation. It tells you clearly:

1. what should be on your leadership agenda
2. who should be in the conversation
3. and how to influence the people around you to bring the strategy to life.

We address our ideas around the *Leadership Unplugged* agenda in the early chapters of the book. But also, in a real sense, the book is part manifesto, part collage and part travelogue, as it describes the route we've taken through the leadership minefield and the artefacts we've picked up along the way. We make neither concessions nor apologies for the eclectic mix of ideas and tools in the book. This mirrors our broad interests in new leadership theories and has helped us reach a new level in our own thinking and our own consulting work with global corporations. The conclusions we reach at the end of the book, after some years of exploration, are related to the power of conversation, the use of questions and the value of listening to the people around us. In short, we believe that leadership is about an intense consideration of values, for us as individuals and for our organizations, made explicit through what we call strategic conversations. For too long our western corporations – and our business schools, incidentally – have continued to perpetrate a selfish way of managing, a selfish way of conducting business. We're reaping the rewards now, watching business after business fold and seeing senior executives on our television screens arrested by the FBI and investigated by the world's authorities.

Perhaps this way of conducting business can be traced back to Adam Smith, one of the founding fathers of modern-day economics, who said that if individuals look after themselves then the market will look after itself. But as researchers intimately tracking the way people relate together in the modern corporation, we have come to the conclusion that leadership is – or should be – more about other people, and not about ourselves. We invariably do better as people and as organizations if we focus our attention on our employees, our colleagues and (at the risk of sounding too New Age for comfort) our families. Extending this further, to the organizational level, leadership is principally about giving stakeholders what they need and want. More on this later in the book. This, of course, could be seen as a very old saw, and we imagine cynics saying there's nothing new here. Not so. The newness comes in seeing how and why we should lead in a different way. Like any developmental or learning experience that changes the way you see the world, *Leadership Unplugged* isn't about facts or content. It's about the process of leading.

It is these reflections on leading through an intimate consideration of personal and organizational values that prompt our sub-title *The New Renaissance of Value Propositions*. In essence we believe that we are seeing a return to the traditional values of leadership, touching one person at a time using a variety of existing and new skills. More on this at the end of the book as we synthesize both the philosophy and the practice of *Leadership Unplugged*.

Before we get much further, though, let's set to one side the question of what *Leadership Unplugged* is to reflect on another question. An equally significant query has driven us for many years: what is leadership itself? For without a clear picture of what leadership is, how can we know where *Leadership Unplugged* might take us?

It is astonishing that there is still life left in this question. Yet no one is really any nearer knowing what leadership is, even after thousands of years of scholarship and debate. Dozens of different definitions exist. Executives and MBA students the world over are exhorted to engage in this or that behaviour and to try a multitude of procedures or policies to achieve their vision, goals or strategy. And we try – executives and academics the world over certainly do try. We have constantly launched change programmes, re-engineering initiatives and new strategic directions. We want to turn ourselves, our people and our businesses into the most X, the most Y or the most Z corporations. We are ever eager to learn what will make us The Best. And while striving to be The Best, and encouraging others to be The Best, is to be applauded generally, in our experience it can sometimes be counterproductive.

It can be counterproductive when it's time to stop trying to be someone – or something, or some corporation – that we quite patently are not. We believe now is that time. Time to take stock of what we've learned from our own lifetime's experience. Time to set aside all the styles and traits and other bolt-on leadership extras we've been toying with for who knows how long. Time to focus on the realities of day-to-day business life. We need to be really clear about ourselves (who we are, what we stand for), our objectives (both personally and for the organization) and our relationships with those significant other individuals who make a real difference (both inside and outside the organization). In short, we believe that leadership itself is not necessarily something we do. It's something we become and are.

It's About Leading the Strategy Process

Most books on leadership recycle old theories of leadership and focus at a theoretical level about what leadership is, or whether leaders are born or made. *Leadership Unplugged* builds on new theories of leadership, more appropriate for our turbulent, uncertain present, but also tells you in a very practical way what to do and why. And the 'what' to do is actually more concerned with the *process* of leading change than executives normally expect. It's more concerned with the process of leading than many will *accept*, too. 'Isn't leadership about taking action?' some say. 'Isn't it about getting my people to do what I want? And don't I need rewards, punishments, if I can't make them do it by telling them?' Well, that is possible. But change delivered through coercion will never be long-lasting change. A strategy delivered by strangling freedom is not a sustainable strategy. No, as the song goes, 'It ain't what you do, it's the way that you do it.'

And we believe that the 'it' is conversation, because research tells us that the work of managers is all talk. (More on this in Chapter 1.) That being so, we need to know how to talk effectively and – more importantly

– to remember how to listen. So this book focuses on the complex processes of leadership communications and offers an important simplification: *Leadership Unplugged* is about debate, discourse and dialogue.

It sounds simple, but we still find clients struggling to balance the technical frameworks and knowledge of their functional roles with the mastery of interpersonal communications skills. In *Leadership Unplugged*, then, it's no surprise that we talk about letting go of the complex, bolt-on extras of business life and focus on the basics of everyday business conversation. You cannot, we believe, control an abstract concept of organizational strategy that's out there, somewhere in the future. The only thing you can control – or rather have any influence over – is the conversation you happen to be in at the moment. So *Leadership Unplugged* is fundamentally about influence. But it is not about getting people to do what you want. And this is the paradox at the heart of the book.

The Paradox of Leadership Control

Our journey – to bring you this framework of *Leadership Unplugged* – has confirmed for us that executives don't find it easy to let go of the idea of control. 'Well, I'm in charge, I carry the can, so don't I have the responsibility to tell everyone what to do and how?' And yet those executives who are able to delegate and are able to let go paradoxically have greater control than they dreamed, especially over the process of managing and leading. (We call this the paradox of control and it's definitely a place where less is more. More on this in Chapter 5.) What we are definitely *not* saying, however, is that managers and executives should abdicate responsibility – for themselves, for their teams or for their organizations. We are suggesting that through a different focus – on the art and science of strategic conversation – there may still be something special, something we still haven't figured out, about leadership. We hope you'll join us in this book to explore the issues and context for our interpretation of leadership behaviour. We believe that *Leadership Unplugged* isn't that complicated. We look forward to joining you in the conversation.

Who Is *Leadership Unplugged* For?

The purpose of *Leadership Unplugged* is to broaden readers' understanding of the interpersonal nature of leading change, of the personal challenges involved in leading change, and of how to develop the personal capability to deal with these challenges. Currently, research on strategic leadership is conducted at many levels, although much of the leadership research actually focuses only on an individual executive – often a chief executive officer (CEO) or business unit head. Strategic leadership can also be considered, though, at the group level, usually focusing on the small group of (say) three to ten top executives known as the top management team: in other words the CEO and those executives who report directly to him or her.

The book aims, therefore, to expose readers in these senior executive positions to a range of interpersonal tools and techniques for leading effective change and implementing strategy. Not only will this be useful in supporting the management of change in organizations. It will also prepare leaders for more effective process roles – the roles increasingly called for by governments and researchers around the world – in their organizations. In addition, the book will be of real practical value to managers and executives with substantial responsibility – for a product line or business unit, for example – but who perhaps feel they haven't been able to achieve their full potential in implementing business strategy. This book explains the thinking and theories behind the practical leadership we need to bring to bear. Of course, the book will also be useful for students on MBA and other Masters-level programmes intending to pursue careers in business, notably in consultancy. And finally, the book acts as a course text and *aide memoire* for our *Leadership Unplugged* workshops.

The *Leadership Unplugged* Style

The book uses a range of devices in support of each chapter, including mini-case studies and QuestionBanks, or short checklists designed to provoke action conversations within the organization. Perhaps the most important aspect of the book is our intention to provoke readers, through the constant use of questions, to get feedback on how they lead. This is crucial if communication by action conversations is to create the backbone of day-to-day business life, for consultants, managers and leaders.

Cases in *Leadership Unplugged*

The intimate and sensitive nature of our research over the past five years means that we can't always reveal the sources of our information or ideas. But a number of key organisations we've worked with demonstrate many of the aspects of *Leadership Unplugged* and where possible, we've included these in the book as mini-cases at appropriate points. Examples and anecdotes in the text either come from our own interviews with executives or from the research literature, and you'll find these references either in the chapter endnotes or in the References section at the back of the book.

How To Use This Book

This book unravels in a definite sequence to help you appreciate the sweep of the *Leadership Unplugged* approach. However, elements can be taken out of sequence if you have a particular interest in assertiveness, say, and dealing with toxic co-workers (Chapter 9). Maybe feedback you've received suggests you need to listen more, or you're not sure how to raise those uncomfortable subjects with your peers? Try Chapter 11. So feel free to dip in and out and explore the issues the text raises, but do challenge us on the structure, or the issues. We welcome your feedback.

What follows is a chapter-by-chapter account of the book to help you structure your reading.

If you want to understand the business case for adopting and supporting this leadership approach read Chapter 1, 'What is *Leadership Unplugged*?'

To understand the key frameworks underpinning the book, how they fit together and how you can use them, read Chapter 2, 'Debate, Discussion and Dialogue.'

To explore methods of communicating your strategic vision, at both the personal and organizational levels, read Chapters 3 and 4 in the 'Debate' section.

The following chapters are in Part II, on discourse or discussion.

Read Chapter 5 if you want to explore methods of improving your personal dealings in organizational politics. Go straight to Chapter 6 to learn about and appreciate the real complexity of organizational life today

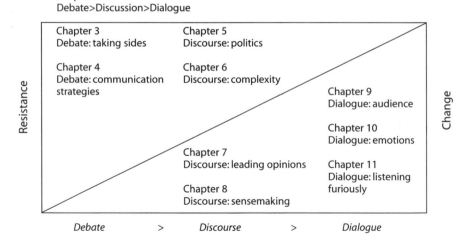

Figure 1 Structure of the book mapped against the *Leadership Unplugged* continuum which we cover in Chapter 2

– this should help reduce any anxieties you have about adopting the *Leadership Unplugged* approach. More information on the paradox of control is also available here.

To find out about effective methods of influencing opinion in written documents and in presentations read Chapter 7, 'Leading Opinions', and to add mechanisms to your repertoire for helping people to make sense of these turbulent and uncertain times, read Chapter 8, on sensemaking and sensegiving.

The final section, Part III, deals with dialogue.

Chapter 9 will help you to connect with your various audiences and begin to understand how leadership can be a performance art without being false or manipulative in any sense. Chapter 10, on the other hand, gives you some practical tips on managing or dealing with emotions – both yours and others' – in the workplace. In Chapter 11, we help you explore the crux of the *Leadership Unplugged* approach and help you get to grips with possibly the most useful tool in the whole book, *listening furiously*.

The final chapter attempts to redefine leadership behaviour in terms of what we've learned over the years about *Leadership Unplugged*, which by this stage you will appreciate is a simplification of our day-to-day business role into its key elements of debate, discourse and dialogue. Understanding and playing an effective role in the ebb and flow of strategic conversations is a strategy few senior executives knowingly engage in. They should.

Thank yous

Many of our colleagues – both wittingly and unwittingly – have been involved in our conversations for *Leadership Unplugged*, both at the *Financial Times* and at London Business School. These conversations have invariably helped shape our thinking over many months. Jacqueline Moore would especially like to thank Diane Summers, Managing Editor at the *Financial Times*, and Steven Sonsino would like to thank Ian Hardie, Associate Dean of London Business School, and Guy Saunders, Director of Open Programmes. Also, Steven would like to thank Professors Jay Conger and Rob Goffee at London Business School, who gave their valuable time to discuss key facets of the work. To Jay Conger go our very special thanks for writing the Foreword. Philippa Morrison, Director of Professional Development at London Business School, also deserves our thanks. She has inspired us to explore the philosophy of living in real-time in organizations and has challenged our thinking on more than one occasion. We'd like to thank Professor Christine Kelly, Director of the International Teachers Programme 1999–2001 and formerly Chair of the Management Communications Department at the Leonard N. Stern School of Business, New York University, for her support and unflinching belief in dialogue. As well, Christine inspires us to remember that significant but all-too-often forgotten arena of communications, leadership and performance.

Our material and teaching on organizational life as drama is very new, and certainly the idea of the organizational leader as director of the drama has not been developed as widely as it could have been. But this is still a work in progress, so we owe some thanks to the people who have motivated us here. Our thinking has been driven by working all too briefly with the Actor's Institute in New York – we hope this relationship will continue – and with Richard Olivier of the Globe Theatre in London, whose work on *Henry V* and inspirational leadership is now more widely available. We must also thank Yvonne Gilan at London Business School for allowing us to explore her exciting work teaching leadership as performance at the senior executive level.

The following were especially helpful and generous with their time and insights: Gifford Booth at the Actor's Institute in New York; Julian Garrett at BT Ignite Solutions in London; and Hetty Pye and Keith McCambridge at Whitehead Mann in London.

We must also acknowledge the following:

- Hugh Carnegy, Deputy Managing Editor, for allowing publication of *Financial Times* extracts illustrating the Daimler-Chrysler and Vivendi case studies (Chapter 1), together with Andrew Gowers, Editor of *Financial Times*; George Graham, Head of Lex, *Financial Times*; and Sarah Jezzard, Head of FT Reprints and Copyright Requests.
- Rod Sievers, Southern Illinois University Carbondale, for permission to feature the Carbondale Oxford debating case study (Chapter 3).
- The European Union, for its permission to draw on case research from across Europe undertaken by our friends Bethan Devonald and Richard Meads at Business Decisions Limited, Cardiff, UK.[2] The Fiat (Chapter 3) and the Fasson and Brabantia investigations (Chapter 6) took place on behalf of the European Commission DG Social Affairs.
- Catharine Guelbert, at the NHS Leadership Centre in the UK, for permission to reproduce the Leadership Qualities framework in the minicase on the work undertaken by the Hay Group which inspired the generation of the NHS's leadership competencies framework in 2003 (Chapter 6).
- Murray Steele, Head of the Strategic Management Group at Cranfield School of Management for permission to draw on the work we did on the Microsoft Business Barometer in 1999 and 2000 (Chapter 8).

- Ben Dunn, Emma Mitchell, Guy Millar and Stephen Barrow at HSBC in London for permission to highlight their early successes in Mexico (Chapter 4) and in knowledge management (Chapter 12).
- David Boje at New Mexico State University, Tom Pugel at New York University , Jeff Skinner at 3M in the UK and Kay Grenz at 3M in the US for sparing their precious time to read our material.

At Palgrave Macmillan, our publishers, we would like to thank Stephen Rutt, Publishing Director, for listening so thoughtfully to the *Leadership Unplugged* concept on perhaps its first airing outside the crucible of the classroom, and who – together with Palgrave's Jacqueline Kippenberger – must have wondered from time to time if there was going to be a manuscript at all. (Patience is a virtue.) Of course, our immense gratitude goes to Curran Publishing Services, and to copyeditor Trevor Ashwin, for helping us turn our concepts into the reality you now hold in your hands.

Most of all, however, we want to thank the many dozens of unsung interviewees, and the hundreds of participants in our workshops and consulting practice, who have helped us define and refine both the theory and the practical tools in *Leadership Unplugged*. Please tell us how you continue to fare.

Jacqueline Moore, *Financial Times*
and Steven Sonsino, London Business School
London, February 2003
www.leadershipunplugged.com

Notes

1. Tolstoy, Leo. *Three Questions*. Mankato, MN: Creative Education Incorporated.
2. Business Decisions Ltd, 1998. *New Forms of Work Organisation: Case Studies*. Brussels: European Commission DG Employment and Social Affairs.

CHAPTER 1

What is *Leadership Unplugged*?

'When one person is speaking on their own that is a monologue, they are doing a monologue. So then, what is dialogue?'

'I know, I know!', answered one of the patients eagerly ...

'It's when there are two people talking on their own.'

Augusto Boal[1]

Headlines

Leadership Unplugged is a practical guide to the art and science of strategic conversation. It tells you clearly:

1. what should be on your leadership agenda
2. who should be in on the conversation
3. and how to influence the people around you to bring your strategy to life.

Leadership Unplugged involves strategic conversations. These conversations tend to occur in a sequence of three phases: debate, discussion and dialogue.

Leadership Unplugged rests on three pillars: strategic leadership (long-term vision), people skills and communication skills.

The leader of a team or of an organization is the most important single agent for change, and leaders' interpersonal skills are therefore crucial.

Leading the change process is a key leadership role and should not be delegated to outside parties such as consultancies.

The *Leadership Unplugged* concepts are underpinned by existing academic research, while practitioner evidence makes a persuasive business case that the *Leadership Unplugged* skills urgently need to be shared with managers and leaders in business today.

Leadership Unplugged is the chief executive motivating the firm's employees to even greater achievements with a rousing speech at a product launch. It's the global bank bringing together specialists from around the world for the first time to talk about the challenges and opportunities of their work. And it's the organization introducing counselling and coaching so that members of the team can explore their job and career needs in confidence. These, and many more examples of the unplugged leadership style, are offered throughout this book. There are many examples because an unplugged revolution is taking place at the grassroots level. Individuals and groups of managers are beginning to understand and to implement certain aspects of *Leadership Unplugged*. Few organizations have a grasp of the big picture, however. No organization we've seen, in fact, has a strategy to develop the full potential of *Leadership Unplugged*. This is a mistake. For the first time, this book gathers together the tried and tested concepts of *Leadership Unplugged*, as well as an armoury of easy-to-use practical interpersonal tools.

So what is *Leadership Unplugged*? It is a practical guide to the art and science of strategic conversation. It tells you clearly:

1. what should be on your leadership agenda
2. who should be in on the conversation
3. and how to influence the people around you to bring your strategy to life.

We asked one workshop participant to sum up how we should describe this to potential participants. 'Listen up', he said. 'Your job just might depend on it.' We believe the speaker was saying that leadership isn't necessarily about the things we do – it's about the things we say. This means, in turn, that leadership is about something we *are* and something we *become*. It's about who we are as individuals and what we stand for. Understand these fundamental leadership issues in terms of understanding and influencing identity and the rest – deciding what to do on a daily basis – follows.

Is the Pen Mightier than the Sword?

Do you believe that actions speak louder than words? Or is the pen mightier than the sword for you? You need to be clear on this point. From our perspective, we do not believe that actions always speak louder than words. We believe that language – debate, discussion and dialogue – can be mightier than the sword. So in *Leadership Unplugged*, without apology, we take as our starting point that leadership, when all is said and done, is about what is said. Language, we believe, is the single most powerful tool at the disposal of executives today. We are unashamed extremists in advocating this view and we are prepared to suggest that language, in the form of real two-way conversation, is in fact the only leadership tool at our disposal. Building on this view, organizations can be seen as networks of conversations between countless stakeholders, and the role of the senior executive becomes that of a perpetual agenda setter, discussion leader and listener.

But we're getting ahead of ourselves. Let's take a step back.

Leadership is Conversation, Conversation is Leadership

Take any in-depth study of managerial behaviour from the past hundred years – from Fayol's planning, organizing, co-ordinating, commanding and controlling checklist, first published in 1916,[2] to John Kotter's exploration of what leaders really do[3] – and the essence of executive behaviour is quite clear. Our role as executives is composed of little more than talk. Most senior executives don't actually 'do' anything. No – senior managers *talk* for a living. The research shows that if you follow us around for a sustained period you will find that most of our time is spent in conversation with others. These people could be our peers, suppliers, subordinates or customers, depending on the issues of the day. So there's no getting away from the fact that we talk. The editor of a management magazine we know described the day he introduced a junior reporter to the staff. He showed her round the various departments, describing the work of the deputy editor, the features editor, the production editor, the news editor, the sub-editors, the other reporters. Then, when they had met and spoken with everyone, the editor asked, 'Is there anything else I can answer for you?' He beamed, pleased with his morning's work. The question that came may have been the most difficult the editor had ever faced. 'What do you do, then?' the new reporter asked. It had never occurred to the editor to articulate his role in leading the team.

'A Little Less Conversation, A Lot More Action'

What do people mean when they disparage someone as 'all talk and no action'? It usually means that he or she, in their view, engages in a good deal of unstructured or pointless conversation that goes round in ever-decreasing circles. Equally, it implies that nothing happens as a result of all the conversation; that there's little change, if any, in the status quo. The phrase represents more than an explosion of frustration, however – it's an extremely helpful indicator. If it were ever used of you, for instance, it could help you appreciate that you might need to reappraise and develop your business conversation skills. Some additional guidelines on debate and discussion skills, along the lines outlined in this book, might be particularly useful for you. More often than not, though, your audience wants you to *listen*. If you're described as 'all talk' then you can bet that your audience has a low opinion of your listening abilities. So your number one task is learn how to listen more effectively. Please don't take it personally when you're told this – very few people are explicitly taught how to talk, persuade or listen. Take it instead as extremely useful feedback, to which you can now respond with some action.

But what about the 'no action' element of the judgement? What does that tell us? Well, first it tells us that nothing actually happens as a result of engaging in conversation with you. This cuts both ways. It can mean that you don't do anything as a result of the conversation (which may sometimes be intentional), but it also tells us that your critic doesn't do anything either. This may be deliberate, too, but may not be what you hope for at all. You may have some work to do to get this person to commit themselves to doing something – clearly they don't feel any pressure to do anything at the moment. (This may well be a second reflection on your conversational prowess. How can we use conversation effectively to get people to do what we need done?)

Most of all, though, the phrase 'all talk and no action' tells us that the critics do not necessarily understand the role of business leaders. This is clear to us because we take the view that the role of business leaders, frankly, is nothing but talk. First, let's look at this from the action perspective. What is 'action', in the context of business managers and leaders? Is it making things? Is it building things? No. Action represents nothing more than reaching agreement that someone will undertake something in the future. Leadership action is 100 per cent focused on getting others to do things. This action may involve an informal conversation or a formal meeting; it may involve getting a signature on a contract, but that itself is nothing more than a highly formal agreement. No, the role of leadership is purely to engage in conversation and to reach a series of agreements with stakeholders, be they employees, suppliers, customers or governments. And because your critic thinks leadership is about 'action', part of your role has to be to educate them. Get them to think about what leadership is and what it is not. Ask them how they would judge an outstanding manager or leader. Most people describe leaders as motivational, inspirational, as good communicators. In other words, as people who get other people to do things.

To conclude, the criticism 'all talk and no action' tells us one thing only – that we as leaders need to become ever better at conversation. As part of the deal we must also become better at educating others, and helping them to realize exactly what leadership is. Leadership could be described as a place where talk *is* action.

Case 1. All Talk at Daimler-Chrysler – the power of conversation

In a 2002 conversation with a Financial Times journalist, Jürgen Schrempp of Daimler-Chrysler explained his recent actions as chairman of the management board. (Was this simply conversation or was it marketing?)

He had announced the formation of an automotive executive committee to make savings through component sharing (conversation or operations management?). 'The Automotive Committee was actually established to make all of the decisions involved in the integration of the company', he said. In describing how the committee works he explained how he used questions to drive the group.'You just put them up against a wall and make a few points. What does this group need? Where can we actually achieve savings? Do we need so many different transmissions, so many different diesel or gasoline engines?'

He moved on to talk about the financial performance of the business and relations with the financial markets (conversation or stakeholder management?):

> The only problem is people say, 'Okay, where is the evidence?' We will show the evidence as the years come. When I talk to financial markets more and more they believe us. In fact we have a situation where they say: 'Okay, fine, we give you the benefit for the right strategy. However, we still have doubts about whether you're able to implement it.' Let's show you how we can implement it.

He described the rejection of a takeover bid for Nissan (conversation or board membership?). 'We were sitting together as a management board in Geneva, 1999, and asked ourselves "Can we go through with it?"'

He also related his views on union involvement in management practices (conversation or industrial relations?):

> What we need is greater labour flexibility. … I find that some partners at union level understand it; it's just a matter of what can be done. I would wish for more labour flexibility, and all those sorts of things, but I wouldn't give co-determination a negative spin. … Everything gets extensively discussed [on the supervisory board] and once a decision is taken you have a good chance of implementing it quietly. … When you look now at the labour representative side [on the board], make no mistake – they have a very powerful position, and are very constructive in our company. We are often in disagreement but we find a solution because their heart is as much in the company as my heart is in the company.

On promoting the business internally (conversation or people management?):

At one of the roadshows I pointed out that every business unit within the company had at one stage or another been loss making. If I'd got rid of everything in a negative situation, I would sit here, but not representing a motor company! I feel very strongly that if you have a strategy you believe in then you should stick to it. Try to get the operations right, instead of changing the strategy.

On being a global statesman (conversation or corporate social responsibility?):

Nelson Mandela comes to me and says 'You can do me a favour', and he has a way of selling it to you – there are these school kids who have to walk over the mountains for two to three hours to come to a school, which is basically under a tree, where they get some information and then walk back for two or three hours. If he says 'Jürgen, I need a new school in the Transkei' then that's what you have to do, and I had the pleasure of actually leading them to the school after two years.

On international relations (conversation or troubleshooting?):

I see myself as a bit of a bridge-builder, because after all we are an American–German company and that's why I spend lots of time in Washington, I spend time in Brussels and obviously in Berlin to sort of say:'Okay, if you have a steel issue or other issue we have to come together and sit around the table and say, let's find a solution and use that.' Two or three years ago, I was the European chair of the Transatlantic Business Dialogue. This was created by the former trade secretary Ron Brown, and by Brussels, for that particular purpose. They said:'Okay, let businessmen come together. Let them make European–American proposals to the administration in Washington/Brussels as to what should actually be done to close the gap', and we have done a lot.

On morale (conversation or leadership?):

I have lived through many [difficult] issues and that's why I am pleased with the mood in the company. We did a survey a year ago, in Germany, of middle-management opinion on whether the strategy was right. It was a resounding success: more than 80 per cent said 'that's the right thing we do', and then there came the little questions. Do we have the money to do that? Do we have the people to do that? All useful questions.

Questions:
1. What work does Jürgen Schrempp actually do?
2. What actions does he take?
3. What kind of talk does he engage in and what does it achieve, if anything?

Extracts reproduced by permission of *Financial Times* Ltd.

Just as there is no doubt in our minds that leadership is about managers sustaining conversations with key stakeholders, there is no doubt in the minds of many others that the role of senior executives should be *action*-focused. It's about 'leading from the front', they say, 'getting the job done' or 'telling us what to do'. So where does the 'action' come in? Who actually gets the job done in organizations? We believe that the majority of statements, views, opinions and decisions of senior executives are transmitted, and translated into action, by the colleagues and peers of senior executives in other ranks of the organization. Senior executives 'do through others'. Others realize what we say as senior executives.

In *Richard II*, one of William Shakespeare's most riveting political dramas, Henry Bolingbroke has stolen the crown to become King Henry IV and has imprisoned his predecessor, Richard II. To pre-empt anyone rallying round the former king, he asks rhetorically: 'Have I no friend who will rid me of this living fear?' He knows full well, even though he is addressing no one in particular, that someone will hear it as a command and will indeed 'get rid' of Richard. While specific examples of this kind are somewhat out of the ordinary today, this kind of signalling is extremely common in our corridors of power. So, it really is true that senior executives 'do through others'. That being so, we need to become far better at clarifying our vision for the future, at leading opinions within the business and at finding out what others think – without the active support of our network, we as senior executives won't be able to achieve anything.

Of course, measuring and managing the performance of the people around us poses questions – about reward systems to motivate and 'incentivize' the workforce; about power tools to coerce reluctant participants. But that's simply another agenda, another set of conversations to hold.

As if using our network of conversations to deliver results isn't complex enough, there is an added complication. When what we say publicly differs from what we say or think privately – when our people share the impression that we say one thing and don't believe it, or don't 'practise what we preach' – can also be a dangerous time. And sadly, for most business leaders, the gap between the saying and the perceived 'doing' is a chasm. It's no surprise, then, that leadership rhetoric is often seen as a blatant attempt at manipulation and the language of leadership as nothing more than a charade: a sequence of soundbites from 'MTV-generation' leaders. The logical conclusion of this perceived manipulation is often the removal of senior executives by the board or by the shareholders themselves. Data on tenure – the length of time executives manage to hold on to their posts – has remained constant over 20 years. Surveys show that senior executives face a major hurdle about 18 months into their role – that's when the honeymoon period is over, and when bottom line financial returns need to be demonstrated.

Bottom Line Symptoms

The constant focus on the bottom line, to the exclusion of all other issues and performance metrics, is a real distraction to effective leadership within the firm. We believe that poor financial results by a unit or business are symptoms, and not the cause, of poor organizational performance, but too often firms forget this. Too often the numbers are not used in any meaningful way – in other words, to unpack what happened or what might have happened. Too often they are simply used as a mechanism for allocating blame, and subsequently as an excuse to remove the senior executives identified as 'carrying the can'. What happens next? A new manager starts all over again, applies his or her own success formula and – in 18 months' time – faces the same backlash. This must change.

In the opposite case – when the numbers are good, or even just OK – there's a feeling that may be summed up as 'why change a winning formula?' If customers are lining up round the block for your service, why improve it? This is surely another example of corporate blindness, but again one that we seem unable to shake. We must. There are too many examples of firms resting on their laurels and being overtaken by their competitors for us ever to stand still. It is better, perhaps, to keep debate, discussion and dialogue alive, and to maintain real clarity in the minds of all stakeholders about the future direction of the firm.

Case 2. Vivendi Universal – the penalty for losing stakeholder clarity [4]

Jean-Marie Messier's gamble to transform Vivendi Universal from a French water utility into a global media empire required a huge leap of faith on the part of investors. The vision was bold enough – to bring together the best content in the world with distribution across all main platforms, from TV to mobile phones. But it relied on one man's vision. Messier was self-styled director producer and lead actor of the of the Vivendi Universal blockbuster. He is not living up to his billing.

Two years after the acquisition of Seagram's entertainment business, there is scant evidence of synergies within the group. The strong set of the US entertainment assets centred around Universal sits uncomfortably enough with Canal Plus, the European pay TV group. But the logic of the 44 per cent stake in French telecoms group Cegetel looks particularly weak – especially as hopes of piping content through Vizzavi, its joint venture portal with Vodafone, have come to nothing.

Houghton Mifflin the educational publisher produces content, but of a very different nature to Universal's films and music. The 63 per cent stake in the vendor's original water utility is pure historical legacy. Moreover sewage makes a formidable poison pill.

Not only has Mr Messier's vision lost its allure since the media bubble burst. It no longer looks achievable. Vivendi is overburdened with debt, forcing it to rule out further deals it might attempt in order to complete the jigsaw it has started. The strategic problems and the debt load have contributed to the share price slump.

On top of that, a more personal 'Messier discount' has helped push Vivendi's market value down to more than a 30 per cent discount to the sum of its parts. Mr Messier has bought some decent assets, and has hit some financial targets. But too often his unpredictability has tested investor patience.

The latest plan to reduce Vivendi's stake in its utility subsidiary is a case in point. It would cut debt and helped focus Vivendi on media, yet it comes only a month after Mr Messier ruled out such plan. Coupled with Vivendi's poor financial transparency, investors struggle to understand what they are investing in, let alone what it will be in a year's time.

Vivendi is trading at a discount to its breakup evaluation. The company requires a clear strategy, new leadership, and in all probability radical surgery. Mr Messier created the empire. It will be hard to convince investors he is also the man to take it apart.

Reproduced by permission of *Financial Times* Ltd.

What is *Leadership Unplugged*?

Our views on the key skills and tasks of leadership are driven by our perspective on the nature of organizations, developed over a number of years of researching the related questions of leadership (what is it?) and the environmental context within which leaders work (where do they practise it?).

In *Leadership Unplugged* we argue for *authentic* leadership behaviour, where what senior executives do, or are perceived to do, rests squarely on what they say. We take as a given that organizations are not, as economists would have it, a nexus of contracts or treaties. Instead we see organizations as a nexus of conversations. It isn't possible, we believe, to control some abstract concept of a future strategy, somewhere 'out there'. The only thing we can control, or rather 'influence', is the conversation we happen to be in at the moment. This means that leaders had better be sure they are effective at engaging people in building 'action conversations' – conversations that jointly construct a way forward for all parties. This leads logically to the questions 'What is conversation?' and (equally logically) 'Can the act and art of conversation really be regarded as a strategic activity?' We believe *Leadership Unplugged* answers those questions and that conversation can and must be a strategic activity, engaged in consciously and sensitively by senior executives.

Leadership as Identity Work

Taking the 'nexus of conversations' view a stage further, *Leadership Unplugged* builds on the related concepts of leadership as the management of identity and leadership as the management of meaning. However, we take issue with the current prevailing concept of 'management', which to most people usually means 'control' or 'power over others'. We do not believe that people, let alone organizational identity, can be controlled. In today's chaotic and hyperturbulent business world, we believe the only thing executives can actually do is influence the status quo, or perhaps merely disturb it. Perhaps we cannot even affect the status quo: the way things happen round here. Perhaps the only thing we can influence or disturb is our sense of who we are – both as individuals and as an organization. And this raises a major paradox for most business executives. 'I'm in charge, but you're telling me I can't be in charge? What gives?'

In order to explore this paradox of leadership, *Leadership Unplugged* interweaves core ideas from strategic leadership, change management and complexity theory. We build an innovative argument for both improvised and routine senior executive behaviour around the key action conversations of debate, discourse (or discussion) and dialogue. Overall, the book is intended to explore the two key questions in the authentic leadership vision of *Leadership Unplugged*:

1. exactly who am I talking to?
2. and what exactly do they need from me?

We will use the *Unplugged Continuum*, a debate–discourse–dialogue model covered in the next chapter, as the book's key dynamic framework. We will also address the following three implicit themes repeatedly throughout the book:

- the leader as change agent
- the interpersonal skills of the leader
- and the implications of change processes for the work of leaders.

The Leader as Change Agent

We believe that board level senior executives cannot abdicate the responsibility for change to executives at lower levels in the organization. The responsibility to see change through to a successful conclusion belongs with the senior executive cohort. All too often, firms employ project managers or other toothless 'champions' to take change forward. Often organizations use consultants, but usually only as scapegoats if things don't go according to plan. We believe that senior executives need the emotional intelligence and 'change maturity' to deliver difficult, if not uncomfortable, messages about strategic change. And they need the political intelligence and influencing skills to be able to handle the gamut of experiences and emotions that their supporters, and their inevitable detractors, will experience.

The Interpersonal Skills of the Leader as Change Agent

In many ways the savvy business leader knows intuitively how to get things done through people. But most of us were never taught what makes people tick, or how to articulate a convincing argument – either on paper or in person. *Leadership Unplugged* begins that process by helping readers to understand how to build credibility, both as an expert in what you do and as an expert in how to do it. The book helps readers explore how to develop compelling arguments that matter to different stakeholder groups. And it helps readers to become increasingly aware of the impact and importance of emotion in leadership – what it means for us all, and how to use that knowledge wisely.

Leading the Change Process

How do we manage cultural change? Precisely how do we manage change transitions? Precisely how do you lead at the edge of chaos? There are many, many tools and frameworks for managing change processes. But the reality is that no one really knows how change works. Every project is utterly dependent on its own particular time and context. Worse, there is no unified change theory that we can draw on to support or bolster our own personal change projects. That being so, what can we learn from the highly structured strategic change frameworks and programmes that do exist? How can we use them effectively, efficiently and successfully? These are significant issues that we rarely understand intuitively, and rarely are we taught how to accomplish them.

Why Do We Need A New Theory of Leadership?

The Theoretical Reasoning

There is still a need for a theory of strategic leadership in complex organizations, because while leadership research has long taxed management researchers, the leadership theories that have been developed have focused largely on the personality characteristics of individual leaders. It doesn't help, either in our teaching or our consulting practice, to have to tell senior executives that 'it's down to your personality and we can't change that'. What makes the psychological leadership literature even more difficult to build on, for practitioners at least, is that many of the studies underpinning those theories tend to describe leadership personality in terms of simplistic, two-factor models. In other words, you're either a transactional or transformational leader, or you are charismatic or non-charismatic. This doesn't help executives improve their leadership skills.

While these 'either/or' theories – and the massive surveys of leadership competencies such as Robert House's GLOBE survey – provide many insights, in essence they oversimplify a complex phenomenon and contribute to stereotyping.[5] It's no surprise that many management commentators are cynical of leadership theories. This in turn reinforces the tired view of leader as superhero or as 'born and not made', both themes we've addressed elsewhere.[6]

One appealing explanation for our inability to define the competencies of leadership is the fact that they are intangible and tacit. In other words, leadership is the way we create, formulate and implement strategies, but exactly what people do and how they do it is unspoken. 'It's the way we do things round here.' This powerful explanation – that the organization's culture is somehow responsible for effective leadership within it – is supported by the 'core competence' or resource-based view of the firm. This valuable, if exasperating, theory leads to the suggestion that a firm's top management may well be one of those rare and difficult-to-imitate internal resources that leads to increased profitability. 'Now, if only we knew how they did it, maybe we could identify it or replicate it with other managers.' This is just one angle on the increasingly persuasive argument that the intellectual and social capital of firms – an organization's people and their interrelationships – are their most valuable asset. But of course this isn't necessarily something you can measure by checking your firm's stock rating.

A distinct strategic leadership literature has developed in parallel with what might be called the 'traditional' or 'old' leadership literature rooted in psychology. This largely defines leadership in terms of top executives and their roles, offering the view that a combination of positional power and functional experience drives leadership behaviour. In other words, an effective leadership theory building on this tradition should be rooted in the behaviour of senior executives.

Perhaps the most significant issue for strategic leaders today, then, is how through their behaviour they can create continuously adaptive organizations that will survive the turbulence and complexity of the age. This emerges as a central theme in much of the strategic change research taking place today. Many commentators are still exploring whether change can be directed strategically and then planned and logically executed, or whether it is emergent and brought about by the interplay of competing interest groups.

All of this suggests a role for leadership in the context of organizations that is far from the command-and-control style of a general. *Leadership Unplugged* supports the view that the need for strategic leadership behaviour shifts the burden of responsibility for the formation of adaptive solutions from the organization's leaders to the employees in the wider organization. The senior executives can't do the job alone. While this appears to be an argument for empowerment and the participation of the workforce in the management of the organization, the task of charting the direction of the firm through the complexity rests squarely on the shoulders of the chief executive officer (CEO). Extending the boundaries of responsibility, the top management team must remain accountable for the entire firm's performance. And this accountability of senior executives, combined with their positional power, makes them the ideal cadre of managers towards whom to direct our theory of *Leadership Unplugged*. This book fleshes out our thesis and provides rich empirical evidence, in the form of multiple case studies, in order to support the development of a leadership theory based round debate, discourse and dialogue. But before we get to the key frameworks, let's take a look at some evidence from managers themselves as to why this may be a valuable approach.

The Practitioner Evidence

A two-year study of management and leadership by the UK's Centre for Excellence in Management and Leadership headed by Tony Cleaver, former chief executive of IBM in the UK, has concluded that British organizations need to raise their game in terms of leadership performance.[7] The Centre's vision is that by 2010 the UK will be seen as a world leader in the development and application of management and leadership capabilities in all sectors and at all levels, though there's every reason to think that the rest of mainland Europe, Scandinavia and the United States could also benefit from the findings.

In essence, the Centre's two-year research programme has produced real hard evidence on the state of the UK's management and leadership capability and its relationship to corporate performance. Indeed, opportunities for improvements in leadership skills are so widespread – says the Centre tactfully – that only a broad-ranging approach can meet them. The organization has made no less than 30 specific recommendations for governments and corporations to take forward as they develop better leaders for the future. For instance, there's much dissatisfaction from managers at all levels at the poor quality of leadership in their organizations. Interestingly, leadership development providers, beyond a handful of world class institutions, on the whole don't seem up to the task of rectifying the situation.

As an incentive for firms to improve their leadership pool, one of the Centre's major recommendations is that of promoting voluntary corporate reporting of firms' management and leadership capabilities. The Centre believes that this will become a requirement in the future anyway, in much the same way that environmental and corporate social responsibilities are now being addressed. This is because stakeholders, and notably investors, are discovering the importance of non-financial benchmarks. The highly regarded Ernst & Young *Measures that Matter* study, conducted in the United States and subsequently in the United Kingdom, concluded that anything from 20 to 60 per cent of decisions to invest or sell stock were based on non-financial attributes of the firm. Additionally, the consultancy found that earnings forecasts were much more accurate when non-financial factors were taken into account, thus reducing the financial risk to investors.

From a *Leadership Unplugged* perspective, the top two 'measures that matter' are rather interesting:

- how well does a firm execute strategy?
- how good is that strategy?

With regard to execution, read: 'How well does a management team leverage its skills and experience, gain employee commitment and stay aligned with stakeholder interests?' Quality of strategy, on the other hand, refers to whether or not management actually has a strategy or vision for the future, whether it can make tough strategic decisions, how quickly it seizes opportunities and how well it can allocate resources. All these are key aspects of the *Leadership Unplugged* philosophy but another point, emerging explicitly from the CEML research, needs yet more emphasis.

One of the most exciting findings of the CEML study, we believe, is that the research reveals serious deficiencies in the following leadership skills:

1. the ability of leaders to create a sense of vision in a fast changing environment
2. motivating teams of people and leading them through change
3. and being innovative in developing services and products and finding new ways of working.

All these skills were found to be in short supply in organizations, from top to bottom. So while managers at middle-ranking levels are under increasing pressure to 'perform' (that is to generate bottom-line revenues and profits), the latest research is putting more emphasis on the importance of leadership development. Why? Because firms are less hierarchical, the pace of change is relentless and there is greater public scrutiny than before with more demands for compliance. All of these point to the need for a judicious mix of leadership skills, now and into the future, to cope with the new and more demanding challenges that organizations face today.

If the CEML study scares you, it should. It builds and expands on other studies that have shown a similar deficit in leadership skills. Despite the increasing number of management qualifications completed and training programmes undertaken in recent years, the Workplace Employee Relations Survey conducted in 1998 showed that:

1. 24 per cent of managers were poor are dealing with work-related problems
2. 30 per cent of managers were poor at keeping everyone up-to-date with proposed changes
3. 34 per cent were poor at responding to suggestions from employees
4. and 38.5 per cent were poor at providing everyone with a chance to comment on proposals.

In conclusion, it seems that this expansive two-year study lays real emphasis on aspects of management competence and leadership ability that have received less attention to date than they should have. These include the ability of leaders to inspire and motivate, to enable people to do things differently, and to achieve new levels of customer satisfaction and organizational performance. CEML reminds us that employers will need more people in their workforces with these leadership skills in the future if present trends continue. There is a greater need to devolve decision making further down the line. The Centre also reports that most future managers will come from a wide variety of backgrounds, with management less likely to be their first choice. This points to the importance of laying the developmental foundations of leadership abilities as early as possible and building on them as managers' careers are developed within organizations. Much of the work of leadership development must therefore also focus on the quality of leadership learning. We have to equip tomorrow's leaders with a basis of effective management and leadership skills today – otherwise we will be suffocating the talent pool from which the managers and leaders of tomorrow are selected.

Case 3. Chartered Institute of Management Accountants – what is the leadership debate?

The UK's Chartered Institute of Management Accountants (CIMA) commissioned a survey to explore the debate about leadership at senior levels within 400 global organizations, and involved us in commenting on the results at the survey's launch.[8] The research provides a fascinating insight into what senior executives believe the most important leadership issues to be, both at a corporate and a personal level (Table 1.1).

Asked to identify the key business issues for the future, the group – made up of CEOs, finance directors and board-level executives from around the world – suggested that finding and retaining good people was by far their number one priority. (French and German firms, Middle Eastern firms and those from the United States rated this significantly more highly than did those from the United Kingdom.) The intense speed of change was ranked their number two concern, alongside the impact of IT on their businesses.

Interestingly, the issues of regulatory impact and shareholder demands came significantly lower in the list. We often find organizations using these as reasons or excuses for pursuing a certain strategy, but CEOs and finance directors clearly find them of less concern than people issues and the pace of change.

When it comes to the personal qualities and skills required by leadership there's an equally interesting outcome. In Table 1.2 the skills appear to be ranked by survey respondents into three distinct groups: interpersonal and motivational skills, business-related skills and functional knowledge.

Table 1.1 CIMA survey of global leadership issues

Important issues for the success of future businesses
(on a scale of 0-10, from telephone interviews with 396 respondents)

Finding and retaining quality people	8.8
Impact of IT	8.2
Speed of change	8.2
Intellectual capital	7.9
Impact of e-business	7.6
Global competition	7.6
Shareholder demands	7.1
Environmental or ethical or social responsibility	7.0
Impact of regulation	6.5
Cultural differences within or between companies	6.2

Table 1.2 CIMA survey of global leadership skills

Important skills for successful business leaders of tomorrow

Skill	Scale of 1–10	Single most important
Leadership	8.9	34%
Vision	8.6	16%
Communication skills	8.5	7%
Swiftness of response to change	8.5	16%
Business acumen	8.0	7%
Entrepreneurship	8.0	9%
Creativity	7.8	4%
Financial management skills	7.4	3%
International experience	7.2	4%
IT skills	6.9	2%

Take this along with another survey finding – that the qualities most admired in successful leaders today are vision, people management abilities, an ability to motivate people and a focus on strategic goals – and you can see that strategic leadership competencies are articulated around strategic focus, people skills and communication skills.

What Does *Leadership Unplugged* Cover?

Following this introductory chapter, where we set out the groundwork for *Leadership Unplugged*, the key framework of the book – debate, discourse and dialogue – is outlined in Chapter 2. Here we introduce what we call the *Unplugged Continuum*, a relationship between the different conversation stages of debate, discourse (or discussion) and dialogue. We examine how these different communication forms appear to build, one on the other, over time. We also explore where the different forms of communication offer greatest promise and application, as well as where executives seem to have the greatest difficulty in using or applying the ideas.

In Chapter 3, 'Taking Sides' – the first of two chapters addressing 'debate' in Part I – we explore the early phases of leading change, often built around concepts drawn from the application of formal communication strategies. We look at these formal communication strategies explicitly in Chapter 4 and discuss how firms are actually engaging in mass communication. There is little doubt in our minds that some firms' emphasis on mass communication – concentrating on efficiency in information delivery through intranets, newsletters and e-mail systems – can be detrimental to the successful communication of leadership messages.

In Part II, 'Arguing the Vision', Chapter 5 looks at the context of interpersonal discourse (for instance interpersonal political issues) and the issues and implications around organizational complexity are considered in Chapter 6. How leaders can frame and position their opinions, making the best business case for them, is addressed in Chapter 7, 'Leading opinions'. Chapter 8, on sensemaking and sensegiving, helps people make sense of what's happening in the conversations around them, addressing the idea of leadership as the management of meaning.

In Part III – possibly the most important part of the book – we explore our version of the concept of dialogue and the dynamics of dialogue. Chapter 9 looks at connections with an audience, Chapter 10 with handling emotions and Chapter 11 with what we call 'Listening Furiously', or the zone of uncomfortable debate. The book closes with a reappraisal of our key concepts. It paints a picture of the organization as a network or nexus of conversations, and considers the roles we all must play in keeping its conversations alive.

This book argues that the constant conversations an organization must initiate and engage in to sustain competitive advantage are essential. By engaging multiple stakeholders in real conversations about an organization's strategy and leadership, we believe that the stop–start leadership of organizations, involving management by unrelated project after unrelated project, can be redefined. Firms need clear strategies – clear at the top and throughout the organization. The skills and tools in *Leadership Unplugged* can help. We only hope that enough people will listen.

Conclusion

The key points we wish to establish at the end of this chapter are:

- *Leadership Unplugged* rests on three pillars – strategic leadership (long-term vision), people skills and communication skills – that are integrated in a very specific way.
- The skills involved in *Leadership Unplugged* are important today because an organization's leaders are its most important change agents. Their interpersonal skills are therefore crucial.
- Academic research and practitioner evidence makes a clear business case for the development of these skills at all levels in an organization, not just in the senior echelons. Tomorrow's leaders need to develop the skills of *Leadership Unplugged* today.
- The single most important point emerging from this chapter is that *Leadership Unplugged* focuses on the simple art of engaging in strategic conversations, where the conversations tend to occur in three phases: debate, discussion and dialogue. The rest of this book explores the context and skills for doing just that.

So, the overall objectives of this book are:

- To enable readers to lead themselves, their teams and their businesses authentically and more effectively.
- To enable readers to act as effective change agents, either internally or as consultants, and to help them implement organizational strategy better.
- To help readers develop a deeper understanding of themselves and of their peers and colleagues, and to understand the practical implications of this for their work as change agents in business.

- To introduce readers to a range of practical interpersonal communications tools and frameworks, developed from the related disciplines of leadership, strategy and change management.

QuestionBank

At the end of each chapter we pose a series of questions, drawn from the discussion in the text. We urge you to take time out to answer them.

You can use the QuestionBank in different ways. First, consider how you personally would answer them as you go through each chapter. We suggest you write down your answers as an *aide memoire*, or treat them as a line in the sand that says 'I was here'. Then – or instead – explore your team's, or your whole organization's, responses in a workshop. The worst thing you can do with these questions is ignore them.

1. Do you believe in the power of language? Do you believe that actions speak louder than words? Or is the pen – language – mightier than the sword for you? How do you live this philosophy? What does it mean for you on a day-to-day basis?

2. Do you believe senior executives are best placed to act as change agents? To what extent does your organization rely on consultants to develop strategy? To manage change?

3. Do you believe an organization's leadership capability is intimately associated with its ability to create strategic and local vision? How clearly are the vision and strategy articulated? How widely are the vision and strategy understood, by those within the organization and outside it? To what extent do the people inside and outside the organization believe in its vision and strategy? To what extent are those within the organization engaged in the pursuit of the vision and strategy?

4. Given the requirements of the vision and strategy, what are the implications for management and leadership capabilities? How can we best communicate to investors and other external stakeholders the value that we derive from our management and leadership capability?

Notes

1. Boal, Augusto, 1998. *Legislative Theatre.* London: Routledge, p. 3.
2. Fayol, H., 1949. *General and Industrial Management*, trans. Straws, P. London: Pitman.
3. Mintzberg, Henry, 1973. *The Nature of Managerial Work.* New York: Harper Collins. Kotter, John, 1999. *What Leaders Really Do.* Boston: Harvard Business School. Mintzberg, considering the nature of managerial work, and Kotter, describing what leaders really do, provide probably the most effective explorations of the day-to-day reality of senior executives as a string of conversations.
4. Reprinted from the Lex Column, *Financial Times*, 27 May 2002.
5. The GLOBE survey in the USA uses the multi-factor leadership questionnaire (MLQ) to assess the competencies of transformational leadership. It has been established for almost two decades and is now being applied around the world through a network of 170 academic scholars. Perhaps conscious of critics charging the difficulty of measuring leadership behaviours, Bass (1999) explores the empirical data derived from work with the questionnaire. He concludes that although applied research has been abundant, usually correlating transformational factors with outcomes in effectiveness and satisfaction of colleagues, basic research and basic theory development have been in short supply. Bass, Bernard M., 1999. Two decades of research and development in transformational leadership. *European Journal of Work and Organizational Psychology* 8(1), pp. 9–25.
6. Sonsino, Steven, 2002a.
7. Council for Excellence in Management and Leadership, 2002. *Managers and Leaders: Raising Our Game.* London: CEML.
8. Coulson, Catherine, and Conforti, Daniela, 2000. *Global Business Management Survey 2000.* London: CIMA.

CHAPTER 2

Debate, Discussion and Dialogue

People are no longer primarily in opposition [debate], nor can they be said to be interacting [discourse], rather they are participating in this pool of common meaning which is capable of constant development and change [dialogue].

David Bohm[1]

Headlines

Leadership Unplugged is a practical guide to the art and science of strategic conversation. It tells you clearly:

1. what should be on your leadership agenda
2. who should be in the conversation
3. and how to influence the people around you to bring the strategy to life.

Strategic conversation takes three forms – debate, discourse (or discussion) and dialogue – and the three forms tend to work in sequence in a programme of change.

In the early phase of a process of change, methods of opening up the debate and promoting a vision for the future are required – this is the 'telling' phase of change.

The debate phase is the most likely to be confrontational and usually involves the senior executives' own perspectives on the future.

As the people in the organization adjust to the idea of change, and to the senior executives' view of what the future holds, discussions take place among and within the different stakeholder groups.

As people develop their own concepts of where the organization might be heading, true dialogue becomes both possible and increasingly important.

Dialogue is more of a 'listening' than a 'telling' phase of the process and should not be curtailed prematurely, if at all.

Most executives are criticized for not listening, which can make entering the dialogue phase problematic.

In framing *Leadership Unplugged* as the art and science of strategic conversation we are building on a well-grounded history of language and its importance to leadership. Many authors, notably Jay Conger, Barbara Czarniawska and Kees van der Heijden, have explored conversation as a mechanism for communicating change and for understanding the role of executives in organizations. Some of the works that have influenced our thinking are listed in Table 2.1, with Conger and Kanungo's call for future research into the language of leadership a key driver.[2]

> [An] aspect of the visioning activity that requires researchers' attention is the use of language that gives shape to the vision of the organization. The issue is: how to frame and articulate a vision for maximum impact?

They articulated the following explicit research questions on the structure and content of strategic visions:

1. What are the unique components of a vision?
2. Are there different types of vision, based on unique configurations of various contents (such as corporate values, missions, specific goals or purposes etc.) or on their scope, time frame, specificity and complexity?
3. How should senior executives structure a vision, and what aspects of a vision are universally important (for example risk propensity and degree of detail necessary)?

This is significant for us, the authors, as it was our starting point for exploring the language of leadership. At the time we were increasingly being called upon in our teaching and consulting to help individuals and firms articulate their strategic vision. Since then, however, our canvas has enlarged because we found that even when an organization had a vision – usually captured in the form of a strategic plan, presented as a bound report with copious pages from spreadsheets and PowerPoint presentations – that vision was simply not implemented. Managers, having created the plan, assumed that the living strategy would simply happen. Not so. Developing the vision, mission or plan is only the beginning. A dance-like process of interchanges – some formal, others informal – usually ensues as the interested parties strive to figure out what's happening and what to do next. This continues until elements of the plan that are important for key individuals are actually instigated, or until the whole thing is ignominiously dropped and swept under the carpet. Or dropped until the next planning round, at least. This is why we began to explore the reality of strategy development processes in organizations – rather than how it was *supposed* to work. Now we've reached a point where we can share with you our conception of strategic conversation – focusing not only on what it is but also, importantly, on why and how to do it.

Strategic Conversation as Debate, Discourse and Dialogue

Our articulation of strategic conversation as the three sequential phases of debate, discourse and dialogue has come directly from our research over the past five years. This has involved workshops with hundreds of executives, interviews with dozens of executives, and shadowing executives on a

Table 2.1 The heritage of strategic conversation

Authors	Value to senior executives	Key mechanisms
Conger (1998) *The Necessary Art of Persuasion*	Influencing skills	Use of language
Eccles & Nohria (1992) *Beyond the Hype*	Better strategy development	Strategy as a language game
Taylor (1993) *Rethinking the Theory of Organizational Communication*	How to read an organization	Conversations (and text)
van der Heijden (1996) *Scenarios*	Better strategy development	Scenario planning process
Czarniawska (1997) *Narrating the Institution*	Conversations and human actions as organizational (institutional) narratives	Using narrative theory as a tool to understand organizations
Conger (1998) *Winning 'em Over*	Influencing skills	Building expertise and relationship credibility
Conger & Kanungo (1998) *Charismatic Leadership in Organizations*	How best to articulate a firm's strategic vision	Research questions address exactly this point

day-to-day basis as they go about their business. When shadowing executives we hear an immense variety of different communications styles, depending in part on the issues they are addressing and on the individuals they are communicating with. The common thread, however, uniting all these different communications is usually conversation of the most informal kind. And the more conversations we hear, the more we have begun to appreciate that they fall largely into one of three types: conversation as debate, conversation as discussion (or discourse) and conversation as dialogue. Each of these different conversational styles has different characteristics and different dynamics and this chapter aims to explore and unpack those differences.

Leadership Unplugged: Key Definitions

Debate

In our debate–discourse–dialogue model, which forms the backdrop for *Leadership Unplugged*, we maintain specific meanings for each of the three phases. By 'debate', for instance, we refer to a communication style where the participants articulate their positions as being different from, and frequently opposed to, one another. Debate is therefore a strategy of *conversational confrontation*. The parties do see a range of opinions, which is to be applauded, but they focus exclusively on the differences between their positions rather than the similarities. Notably, each party espouses their own position as superior to others. This is the traditional rough-and-tumble style of party politics – think of the despatch box at Prime Minister's Question Time in the British House of Commons. Indeed, a participant in a formal political debate aims to marshal facts and opinions in order to create the best possible case against the opposition.

Debate, in our terms, is therefore to be regarded as a mechanism for crystallizing opinion so that an audience can decide for themselves which version of events out of several they prefer. As an aside, at this point, it's worth remembering that in most formal debates very few members of the audience actually change their minds, take new sides or adopt new positions. The debate may have been an interesting experience – even an enjoyable one – but very rarely do participants' opinions shift, if they are honest with themselves. There will be more on this in Chapter 3, along with the results of an experiment that is intended to change people's minds. Our conclusion is that engaging in debate – no matter how articulate an orator you might be – cannot represent an effective way of influencing people and bringing them over to your way of thinking. Or not, at least, without subsequent exploration of the issues in discussions.

There's an added complication here – senior executives often love to talk. Many of them regard talking or 'telling' as their sole role as leaders of the organization. They may come across much as General Peckem in Joseph Heller's novel *Catch-22*, who 'liked listening to himself talk, liked most of all listening to himself talk about himself'. This is, of course, a sure-fire way of 'switching off' those whom we seek to influence.

All of this doesn't mean that you should avoid the debate phase. In fact, it is an integral part of the change process and one that shouldn't be ignored. Chapter 3 explores debate in much more detail, while Chapter 4 explores mechanisms for engaging the whole organization in debate.

Discourse or Discussion

The roots of the word 'discussion' are similar to those of the words 'percussion' and 'concussion', and are related to 'breaking up'. So, in the dynamics of discourse or discussion we may break up the agenda of a larger debate and begin to build a different framework or system of ideas. We may begin to deconstruct a debate and then to integrate different parts of the conversation. We will build links between certain ideas from the debate and will exclude other elements. In this way we start to build links between different ideas or elements of the different debates that make sense to us, and that we have been involved in. Inevitably, we also begin to build links and relationships between the ideas and the people whose ideas they were. Some relationships are positive and constructive; others less so. Instead of simply discussing our own positions we also begin to introduce and explain ourselves, and our feelings, into the discussion at this point. This explains why strategic change and moving away from the status quo are usually very sensitive subjects for discussions. We often begin to take criticisms of our ideas personally, which greatly hinders the conversation moving forward. This can escalate tensions between individuals in an organization, which can be especially difficult when the individuals in question are senior officials, and highlights why knowledge of how to deal with organizational politics becomes important here. This is a topic we address fully in Chapter 5.

In conclusion, the various discourses or discussions that we become involved in during a programme of change are fundamental to our paving the way for the successful implementation of strategy. Therefore, knowing how to get into and out of tricky conversations safely is a key interpersonal skill that all executives – not just those in the senior echelons – must build and nurture. This is such an important part of conversational strategy that we deal with it explicitly in Chapter 11.

Dialogue

Dialogue is the most difficult of our three conversational phases to define, and yet it is the most important. The word 'dialogue' has been taken to mean discussion between two people – in other words, as a synonym for discussion. Being cynical for a moment, we find that executives often *talk* about entering dialogue, but we sense that they don't always really mean it. Often it seems to be an attempt to get the other party to reveal information about their position, make concessions, or even capitulate.

Many people simply do not grasp how different the *listening* aspect of dialogue is from simply *hearing*, nor how difficult it is. On taking a role in a film as a therapist, Greg Wise, the actor partner of Oscar-winner Emma Thompson, described what a therapist does as 'glorified listening'.[3] We think there's more to it than that, and that there are valuable lessons to be learned from the way therapists actively listen. There's more on this in Chapter 11.

In our terms, then, dialogue is a process of seeking common ground where both parties, often from different sides of a fence, build meaning through conversation. Here we begin to integrate our selves and the ideas we hold with the ideas held by others. Our intention in dialogue is to pursue unity, or the possibility of unifying our different ideas. Perhaps the defining element of dialogue is actually nothing to do with talking at all, but is connected with listening. And by listening we don't mean just hearing – we mean really *listening*. Ruth Gillespie, the human resources director at the business publishing arm of Anglo-Dutch publisher Reed Elsevier, captures this activity perfectly. She describes it as 'listening furiously'. This is listening as an active skill, not as a passive 'receiving' state.

Listening furiously is the act of bending all your attention towards the person with whom you're speaking, trying to shut out everything else that might be going on around you and giving your conversation partner your full attention. This is being in the room with the other person and focusing on them exclusively. Listening furiously is perhaps what Mr Spock, the science officer from *Star Trek*, is trying to achieve in a Vulcan mind meld. Interestingly Leonard Nimoy, the actor playing the *Enterprise's* Science Officer, often portrays the act as emotionally and physically draining. So is listening furiously. The challenge is magnified when the individual you're listening to is someone whose views you may disagree with, perhaps even someone you dislike as an individual. Giving your conversation partner that focus of attention is imperative, however. The Greek roots of the word 'dialogue', *dia* and *logos*, suggest 'through meaning' or 'stream of meaning'. We see dialogue, then, as intended to help us jointly capture or create shared meaning. And this forms the very basis for people understanding each other. We'll revisit the elements of dialogue, and listening furiously, in Part III of this book.

Integrating the Three Phases

Positioning the Vision

Many individuals at senior levels in organizations are powerful speakers. They marshal facts carefully, create arguments convincingly, and seem to have boundless confidence to speak at the drop of a hat on almost any topic. This is helpful in the debate phase, as a vision for the future needs to be supported by the best business case possible to get debate, discussion and dialogue rolling. We call this *positioning the vision* (Table 2.2), and there are some tools to help you articulate the vision in Chapters 3 and 4. Some strategy consultants advocate creating crises to 'mobilize the troops' and overcome organizational inertia, but this is usually unnecessary if the vision is positioned in a compelling way.

Many senior executives, however, make the mistake of articulating their vision as a *fait accompli*: 'There will be no further discussion', they announce. They have had endless board meetings and have the benefit of full information about all the relevant issues, so clearly there is nothing more to be said. They don't appreciate that this positioning of the vision, this debate phase, is an opening salvo – an introduction to the real strategy development work to follow. Unlike in formal debates, however, an organized, well-prepared opposition speaker is rarely in evidence. This occasionally leads to audience feelings of frustration, as they feel uninvolved in the process. But this frustration is important, and indeed essential, to getting the discussion phase moving. So let the audience – who are usually

Table 2.2 The objectives of debate, discourse and dialogue

Phase	Conversational dynamic	Transition triggers	Strategic objective
Debate	Telling	Emerging arguments	Positioning the vision
Discussion	Exchanging	Vision echoes	Arguing the vision
Dialogue	Listening	Emerging debates	Listening to the vision

employees within the firm but occasionally outside stakeholders too – begin to develop their own arguments as to why this or that policy won't work. Let them be part of the process. They will then begin to exchange fire with other members of the audience, and occasionally with the senior executives whose vision it was. This is a good sign that the change process is under way. It may be uncomfortable, but executives usually appreciate that it won't be easy.

A danger point in the process arises here, as senior executives inexperienced in interpersonal communication take resistance personally. They often respond by trying to justify what they originally intended, or even by cutting off the debate. Instead, executives should express their gratitude for the feedback – say 'Thank you', even – and continue to listen to the currents of opinion within the organization. They should also listen to what's being said informally, as well as formally. Ideally, you should encourage public exploration of these early audience responses. Making instant off-the-cuff responses to quell fears or anxieties during the early stages of a discussion is extremely counter-productive. Never, ever, cut off the debate. Unlike the evil Vogon aliens from Douglas Adams' cult book series *The Hitchhiker's Guide to the Galaxy*, who screamed 'Resistance is useless!' at the tops of their voices, you must take the position that 'resistance is *useful*'. Resistance provides information about the sensitive issues on the corporate agenda that people care about. Remember, you may need to dig deeper to establish the real reasons for resistance, if they are not immediately obvious. Resistance also gives you clues as to who the movers and shakers within the organization might be. This can help you identify whom you might need to lobby and win over, or who to engage in support of your vision for the future.

After beginning the debate phase, then, senior executives must listen for emerging arguments and to identify people who are standing up for their views. This is the signal that you are ready to begin the next phase – discussion.

Arguing the Vision

Because there is no formal process counterbalancing the debate initiated by senior executives, the next phase – discussion or discourse – is extremely important. It is here that the interchanges really help participants refine their own views and reinterpret the vision articulated by the senior executives. It is here, therefore, that the real collective vision of the organization emerges (as opposed to the senior executives' version of the vision). However, because the debate largely goes underground at this point, taking place outside the formal arena, it is now impossible for executives to control. It can only be influenced: even then, this is very difficult to do in practice. This is where involvement by 'movers and shakers' in the organization must begin. Other commentators describe these individuals as champions of change. In fact, the most appropriate champions invariably step to the fore naturally, so executives shouldn't worry about overtly 'choosing' key individuals way ahead of time – it is usually obvious who they are. If senior executives themselves cannot identify them, often someone in their immediate network can. So find them, and give them space and time to articulate their view of the vision.

Interestingly, the movers and shakers' version of the vision won't be exactly the same as that espoused by senior executives but will be closer to the coalface, and more accessible and readily acceptable to broader numbers of people than that devised by senior management. Encourage this discussion; give it space. The payoff will lie in faster acceptance of the vision.

Inevitably some individuals will articulate a strong antipathy – if not outright opposition – to the vision promoted in the debate phase. These people must also be given space or airtime to articulate their view. The worst thing a senior executive can do at this point is try to silence opponents' views, or attack them as individuals. An individual's opinion can certainly be challenged, but in ways that don't prevent him or her from participating in the discussion again. There are other reasons why opposing views must actively be sought, and their supporters challenged but not quashed. We'll deal with these in more detail in Chapter 5, on politics.

Not surprisingly, some executives report the onset of panic at this point. They fear they are losing control, and find that the revised vision they are hearing isn't quite what they had in mind. The answer is to make sure the participants to the discussion have as much information as possible. Allow them access to the deep insights, facts and figures you yourself have; allow them to work through the thought processes. Then they are more likely (although still not guaranteed) to see the world more as the senior executive does. So resource your champions – give them all your information and data but let them make up their own minds. If they make a rational decision, based on logical analysis and thought processes, their take on the vision and its implementation probably won't be a million miles from yours. Indeed, it may be a better one. Perhaps the senior executive team has forgotten something in the mix. Not to worry – the discussion phase is where this will emerge. It gives everyone time to reappraise the situation, rework their thinking and reframe the vision.

It is at or around this point – when the vision is reflected or echoed back from the participants in the discussion – that the time is right to engage with the third, and perhaps the most difficult, transition phase. This is dialogue.

Listening to the Vision

The task facing senior executives in the dialogue phase, following a robust give-and-take discussion, is to listen to the 'echoed' vision as it is reflected back from the organization. The challenge is to listen hard to how people articulate the vision, and not to reject their perspective out of hand just because it's 'their take'. At this point there should be minimal confrontation or direct disagreement – that should have taken place earlier, during the discussion phase. Now it's time to listen clearly to the wider vision for the organization.

Listening to the key players articulating how they see things working is the surest way to help them engage with the detail of the vision or strategy. It's the easiest way to help them find its weaknesses and its strengths. It's when listening to someone describing how the organization could be – or should be – that you get a real sense of whether they have caught it well enough. Maybe another question or two needs asking to help them clarify their thinking on what needs to be done. The astonishing spin-off here is that the individual, through being listened to, gains a tremendous sense of self-respect and is thus motivated to get the picture 'right' to the best of his or her ability. Listening to people gives them immense confidence. Sometimes senior managers forget how powerful this can be.

We call this phase 'listening to the vision', and there are two significant hurdles to overcome here. The first – as always – is senior executives' desire for control and clarity. (We call this the *paradox of control* and deal with it in more detail in Chapter 6, on complexity.) Second, and perhaps more importantly, the criticism most often levelled at senior executives is that they don't listen. They always want the last word. They can rarely let someone else manage or close a conversation. That can make this phase – whose sole purpose is listening – tremendously difficult. What to do? We hope that some of the tools and techniques explored here will help.

Integrating the Three Phases: Coda

What we tend to see in organizations is the effective articulation of business cases, strategies and visions, along with reasonably effective processes for dealing with political issues. This is largely dependent, however, on the effectiveness of *informal* networks within organizations and often occurs only by chance. What we don't see happening very effectively in organizations is *listening*, and this hinders the implementation of strategy at a fundamental level. This may be due partly to the length of time that strategic change programmes take. By the time a senior executive has engaged in debate to

kick-start change, entered discussions on key issues with the various stakeholder groups and passed through the dialogue phase, he or she may well
have moved on within the organization, or even have left. Any new incum-
bent must start the dialogue process all over again, usually to the groans of
the staff members who respond with the now-classic line, 'Oh, no! Here we
go again.'

Another major challenge for senior executives in the dialogue or listening phase is that by this stage of the change process many people within the
organization have had the chance to be part of the strategy development
process, and have developed their own ideas and concepts about the way
forward. So at this stage senior executives need to listen very carefully to
the vision coming back at them, like an echo but with subtle, sometimes
significant twists. This is what we mean when we say this phase's strategic
objective is 'listening to the vision'. The vision may come directly from
mainstream employees of the organization or be refracted via their peers,
depending on the strategy development processes in place. The value of
devolving participation in the strategy development process lies in the fact
that a revised vision, developed in reality at grassroots level, may well
contain excellent and pragmatic ideas about where the organization should
go, and on how really to implement the strategy. This wider participation is
often difficult for senior executives to accept, however. They usually
perceive motivating the firm to realize the strategic vision as their own
unique role, despite any lip service they may pay to participation and
empowerment as mechanisms for achieving and sustaining competitive
strategy delivery. Most senior executives don't see their roles as facilitating strategic change at all – they are more likely to see themselves as
driving it and leading from the front.

With this in mind, the concepts within *Leadership Unplugged* and the
frameworks set out here will help individual senior executives develop
their own influencing skills with multiple stakeholder groups. They reflect
the very best practice in engaging the hearts and minds of employees
within an organization.

Having explored the definitions of debate, discourse and dialogue, it's
now worth looking at the dynamics of how they fit together in a little
more detail. Then, in the subsequent sections of the book, we can explore
the detail of the three phases and establish an overall context into which
the elements can fit. In some respects, positioning these frameworks here
at the front of the book – at the start of the *Leadership Unplugged* debate,
if you will – represents our attempt at articulating the 'big picture' for our
readers before getting into discussion of the elements of the framework
(Table 2.3).

Table 2.3 The *Unplugged Framework*: making leadership strategy live

Phases	Management role	In the organization	Objectives
Debate	Position the vision (sensegiving, focus on others)	The losing stage (transition stage I, unfreezing, where many feel anxious, uncertain)	1. Build best business case 2. Choose compatible channels 3. Open conversations at every level 4. Expect resistance, (but know that 'resistance is useful') 5. Listen for emerging arguments (transition signals)
Discourse	Argue the vision (sensemaking, joint focus with others)	The learning stage (transition stage II, where some feel excited, motivated)	1. Identify cynics and supporters 2. Kickstart mini-debates (keep them small) 3. Scale debate to the speaker 4. Lobby, listen and learn from cynics and supporters (ask questions) 5. Listen for vision echo (transition signals)
Dialogue	Listen to the vision (sensemaking, focus within self)	The leading stage (transition stage III, where most feel responsible on a day-to-day basis)	1. Resource the supporters 2. Listen to cynics 3. Respect the re-vision

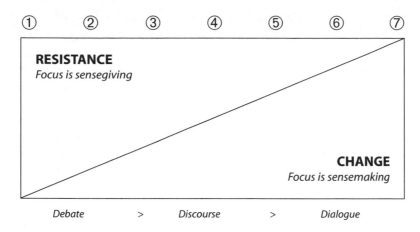

Figure 2.1 The *Unplugged Continuum* – how the phases are integrated

In our work on debate, discourse and dialogue within firms we have seen that under the status quo (Figure 2.1: marked with a ①) there is huge resistance to the idea of change – *any* change. Inertia and 'the way we do things round here', the very fabric of organizational culture, preclude it. At point ② however, once the debate is under way, we find some people responding positively and welcoming the idea of change. ('At last!', or 'it's about time!', are common exclamations from individuals at the beginning of change programmes.) We need to keep these people engaged in discussion, and to engage them in talking to others in an informal communications cascade. (Formalizing this cascade rarely seems to work, but for more on organization-wide communication strategies see Chapter 4.) We need to help these people keep the discussion alive.

At point ④, the discussions and lobbying taking place around the organization are at their height. Importantly, something that senior executives often fail to take into account is that change programmes are relatively easy to initiate but that sustaining the required effort – especially through this central discussion phase – is immensely time-consuming and draining. The processes are draining both for the organization and for the senior executives driving them. This may explain why consultancies are so often drafted in to project-manage change programmes. This decision represents a major error of judgement, however. By using consultancies to project-manage change, senior executives lose the opportunity to explore and understand in real detail the issues and concerns of the people within the broader organization. This kind of engagement is also part of the process of building trust, and one that employee surveys always rate as an important requirement. Only rarely is this aspiration met.

Consultancies do have an authentic role, we believe, but more as coaches and counsellors to those within firms who undertake the change agent's role – in other words, to the senior executive pool. Senior executives invariably make the best change agents. Indeed, practising leaders actually provide instruction for some of the world's high performing organizations. In the words of Jay Conger and Beth Benjamin:[4]

> Because leadership development programs aimed at socialization seek to impart a greater understanding of a firm's guiding philosophy, core values, and particular strengths, many programs increasingly use their own executives as instructors. Though a well-known leadership guru or knowledgeable business school professor can provide insight into the latest theories on leadership or competitive strategy, outside experts typically have less to say about the strategies or practices that have worked well for one's own firm. Moreover outside experts may only have superficial knowledge of a firm's culture or history and little understanding of the idiosyncratic relations that dictate current practice.

Once points ⑤ and ⑥ are reached, the effort expended begins to reduce as the baton of responsibility is picked up by increasing numbers of individuals and teams around the organization. However, the personal effort for senior managers increases as the effort of engaging in dialogue – true listening – takes hold. There is more on this intra-personal dynamic in Chapters 9, 10 and 11.

Point ⑦ is seldom reached at all. A change programme rarely reaches a point where everyone is on-board or on-side and fully committed. There is almost always a group of people who will resist change, come what may. Such a group may oppose the proposed change for various fundamental reasons, often associated with the history and heritage of the firm. The mistake that some senior executives then make is to ask these people to leave, to remove the need for their jobs or to close down their business units. This is a mistake. When antagonistic voices are silenced so blatantly, others will step forward to replace them. Their speaking out will then be all the stronger, and will be perceived to have heightened validity given the way their predecessors were treated. No – the best way to deal with cynics in the organization is to give them airtime. Channel their conversations constructively to a wider audience, knowing that their extreme antagonism will probably help others see the views of the more moderate majority.

This probably represents an acceptable state of affairs. At this point the majority of people within the organization understand the organization's vision and can articulate it themselves. They can engage in dialogue and can 'listen furiously'. Few organizations, of course, have achieved *Leadership Unplugged* nirvana, travelling the journey from debate through dialogue, but there are business units and smaller, entrepreneurial organizations that do create active and open platforms for dialogue.

Case 4. 'It was the best of times' – the e-business debate

In the 1990s one word, 'e-business', seemed poised to change business for ever, and not just in the Silicon Valley heartland of the internet. The word 'e-business' appeared across the business pages of newspapers around the world, every one of them full of tales of young entrepreneurs who had set up internet-based information or e-commerce services and become million-aires overnight. At one stage, any company that announced an e-business strategy was rewarded with a sharp rise in its share price on the stock market, as investors hoped to share in the riches of the new economy.

It was hard at this time for business leaders of even the biggest compa-nies to ignore the 'dotcom revolution', but most of them were unsure how to respond. Some, like media mogul Rupert Murdoch, were sceptical at the outset. At the beginning of 1999 Murdoch declared that the Internet 'would destroy more businesses than it creates'. Later, however, he appeared to succumb, talking about a future in which the bulk of his media group News Corp's value would be 'internet related' and earmarking an estimated $2.3 billion for internet ventures between July 1999 and June 2000. Come June 2000, however, he seemed to have changed his mind again: 'News Corp and its subsidiaries began shelving online plans, firing dotcom employees, clos-ing down start-ups, cancelling investment plans and reducing the web ventures to their bare bones.'[5]

Other global companies responded to the internet challenge by setting up e-business groups, but groups with very different functions and purposes. Some set up a separate e-business division where these projects were handled, perhaps in a somewhat traditional way. At one pharmaceuti-cals group, the division did not have its own strategy. As the head of e-busi-ness projects explained, 'e-business is not a separate strategy' but 'an integral component of strategy'. The division's role was implementation of *group* strategy.

In contrast, one global manufacturing group set up something more closely resembling an e-business talking shop. Senior executives from the group's companies around the world would meet for a couple of days every month to consider e-business strategy. Often the chief executive would attend the discussions, allocating whole days of his valuable time to the group. The meetings gave executives opportunities to debate the value and the challenges of e-business and discuss how it should affect corporate strategy.

Response from the participants was enthusiastic. The regular meetings were seen as a chance to talk with peers and to influence discussions (or 'sharing') with individuals in the rest of the organization. The group discussed not only the pros and cons of e-business but also the virtues of setting up the discussion forum itself. The forum chair said:

> We've had a discussion about the value of doing this. It's not only about us getting together physically in order to share, but it's about creating the right tools, mindset and behaviours in the organization for the sharing to go on.

This meant that e-business strategy was still in the debate stage in early 2001. The forum allowed the expression of views from all sides of the debate. This becomes clear when looking at the range of comments made at one meeting held in March that year. On the one hand, one participant argued:

> The more I get into this, the more I'm beginning to think the 'e' thing should be dropped. If you look back over the last 20 years, or if you think about the telephone, the car, other technologies – all businesses went through major changes, right back to Henry Ford, and the winners were the ones that adapted, and the losers were those that didn't. I'm beginning to think that e-business is probably less significant even than the telephone.

However, another participant said:

> Even the people who think e-business is irrelevant need to embrace it, because it is just going to be part of business. So there's this dangerous view that says: 'Well, dotcoms – obviously they're all a load of rubbish, so e-business is over.' That's just as dangerous as being a full e-business convert.

The advantages to business leaders of addressing turbulent times through discussion are clear. In this way leaders can influence individuals within the company, and so influence the company's culture. As the forum chair said:

> Leadership has a lot to do with either changing or developing the right culture – culture around risk profiles and the amount of risk we can take,

around change and learning, around sharing. Success really starts with the leadership. So the leaders who 'get it' and influence the rest of the organisation to move on in a certain direction are the ones who are most successful.

As one of his colleagues put it, 'it's all about walk the talk'.

Leaders can take advantage of times of flux and uncertainty, such as the e-business boom. The optimism of those times led to a change of culture at many big companies, because individuals were more prepared to open their minds to different objectives and ways of working. Global companies found themselves wondering who their competitors were. As one senior executive said: 'We used to know who our competitors were, and now we don't.' Another, from a different group, asked: 'Who are our competitors? It could be [traditional rival] companies, [information agencies], healthcare portals – the competition is different.'

The last speaker encapsulated how the 1990s changed the way many business people thought:

E-business is change all the way through. It has created an opportunity. Organizations change anyway: people change in roles, products change. E-business is just another thing, but resistance that might have been there before is not happening. People are embracing change.

The Dynamics of Strategic Conversation: Coda

As the sequential phases of debate, discussion and dialogue progress, more and more members of the organization can be expected to join the movement towards adopting change. What we've seen is that distinct groups of people with different communication needs tend to be involved. It is helpful, therefore, to change or amend the nature of debates, discussions and dialogue to suit the different participants (Table 2.4, Figure 2.2).

Conclusion

The key points we want to remind you of at the end of this chapter are:

- Strategic conversations involve debate, discussion and dialogue in sequence.
- Unlike the dialogue phase, which is characterized by listening, debate is a phase characterized by telling, where senior executives articulate their vision for the future.

Table 2.4 Changing characteristics of the change audience

Broad categories	Typical characteristics	Comments
Change extremists	Will adopt almost every change Happy with change for change's sake	In some respects it is not necessary to worry overmuch about individuals in this category, they will adopt almost any proposed change. However, there may be movers and shakers useful to draw on during the discussion phase. The downside of using extremists as advocates, however, is that many people elsewhere in the organization will recognize participants in this category and therefore may resist – 'I'm not like them'.
Change champions	Enthusiastic, forward looking, comfortable with change, comfortable with uncertainty, often a limited power base, no or only a limited empire to protect	This is the key target for the early messages of change. Early debates and early positioning must be about the future of the organization, its very existence, 'it's time for a change'.
Change followers	Stalwarts, believers in the organization, often powerful, often with significant empires and therefore a useful powerbase	As the discussions get under way this group becomes significantly important. They need lobbying and listening to, both the cynics and supporters. With many of this group on board the work of the change agent in mobilizing the workforce is almost done.

Table 2.4 (continued)

Broad categories	Typical characteristics	Comments
Change inevitables	Astute group of people, often with large empires, usually favour the former heritage of the organization but know that eventually change will come	Many of these are powerful individuals associated with the success of the organization in the past and so need careful managing; however, given the swing of the organization to the new way of working/ thinking, their commitment is, as their name suggests, inevitable
Change reluctant	Unhappy with the idea of change at this time for various, often personal reasons	A diverse and therefore difficult group to win over in their entirety. Given the group has resisted change for so long at this stage, they are unlikely to be swayed by the flush of the new, or of the growing numbers of people now adopting or espousing the new vision. Use the movers and shakers closest to this group to engage with individual members that would be useful supporters.
Change challengers	Unwilling to consider change, becoming more vociferous and antagonistic over time as change becomes inevitable, occasionally very powerful	It would be very unrealistic to think these powerful individuals (in stature if not in rank) can be persuaded actively to adopt the changes others have adopted. Don't make the mistake of removing them though. Give them airtime. Channel their arguments into forums that will help show how different your own position is, but allow them to make the running.

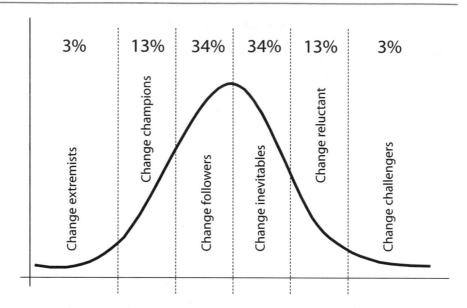

Figure 2.2 Dynamics of the change audience and how it changes over time

- Expect resistance, and know that resistance is useful.
- Emerging arguments are a signal to move into the discussion phase.
- Discussion with multiple stakeholder groups is time-consuming.
- Hearing the vision echoed back to you is a signal for dialogue to commence.
- Dialogue involves 'listening furiously'.
- Not every member of the firm will embrace change wholeheartedly – but give dissenters airtime.

QuestionBank

1. Traditionally, how do you initiate a change process? How effective is this? What is the normal response of organization members? How personally do you deal with vociferous opposition? How does the organization tend to deal with it?

2. How effective are you at recognizing and developing high potential managers within the organization? What prospects are there within the organization for movers and shakers? What development opportunities do you offer high potentials? What proportion

3. of their development is functional? And what proportion is interpersonal, revolving round communication, team building and influence? How much attention is given to the skills needed to identify high potential managers within the firm?

3. How well do senior executives within your organization listen? What evidence do you have to support your view? How can the organization's 'listening quotient' be improved? How comfortable are senior executives with giving up control of the strategy-making process? How comfortable are they with uncertainty?

4. How familiar is your organization with change? With unsuccessful change? With successful change? Who tends to oversee change programmes within the firm? Who is responsible for overseeing and developing the change agents?

Notes

1. Bohm, David, 1996. *Unfolding Meaning.* London: Routledge, p. 175.
2. Conger and Kanungo, 1998, p. 247.
3. The actor Greg Wise was interviewed on his role in *Sirens* for *Radio Times*, 25–31 May 2002 (London: BBC Publications). His full sentiments on therapy were: 'It's just glorified listening, isn't it? You give me a hundred quid and I give you a bit of useful advice that you might get out of a cracker.'
4. Conger, Jay A., and Benjamin, Beth, 1998. *Building Leaders: How Successful Companies Develop the Next Generation.* San Francisco, CA: Jossey Bass, p. 101.
5. Daniel, Caroline, Harding, James and O'Connor, Ashling. The internet retreat. *Financial Times*, 16 January 2001.

PART I

Debate:
Position the Vision

Debate:

1. Strife, dissension, quarrelling; a quarrel
2. Contention in argument; dispute; controversy; discussion; especially discussion in Parliament; a discussion.

Shorter Oxford Dictionary, 3rd edn.

CHAPTER 3

Debate: Taking Sides

Words are witnesses which often speak louder than documents.

Eric Hobsbawm (1962)[1]

Headlines

Strategic conversation takes three forms – debate, discourse (or discussion) and dialogue – and the three tend to work in sequence in a programme of change.

In the early phase of change, methods for opening up the debate and promoting a vision for the future are required – this is the telling phase of change.

The debate phase is the most likely to be confrontational, and usually centres on the senior executives' own perspective on the future.

The fundamental objective of debate is to get as many people to support you as possible. Debate is about winning a mandate.

There is little evidence that debate ever changes people's minds.

Debating Debate

Debate is the first of the three forms of strategic conversation that executives tend to engage in. They must pass through a phase of debate before entering the discussion phase, and before passing on into the phase of dialogue. In this chapter we'll explore in some detail how debate works, both in theory and in practice, and how it might work even more effectively for senior executives in the future. We'll explore the five strategies of debate. In particular, we want to draw the attention of executives to the extreme significance of the structure of debate. Furthermore, we want to point out how the debate itself merely acts as a platform for the detailed discussions, and the subsequent interpersonal dialogue, that needs to occur. Only the full three phases of conversation can pave the way for real, long-lasting change. The main point we make in this chapter is that it's the structure of the communication form we call 'debate' that tells the story.

The Dangers of Debate

Throughout the chapter we explore the current practical realities and dangers of debate. We acknowledge that many senior executives – groomed at making business cases, adept at mobilizing facts and figures in their favour – are very effective at this stage of mobilizing change. Often, however, these same executives hold misguided views about the likely outcomes of debate. They are impatient, and expect their peers and subordinates to be won over by the charm and power of their oratory. We make the point that this impatience kills the power of debate. If executives expect the barnstorming speech and the crystal-clear logic of their public speaking to win the day in one fell swoop, they will be disappointed. This kind of transformation rarely happens in a debate audience. So this chapter also explores the incorrect assumptions and expectations of the impatient leader and, we hope, opens the way for a more considered, unplugged style. We will develop this further in subsequent chapters.

Furthermore, this chapter explores the idea that debates can take place with audiences of different sizes (yes, there is a such a thing as a debate with an audience of one). These can (must) have differing outcomes, both intended and unintended, so there are dangers here for the unwary. If we expect all debates to be structured in the same way and to deliver the same kind of results, we can expect to be surprised. So we'll also explore these expectations and – we hope – help senior executives scale down any expectations of instant success.

In short, we must view engaging in debate as a necessary scene-setting practice for senior executives – one that begins the process of change by flushing out arguments and concerns, and by allowing those in direct opposition to us to identify themselves in a constructive way. Without this essential stage executives in opposition often go underground and engage in subversion. Better to have things out in the open.

In conclusion, we argue that debate is not an end in itself. Debate leads the procession of strategic conversations, and is followed inexorably by discussion and dialogue. But there's a real challenge here. Executives usually fall into one of two camps. They tend either to be excellent at debate and reasonable at involving stakeholders in discussion, or very good at discussion and reasonably adept at dialogue (Figure 3.1). We have come across very few executives who have skills spanning the entire range of the *Leadership Unplugged* continuum, from debate through discussion to dialogue. Why? Common sense indicates (and our research supports the idea) that good tellers in debate often aren't good listeners in dialogue. More on this in Part III. We end this chapter by reinforcing the book's main

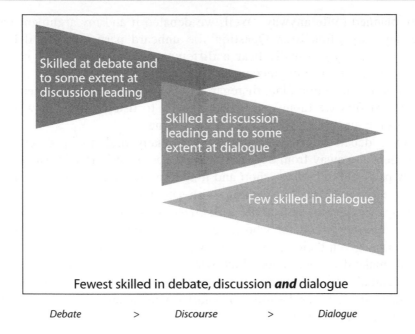

Skilled at debate and to some extent at discussion leading

Skilled at discussion leading and to some extent at dialogue

Few skilled in dialogue

Fewest skilled in debate, discussion **and** dialogue

Debate > Discourse > Dialogue

Figure 3.1 The *Unplugged Continuum* revisited

message – that the executives most likely to succeed in leading change are those who appreciate the completeness and interrelatedness of the three conversation processes, and how communication dynamics must change over time.

What is Debate, and What is It For?

If debate doesn't represent the great orator at work, beating the crowds into submission with the power of her words, what is it? And – more importantly – what is it for? In essence, we believe that engaging in debate is about taking sides. It's about getting people to say yes or no. And it's about creating confrontation. It's widely held that this conflict stage can be tremendously productive and creative. We agree, but with one caveat – it can be productive so long as all parties to the debate understand the place of debate in the continuous cycle of conversations. In reality, however, when leaders or managers say 'Let's debate this', often they mean 'Let's get the issues out into the open'. And that doesn't usually mean they're about to agree with, or build on, an opposing view. More likely it means that when they identify contrary arguments they will proceed to shoot them down and drive ahead relentlessly, doing what they planned to do anyway. 'Well, we debated it and my argument won the day', we often hear. Question the unheard parties to the debate, however, and you usually hear a different story, frighteningly similar from organization to organization: 'It's just the CEO railroading his/her ideas on to the action plan, disregarding the opinions and experience of others. At first we thought they were going to listen to us, but when it keeps on happening you know it's just a game.'

While debate is confrontational – and many mid- to lower echelon managers shy away from exposing themselves directly in this way – it is really powerful in both the short and long term. But this is only the case if it is used in a constructive fashion, with safeguards in place to encourage participation. Senior executives must make it safe to engage. If debate is used with due regard for who is taking part and their emotional needs (especially given their status in the organization), and if it is used to help people make decisions about which way to go, it can be extremely powerful. It can also be used to encourage people to get off the fence or to stop procrastinating. It can be used to polarize your audience and to identify voting intentions within it.

Positioning the Vision

It's because of debate's power to articulate simple messages that we describe the debate phase as 'positioning the vision'. What we mean here is that the simple structure and style of the debate phase can be used to great effect to convey a senior executive's vision for the organization. We believe that senior executives who use debate as a fundamental communications tool in this way will provoke discussion and generate some agreement about the way forward for an organization. Before we get much further into what we mean by *positioning*, though, let's look in a little more detail at *vision*.

Organizations have long talked about the need for vision, whether strategic vision, organizational vision or leadership vision. But what do they mean by 'vision'? Management gurus the world over – from consultants and practitioners to academics and writers – have long talked about it. Vision has been defined, variously, as 'the big picture', 'a compelling future' and 'audacious goals', among many other things. Generally it is construed as some visible, almost tangible, description of the future: a future that is worth struggling for, worth fighting for. But the point we make at the beginning of the previous chapter is that we are actually no nearer knowing or understanding what 'visions' are, or how to encapsulate them, than we have ever been. So we ask managers what they mean by 'vision'. Inevitably people's answers are individual. This apparently trivial exercise almost always halts executives in their tracks and it's worth exploring why.

If it is a truism that every single executive sees the world in a different way how, then, can any vision appeal to every single individual? How can any of us as individuals – seeing the world through our own individual filters – paint a picture that has meaning for anyone else? We are all governed by our own ways of making sense of the world and how we absorb information. But we are also driven by how that information builds on, or relates to, our previous experience. And we all give different weights to different aspects of the data that we think are particularly important. Further, any final decisions we take on the basis of a body of data will be different from those that any other individual might make. This difference reflects our differing criteria of value. In this sense, what is usually described as 'common sense' doesn't exist. At the very least, it isn't common.

Filtering the Vision

Why do executives perceive only a small portion of the available information, attach idiosyncratic interpretations to that data and then assign peculiar weights to different possible outcomes? Researchers have found that a three-stage filtering process (Figure 3.2) occurs. All of us:

- have a limited field of vision
- display selective perception
- and practise selective interpretation.

Much research has been conducted into how we scan the world about us, and into what it is that executives focus their attention on. For instance, while some executives spend a great deal of effort reading formal reports from external consultants and research organizations, others rely on a network of more informal contacts to find out what's going on. However an executive tries to get information, though, he or she cannot be looking in every direction at once or listening for every piece of relevant news and this limits his or her field of vision.

Additional filtering occurs because executives perceive only a fragment of the data within their field of vision. When reading a consultancy report, for example, secondary issues will interfere with an executive's comprehension – his or her regard for the consulting firm, for instance, or whether or not he or she likes the editorial style and layout of the report.

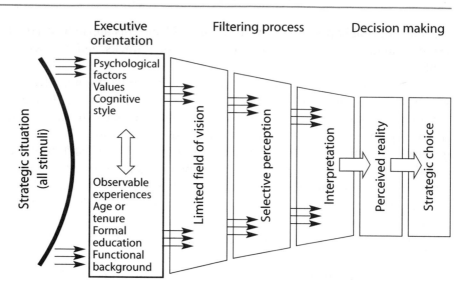

Figure 3.2 Executive reality – the route to strategic choice is filtered by what we see, what we think about what we see and our previous experience of what we see (after Finkelstein and Hambrick 1996[2])

Finally, the executive will interpret or attach meaning to the information received. For example, does she perceive an opportunity or a threat in the data?

As if the three steps in this filtering process were not complex enough, they may also interact out of sequence. An executive who regards a particular information source as valuable, for example, is more likely to rely on that source in the future. In this case, selective perception will affect that person's field of vision in the future.

The overall result of the filtering process is that an executive's picture of the strategic situation his or her firm faces may correspond only vaguely, if at all, with the objective facts – even if those could be ascertained.

A useful conceptual approach to considering an executive's cognitive style is based on the work of Carl Gustav Jung, a classic psychology theorist and a student of Freud. Jung's theories identify two dimensions of cognitive style captured effectively by Katherine Briggs and Isabel Myers[3] (Figure 3.3):

- information gathering (or perception)
- and information processing (or judgment).

The perception dimension maps an individual's preferred way of seeing the world, whether by sensing the world through the five physical senses (S in

Figure 3.3) or by intuition (N in Figure 3.3). Likewise, judgment or information processing occurs either through thinking (T), linking ideas logically using notions of cause and effect, or feeling (F), basing an evaluation on personal or group values.

Appreciating how we prefer both to gather information and to process it can help us understand how we make decisions. For instance, the ST executive tends to be fact-oriented, practical and orderly, relying heavily on written, formal sources of information. In a study of how executives responded to capital investment proposals, those with an ST profile showed a general aversion to investing, given the limited data available, and usually rated proposals as highly risky. SF executives, in contrast, were most inclined to accept the same proposals and rated them as relatively low risk.

This relatively simple example shows that what we think is largely driven by how we think. The implications of this are striking. Gaining consens-pus on significant issues from peers, for example, is no longer a question of understanding *what* they think but of understanding *how* they think.

This simple insight can lead to extraordinary gains in how we communicate or position the vision. If we can do this in such a way as to tap into

Information processing

		Thinking (T)	Feeling (F)
	Sensing (S)	ST: administrator Fact-oriented, practical, orderly; relies on written, formal media	ST: coach Tends to be fact-oriented, friendly, spontaneous; relies heavily on oral, informal media
Information gathering	INtuition (N)	NT: strategist Tends to be possibility-oriented, impersonal, integrative; relies primarily on written formal media, engages in little scanning	NF: visionary Tends to be possibilities-oriented, enthusiastic, insightful; engages in little scanning, relies on oral, informal media; thinking patterns original

Figure 3.3 How your thinking style affects decision making – Myers-Briggs Type profiles

the very different way individuals see the world and make sense of it, then we've gone a long way towards getting our message across to them. In other words, because a vision or strategy for the future must be communicated in three, or perhaps four, different ways to reach an entire audience it must as be clear and unambiguous as possible. Striving for this clarity can often help you develop a communicable and memorable view of what the future might look like; of what it involves us doing today to get there. In Figure 3.4, there's a simplified framework to help you understand how others might be thinking and to help you develop a position that others can appreciate.

This communicability is essential, because what you are looking for in the debate phase is nothing more than a simple agreement. You're looking for the 'yes' vote. The fundamentals of the debate phase boil down exactly to this decision point – do I agree or disagree? The twin forces of logic and language are all drafted to help you persuade others to say 'yes, I agree', and to line up behind you. It's the ultimate in democratic forms of leadership.

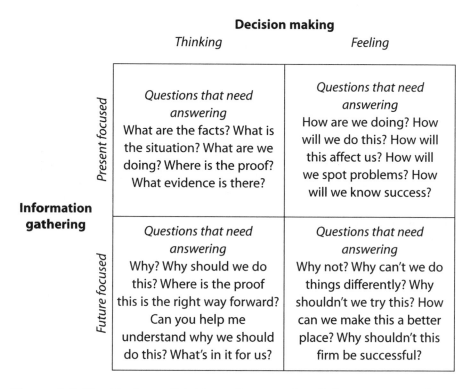

Decision making

	Thinking	*Feeling*
Present focused	*Questions that need answering* What are the facts? What is the situation? What are we doing? Where is the proof? What evidence is there?	*Questions that need answering* How are we doing? How will we do this? How will this affect us? How will we spot problems? How will we know success?
Future focused	*Questions that need answering* Why? Why should we do this? Where is the proof this is the right way forward? Can you help me understand why we should do this? What's in it for us?	*Questions that need answering* Why not? Why can't we do things differently? Why shouldn't we try this? How can we make this a better place? Why shouldn't this firm be successful?

Information gathering

Figure 3.4 The *Unplugged Matrix* – a framework to help you communicate through understanding the questions different people ask

Coercion and human rights – the dark side of leadership

Coercion still works today as a form of leadership. It's fast – you can buy compliance quickly – but it is not effective or moral leadership. Dictators, both in organizations and on the world's political stage, know what they want. But they need much more than conversation, logic and language to ensure they get and keep their 'peace'. They need Draconian measures, guns and punishment. They actually don't want any form of discussion – they want fear, compliance and silence. This is not good leadership. It isn't leadership borne of values that respect people.

If ever you fear that you as a leader may be tempted towards the powers of the dark side – 'I'm in charge, surely they must do what I ask? I'll show them …' – we urge you to read and review the Declaration on Human Rights issued by the United Nations over 50 years ago. Look on the web at http://www.un.org/Overview/rights.htm. Then think about your own organization, and see whether your people in truth have freedom of speech and freedom of thought. It's a sobering exercise.

Positioning the vision, then, is the purpose of debate. It's important to remember, however, exactly what it is that you're attempting at this time. You are trying to portray the vision in the best possible light, as well as you are able. In reality, all you're trying to do is kick-start the debate. You must remember that communication is dynamic and the message invariably changes over time. Too many senior executives forget the speed with which this happens, but they must remember that it is the participants in the implementation process and the organization's other stakeholders who will amend and tweak the vision as they see fit. They do this as they come to know the vision and as they get to implement it. This is the inevitable side effect of everyone seeing the world individually – that they will see your own vision and its implementation differently from you. And if they manage the implementation, you had better believe that it will be *their* version of the vision that will be implemented.

Many senior executives give up striving for employee participation at this point and try to haul the process 'back on track' with a dose of coercion. This is the worst thing that can be done, since handing ownership of the vision and its implementation to the team is exactly what most executives want in the first place. It's purely the feeling of losing control that causes the teeth to clamp shut and leads to the process being 'hauled back on track'.

So does this tell us anything more about what vision *is*? In the *Unplugged* view of leadership, vision is the best business case for our chosen strategy. You have to go to your stakeholders with all guns blazing to persuade them that yours is the only appropriate way to tackle the future of the organization, but you must also remember that it won't win every- one over – not by a long chalk. Its function is as a line in the sand or stake in the ground marking where we, as the organization's senior executives, want to go. More than anything, it's a clarion call for change.

The Five-Point Debate Strategy

Looking in detail at the debate phase, it is clear that it comprises five distinct stages. So in engaging with your audience, whoever that might include, there is a five-point debate strategy that you need to prepare and put in place:

1. research and build the best business case
2. choose compatible channels for the message
3. open conversations at every level
4. expect resistance, but know that resistance is useful
5. listen for emerging arguments.

Case 5. Southern Illinois University Carbondale – learning to debate

April 12, 2002
Debate format to follow Oxford University model
By K.C. Jaehnig

CARBONDALE, Ill. – a small but determined band of planners is working to transplant a 175 year-old Oxford University tradition from its native England to the campus of Southern Illinois University Carbondale (SIUC). In what donor Barbara J. Schwartz dubbed an 'organized experiment', SIUC's new Center for Civil Discourse has devised a programme for debates modelled after those held by the famed Oxford Union each year since 1873.

'This is not debate as practised by school debate teams', stressed Schwartz, whose 1999 gift of $100,000 in stock endowed the new center. 'This is a platform for all students from every discipline to talk about the issues of the day that are important to them', said the Makanda resident.'We would like to encourage them to look below the surface, beyond the hot buttons – to question the platitudes in the press and from the podium. We also want to help the participants develop techniques for defending their positions in a civil fashion.'

The inaugural debate – on the question of whether guided prior should be part of SIUC commencement exercises – will take place from 7.28 pm Wednesday April 24 in the auditorium of the Hiram H. Lesar Law Building. It costs nothing to watch, and area residents as well as members of the university community at large are welcome not only to attend but to take part if time allows.

'Jonny Gray (assistant professor in speech communication at SIUC) informally sampled the group of students to come up with the first topic and this was the one that emerged', said Nathan P. Stucky, chair of SIUC's speech communication department. 'It's a topic that can stand some careful thinking about.'

Stucky and Gray have some experience with the style of discourse that underpins the new center. They both taught for several years at Louisiana State University, where a speakers' forum draws hundreds of student participants each semester. 'You'd see incredibly committed students vigorously defending their positions on topics with a great deal of enthusiasm', Stucky said.

They weren't just getting together to have a talk. They did research, constructed a cohesive, articulate argument and tried it out in the forum of public opinion. That's what we want to encourage here. Our students will find themselves having to do that repeatedly in their lives and careers, whether it is talking to the city council about the need for a stoplight at a school crosswalk, or making a presentation to a Board of Directors. These are skills we're hoping to foster.

Stucky, Gray and SIUC Crime Study Center Director Thomas C. Castellano, chosen for his wide-ranging involvement with contemporary social problems and issues, serve on the fledgling center's executive committee. They have been working for nearly a year to establish guidelines for running its debates. Right now, this is how they think it will work. First, students will choose a topic. Next, an advisory committee of students and faculty will hold open auditions a week before the debate itself, choosing one speaker to argue in favor of that topic and one to argue against it. These students will begin the actual debate with five-minute speeches. Afterward, students who audition may present their positions. If time remains, members of the audience may also speak.

Even if they do not choose to speak, debate observers will still have a role to play. Organizers will divide the auditorium into 'for' and 'against' sections. Audience members can vote with their seats as to whose argument is most persuasive by changing sections as they change their minds. In a vigorously argued debate, it could well be that everyone would be on their feet at the same time. If that's the case, it might be just what the donor ordered.

'The debate has been an American tradition, but it's kind of died out', Schwartz said.

People will sit and listen to all sorts of disruptive and disturbing ideas and never speak up. Maybe it's because they don't feel comfortable expressing an opinion when there are so many 'experts' around. Maybe they don't think they can make a good argument. We need a way to balance this. People need to know that their opinions are important.

Public Affairs
Southern Illinois University
Carbondale, Ill. 62901–6519
618/453 2276
Sue Davis, Director

Building the Best Business Case

> The five-point debate strategy:
>
> 1. **best business case**
> 2. choose compatible channels
> 3. open all channels
> 4. resistance is useful
> 5. listen for emerging arguments.

If reading the SIUC case is your first exposure to formal debate procedures since high school, you will get your first reminder that structure plays a significant role in the process and that there's more to setting up formal debates than you might think. Note that the SIUC spent a year figuring out the best way to structure the formal debates. And they're very clear, too, about the heavy upfront commitment to planning on the part of the debaters themselves. There's research to undertake and a cohesive argument to artic-ulate, and there are rehearsals to attend. How much preparation on this scale do most senior executives undertake before foisting key issues on stakeholder groups? Some, we know, undertake a good deal of preparation, but the vast majority don't spend half this much time planning their communication to this level of detail. They should.

Now, we are not at all suggesting you establish formal debates to get your organization's key issues out into the open, though this wouldn't necessarily be such a bad idea. What we are suggesting is that by looking at how debate is structured, we can adopt some of its more powerful aspects informally into our portfolio of leadership skills.

Case 6. International debating rules – learning to use debate processes

What's the Issue?
Every debate revolves around a specific topic or theme, known as the resolution or motion. The 'government' usually proposes the motion and the 'opposition' opposes it. If the resolution or motion contains vague phrases or words, the government team has to clarify the vague terms at the beginning of the first speech. The clarified resolution is then called the *case*. In essence, this is the issue that the debate has to resolve.

Significantly, many different cases or issues can be derived from each resolution, and the important point for us as executives is that it is the issues that must be dealt with in the debate. The motion itself (for example, how we as an organization, or how organizations generally, become more competitive) may

Table 3.1 Debate styles compared

Debate styles	Order of speeches and length
Japan and USA	Prime Minister constructive, 7 minutes
	Leader of the Opposition constructive, 7 minutes
	Member of Government constructive, 7 minutes
	Member of Opposition constructive, 7 minutes
	Leader of Opposition rebuttal, 4 minutes
	Prime Minister rebuttal, 4 minutes
British	First proposition, first speaker; 7 minutes
	First opposition, first speaker; 7 minutes
	First proposition, second speaker; 7 minutes
	First opposition, second speaker; 7 minutes
	Second proposition, first speaker; 7 minutes
	Second opposition, first speaker; 7 minutes
	Second proposition, second speaker; 7 minutes
	Second opposition, second speaker; 7 minutes
Canadian	Prime Minister constructive, 7 minutes
	Member of the Opposition, 7 minutes
	Minister of the Crown, 7 minutes
	Leader of Opposition, 10 minutes
	Prime Minister rebuttal, 3 minutes

simply be too big to deal with in one session. For this reason the case must be clear, debatable and directly derived from the resolution. An example of how to develop a clear case is as follows.

Resolution, motion or strategy: Within organizations, all departments should be more competitive.

Link or definition: By 'organizations', we mean private rather than public sector organizations. By 'departments', we mean autonomous business functions such as manufacturing, research and development, accounting, marketing and human resources, among others. By 'competitive' we mean able to generate more revenue than other firms in the industry. Therefore it can be argued that all a firm's functional departments should generate revenue. However, some functional departments can't generate revenue on the open market; they must service internal clients.

Therefore our case is:

Case or issue: Service departments should not have to generate revenue. The case is relevant to the theme or topic of competition, but it is clearly a subset of the issue. Breaking the theme down into issues in this way helps us to identify what competition, for instance, actually means to us in the here and now. And by articulating the case, as distinct from the resolution or motion – the short-term tactics rather than the long-term strategy, if you will – we're simplifying the debate and making it easier to involve our audience in addressing the issue. Also it's easier to do something about the issue, if necessary.

This process of elaborating cases or issues from themes is extremely relevant and important, because it is the case that the opposition must attack and not the resolution. Too often in business debate we attack the bigger picture or theme of the debate, as opposed to the smaller, more focused issue that may indeed be possible to overturn. When deriving an issue to debate in organizations, it's important to make sure that the links are tight and clear; otherwise the debate becomes fragmented and the participants can't see the point. (In formal debate processes, loose links between motion and case are common and can lead to stimulating and interesting debate. In the corporate arena this probably wouldn't help, however.)

Dealing with a Counter Case
If the government proposes a policy case – saying 'We should do X' – then the opposition usually defends the status quo with 'We should not do X'. This often happens by default in the informal strategy debates that take place in companies. For instance, if the resolution (or strategy of a firm) is that firms, in order to be competitive, must expand overseas, the case or issue to address might arise when one director says 'We should move into

Asia, and here's why'. Another director disagrees. 'No, we shouldn't move into Asia. Here's why not.' Often what results is a standoff.

The situation becomes increasingly complex when the opposition raises a counter case that runs against the original case. 'No, we shouldn't move into Asia, we should move into Scandinavia.' A counter case is usually wholly at odds with the case up for discussion, and is almost always unhelpful. In the strategic expansion example, the organization probably doesn't have the resources for such a strategy – 'Asia and Scandinavia? No, thanks.' What's needed at this point, then, is a clear procedural decision on how to deal with the opposing cases arising in debates. Interestingly, formal debate procedures are sketchy on how to handle counter cases. Japanese debating guidelines suggest that counter cases are a relatively new phenomenon, and that there is little consensus about how to how to structure them formally.

One way to deal with this most lifelike of dilemmas is to use Australasian debating rules, which some in international debating circles regard as controversial. Normally the government team making a proposal has the exclusive right to define the case from the resolution. Not in Australasian debates, however. The opposing team has an equal right to launch a case from the definition. In the expansion example this might very well be a counter case, such as 'Let's expand into Scandinavia'. So then the debate considers the case for Asia, the case for Scandinavia and a third case – which of the cases best addresses the resolution (or strategy)? All very time-consuming, but essential if real participation and effective implementation are to be achieved in the medium to long term.

Clarity of Debate

A widely held rule on the international debate circuit is that debaters may not read their arguments from notes. Governing bodies almost always demand that participants not make cases that require excessive specialized knowledge in order to debate. Such cases are considered undebatable, and running against the grain of clarity and communicability. Another indication of the significance that debate organizers attach to this issue is that debaters who wish to reject a case as unclear or undebatable must make their point as soon as possible, and usually within the first three minutes. After this time the case is presumed valid and may not be challenged on these grounds. In the real world, too, there is a corollary – analyse situations quickly and tackle the false logic in any debates or issues that arise.

The Team Line and Team Roles

Supporting the team line, or singing from the same hymn sheet, in a debate is extremely important, as veering away from the agreed thread exposes your team to attack. The team line need be nothing more than a one-line summary of why the house should adopt or reject the case under discussion. Keep it simple. A clear allocation of roles in debate is also helpful and should be adhered to. Departing from agreed roles is described as 'knifing' your own team. Invariably it leads the opposition to quote the opposing views fielded by your team and accuse you of contradiction. Get the allocation of roles right first time.

The Burden of Proof
The burden of defining the case from the resolution usually lies with the government, and there must be a clear and debatable case. The burden of proof also lies with the government, and ties are awarded to the opposition. The opposition, importantly, has what is technically called the burden of clash. In other words, they must attack the case. For the most robust argument to win the debate it is important that the participants make the best case they can for each side of the argument. The opposition must disprove the case, with logic and evidence, or show that the case is undebatable or does not directly deal with the resolution. In much the same way that scientific theories are tested by attempts at disproving them, so too in debate. An innovation here is provided by the situation in Canada, where the burden is on the opposition to disprove a case. Here ties go to the government. This often demonstrates forward thinking, and represents a significant move away from the status quo.

Microtactics of Debate
No new material or new arguments are allowed in rebuttal speeches and conclusions. It's simply too important a point at which to keep re-opening the debate. The rebuttal and conclusions are about ending the debate, and moving to a decision and closure. Not only does it hold up the decision-making process – it's also confusing for the audience. New and exciting examples to illustrate your points are welcome, however, and will help you win the argument.

You'll see from the table at the head of this case that there are some minor differences in the sequencing of debates. The data shows that it is difficult for the opening party to be perceived as the winner at the conclusion of British-style debates. They, and their arguments, have usually been completely forgotten after the half dozen or so speeches in the interim. A really important lesson here, then – speak last if at all possible.

Organizers of debates round the world recognize the importance of these hot spots, and don't allow interruptions from opponents or from the floor in the first and last minutes of the debate. If these are critical moments in your communication make sure you use them. Never, ever, simply run out of time. It's a waste of key airtime.

Other advice to debaters:

- Use the conclusions and rebuttal periods to explain why you have won the debate.
- Offer points of information to remind people you exist.
- Accept points of information to demonstrate how magnanimous you are.
- Defend yourself if you're insulted or misquoted.

How Long Do You Need in a Debate?
There is worldwide consensus as to how long it takes to make a point in a debate. In seven to eight minutes you can make a phenomenal contribution, says debate theory. You do not need any more time. After all, with a simple, clear issue to resolve all you want from your audience is a simple 'yes'. Further, rebuttal speeches need only three or four minutes to deliver a barnstorming conclusion. How long do you spend trying to browbeat the opposition into submission?

Judging Performance in a Debate
Besides the eventual vote outcome, debaters are scored by a judge or panel of judges. Here 60–70 per cent of the marks are awarded for the substance of the debate, the logic and rational argument, and 30–40 per cent for style (including body language, grammar and vocabulary). In Britain more weight is given to debaters who are confident and display wit, imagery and erudition, which may explain why US debaters claim that British debate lacks substance and does not always bring disagreements into sharp focus. Britons, on the other hand, often think that American debate is rather dry and misses the fundamental point of debate – to inspire, move and use language beautifully.

Questions:
1. What does the development of clear, debatable issues derived from resolutions achieve for the parties to a debate? Why might it be valuable for executives to consider this in the context of their own organizations?
2. How does the intensely formal, alternating-speaking schedule enhance the debate? How might this type of discipline be applied in organizations?
3. What can we learn from the brevity of debate speeches, and from the importance that organizers place on the correct sequence of speakers?

The Business Lessons from Formal Debate Processes

Define the Issues

Formal debate procedures from round the world can teach us powerful lessons we can apply in the business arena. First, that we can use general themes – or resolutions – from our business strategy (be competitive, be global, be ethical) to develop simple clear issues (or cases) to debate within the organization. Many issues can be identified and dealt with in this way. This is reminiscent of the 'salami' approach to problem solving, where complex and apparently insoluble problems are broken down into smaller issues of manageable size.

Make Every Word Count

In your simple one-line definition of the issue, make every word count. What exactly is the issue that needs addressing, the thing you believe, the action that needs taking?

Attack the Issue, Not the Strategy

If you are opposing some development, the burden is on you to attack the issue. If it survives your attack, or comes through modified in some way, that's a good outcome for the organization. Remember to attack the issue, as defined by the protagonist, and not the bigger theme or the strategy generally, which is probably too big. A broadside along the lines of 'I disagree with your strategy' is not as helpful to your argument as 'I don't think we should launch this product now', or 'I don't think we should open offices in the Far East.'

Attack Early

If you are opposing an issue, remember to attack its logic early. Is the one-line issue clear? Can it be tackled or addressed by this group of people? Does it support the overall theme or strategy of the organization? Use logic and rational argument to make your points here. Emotional blocking and posturing is not helpful in promoting your viewpoint.

Simplify a Complex Debate

If mutually exclusive proposals (or counter cases) are made in a strategy development meeting, have a clear process in your own mind for dealing with them. You could deal with each one separately on its own merits, and then appraise each one against the overarching strategy of the organization. Finally, address the proposal that best fits the strategy. (This is subtly different from debating which is the best proposal.)

Keep It Simple and Short

If you need a mass of specialized knowledge to make or to understand an argument, then the issue is not simple enough. And you don't need more than seven minutes to make three key points, which is all anyone needs to make a decision. So you must be able to communicate what's on your mind without resorting to a three-hour laptop presentation with supporting spreadsheet appendices.

Use the Hot Time Slots

The first minute and the last minute of every speech are the most important. Use them wisely. Always remember to speak last or to sum up, if you can, if there is a sequence of speakers.

Support the Team Line

Select two or three people; ensure that each of them are lined up to support and argue different elements of the debate. Make sure they are clear about what their roles are so that they can support the team line honestly and effectively.

The Burden of Clash

Although the burden of proof on any particular issue is with the proponent, it's worth being an aggressive opposition. Disprove the case if you can, rather than merely let the other side make a poor case for their issue. This means you must engage in the debate. Don't abdicate your responsibility to be party to the discussion. It's your responsibility to clash but remember to clash with the issue, not the people behind it.

Style and Substance

Remember that most of the general corporate audience regards logic and analysis highly, but many will also be won over by your confidence, clarity and conversation. You need to bring both substance and style to your debating performances.

Choose Compatible Channels

> The five-point debate strategy:
>
> 1.   best business case
> **2.   choose compatible channels**
> 3.   open all channels
> 4.   resistance is useful
> 5.   listen for emerging arguments.

Considering whether the issue is routine or something out of the ordinary – a bit more complex – should help you decide how to communicate with your various stakeholders. A seminal research project by Robert Lengel and Richard Daft[4] showed that complex issues such as organizational strategy and change management demanded rich, usually face-to-face, communication channels. Too little information on complex issues would often lead to mistrust and a lack of commitment, while also probably leading an audience to imagine that things were being kept from them. If rich communication channels are used to deliver routine news or data, on the other hand, all too often the natural outcome is confusion and again uncertainty. The natural questions may become: 'What's going on here? Why am I being told this?'

There is a real skill involved in choosing the right medium for the message. This is so important that we've devoted much of the next chapter to this topic.

Open All Channels

> The five-point debate strategy:
>
> 1.   best business case
> 2.   choose compatible channels
> **3.   open all channels**
> 4.   resistance is useful
> 5.   listen for emerging arguments.

Having identified, clarified and simplified the issue, it's time to begin the communication process. The debate must be 'seeded' by opening as many communication channels as possible, each delivered with a style or richness appropriate to the message. These are the first tentative steps towards actually positioning the vision, and as such are crucial to the success of the venture. This part of the visioning process – the opening up of the debate and the clarion call to different stakeholder groups – is critical. If it is done well it gives everyone confidence that the top management team has a vision for the future, and that they are willing to engage in discussion about it. If done badly it can mar the entire leadership process, and often leads to an irrevocable breakdown in trust. This is illustrated in the Greek myths by Cassandra, King Priam's daughter. The sun god Apollo granted Cassandra the gift of being able to tell the future but tainted this with the knowledge that no one would trust her. The message for senior executives, then, is engage in visioning by all means but also position the vision. The penalty for failure is being labelled a corporate Cassandra. More on this in the next chapter.

Expect Resistance

The five-point debate strategy:

1. best business case
2. choose compatible channels
3. open all channels
4. **resistance is useful**
5. listen for emerging arguments.

What we've seen in working with executives over the years is that they are almost always astounded that so few people buy in to their visions of the future. They never seem to expect wholesale resistance to their ideas. This must change. Expect resistance, but know that resistance is useful. What people say, if they are given airtime, tells us many things about their concerns for the future of the organization. How explicitly emotional the resistance is, and in what forms people reveal their concerns, tells us much about the significance or importance of the issues at a gut level. Armed with this information, we can then revise the message and recast it as necessary – changing the story, making it more relevant. Of course, executives must also recognize the subtle but significant shift in power taking place here. Here are the earliest signs that you must relinquish your vision of the future at some point and allow others to carry it forward as they see fit. Start getting used to the idea that eventually the organization's vision will not be wholly yours.

Case 7. Fiat Auto – overcoming biases, opening the debate

A good area to witness the confrontational aspects of the debate phase of change is in industrial relations between an organization's management and its unions or union officials. Nowhere in the history of management practice has this been more problematic than in the automobile industry.

In the 1990s, Fiat Auto in Italy faced major problems. Europe's automotive markets were highly competitive, caught between the rock of Japanese imports and the hard place of static demand. These problems, together with a recession in Italy, created a major financial crisis for Fiat. Their response was innovative and uncompromising. New plants were planned for Melfi in southern Italy. These plants involved high technology but also – and most significantly – new forms of work organization. A leaner management structure combined with a system of cell or team working formed the blueprint, but would it get past the unions? Fiat was heavily unionized, and major difficulties were foreseen in overcoming the legacy of 'them and us' distrust that had built up over decades at other plants in Italy.

Early discussions about how the workforce would be involved in communication on an ongoing basis were very positive. A system of horizontal communication, based on processes rather than functions, was developed. Each team was expected to talk to others in a supplier–customer relationship and team leaders' effectiveness was measured in terms of how effectively they communicated horizontally, as well as vertically. A major investment in training was planned and delivered, and not just in technical or functional skills. Teamworking, problem solving and communication skills were also major planks in the strategy. As well as formal off-the-job training, Fiat also used on-the-job training, focusing especially on the employees responsible for the integration of processes within teams.

The unions and management signed a formal accord to work together in this way, and that in its own way was also innovative. An accord? To address how we work together as opposed to targets? Unheard of! The upshot was extensive and regular consultation between unions and managers, designed explicitly to prevent disputes and to provide regular opportunities 'for communication and debate' (quote unquote).

The results? Large-scale investment, at a time when cash was scarce, made Melfi one of the most competitive automotive assembly plants in Europe. (One important indicator, inventory, was reduced to 11 hours' production in Melfi. Comparable German plants held 25–30 hours' inventory.) Finally, Melfi is indeed a profitable plant, delivering a higher return on investment than other comparable Fiat plants.

Case included by permission of European Commission DG Social Affairs, the European Union.

Listen for Emerging Arguments

The five-point debate strategy:

1. best business case
2. choose compatible channels
3. open all channels
4. resistance is useful
5. **listen for emerging arguments.**

When the various debates you might launch have been under way for some days or weeks – listen. What are people saying to you, directly and indirectly? What do you hear on the organizational grapevine? When you start to hear small voices picking arguments with you the debate has started in earnest! You need to be really sensitive and attuned to this, especially if your organization is not used to people speaking up. It may take time for staff to pick up the gauntlet that we described earlier as the burden of clash. You may need to teach them how to make sense of what's going on and coach them how to argue. (You may need coaching yourself – few of us are really effective at logical argument.) You'll certainly need to acknowledge the efforts people make when they engage in the debate.

In essence, these early opposition voices are the signal that it's time to move on. But you need to know what the arguments look and sound like before you do move on, so listen a while longer. Ask yourself who is taking part in the debate. Are they behind the issue or against it? When you have enough information about what's on the agenda and who the speakers are, then you can move on. Open the discussion.

Now Just Wait a Minute

It's at this point that authoritarian leaders usually say to us: 'What you say sounds interesting, and backs up much of my thinking, but shouldn't people do what I tell them?' Well, no. That's not our experience. And if you're reading this it probably isn't your experience either. Authoritarian leaders can get this far into the process many times but then they run out of ideas, or energy, or belief that anything can happen fast enough. We'll explain in the next chapter how time isn't on your side, and yet paradoxically how patience really *is* a virtue. So stick with it. It's a process; you've engaged in debate many times before; now we're asking for a change. Don't get attached to the debate phase just because you're good at arguing. Get ready to step aside and to listen.

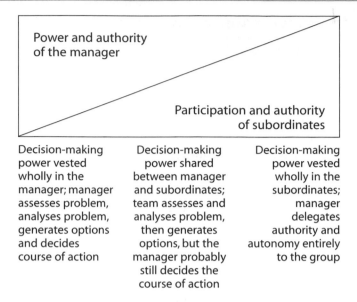

Power and authority of the manager		Participation and authority of subordinates
Decision-making power vested wholly in the manager; manager assesses problem, analyses problem, generates options and decides course of action	Decision-making power shared between manager and subordinates; team assesses and analyses problem, then generates options, but the manager probably still decides the course of action	Decision-making power vested wholly in the subordinates; manager delegates authority and autonomy entirely to the group

Figure 3.5 The power–participation continuum

There are some challenges on the way. Many executives, for instance, equate employee participation with the giving up of decision-making power. Not so. Just be clear what you are giving. Interestingly, many executives are afraid to ask for their employees' participation, and even to ask for their opinion. 'Doesn't it show I'm weak? That I don't know what to do?' Well, no. Most employees, when you ask them, see it as a sign of mature leadership. Just be clear. Some employees do confuse opinion seeking with power sharing. So be clear what you're asking for, and what you're giving. Where do you fit on the participation–power continuum in Figure 3.5? Does everyone in the debate know where they are? Make sure they do.

Changing Minds

Despite what we would like to believe, debate doesn't change people's minds. Our experience has been that people don't change their minds in debates that matter. Interestingly, the organizers of the 2002 debate held by the Oxford Union explicitly attempted to change people's minds.

Case 8.   BBC – can debate change people's minds?

Friday 7 June, 2002, 08:27 GMT 09:27 UK
The debating chamber: hear Count Tolstoy and Bonnie Greer speak

What will the future hold for the British monarchy?
A head to head debate at the Oxford Union covered some of the issues surrounding the Royal Family in the wake of the Queen's Golden Jubilee celebrations. The Union is the world's foremost debating society, with a reputation for bringing international guests and speakers to Oxford. It has been established for 175 years, aiming to promote debate and discussion not just in Oxford University, but across the globe.

Count Nikolai Tolstoy, great-nephew of the Russian author Leo Tolstoy and chairman of the International Monarchist League – which aims to support the monarchical system throughout the world – spoke on behalf of the royalists. Alongside him was the playwright and critic Bonnie Greer, who spoke for the republicans. She has lived in Britain since 1986, where she has worked mainly in theatre with women and ethnic minorities.

Silver Jubilee Babes
Our Silver Jubilee Babes – Deborah, Lucy and Dougald – also attended the debate. Deborah, Lucy and Dougald took part in an experiment to see if experts, celebrity guests and yourself – the general public – were able to change their minds about the monarchy.

Conclusion

The key points we want to emphasize at the end of this chapter are:

- Debates have a very clear issue or resolution, and this is almost always known before the debate begins.
- Debates are structured round a closed issue ('this house believes that …'), requiring from an audience only agreement or disagreement. ('All those in favour? Those against …?')
- Debate is a highly structured form of communication and the structure itself tells the story.
- Debate – used early – can help establish an effective position and a line of argument.
- The principles of debate tend to be used for argument in governmental and public fora.
- Debate is a simplistic form of communication, in that it is one-way (speaker to audience).
- Logic and analysis (substance) are highly prized in debate, but skilful style and presentation also have significant roles to play.
- The fundamental object of debate is to get as many people to support you as possible. Debate is about winning a mandate.
- There is little evidence that debate ever changes people's minds.

QuestionBank

Take time out to answer these questions.

1. How much do you encourage a culture that encourages debate within your organization? What could you do to open up the culture still further? How could you nurture the concept of the burden of clash? To what extent do you and the people you work with take criticism of your ideas personally? How can you de-personalize criticism? To what extent do you believe that ideas tested by rigorous debate are better than ideas that haven't been tested in this way?

2. How perceptive are you, and how sensitive are you to the under-currents in the organization? How can you tell what people are thinking and what questions they might have about the organi-zation's strategy? How good are members of the top manage-ment team at encouraging openness? What does openness mean for you on a day-to-day basis?

3. How impatient are you? To what extent do you believe people should hear your message once and then immediately align themselves with it, and behind you? How much do you believe your position confers power on you, and that people should simply listen to you and fulfil your demands? When might senior executives' impatience be a hindrance? Why don't people do what you want when you want?

Notes

1. Hobsbawm, Eric, 1962. *The Age of Revolution* 1789–1848. London: Weidenfeld & Nicolson.
2. From Finkelstein, Sidney and Hambrick, Donald, 1996. *Strategic Leader-ship, Top Executives and Their Effects on Organizations.* 1st edn. Reprinted with permission of South-Western, a division of Thomson Learning: www.thomsonrights.com. Fax 800 730-2215.
3. Briggs Myers, Isabel with Myers, Peter B., 1980. *Gifts Differing: Under-standing Personality Type.* Palo Alto: Davies Black.
4   Lengel and Daft, 1988. p. 13–

CHAPTER 4

Debate: Communication Strategies

This is not the end. It is not even the beginning of the end. But it is perhaps the end of the beginning.

Winston Churchill (Mansion House speech, 1942)

Headlines

In the early phase of change, methods of opening up the debate and promoting a vision for the future are required – this is the telling phase of change.

The debate phase is the most likely to be confrontational, and usually deals with the senior executives' own perspective on the future.

There is little evidence that debate alone ever changes people's minds.

Communications are often seen as a singular event – instead they should be regarded as part of a sustained process.

Organizations must move into the discussion phase when appropriate.

A range of different communication channels should be used to initiate and sustain debates, but these should deal with different aspects of the same debate theme.

The essential task of communicating corporate strategy and change is usually carried out half-heartedly, and in a manner that is blatantly manipulative and not at all sustained.

Most communications programmes change neither the message nor the medium over time.

No One Receiving

What is your organization's communication strategy? Who is responsible for deciding what to send, to whom and when? When was the last time you asked recipients of your communications (whatever they might be) whether what you were sending them was appropriate, or even whether it had been received? One communications business we were involved with sent paper copies of important documents to everyone's desk. However, because so many of the staff were hot desking (never sitting in the same place from day to day) they never received any of this material. The problem was exacerbated by the fact that these itinerant workers couldn't access e-mail except over the web; further, because of the company's firewalls they never received any of the attachments or files sent to colleagues who could access the networks internally. A well-thought-out communication strategy, focused on the needs of the recipients rather than of the senders, might have spotted some of these difficulties.

This particular organization is not alone in forgetting its employees. In most organizations the communication strategy is often regarded as part and parcel of the human resources workload. Occasionally it is treated as the responsibility of marketing instead, to keep internal customers informed as to what's going on. But it is always regarded with disdain and resignation. It's just something we have to do, or be seen to be doing. This must change. Because the most fundamental task of an organization's leaders is to communicate, and because the workforce of an organization is responsible for organizational performance, the company's employees are key stakeholders in the business. It is a major error of judgement to delegate communications strategy, either internal or external, to an outside organization, or to someone who doesn't possess full knowledge of the issues and of what's going on in the organization.

If, as we suggest, leadership is solely about communication, then developing and implementing the communications strategy is a fundamental element in the role of all senior executives. This is primarily because the early conversational phase we call debate offers your best opportunity to capture and convey the best business case for your version of the organizational vision or strategy. This was Step 1 in the five-point debate strategy we introduced in Chapter 3. As you can see from Table 4.1, this chapter

Table 4.1 The five-point debate strategy

1. Best business case	Chapter 3. Debate and also Chapter 7. Leading opinions
2. Choose compatible channels	Chapter 4. Communications strategies
3. Open all channels	Chapter 4. Communications strategies
4. Resistance is useful	Chapter 5. Politics
5. Listen for emerging arguments	Chapter 4. Communications strategies

deals with Step 2 (choosing compatible channels) and Step 3 (opening all channels) in the five-point debate strategy. We conclude this chapter by looking at how you recognize Step 4 (resistance) and Step 5 (emerging arguments). This final step, involving the emergence of arguments around the vision, is the transition trigger that tells you you're moving into the Discussion phase, which we will look at in Part II.

Before we explore the five-point debate strategy in more detail, however, we need to look more closely at the reasons for opening the debate, the three ways in which the debate phase can be used, and the purpose of organizational communication strategies generally.

Opening the Debate

Our major reason for wanting to communicate with as many people within the organization as possible is because being involved in communication – either transmitting or receiving – is to be involved in organizational decision making. And employees tend to feel that if they are not involved in organizational decision making then they are not involved in the organization. So the communication strategy of the senior executive team represents your first – and perhaps your only – opportunity to open the debate with the organization. As we saw in the last chapter, opening the debate is one of the most important aspects of the debate–discussion–dialogue continuum. Abdicate responsibility for this at your peril.

Most senior executives appreciate that leadership involves decision making. They also know that decisions – however they are arrived at – need to be communicated to employees, shareholders or customers. However, a surprising number of those senior executives believe that decisions should made solely by the top team – always behind closed doors – and that the staff should be told of a decision in a memo, a company-wide e-mail or a 30-minute presentation. Their perspective is that the role for leaders is to lead. The role for everyone else is to listen and get on with it.

Our view is that this method of communication may be fine where the decision concerns relatively simple operational aspects of the business. We're thinking here of ordering stationery, office refurbishment or even restructuring of the board. None of these things usually requires a two-way flow of information, or an exchange of views about possibilities and options. However, many of the most successful leaders believe that communication on strategic issues should start well before any decision is made. Indeed Andy Grove – chairman, co-founder and former CEO of Intel, the chipmaker – suggests that leaders should kick off the communication process in order to find out whether a decision needs to be made at all.[1] 'The most important tool in identifying a particular development as a strategic inflection point is a broad and intensive debate', he says. In other words, to see if the firm has reached a point where the old strategic picture dissolves and must give way to a new vision, put out the question: 'What's going on here? We think it might be this.' This is about seeing what messages come back from the opening salvo; it's about testing the organizational ground. This is a powerful way to engage the organization in scanning the immediate environment. Over time, key individuals – the leaders of tomorrow – will learn to become more attuned to organizational issues of significance. In addition, because they are experiencing the powerful communications medium of debate at first hand, they will be better placed to use it and its key variations in the future.

Three Ways to Use the Debate Phase

Although some executives we've worked with find the apparently highly structured character of the debate phase restrictive, it can be used in three quite different ways. First, to identify where a problem lies within an organization or unit; second, to work out how to tackle the problem in an appropriate way; and finally, to initiate any changes required within the organization. We'll take a look at each of these in turn.

Identifying the Problem

Let's say that you know you are losing market share. You want to know why. By engaging in debate with executives, managers and employees from a wide range of functions you can explore all aspects of product development, marketing strategy and customer satisfaction or dissatisfaction, and pinpoint any changes that need to be made.

Peter I. Bijur, chairman and CEO of oil group Texaco until his retirement from the group in 2001, was a business leader who believed firmly in communication, regarding it as one of the key skills of a leader.[2]

> To be an effective leader … requires the desire to communicate and the skill to engage in dialogue. I suspect that many CEOs get frustrated at the intractability of human issues. True enough, people are difficult: often slow to change, sometimes unable to understand messages. If a CEO is going to be involved in personnel development activities, he or she must work exceedingly hard to make contact with the people, to build bridges throughout the organization.

Bijur actively tried to find out about problems by setting up debates with groups of employees.

> My own preference is for open-ended get-togethers with about a dozen employees at a time – to which their managers are not invited. I share with them a lot of my views on things, and I stimulate them to share their views. Sometimes it isn't easy to persuade them to be candid. So I take my jacket off and I sit down and kick off a very informal chat about a wide range of things. I accept that there are things on their minds that I won't hear about. If people are going to ask me questions, it won't be about minutiae. It will be about macro issues that they think I might be interested in.
>
> I also recognize that they are anxious not to embarrass themselves by asking me a question I might regard as dumb. But I try diligently to treat with respect every question that is asked of me. I tell people all the time, 'There is no such thing as a stupid question. If it's important to you, I'm happy to answer it.' I end these meetings by saying, 'I read my e-mail everyday and I always respond.'

Identifying the Solution

You can also use debate to decide on a course of action. You know you need to cut costs, but how? In a debate with your top team, the finance director says the marketing budget must be cut. The marketing director responds that the most recent advertising campaign has been the most successful yet – it needs to be expanded, not cut. You then widen the debate to include other members of staff. You tell them you would like to cut costs but that you don't want to harm your marketing advantage, and you explain why. An employee in the post room suggests that you can save a few cents per package by reducing the weight of your marketing packs. And this would amount to a saving of several million dollars a year.

Initiating Change

Debate is also the first stage in initiating change. Your problem has been identified – costs are too high, for instance, and are growing fast. You have identified what you think is the correct solution – you need to move your headquarters to a city where real estate is less expensive. How do you persuade your head office staff to relocate without losing their commit-ment? One company facing just this challenge organized a series of meetings of its top executives, but foolishly kept the subject of discussion secret.[3] The staff noticed their bosses spending a lot of time in secretive meetings. They concluded that something big was going on, and that it must be horrible because they hadn't been told what it was. When the relocation was finally announced, in a way that allowed no time for discussion or questions: 'Managers and workers felt alienated and devalued. Their opinions had never been sought; their concerns and feelings had never been considered.' Some head office staff refused to relocate and left the company. Others went along with the move but their loyalty and commitment to the company had been destroyed. It's been proved time and again that clarity, openness and honesty are essential throughout the leadership communication process. The highly structured phase we call debate allows you to do this.

Engaging others in debate, seeking their views and opinions, is not an easy option, however. As Andy Grove points out, in a real debate your decisions will meet strong opposition and your point of view will come under attack.[4]

> This kind of debate is daunting because it takes a lot of time and a lot of intellectual ergs. It also takes a lot of guts – it takes courage to enter into a debate you may lose, in which weaknesses in your knowledge may be exposed and in which you may draw the disapproval of your fellow co-workers for taking an unpopular viewpoint. Nevertheless, this comes with the territory.

He continues, building a powerful case as to why it's essential not to shy away from difficult debates:

> If you are in senior management, don't feel you're being a wimp for taking the time to solicit the views, convictions and passions of the experts. No statues will be carved for corporate leaders who charge off on the wrong side of a complex decision. Take your time until the news you hear starts to repeat what you've already heard, and until a conviction builds up in your own gut.

You also need to remember that debate is not the end point, the final whistle – it is just the beginning. Says Grove:

> It is important to realize what the purpose of these debates is and what it isn't. Don't think for a moment that at the end of such debates all participants will arrive at a unanimous point of view. That's naïve. However, through the process of presenting their own opinions, the participants

will refine their own arguments and facts so that they are in much clearer focus. Gradually all parties can cut through the murkiness that surrounds their arguments, clearly understand the issues and each other's point of view. Debates are like the process through which a photographer sharpens the contrast when developing a print. The clearer images that result permit management to make a more informed – and more likely correct – call.

If the prospect of a vigorous debate scares you, it's understandable. Lots of aspects of managing an organization through a strategic inflection point petrify the participants, senior management included. But inaction might lead to a bad result for your business and that should frighten you more than anything else.

Note here that 'inaction', in Grove's lexicon, is the logical conclusion of ignoring the call to debate.

What is the Purpose of Organizational Communication Strategies?

Leaders usually need to communicate with others in their companies because of some necessary organizational change, or at least because of their perception that change is needed. The purpose of the communication, then, is either to explore what change is needed or to start implementing the change. All too often, however, the senior executives hide themselves behind locked doors and decide to change something about their business. They work out the implementation in detail and then decide to tell the staff what is happening. They organize a presentation or series of presentations, and tell employees the great secret, such as: 'Our company will become more customer focused.' The employees sit there, listen to the message, go back to their desks and behave exactly as they did before.

Not only is the content of the message ridiculed, but the way it has been dreamt up also comes in for criticism. And senior executives don't learn. Having been burned once for ignoring the brainpower of the workforce they do it again the following year. Why do senior executives continue to make these errors of judgement? Does self-confidence naturally breed the arrogance that makes them forget the impact of their approach on the workforce? This behind-closed-doors decision making is about as effective as sending people their New Year's resolutions through the mail and expecting them to be kept whatever they may be. Bill Quirke, formerly a director at major international public relations consultancy Burson Marsteller, puts it this way:[5]

At the outset of change, the board goes away for a three-day off-site retreat. They are the best informed, the most strategically minded and take the long-term view. When the change has been decided they come back to present the future to their employees. Employees, who are least well informed, least involved in the background thinking and critical to the strategy's success, get only a two-hour slide presentation, after which they are expected to be enthusiastically committed.

It really should come as no surprise when the criticism 'all talk' is levelled at boards behaving like this in this day and age. They must continue to make their views known, but they must also encourage participation through sharing knowledge and information in new and innovative ways. This is important because all business leaders today are bombarded with information. How do they sift through it all while at the same time ensuring that they hear all the important voices? One of the ways of avoiding information overload is to set up systems that delegate the responsibility for keeping informed, following corporate strategy and innovating to other groups of leaders within the company. However, these systems have to be ones that these different groups within the firm themselves value.

This is a tough challenge but one that represents a particularly valuable approach in an international company, for instance. How is the chief executive or the top team going to keep track of all developments in all aspects of their business in each country, while ensuring that the corporation is offering a standard service to its customers throughout the world? In the past, each national arm of the company would have functioned almost as a separate unit, with regular communication existing only between the top executives in each national centre. Today, a company is more likely to set up international groups of peers, who are in constant communication with each other and who are able to ensure that the corporation is offering a standardized service in all countries in which it operates.

Keith McCambridge of Whitehead Mann, a consultancy firm specializing in executive assessment and leadership development, explains how such peer groups work within his own clients.[6]

For example, if you had a global financial services business, its IT peer group would be composed of all the IT directors from all the different countries around the world. They would work as one team, they would share their experiences and knowledge, they would share their development, and they would help each other out. This prevents regional efforts that aren't integrated on a global stage. It avoids duplication of effort, or contradictory approaches to customers. [After all,] the reason why they're doing it is that their customers are global and expect the same level of service across the globe.

The ways in such peer groups communicate vary. Many not only communicate electronically but also get together in person. McCambridge says that the global oil group BP Amoco, for instance, uses peer groups intensively.

> They have discussion forums on the internet, they have video conferencing, and they have 'peer assist', where someone on the other side of the world in the peer group says: 'Right, I need some help here, and you in America have got the expertise that I need. I'm going to "play the Joker" – I need a peer assist.' That guy has to get on a plane, fly over and help him out.

McCambridge says this is a way of turning a group of national units that are operating almost as separate companies – 'America is doing its own thing, not talking to Australia or New Zealand' – into one integrated, global company. 'Setting up a peer assistance scheme is a way to build truly global communities in functional areas', he says.

As McCambridge suggests, the debates and conversations taking place throughout a company are sometimes face to face – and these conversations are almost always the most effective – but other methods, such as e-mail, also offer effective communication media. Just as long as the medium doesn't swamp other channels. The local government offices for one major European city we know of proclaimed Wednesday 'no e-mail day', in order to bring conversation and relationships back into the workplace. A Draconian measure, perhaps, but the point is well made.

Many business leaders welcome e-mail, suggesting it opens up new and direct channels of communication, enabling them to reach and hear from individuals with whom they would not make direct contact in any other way. Peter Bijur, former chairman and CEO of Texaco, said: 'E-mail is a wonderful medium. Just three or four sentences, then the person pushes the "send" button and the dialogue has begun. People feel free to send e-mail where they'd not ever think of writing me a letter.' He recalled one big CEO conference that he attended where delegates were asked if they had made their e-mail address known to the whole world. 'To my surprise, less than half of the group raised hands. I think those CEOs who don't broadcast their addresses are missing a great opportunity to create connections outside the executive suite, be it with employees or suppliers.'

In Bijur's view, not taking advantage of the benefits of e-mail communication not only risks missing out on some key conversations. It also gives an impression of unapproachability. 'Those CEOs who don't give out their e-mail addresses symbolically convey a message that they live behind some executive barricade.'

Inviting further communication may seem self-defeating in an age where a business leader may receive hundreds of e-mails a day. However, the time spent dealing with it can be worth taking. Bijur believes that a leader who guards his or her e-mail address as though it were sensitive corporate information is not only unapproachable, but is also deficient in a key leadership skills. 'They are tacitly admitting that they are not good listeners', he says. 'Listening, sounding people out, taking the pulse of the climate of an organization are a big part of my agenda.'

Choosing Compatible Channels

In seminal research conducted in the late 1980s, US academics Robert Lengel and Richard Daft established beyond doubt that some managers were smarter than others at choosing the right communications medium for a particular message.[7] They proved for the first time that what they called 'rich communications styles' – invariably face-to-face, usually one-to-one – were far more effective at communicating complex messages than what they referred to as 'lean' communications media, such as memos or newsletters (Figure 4.1).

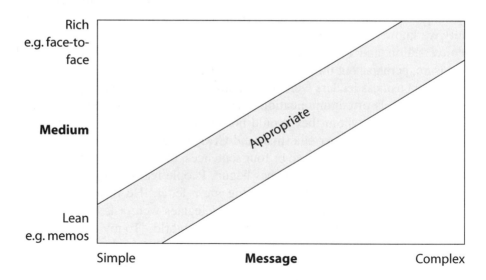

Figure 4.1 The medium and the message – communicating complex messages demands rich communication channels

Lengel and Daft's main findings may seem obvious today but no one had had such an impact on the thinking of communications professionals before, and few people have since. Sadly, the message has been lost on the vast majority of management practitioners, some of whom understand this intuitively but most of whom don't fully appreciate it. One executive who did was Harold Geneen, the ITT CEO, who said:[8]

> If I and my headquarters team intended to monitor and oversee the European operations, I owed it to the European managers to be there on the spot. … It became our policy to deal with problems on the spot, face to face. … In Europe [as opposed to New York] I could see the man's face, hear his voice, understand the intensity of his conviction.

Sadly, business leaders often fail to see that their choice of medium (Table 4.2) affects the meaning of a message as it is received by its audience. This is despite the fact that it is now clear from communications research that communication will only be effective when the richness of the medium matches the complexity of the message. By 'rich' media, we mean channels that convey what researchers call 'social presence'. Rich media have the ability to convey multiple information cues simultaneously, facilitate rapid feedback between the parties and establish a personal focus. In other words, they allow the parties involved to learn what's going on as quickly as possible, both at the explicit level of content and at a subliminal emotional level. This probably explains why research shows managers spending upwards of 80 per cent of their time in personal, face to face discussions. They want to learn as much as possible as quickly as possible. Electronic media and newsletters,

Table 4.2 Making the medium match the message: Lengel and Daft's six rules for choosing the right medium for your message (Lengel and Daft, 1988).

1. Use face-to-face channels for non-routine, difficult communications

2. Send routine, simple communications through a lean channel

3. Use rich channels to extend your reach across and outside the organization

4. Use rich channels for implementing corporate strategy

5. Don't censor information about critical issues – be honest

6. See electronic media as just one channel in a communications spectrum

for instance, fall short in this sense because generally they convey limited cues and are slow to provide feedback.

Don't misunderstand us. Astute business leaders don't shy away from the blunt memo and the routine e-mail, but they choose it only when the message to be conveyed is routine and simple. A memo, after all, saves time and prevents information overload. It is best not to use a memo or report for the non-routine or the complex, however, as this will invariably be perceived as a smokescreen to bury unpalatable issues. Lose the trust of your audience and you'll never rebuild it completely.

Open All Channels

Communications techniques should kick-start debate at the early stages in change programmes. They include all forms of public speaking, large-scale video presentations and, interestingly, the judicious use of the open letter.

Case 9. Eli Lilly – Sydney Taurel puts the moose on the table

In February 2000 Sydney Taurel, after two years as CEO of Eli Lilly, the pharmaceutical company famous for Prozac, issued a 6000-word white paper entitled *On Leadership* to every member of the firm. It ranged widely across the issues you would expect from the leader of such a major player on the world pharmaceutical stage. But it also raised issues that many might think inappropriate – about the sensitivities of the organization, for example, and about Taurel's perceptions of the organization's strengths and weaknesses, some of which were interlinked.

Headed boldly 'to my colleagues', Taurel's paper opens by emphasizing the growth opportunities available to Lilly. But he also makes the point that these opportunities are in no sense entitlements. 'They will not fall into our laps simply because we have devised a strategy for pursuing them. We will realize them only if we can implement our strategy fully, efficiently, and effectively.'

Taurel's faith and confidence in the firm's potential is clear, but he isn't afraid to challenge the organization either.

> We need to bear down on implementation with a focus and a force many times greater than we have mustered up to now. ... I know that many of you share my sense of frustration when we don't consistently meet our own expectations. And perhaps, as you begin to read this, the thought uppermost in your mind is: 'Can't we stop talking about it and just get on with it?'

Well, yes, he says, but first they have to identify clearly what it is they want to do. And the purpose of his paper is to describe a framework for more thoughtful and productive action.

> I want to engage the entire leadership team in a dialogue about how we can bring about necessary changes in our company. This is intended as a background or reference document for a series of discussions that will begin in the very near future. But in fact, as I have indicated in my last two business television broadcasts, most of these concepts are clear and straightforward. I would like to see our management team begin acting on them right away.

Despite having a strong sense of purpose in his communications, Taurel is not under any illusions. 'Transformation cannot be achieved merely by issuing new policies and making a few speeches', he says. 'It requires a patient, sustained effort to educate people to a new way of doing things, to eradicate the old habits that no longer work, and to validate the benefits of change as they occur.' Importantly, he believes that:

> ... it requires honest introspection and change at the personal level. This is one process that absolutely must come from the top down, for the simple reason that, if management behaves according to the old culture, everyone else will receive implicit permission to do so as well.

Interestingly, Taurel highlights one of Lilly's strengths – the high value the company places on people, which makes it one of the world's most admired companies to work for – as a possible hindrance to future competitiveness.

> As a group, we fear failure, we love harmony, and we live in a world apart. ... The deep fear of failure in our culture engenders an aversion to risk, which in turn manifests itself as indecisiveness, paralysis by analysis, and a penchant for passing the buck.

Importantly, he adds, it also works to suppress the flow of bad news that may signal failure to come.

Taurel begins to tighten the emotional screw by describing Lilly's 'love of harmony' as potentially having what he describes as 'toxic' side effects, and a negative synergy when compounded with the fear of failure.

> It urges us to avoid confrontation and healthy debate. It drives us to mimic consensus where none really exists. And it makes us shun the mavericks

who want a better answer or who see a different way. Thus we inoculate ourselves against uncomfortable questions and, all too often, great opportunities.

Taurel's tough take is not simply the ranting of a single-minded CEO, he says.

They are the composite of the negative features of our culture produced by one confidential survey after another, in virtually all parts of the business, over the course of [the last] decade. A supplemental analysis of our cultural history traces them back to practices and principles established in the early decades of the company.

Despite everyone's respect for the past, he says, the firm must not carry these traits into the future, 'or we may never fully realize our true potential'. Instead, says Taurel, Lilly needs to replace what might be seen as negative norms with positive principles of action, instilling new capabilities that will give the organization a competitive edge in implementing strategy. The theme that Taurel reaches towards here is innovation.

Our business runs on ideas. We say that the molecule is the core, and it is. But the molecule really is the tangible product of an intellectual process. It is the running total of a long, complex chain of ideas that begins as a raw hypothesis in the mind of a research scientist and ends as a conversation between a physician and a patient.

Taurel lays the responsibility for establishing and driving those conversations – throughout the supply chain – at the feet of his leadership team.

We urgently need to reawaken our leadership capabilities from top to bottom. We cannot build a winning culture simply by being good caretakers. We must also put our energy into becoming great change makers. ... In any organization, this role is not confined to one person at the top.

He goes on to define the key focus for leaders within the organization as aligning the specific direction of each individual part of the organization with the general direction of the whole, and to provide the energizing spark to keep everyone moving forward. This can be achieved, he argues:

... by saying what we mean, by meaning what we say, and by proving both in what we do, day in and day out. In short, this fundamental, ethical dimension of leadership is grounded in what our actions say about our values.

Taurel brilliantly captures the start point for the *Leadership Unplugged* concept here – by emphasizing the values that guide our organizational life. And for organizations such as Lilly there is a tremendous legacy to draw on without hesitation or modification, because the core Lilly values of people, excellence and integrity constitute an ideal foundation for a practical philosophy of organizational effectiveness. Taurel summarizes this in his paper as 'acting on principle'.

The honesty imperative is captured most clearly in Taurel's seventh core value and principle (Table 4.3) – 'put the moose on the table'. Let bad news travel fast, he says.

As you finish reading the case, perhaps you've been asking yourself what Taurel was attempting by writing it? And having finished it – no trivial memo, this – what drove him to issue it across the organization?

Our assessment is that the paper – as an opening salvo in a debate about the future for Lilly – achieved its aims. It was not intended to change the organization – a statesman as experienced as Taurel isn't that naïve. Instead he wanted to get the organization talking, and in this he succeeded. In a workshop with one clinical division within the organization we were able to hear the practical upshot many months later. 'We must incorporate Sydney's themes into our performance metrics', said one director. 'What gets measured gets done.' Whether the metrics themselves would ever achieve anything is debatable, in our view, but Taurel's aim was to kick-start the conversation. Now, following a sustained strategy of communications across the organization, Sydney Taurel's presence is felt everywhere within Lilly. And this is helpful, for his task is not yet over. He knows that probably it never will be. For leadership is a process – a race without a finish – and Taurel is one of the few who realize it.

The Rise and Rise of Stakeholders

The whole purpose of the debate phase comes down to this next point – that keeping stakeholders in the loop of management thinking increases in importance on a daily basis. Why? These powerful groups are able to remove CEOs and management teams that fall from favour with increasing speed. Indeed, their power is such that boards of directors themselves sometimes evict executives whom they fear are out of favour with powerful stakeholder groups. This, in effect, doubles their power. Evictions for fear of stakeholder reactions happen in politics, too – British premier

Table 4.3 Sydney Taurel's seven core values and their allied principles

Key action 1 Model the values Motto: Show us what you're made of	Expect all employees to embrace the organization's values. But expect leaders to model them. Not just in words, but in action.
Key action 2 Create external focus Motto: Look outward – face reality	The principle of external focus encourages the active creation of relationships and networks with with key sources of information and potential support in the world around us. Our scientists do this routinely, and we should have the same approach to other vital resources – financial advisors, management scholars, government officials, members of the media, and so on.
Key action 3 Set direction with strategic thinking Motto: Get to the future first	We must learn to envision the shape of the future marketplace systematically and create plans to take advantage of it. We should depend on – and develop deep capabilities in – strategic thinking, and use them to build competitive advantage. This charge falls most heavily on senior management, but it is usually the people closest to the action who are best positioned to spot new opportunities – whether it is the evolution of a new scientific hypothesis or the emergence of a new trend in customer preference.
Key action 4 Implement with integrity, energy and speed Motto: Provide the powder, supply the spark	To implement with integrity is to focus on doing first what is most important to the success of the team and the company as a whole. Effective leaders communicate the assignment with enthusiasm with feeling, and continue to pump energy into the team to keep everyone on task and at their best. Of all the key actions of leadership, this one seems the most likely to depend on some sort of natural aptitude. It's hard to learn and even harder to fake. But part of it, I believe, is an attitude of optimism – confidence in our personal and collective ability to find winning solutions.

Table 4.3 (continued)

Key action 5 Get results through people Motto: Set people up to succeed	Leaders must set people up to succeed and allow people room to act on their own. This means more than resisting the intrusive and controlling behavior that we think of as micro-managing. It means developing the leader as teacher, as coach, as champion and protector, based less on authority and more on persuasion and mutual trust. Done perfectly, as the Confucian teachers noted long ago, leadership is almost invisible. The people see the results and say, 'Look what we have done.'
Key action 6 Check results and exercise accountability Motto: If you're not keeping score, you're just practising	Lilly is a business and 'winning' means, ultimately, excelling in the measures of the marketplace – growth in sales, in earnings, in economic value added, and in total shareholder return. But our financial results are created out of a vastly more complex interaction of human factors. 'Checking results' means monitoring, through means such as the balanced scorecard, all the vital signs that predict the health of our business performance. The point is, we need to be accountable for whatever is important to our success, whether it can be quantified or not.
Key action 7 Harvest learning and share ideas Mottoes: 'Facts are friends' and 'Put the moose on the table'	'Put the moose on the table' applies to everyone. But the leadership must model it or no one else will. Whether gathering input for the next round of strategy or simply in daily operation, leaders at Lilly must create and preserve a climate where ideas and learning flow freely – within teams, across teams, and throughout the whole organization. Leaders need to confront head-on the fear of failure that so often hamstrings our forward progress. Let bad news travel fast. This holds true for downward communication as well. It's misguided for senior management to try to protect employees from unpleasant news when its emergence is inevitable. Candour is part of respecting people and may be the single most important ingredient in building trust.

Margaret Thatcher was ousted by her party in 1990 when they believed her unelectable in a General Election.

But exactly who to keep informed? What to tell them? How often? After all, we've been complaining of information overload for much of this chapter. How can organizations avoid contributing to information overload, and to annoying the very stakeholders they want to pacify or excite?

The first step here is to map stakeholders onto a grid according to how powerful they are with reference to your organization (Figure 4.2). Then you should plot them on the second axis according to the level of interest – not necessarily financial – that they have in you. 'Interest' in this sense may be related to how closely they are involved with your organization on a daily basis. Shopfloor workers, for instance, will often be highly interested in what happens within an organization but may have no significant power to effect any change, save whatever strength they have as a unionized workforce. On the other hand, some institutional investors may wield tremendous power but are so busy worrying about another client that they don't exert daily pressures.

Gerry Robinson, then chief executive of the Granada media group, courted the 15 or so institutional investors who effectively controlled the Forte hotel group and restaurant chain with a short series of breakfast presentations. By pointing out what was happening at Forte (opening the debate) and by talking to them about their expectations of what Granada might do with the chain in the future, the investors began to talk to Granada, moving from being powerful but not-that-interested stakeholders to powerful *and*

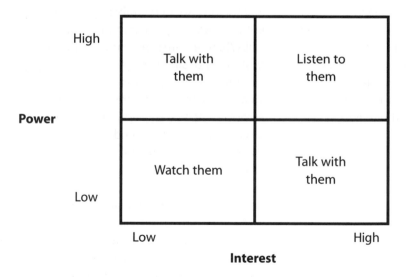

Figure 4.2 Planning stakeholder communications

interested stakeholders. The legacy of the situation is that in the transition period, and in the early years after the sale, Granada had to listen closely to what its stakeholders were saying. By delivering on the numbers and by keeping them informed as to what was happening, Granada – astutely – was able to reduce the interest levels of the stakeholders once again, as other more critical decisions had to be made elsewhere in the industry.

In a television documentary describing the purchase, Rocco Forte spoke tellingly when he said, 'I thought all we had to do was keep delivering excellent service'.[9] Sadly that isn't enough today.

People are usually aware of the concept of stakeholders but most of us forget what to do with this notion. Here's our practical workshop version, based on our research with boards and their stakeholder groups.

Plot the key stakeholders on a matrix of power versus interest, then:

- watch them
- talk to them
- or listen to them.

The critical thing is to listen to key stakeholders who are high in both interest and power. Often while listening to them you help them to articulate a better or different way forward. Research shows that people often change their views when they are listened to, sometimes subtly and sometimes less so.

As you plot your stakeholders against the matrix you begin to realize that while every stakeholder or stakeholder group has their own contextual issues, which you need to understand, they can be communicated with in one of three basic ways:

1. watch what is going on within the groups
2. tell the groups what you're doing (with varying degrees of detail)
3. listen to the groups.

These strategies are expanded upon in Table 4.4.

Plotting stakeholder strategies, as we've done in Table 4.4 and Figure 4.3, suggests specifically that engaging in strategically informed debate with potential allies who are powerful but not yet interested is helpful. Tell them what you are doing, position the vision with these groups and then wait for the resulting discussion. Engaging in debate with these stakeholder groups is the first step towards helping them change their perceptions. Of course, it is also helpful to have them where you can keep an eye on them because you may not want them to change. You should revisit the matrix from time to time during the course of the book.

Table 4.4 Stakeholder strategies: communicating with stakeholder groups

Stakeholder groups	Appropriate strategy	Desired outcomes
Quadrant 1 Low interest, low power	Watch these groups – keep an eye on them	Early identification of trends and movements within the group, towards high interest or high power
Quadrant 2 High interest, low power	Tell these groups what you're doing – keep them informed	You ought to keep the high interest groups' attention in case they gain or take power in the future; to reassure high interest groups with associated stakeholders in the high power low interest quadrant that all is well
Quadrant 3 Low interest, high power	Tell these groups what you're doing – keep them informed	a) To reassure the high power groups you don't want to become interested that all is well b) To entice the high power groups who could support you to become more interested
Quadrant 4 High interest, high power	Listen to these groups	a) Listen to these groups at every opportunity, involve them in discussions, canvas opinions, engage in surveys, constantly test their understanding and support by listening b) Offer relevant information on request to reassure and entice them to remain interested c) If some group is not wholly committed to remaining involved at this level, they will gradually lose interest and therefore day-to-day involvement; they may even abdicate power (by trading in shares or leaving the business)

Case 10. HSBC/Bital – Simultaneously Communicating Change and Stability

Late in 2002 HSBC acquired the Mexican bank Bital, which with its 17,000 people and 1400 retail branches gave it a powerful foothold in the country. In order to get a grip on the communications plan following the acquisition, managers at the Group Headquarters in London wanted a blow-by-blow tactical chart telling them what would be communicated and to whom. However, the manager HSBC brought in from London to manage the communications strategy was also asked to develop a strategy for *what* was to be communicated, and for *how* messages were to be sourced and distributed. Preparing a short-term tactical plan would have limited value without any sense of what the overall communications plan was trying to achieve. HSBC's eventual tactical plan was based on the matrix in Figure 4.3.

The initial objective of the communications team set up to manage the transition to full HSBC management and leadership was 'to gain the support and capture buy-in of any and all stakeholders involved or with an interest in the acquisition of Bital by HSBC, building acceptance, early support and full participation'. They wanted to communicate the benefits of the acquisition, the fact that HSBC was strong and well managed, and that the future for Bital was secure.

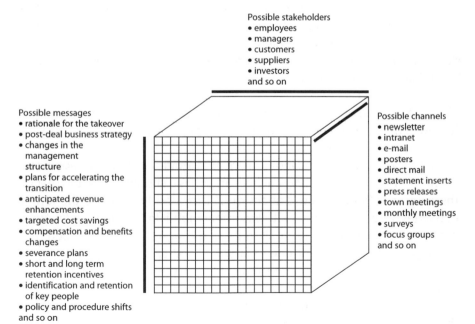

Figure 4.3 The tactical matrix

The communications team wanted to build feedback loops into the exist-ing communications channels to create dialogues where possible. Many organizations putting together a communications plan forget to do this. This results in the creation of a one-way broadcasting plan, disseminating what head office wants the field managers to know but not addressing what those in the field want to ask or propose to central managers.

The team divided the communications process into four broad areas:

1. *The reactive process*: how they would deal with emerging debates and discussions within Bital. These were expected to arise through feedback from customers and employees – perhaps from formal and sometimes informal conversation, the corporate intranet and other sources. 'We need to put in more feedback loops for this', the manager on site said, appreci-ating that without actively canvassing for views nothing would be heard as no one would expose themselves in the climate of uncertainty.
2. *The proactive process*: in other words, messages HSBC wanted to commu-nicate to Bital employees. These were often not directly requested by employees but were thought to be of interest or use nonetheless.
3. *The regular process*: these are the messages that HSBC wanted to update on a regular basis. Wherever possible, deadlines were to be set for post-ing these messages so that the staff knew what to expect and when. One manager was concerned, saying that 'to a degree this will create a rod for our own backs', not least because of the focus on 'telling, telling, telling', as opposed to listening.
4. *One-offs*: the prevailing view here was that their number should be minimized where possible.

The communication team saw these as boxes in a two-by-two matrix and hoped to minimize the reactive one-off messages, while focusing if possible on regular, proactive messages.

Helpfully, the communications team was quite clear that a significant proportion of messages – particularly early ones – should be crystal clear on the subject of 'how does this affect me?'. They had to translate the formal messages into something that was meaningful in different individuals' contexts. 'This will also force us all to think through the reasoning behind a message, and to use every one as a sales tool', said one manager. 'Every group needs to feel that communication is directed at them', said another. 'This is a campaign for their hearts and minds.'

Much of the group discussion in transatlantic teleconferences was about the different stakeholder groups the bank needed to communicate with. Key questions the team had to address round this topic were:

- What stakeholder segments exist today?
- What are their urgent concerns?
- What feedback loops exist today? What other loops should exist?
- Who can we reach with each channel?
- How timely are the channels?
- What message is best for which channel?
- What other channels could, or should, we create?

Questions formed a key part of the communications team's method of working, as highlighted by the sequence of questions in Table 4.5.

The communication structure was developed and built around the idea of 'segment champions' drawn from various levels across the organization.

The group progressed by defining the different media or channels they would use for communications, largely adopting systems and channels that

Table 4.5 Questioning the assumptions behind communicating

	What do we do now?	*Why do we do it?*	*What could we do?*	*What should we do?*
What? (Message)	What Is communicated now?	Why is it communicated?	What could be communicated?	What should be communicated?
How? (Process)	How is it communicated now?	Why is it communicated that way?	How could it be communicated?	How should it be communicated?
When? (Timing)	When is it communicated now?	Why is it communicated at that time?	When could it be communicated?	When should it be communicated?
Where? (Source)	Where does the communication come from now?	Why does it come from there?	Where could it come from?	Where should it come from?
Who? (Audience)	Who is the audience?	Why them?	Who could be the audience?	Who should be the audience?

already existed. It was keen to assess the effectiveness of each channel, and constantly asked: 'What style is most appropriate for each audience?'

The fundamental question constantly on the agenda was: 'What expectations/awareness should we be creating?' This underpinned the organization's strategic objectives – to grow the business in Mexico – but also ensured a constant focus on linking short-term tactical objectives with long-term strategic goals.

In managing the early stages of integration with Bital, HSBC got Bital people and stakeholders around the business to talk, and actively listened to them. Early concerns were for security and job safety, but these changed rapidly to concerns about HSBC's goals and strategic intent for the organization. Creating active feedback loops gave Bital people 'permission to talk' and allowed them to express their anxieties from the past, their concerns and confusion at the present and their fears for the future.

HSBC's third key action was to begin asking questions about Bital's people's own hopes for the future. It also asked them how they thought they might be achieved, and who they felt was responsible for this. In short, nothing was done without involvement from Bital's own managers and human resources contacts.

HSBC's key objective was to develop an implementable communications strategy setting out its business principles and then to move on to a detailed tactical plan, with each channel, message and strategic objective clearly linked.

Reflecting on the process after some months, the organization's very openness may have created problems for the communications team. Many questions and issues were raised which the communications team still feels responsible for addressing. Clearly, engaging with people to build loyalty and commitment takes time and effort. In future, then, the organization envisages being clearer over what feedback and questions it expects to see through the different communication channels and – importantly – who ought to be responsible for responding to the queries. It may, perhaps, be more appropriate for the organization for line managers to field the queries raised by the open communications process.

In conclusion, consider the following questions:

1.   What did HSBC do well in this early integration of the acquired Mexican bank? What might it have done even better?
2.   What, in your view, were the critical features of HSBC's communications plan and what impact would they have had?
3.   What was the reason for involving Bital's local workforce in the communications process? What impact did it have?

4. How could HSBC have improved the development of the open, questioning culture it has begun to create?

Moving On: Listening for Emerging Arguments

It's also clear that communication must continue *after* setting up a debate and initiating a change. Too many leaders and businesses become stuck at this point. Leaders think that simply by telling employees what they want to happen, or by telling stakeholders what their perception of the vision is – and only once at that – change will inevitably result. If only life were so simple. Senior executives who feel that they have the right to demand change because of their position, or seek to preserve some false prestige by keeping knowledge to themselves, are mired in a status quo where to stand still is actually to slide backwards. If any innovation or change is to be achieved in an established company, thousands of men and women must see the rationale behind the change and view it with favour. They must commit to the vision, but that commitment cannot be demanded. It must be earned.

So, to help people understand the rationale for change leaders have to move the communication on. They must take it beyond debate into discussion, and then into the phase we call dialogue. Jack Welch, chairman and CEO of General Electric until his retirement in 2002, explained what these later phases are like in a 1987 speech to employees:[10]

> We've learned a bit about what communication is not. It's not a speech like this or a videotape. It's not a plant newspaper. Real communication is an attitude, an environment. It's the most interactive of all processes. It requires countless hours of eyeball-to-eyeball back and forth. It involves more listening than talking. It is a constant, interactive process aimed at [creating] consensus.

Debate, then, is a crucial phase. It's the basis and springboard for every formal communications strategy that there is. But it is not enough in itself. Debate only stirs the imagination of key stakeholder groups. It motivates certain individuals and groups to oppose the views espoused in the debate. It motivates them to speak up and speak out. So it isn't the people who support our cause that we should be listening for – it's those who voice the counterpoint to our point that we must be sensitive to. Then, and only then – when we begin to hear the arguments against the proposal – can we say that the process of leading change has begun.

Conclusion

The key points we wish to emphasize at the end of this chapter are:

- Communication strategies are usually developed in an ad hoc manner, after change campaigns have begun – this is too late.
- Formal organized communication usually peters out during change programmes, or organizations stay in the debate (telling) mode too long.
- Most centrally issued communications are sanitized by such a lengthy corporate editing process that they offer little, if any, new information. The message itself is usually hopelessly out of date by the time it reaches its audience.
- Because the medium is the message, 'shallow' media such as memos, newsletters and (to a certain extent) e-mail are not sufficiently potent to communicate significant strategic or change issues effectively.
- Corporate communication strategies should not be devised and managed by public relations or human resources departments, but at the highest level in the organization.
- Without top management involvement communications projects often flounder. This may stifle or even kill a fledgling debate.

QuestionBank

Take time out to answer these questions.

1. How much do you involve yourself in developing organizational communication strategy? Why isn't this a higher percentage of your time? How sure are you that the other things you do are more important?
2. How do you know what people are thinking within and outside the organization? Who manages your communications with the outside world? Why do they manage it, and not someone closer to you? Why not you?
3. How quickly do you hear that there is a communication problem within the organization?

Notes

1. Grove, Andrew S., 1996. *Only The Paranoid Survive*. London: HarperCollins Business. This is a helpful guide to competitive strategy.
2   Peter Bijur contributed at length to *Wisdom of the CEO* (2000), in the PriceWaterhouseCoopers CEO series of reports compiled by G. William Dauphinais, Grady Means and Colin Price.
3. Duck, Jeanie Daniel, 1993. Managing change: the art of balancing. *Harvard Business Review* 71(6), pp. 109–18.
4. Grove, op. cit., p. 115.
5. Quirke, Bill, 1996. *Communicating Corporate Change*. London: McGraw-Hill, p. 113.
6. Interview for this book.
7. Lengel, R. H. and Daft, R. L., 1988. The selection of communication media as an executive skill. *Academy of Management Executive* 2(3), pp. 225–32.
8. Geneen, Harold and Alvin, Moscow, 1984. *Managing*. New York: Doubleday & Co., pp. 46–7.
9. From the superb fly-on-the-wall documentary series *Blood on the Carpet, The Forte Story*, originally broadcast by the BBC in 2000.
10. Lowe, Janet, 1998. *Jack Welch Speaks*. New York: John Wiley & Sons, p. 85.

PART II

Discussion: Arguing the Vision

Discussion:

1. Examination of a matter by arguments for and against
2. A disquisition in which the subject is treated from both sides.

Discourse:

1. To discuss a matter, confer
2. To go through in speech; to treat of in speech or writing; to talk over, to talk of, to tell
3. To converse with, to talk to, to discuss a matter with, to address.

Shorter Oxford Dictionary, 3rd edn.

CHAPTER 5

Discussion: The Politics of Change

It must be considered that there is nothing more difficult to carry out, nor more doubtful of success, nor more dangerous to handle, than to initiate a new order of things.

Niccolò Machiavelli (1469–1527)[1]

A politician is a person who approaches every problem with an open mouth.

Adlai Stevenson (1900–1965)[2]

Headlines

During discourse or discussion, strategic conversation should focus more on the arguments raised during the debate phase than the agenda of the debate phase itself.

The discussion phase is characterised by a robust exchange of views and information – it may involve extensive research in order to substantiate lines of argument.

The discussion phase may be characterized by argument but it is primarily a learning phase, where parties explore the positions that others hold through logic and rational challenge.

The fundamental object of the discussion phase is to identify opponents as well as supporters, and to help both sides to clarify their own arguments. Giving them as much help or information as they need will help allay their important fears and doubts, and assist them in making up their own minds.

During the constructive arguments of the discussion phase, a significant number of people may find out enough about the issue at hand to be won over. The important point to note is that they are won over by their own efforts – people invariably persuade themselves.

This chapter is not about political tactics – it aims to address the attitudes towards politics held by managers in firms, and takes the

---

position that politics is a natural and important aspect of day-to-day organizational life.

This chapter takes to task managers who see politics as a 'dirty' or unethical activity, and acts as a wake-up call to those who cannot see political behaviour taking place.

Political competence is an essential skill, not only for change agents (without positional power) who wish to initiate change but also for those in authority (with positional power) who need to motivate the rest of their team or the workforce generally.

The Politics of Uncertainty

At the start of the 21st century business leaders are faced by pressure for change from every side, and on a massive scale. Change has, of course, been something of a constant of business – almost a cliché – for decades now. And it seems likely to continue to accelerate. Why? Well, until recently, strategy was intrinsically about the long-term direction of a business. But the long-term is shrinking. Instead of five-year plans, organizations are working to much shorter time-horizons, looking only three years or even only one year ahead. Some organizations can't plan past the next quarter. This was probably brought to the fore by the e-business boom, when companies of all sizes seemed to be confronted by fundamental questions about their businesses and every organization faced an uncertain future. Large multinational manufacturers, for instance, were no longer certain who their competitors were. How seriously should they take the dotcoms springing up around them, or the portals, they asked? What impact would be felt by the unlikely alliances between corporations in different industries? As the former head of a global telecommunications company said at one meeting of senior executives: 'All I can promise you is change.'

To introduce change successfully, however, leaders must be political. This is both the challenge and the inherent problem of change as 'politics' is still a dirty word today, associated in the eyes of many individuals with immoral, manipulative and dishonest tactics. Others think that 'doing politics' means being particularly brutal, putting your own needs way ahead of those of the organisation and winning victories over your fellow team members. In fact, the reverse may also be true. In the light of the corporate scandals surrounding previously untouchable corporate US icons, however, there is a fear associated with the idea that corporate politics has gone horribly wrong. With the rebirth of corporate social responsibility as a meaningful exercise, we may be witnessing a misguided backlash against political behaviours in organizations.

Building on all of these issues, this chapter is intended specifically for two groups of executives:

1. those who claim the moral high ground by suggesting that politics is an unnecessary aspect of business
2. the less clearly defined group of people who have no idea that political behaviour goes on in organizations at all.

We hope that this chapter – in something of a one-sided discussion – will offer a wake-up call. Its aim is to overturn both of these equally unhelpful attitudes.

Let's open the debate, then, by stating that acting 'politically' does not mean playing a manipulative part, Machiavellian or otherwise. It does mean, however, that executives at every level in the organization need to be aware of the effects of every move and every word they contribute, and it also means knowing how to manage the politics and the way politics is practised. This is a tall order, as it always has been.

The Uncertainty of Politics

The first political act of any leader introducing change is that of outlining his or her initial position through the medium of debate. As we've seen in earlier chapters, other parties inside and outside the organization will automatically start to take up their own positions, either supporting or opposing the change, and the whole programme will begin to move in a halting, juddering fashion as the initial inertia of the status quo is challenged and overturned. To some people we've worked with, this first stage – where leaders face huge resistance to the prospective change – seems an immense hurdle. Garnering support from all key quarters is often perceived as an inconvenience or a hindrance by derring-do managers. 'What the company really needs is immediate action', they tell us.

'Not necessarily', we are forced to remind them. Without persuading enough people in the company that there is a real need for change, the change process is likely to fail. Indeed, change begun without enough support will not only fail. It will backfire, affecting the future ability of managers with low political credibility to launch effective change of any description. And an executive without the credibility to lead change is powerless.

So we must engage in organizational politics if we are to lead change. There is much reassurance for managers here, as research tells us that conflict between the person driving the change and other stakeholders is almost always beneficial.

In a powerful recent research study, Dave Buchanan and Richard Badham at the University of Warwick, UK, capture well the dilemma of 'shall I/shan't I get involved in organizational politics?'[3]

> One voice can claim that these conflicts consume time and energy and attention, thus harming organizational performance. Another voice can equally claim that these disagreements, disputes, arguments, uncertainties, doubts and conflicts can be valuable source of creative energy, supporting positive change and innovation and raising individual and organizational effectiveness.

So where is the truth of the matter? Our research has shown that after the various participants within a company have engaged in the debate phase, effective leaders tend to adopt the 'discussion/discourse' style. In this way they can influence the argument, helping people to articulate their views for and against the idea of change, without forcing issues using Draconian measures that would forfeit the commitment of the staff implementing it. We believe that politic activity is a useful, if not essential, aspect of *Leadership Unplugged*. It represents a skirmishing phase, where we must begin explicitly to identify the movers and shakers within and outside the organization and to ascertain their real points of view on the issue we're addressing.

Don't just take our word that politicking is significant – reflect on your own experience (good, bad or indifferent), and also on independent survey data. The literature surveying middle and senior managers consistently shows that 99 per cent of all managers agree that change agents today need well-developed negotiating, persuading and influencing skills. This is not a 'nice-to-have' set of skills and behaviours – it's a *must*-have skillset. We conclude that politics is a natural part of business, and that leaders expect to practise it and to interact with others practising it.

It's worth seeing organizational politics, then, as an autonomous and self-sustaining phenomenon, and not merely something that happens because an organization has weak leadership or a structural deficiency. It doesn't arise because of the predilections of devious organization members, or because of incompetent managers. All of these factors – structural, personal, and managerial – exacerbate, modify and otherwise colour or texture the organization's political environment. We therefore urge you to regard organizational politics as ubiquitous and to accept that it cannot be ignored, removed or designed away simply by instituting different policies and practices.

We must be clear that organizational politics is a naturally occurring phenomenon. And, because reasonable people will usually argue strongly in support of their personal convictions, they can be expected to disagree on major, uncertain and ambiguously defined issues. Remember that these dynamics yield truly valuable information. (*Resistance is useful.*)

At this point, some readers ask whether the practice of 'politics' isn't merely cynical, unethical manipulation – a means of increasing the leader's power? We usually counter that politics is one of those subjects inevitably scattered with re-presentations of meaning – what some today call 'spin'. One person's influence is another's manipulation; one person's ethical stance is another person's rebellion. If you are to engage successfully in the organizational arena it is important to understand the language you and your colleagues are using, and to avoid these loaded terms where possible. Take the conversation to a higher level. Make it clear that you act in the interest of the company's stakeholders, not to further your own ends, and that you encourage others to do the same.

In other words, as an unplugged leader you must recognize the existence of political manoeuvring – largely enacted through the language of leadership – and act with honesty. This will involve seeking out and engaging with particular 'political' contacts – especially those followers who are ready and able to enter the dialogue phase with you – but to do so with regard for the organization's interests, and for those of the individuals who make it up. It's better (ethically) and more effective (motivationally) to see an organization's human resources as 'human' rather than as 'resources'.

Change and Political Blindness

Sometimes the uncertainty over whether or not to 'play' at politics, and a strong concern with tactics and 'what to do', tend to obscure the fact that leaders need to plan political campaigns carefully. They must identify the people they most need to influence – who can influence others in the organization in turn – and then arrange to engage in strategic conversations with those stakeholders. Hundreds of years after Machiavelli, this is still the way in which leaders need to introduce much-needed change into the political arena.

Business leaders need to engage in organizational politics in order to effect any change in their company. When change is first introduced, for example, most individuals involved in the organization are likely to resist it to some degree. Jack Welch, chairman and CEO of General Electric Corporation for more than 16 years, believed that the ground needed to be prepared carefully for any kind of change – from a move into a new market to an improvement in productivity.[4]

The difference between winning and losing will be how the men and women of our company view the change as it comes at them. If they see it as a threat – as an ill wind to be resisted by keeping your head down and digging your feet in – we lose. But if they are provided with the educational tools and are encouraged to use them – to the point where they see change as synonymous with opportunity; where they become receptive to it, even demand of it – then every door we must pass through to win big all around the world will swing open to us. New markets, exotic technologies, novel ventures, dramatic productivity growth.

Ralph Lazarus – a precursor of Jack Welch's, writing as early as 1963 – was adamant that the best-educated executive would never succeed without the ability to get other people to pursue their goals. This isn't so much about people preferring not to engage in politics – it is more about people who just don't acknowledge that it exists. Lazarus, a former chairman and CEO of Federated Department Stores, owner of premier retailers such as Bloomingdale's, Bon Marche, Abraham & Straus and Filene's, told the story of the failure of one such executive, a good friend of his ('I'll call him Joe'), who came to Lazarus's home one weekend.[5]

At age 42, he said, he [Joe] had just been asked to resign from a vice-presidency in one of the nation's leading corporations. Worse, this was the third consecutive time, he confessed, that he had been forcibly separated from gainful employment. 'What', he asked plaintively, 'is the matter with me?'

... A week or so later I met the president who had fired him.

'What happened to Joe?' I asked.

'Listen', the President replied. 'Three years ago we thought Joe was a real find. I even visualized him as my successor. He knew how to smell out a problem. He knew how to get the facts. He knew how to make a decision. But we learned to our sorrow that that's all he knew. It never occurred to him that the best decision in the world is no good until somebody does something about it. He never learned that an executive has to be effective through other people – and that you make a decision not just on the facts but in terms of who will do what you think needs to be done.'

Buried in the story, Lazarus believed, was a fundamental truth about young executives. Many of them would fail to reach their goals, he said, not through lack of competence but because of what he described as 'people-blindness'. Time after time, this traps them into making a technically good decision that just won't work in practice. It remains true today that executives succeed or fail not so much on the basis of what *they* do but because of what they are able to get *someone else* to accomplish. In our view this is less 'people' blindness than 'political' blindness. It hampers executives badly, not only when initiating change but also as the change programme unfolds.

When debate over a change has begun, for example, it is vital that the leader sustains the change by identifying both the people who agree with the course of action or the issue and those who disagree. Step two is to explore specific areas of agreement and disagreement with them. We know that it's all too easy for leaders to hear only those that support their proposals, and (deliberately or unconsciously) to discourage those with opposing views from speaking. If the corporate culture does not support those who disagree with their leaders – and therefore does not allow for lively discussions – mistakes are far more likely.

A powerful example comes from Willard F. Rockwell, Jr., the man who brought us the first space shuttle and the former president of Rockwell International. He recounts a tale of a (nameless) company that had developed an exciting new product line:[6]

> The marketing people boiled over with enthusiasm. The president, a strongly growth-oriented executive, was swept along by the tide of this fervour. He painted a glowing picture of the potential to the financial vice-president, an astute executive whose views had always been carefully weighed by the president in formulating his own decisions. Privately, the man was not so sure the product line was ready for market. He had heard rumblings and grumblings from Manufacturing and Engineering regarding problems they were running into. But, reluctant to buck such formidable opposition as Marketing and the chief executive, he said nothing. The line was introduced to the marketplace.
>
> As it turned out, the introduction was premature ... Almost from the first day, customer complaints started pouring in. The company's excellent quality image was seriously undermined.
>
> The president, crestfallen, called in a consultant to determine why and how the blunder had been made. His findings, emerging mainly from a series of soul-searching interviews, were blunt and revealing. The financial executive, manufacturing and engineering managers, and others bared their true feelings, which in the main had been squelched by the Marketing–president combine.
>
> 'The devil's advocates were never given a chance to air their view', the consultant said simply.

Rockwell says that meaningful changes were made as a result of the consulting experience. The president learned to side-step the 'yes men' and to conceal his own opinions in order to obtain the free and unbiased independent judgment of others. He told Rockwell: 'I found out, too, that if you want the truth, you have to convince people of your willingness to accept it.' In other words he had learned, perhaps for the first time, to act politically – to behave in such as way that he would hear opinions counter to his own and therefore receive a truer picture of the company's prospects.

In terms of *Leadership Unplugged*, we would conclude that the president had set up the original debate ('We must launch this wonderful new product line') but had then acted, and continued to act, without properly engaging in the discussion phase. At no time was there any dialogue in which listening played a major part. This leader learned the value of discourse and of listening the hard way.

Interestingly, he also learned that leaders must not only be willing to hear the truth, but must also convince people that they really do *want* to hear it. This cuts right to the fundamentals of leadership, and the building of trust and belief that you mean what you say. What makes this challenge even tougher is that if the organization discourages executives from speaking their minds – by blaming them for mistakes, ridiculing them for certain opinions or simply ignoring their comments – you are unlikely to hear the truth. Ever.

Semco, long regarded as an innovative Brazilian company, makes it safe for staff to participate by actively encouraging them to give opinions. A booklet given to each new member of staff says:[7]

> Our philosophy is built on participation and involvement. Don't settle down. Give opinions, seek opportunities and advancement, always say what you think. Don't be just one more person in the company. Your opinion is always interesting, even if no one asked you for it. … Make your voice count.

The Politics of Change

Business leaders tend to practise organizational politics without planning or intending to do so, and certainly without any special training in the subject or in tactics. Political behaviour is widely held to form part of the 'taken-for-granted' routines, scripts and recipe knowledge used by most managers. Political behaviour is used by managers habitually, and usually without prior analysis.

Nevertheless, there is a feeling among a significant number of business leaders that an organization cannot be truly effective if managers feel they must – or want to – spend time, energy and creative effort playing the political game. They see politics as something underhand, manipulative and 'off-the-agenda'. Their fear is that such behaviour detracts from the business of providing services and making products.

Our view, however, is that organizational politics can hold advantages both for the firm and for individual managers. For example, it can help executives who want or need to act as project leaders or change agents, for example, who have to work with individuals or groups over whom they may have no formal authority. They can employ political tactics in order to recruit allies and form coalitions, and to exert influence over current programmes and also over future developments. They must be willing to intervene in the political processes of the organization, to push particular agendas, to influence decisions and decision makers, to deal with (and perhaps silence) criticism and challenge and to cope with resistance. They must also be able to intervene in ways that enhance rather than damage their personal reputations. And they may at times have to avoid such activities, or play down the use of these tactics that some managers regard as so distasteful.

The building of alliances, and the explicit trading of valuable information, is helpful because change agents are largely engaged in facilitating new ways of working. They are often exposed and vulnerable, and so must use political skills to protect themselves from threat, challenge or attack.

Those change agents who do have a tough time with the whole concept of organizational politics, and who think the turf game is unethical, will inevitably find it difficult to succeed. Indeed, a refusal to take part in politics may not only prove a barrier to success but could even be described as immoral itself. If you attempt to defend the high moral ground by saying 'no politics here', then you take issue with the argument that politics is an inevitable companion of change – and even a necessary and desirable one. By taking such a lofty position you automatically sideline and marginalize the right to challenge and protest. If as a leader you insist on cooperation and openness while simultaneously outlawing backstage manoeuvring, you restrict opportunities for discovering more about an individual's, or a group's, ideas, proposals and criticisms. Buchanan and Badham put it this way:[8]

> One moral implication of the 'squeaky clean' imperative is thus to stifle the expression of dissent. And that is not a liberating or emancipatory stance. This may instead be viewed as an extreme and rigid authoritarian position … the emancipatory view, in contrast, involves recognizing the political reality of organizational functioning, exposing political behaviour to

scrutiny, legitimating intervention in political processes, and disseminating more widely an understanding of effective intervention strategies and tactics.

Political behaviour, in their view, can be managed but cannot be managed away. So the successful handling of organizational politics can be related to successful organizational development and change, as well as to personal career success. Executives who are not politically skilled will fail.

The Politics of Power: Written Versus Unwritten Rules

> Computers don't get built, cities don't get rebuilt, and diseases don't get fought unless advocates for change learn how to develop and use power effectively.
>
> Jeffrey Pfeffer[9]

What does it mean to manage with power? One of the world's leading authorities on power, Stanford University's Jeffrey Pfeffer (quoted above), believes it simply means recognizing that there are varying interests at work within every organization. One of the first things we need to do when using an unplugged approach to lead change, therefore, is to assess the political landscape. We must work out what the relevant interests are, and what important political subdivisions characterize the organization. This builds on the perspective Pfeffer offers when he suggests:[10]

> It is essential that we do not assume that everyone necessarily is going to be our friend, or agree with us, or even that preferences are uniformly distributed. There are clusters of interests within organizations, and we need to understand where these are and to whom they belong.

This forms part of the fundamental planning of any political campaign.

The next stage in campaign preparation is to work out what points of view these individuals or groups hold on issues of concern to us, and to understand why they hold them. This often helps executives to realize what is perhaps the most important aspect of politics and power, and the real secret of success in organizations – that power does not come from advising those who know and love us. Power comes from how we deal, politically, with people whom we might actually regard as being dumb, or as less perceptive than ourselves. It's about how we get people who differ from us, and whom we don't necessarily like, to do what needs to be done. Let's be clear. People whom we think of as 'dumb' invariably are not. They just see the world a different way from us. And the ones who are explicitly differ-ent – who we simply don't like – can often scotch our chances of achiev-ing change successfully. Using coercion to ride roughshod over these two camps is not effective. It isn't *Leadership Unplugged.*

Leadership Unplugged means understanding, in a very simple way, where power comes from, and it means seeing the strategies and tactics through which it is developed and used in organizations. Too often, people do not think strategically or purposefully about acquiring power and employing it. This is a mistake, says Pfeffer, who discards the 'knowledge is power' mantra, suggesting instead that 'knowledge without power is of remarkably little use'.[11] The logical extension of this, and the point at which *Leadership Unplugged* picks up the baton, is that power is wasted without the skill to employ it effectively.

This issue is worth pursuing because many of the executives we've worked with in both private and public sector organizations simply don't understand that power isn't a magic wand that can be waved to ensure every-one follows 'The Rules'. A surprising number of extremely senior executives do not appreciate that every organization actually has *unwritten* rules, and that it is these rules that guide the day-to-day behaviour of employees. One of the reasons that this insight is still rare among senior executives is that most employees inside organizations are sufficiently 'political' to pay lip service to formal values or policies while adhering unerringly to an implicit, unwritten code. If leaders do not understand the unwritten rules in their busi-ness it can lead to disaster, however, because these unwritten rules usually obstruct change and undermine new initiatives.

For instance, one consumer products company introduced what we might think of as a 'written rule' – 'To become a top manager, you need broad experience.' People recognized that they had to pass through ten grades in as many years if they were to have a chance for the top. In prac-tice, therefore, an unwritten rule was born – 'To get to the top, job-hop as fast as possible.'

The idea of the unwritten rule ('the way we do things round here') has long been a subject of research into organizational culture. Capturing the unsaid, implicit routines in business has been a fascinating academic pastime. One consultant who helps firms to unpack their unwritten rules in practical terms is Peter Scott-Morgan. He suggests that the first thing to do when introducing a new initiative is to listen to a carefully selected group of people, encouraging them to talk generally around the topic. Uncover-ing the unwritten rules hidden amongst the comments is a hard task, and Scott-Morgan suggests you need the help of three 'magnets' when separat-ing the various important aspects of what people tell you.[12] The first are 'motivators' – the things that make people get up in the morning, or that they perceive as rewards. These are not the things that are supposed to motivate them but the things that *really* motivate them, such as career advancement or being able to pay the mortgage. The second magnet comprises the 'enablers' – the people who can enable employees to get what is important to them. And it's this group of people who are most relevant to this chapter in that they encapsulate, in effect, the power structure of the company as it is perceived by those within it. Scott-Morgan's third magnet is 'triggers' – or the conditions that people think must be satisfied for them to get what they want. In the case of career advancement, for example, the target is gaining promotion.

Thankfully, in order to uncover the unwritten rules in organizations it isn't necessary to arrange vast numbers of interviews or to issue hundreds of questionnaires. It can be done by talking with about a dozen people across the organization and asking them simple questions, such as 'What would you say to a close friend about what it's like to work here?' or 'What do people talk about after work in the bar?'

The important aspect of all this from a political perspective is identifying the questions that reveal the movers and shakers – in Scott-Morgan's, terms 'the enablers'. Because having identified the real power figures in organizations – and they are not always senior board members – we can begin to engage them in discussion about the way forward. If we can do this, then we may at last be able to begin the process of realigning expectations across the organization and leaving the status quo behind.

Case 11. Royal Dutch/Shell – practice, performance and politics

The global oil group Royal Dutch/Shell, for so long one of the most admired corporations in the world, decided to enter a restructuring process at a time when many companies might simply have enjoyed the good times – in the mid-1990s, when it was the most profitable company in the oil sector. Cor Herkströter, then Chairman of the Committee of Managing Directors at the Shell Group of Companies, led this streamlining, which focused on the company's relationship with its investors, the corporate centre's relationship with the operating units and the company's contract with its managers.

The existence – and management – of organizational politics is perhaps clearest in the third of these areas. Under the old contract with managers, Shell's performance expectations of individuals were far from demanding, says Herkströter.[13] Mediocrity was tolerated, while only gross incompetence was punished. There was an unwritten rule that almost anyone could climb the career ladder through a sequence of automatic advances.

Shell proposed a new contract that was designed to add value. The proposals comprised:

- shocking changes in the old system of security
- new objectives tied to new rewards
- structural changes linked to new purposes
- communication as an instrument of change
- positive leadership from the top.

'By far the most difficult thing for Shell people to absorb was the abrupt loss of the guarantee of employment for life', says Herkströter. 'At Shell today no one, no matter how senior, has a job contract that runs to retirement. This created an uproar that is still echoing throughout the organization.'

As lifetime employment vanished, so did the key elements of job security. Appropriately, this transformation began at the top, where the hundred leading jobs were reconfigured. No one in the central organization will remain in his or her present job for more than three or four years. Senior people must then rotate to similar positions elsewhere in the organization – perhaps in the operating companies. The enforcement principle is clear: either people adopt these new behaviours or their future with the organization is threatened.

Changing managers' employment conditions – and with it the culture of complacency that Herkströter suggests existed before the change – represents one of the most highly political actions you can take in an organization. The fact that the 'uproar' is still echoing through the group suggests that the changes were not handled with great sensitivity. But when your goal is to remove job security, make promotion more difficult and shake people up in roles where they might have become comfortable, you are not seeking to be gentle. This is clear from Herkströter's language, where he uses words such as 'enforcement' and 'threatened'.

In this instance the resistance to the change might be expected to be so great that the change would inevitably fail. It is easy to imagine good managers leaving in droves, and those remaining paying only lip service to the new accountabilities, responsibilities and revised performance indicators. So how did Herkströter aim to avoid political meltdown?

His first goal was effectively communication regarding the changes. 'Since clear communication is an essential instrument of change, we have invested in proclaiming the new order and making certain that it is understood in all quarters. The communication process began from Day One.'

He also sought to make the communication process continuous – and an element of discussion was also included in it.

At least once a month, I personally lunch with younger managers, who are free to raise any topic. At first, there was a lot of confrontation as managers came face to face with the new cultural approach. It directly challenged our time-honoured contractual principles – including the old unwritten law that 'in Shell, you never hear about mistakes'.

Changes at the corporate centre meant that job cuts were necessary. Herkströter expected to encounter resistance over this, but met with far less opposition than anticipated. He believes this is because the management's announcement was seen as honest and forthright.

Another key part of the communication programme was designed to deal with the necessary downsizing, since the new reformed Shell would need 30 per cent fewer employees at Corporate Center. The managing directors and I expected negative reactions. But our announcement was seen as honest and forthcoming, and this helped produce a constructive outcome.

Herkströter and his fellow senior executives believed it was important to act as positive role models in the group's culture change. This was a political act, in much the same vein as politicians who sometimes vote not to accept pay increases because they know the public will find them unacceptable at times of wage freezes and growing unemployment.

Herkströter became personally identified with the changes, and made sure that he was the one communicating those changes to the managers. 'I took an unprecedented step in demonstrating commitment to the change process by personally telling people about the new reforms and the effect these moves would have on their lives', he says. He implies that this was not as calculated an act as one might think. He adds: 'My gamble paid off. The new openness and candour spread like wildfire throughout the organization.'

After the changes were introduced, Herkströter spent at least half a day a week dropping in unannounced on company facilities to see how the change programme was faring, 'and to communicate directly with Shell's people'.

He concludes that the changes became firmly established within Shell's new corporate culture. 'And the best news of all is that, as culture shock abates, anxiety is being replaced with a high level of enthusiasm, drive, and commitment.'[14]

The changes at Royal Dutch/Shell appear to have stuck. In April 2002 Phil Watts, new Chairman of the Committee of Managing Directors, said of the structure of the organization: 'Current arrangements have served us well', particularly since the 1996 changes that ended Shell's regional fiefdoms and reorganized it 'on clear business lines with clear business responsibilities'. Questions of any further reorganization are 'just not at the forefront of my mind', Watts says, adding firmly: 'We have business to do.'[15]

The Politics of Motivation

One of the most misunderstood political acts is the giving of rewards. Offering rewards to people to get them to act as you would like is certainly political. Politicians promise voters tax cuts close to an election, and the promises get more generous the closer the election comes. However, one business leader who believes the best way to get managers to perform is to reward them appropriately does not think that 'rewards' should necessarily mean money in their pay packets. Al Zeien was chief executive of consumer products group Gillette until 1999. Zeien, the darling of Wall Street through most of the 1990s, was considered one of the best managers in the United States at that time. He points to the introduction of a new shaver in Japan and describes how he listened to a presentation on the product and thought that the product was 'absolutely fantastic'. But he also told the manager: 'You're not spending enough to get it to market. Now, what would happen if we doubled the rate of expenditure?' Zeien went ahead and did just that – a process he calls 'endorsement' – and the shaver appeared on Japanese shelves a year ahead of schedule and sold very well. 'I believe in individual rewards', Zeien explains.[16]

> When I left that meeting, that guy felt like I had given him a blank cheque. Individuals are individuals, and this guy deserved the reward, even if it wasn't monetary. It's psychological – people like to win, and people have to be rewarded as winners. It's not just passing out a bonus cheque at the end of the year. It's my job, my role, to let them feel that way.

People may like to feel like winners, but if the culture of a company means you can win a pay rise or promotion simply by staying a certain number of years, or by taking as few risks as possible, it is more difficult to motivate them to participate in change. Altering the status quo simply isn't in people's interests if in a short while the status quo will reward them. What happens here is that staff will listen to the board's new change initiative, while all the time comparing it with the unwritten corporate rule that says 'no harm will come to you if you do nothing'. The inevitable result is inaction, and the complete failure of the change programme.

At one company, the top team failed to take into account the organizational politics involved in change and the change programme was arguably a failure. Certainly it became a battleground – and the body count eventually included the chief executive who was leading the change. This was in the mid-1990s and J. P. Bolduc, then chief executive of international industrial conglomerate W. R. Grace, was very aware of the changing world economic order. He saw well educated, multilingual people in other countries turning out products for half what it cost his company and decided he had to create 'a new Grace' – to transform W. R. Grace into a company characterized by openness, creativity, flexibility and boldness. He and his top team set about spreading the message. They made speeches – many of them no doubt inspirational – and held many meetings with employees, shareholders, analysts and managers. The initial reaction, Bolduc recalled, was 'a big yawn'. The reality of the situation was that Grace was so deeply entrenched in bureaucracy and hierarchy that everyone shrugged off 'the new Grace' as 'new CEO sabre-rattling'. 'Nobody believed what the hell we were trying to do, Bolduc said, 'so it became clear we had to break through the sound barrier.'[17]

Faced with the initial failure of his initiative, Bolduc decided to force the changes through. First, he and his senior management team showed they were serious in their intentions by accelerating the sale of several non-core businesses. Then they started rebuilding the corporate structure, integrating functions across divisions and eliminating levels of management. At this point, having sent his company into a kind of culture shock, Bolduc became more overtly political in his actions. Having set the divestment and restructuring plans in motion, he travelled the world with the senior managers he called his Policy Cabinet. First they met with hundreds of key managers, prodding them to develop their global product lines for the year 2000 as well as a strategy that explained, in persuasive detail, why their businesses should remain part of Grace. Next they focused on employees beneath the executive ranks.

'During the first two years of restructuring, I met with every single employee group I could get my hands on, spoke for twenty, thirty, forty minutes. After we'd given them "why" for change', Bolduc recalled:

I'd take my jacket off and say, 'All right, have at me. Let's talk about the company, its future, your job, your career, and our future. Let's talk about how you can make a difference, how you can make Grace a better place in which to work and live.' Some of the sessions would start at seven o'clock at night. We'd have dinner, and by eight o'clock, I'm on the podium. Nine o'clock I'm wrapped up, and then we'd go with questions and answers for however long it took – sometimes until one or two in the morning.

The example of Bolduc at W. R. Grace is an interesting one. His first stratagem for introducing change was simply to tell everyone the company would change – not surprisingly, nothing happened. His second stratagem was to force the change through. This undoubtedly left the staff bloodied and bruised. At this point Bolduc finally began to employ political skills to set about bringing the employees back on board, trying to gain their commitment through discussion and dialogue. The threat remained, however – as Bolduc and his Policy Cabinet travelled the world meeting managers, those managers had to explain in detail why their businesses should remain part of Grace. They were fighting to prevent themselves being closed down or sold off. Even in the ostensibly informal sessions with employees, the atmosphere sounds confrontational. Urging staff to 'have at me' does not sound the ideal way to draw out the most constructive feedback.

In the end Bolduc's tough, perhaps brutal, tactics earlier in the change process seem to have had a lasting effect. According to newspaper reports, Bolduc himself was engaged in a feud with chairman J. Peter Grace and in March 1995 he resigned. Institutional shareholders then pushed through their own changes, including a reduction in the board of directors from 22 to 12 members, the resignation of J. Peter Grace as the Chairman and as a director, and the offer for sale of National Medical Care, Grace's largest subsidiary. Bolduc's restructuring, however, did seem to have had the desired effect on the company's profits. At the time he resigned, W. R. Grace was experiencing its highest earnings in more than a decade, operating margins had risen nearly 100 per cent since he took the reins, cash flow was out of the red and costs were down by hundreds of millions of dollars. Since then, the group has been the target of an avalanche of asbestos-related lawsuits, and on 2 April 2001 Grace and 61 of its US subsidiaries and affiliates, including its primary US operating subsidiary W. R. Grace & Co, filed for Chapter 11 bankruptcy protection.

We are not suggesting that the political style of Grace's management was responsible for the final *coup de grace*, but there are different ways of leading that can result in quite different and sustainable outcomes.

One company that runs on a very different political model – almost that of a socialist cooperative – is Semco, the Brazilian business services and equipment company. Ricardo Semler, the company's leader, says his goal was greater democracy. He has not sought personal power within Semco. Indeed, in 2001 he boasted that it had been 15 years since he had signed a cheque and 14 years since he had had his own office, and added: 'We had a party recently to celebrate 10 years since I had taken a decision.' Many staff at Semco set their own salaries and vacations; they take part in decision making, and there are no rigid financial checks on budgets.

Against the odds, perhaps, the company's recent record is impressive. Revenues have been growing at about 30 per cent a year, and profits trebled between 1996 and 2000.[18] A lot has been written about Semco, not least by Semler himself, so we will not go into detail here. The company is worth mentioning, however, as a successful example of the tie-less, democratic culture at work, where political ideals are part of the everyday life of the company and its staff.

It is worth noting, however, that commercial success has started to compromise the company's ideals. 'The fact that we are growing and will make more money is a sign of success, but we are further from the original goal we set out, that of being a democratic company', says Semler. Rapid expansion has made some of the company's unusual practices less practical. It is no longer possible for all new employees to be interviewed for the job by their subordinates, for instance. And fewer staff set their own salaries – only about 10 per cent now, compared with one-third five years ago. It's a shame that the perceived commercial pressures at Semco are starting to put pressure on the company's political dream. Because unless we sustain our efforts to manage and lead our businesses in a different, more egalitarian, way we will never prove to the world how effective it can really be.

Politics of the Personal

People behave politically in all aspects of life, trying to influence people to adopt a different point of view. Some people have always, and will always, use underhand political methods to achieve their ends. In one survey, managers cited several unethical-sounding tactics and moves in the context of political change:[19]

- 'Wait until it has been successful – then claim credit.'
- 'Never disclose your full hand.'
- 'Slant information, deny knowledge, reveal nothing.'
- 'Create an illusion by excluding information and mystifying concepts.'
- 'Blame others when things go wrong.'
- 'Associate with power bases (i.e. "creep").'

Although political behaviour can be misused in this way – to undermine authority, to appear sincere or to gain the accolades of superiors – this behaviour is difficult to sustain and is almost always uncovered in time.

Our point made throughout this chapter, however, is that political behaviour in itself is not intrinsically a bad thing. When a chief executive and his or her top executive team decide to tackle rising costs, a new competitive threat or a deceleration in new product development, they need to state their intention to introduce change: that is, enter the debate. There will always be those who resist the very idea of change, but that is where 'politics' can be brought in. The leaders need to identify those individuals whose opinions and skills they value and engage them in discussion or discourse. This way, all views on the best ways to achieve change will be heard and considered. The opponents of change, and the subversives, must also have a chance to voice their views. In this way, leaders can influence opinion in an ethical, honest way. If leaders genuinely value the contributions of others, they are more likely to win the commitment of managers and employees to their change programme.

In closing, it's also worth bearing in mind that the way in which the leader exerts influence is particularly important. The difference between motivation and manipulation is the interpretation that those on the receiving end place on attempts to influence them. If they are influenced in a positive and favourable way, people may consider themselves as having been 'motivated'. If, however, attempts at influence are not well planned or well conducted, people often describe themselves as having been humiliated and – particularly – manipulated.

The *Leadership Unplugged* approach to organizational politics does, however, carry a risk. There is a chance that the leaders, while taking part in a lively, honest, searching discussion with their managers and employees, may have their own minds changed. If that is the case, however, in our view the time will have been well spent. You've learned something and are usually in a better position as a result, making more effective decisions that are not rooted in your own experience.

No matter what any author says, research highlights the fact that business leaders will become involved in organizational politics whether they want to or not. It is an autonomous and self-sustaining human activity. But practising organizational politics need not mean compromising your own ethics or morals. In fact, it must not. As the reforms proposed by US President George W. Bush in the wake of the collapse of energy trader Enron suggested, business leaders must be seen to embody the honest practices expected of their companies. As the scale of the Enron scandal rapidly unfolded early in 2002, the London *Financial Times* described it as:[20]

Individual greed on a spectacular scale. A shocking willingness to overlook questionable practices by institutions claiming to uphold the highest standards. A shameful determination to cover up evidence. Politicians eager to accept money from a company subsequently shown to be a sham. These are the hallmarks of the Enron scandal.

The taint of Enron spread, not only directly (notably to its auditor, Arthur Andersen) but also indirectly to boardrooms throughout the industrialized world. Shareholders held boards up to closer scrutiny as the nervousness about corporate governance spread. The shockwaves prompted President George W. Bush to outline a ten-point plan to improve corporate responsibility and protect shareholders in March 2002. The proposals included a call for chief executives to vouch personally for 'the veracity, timeliness and fairness' of their companies' public disclosures and financial statements, and suggested that officers who abused their power should be banned from corporate leadership. Obviously, these measures were proposed at a time of public suspicion about business leaders. However, the idea that leaders should be able to vouch personally for corporate veracity and fairness is a useful one to consider when engaging in corporate politics.

Conclusion

The key points we want to emphasize at the end of this chapter are as follows.

- Being in a position of formal authority is not sufficient in itself to engineer and initiate wide-ranging strategic change. All too often an unacceptable boss finds that he or she is blocked, out-manoeuvred or even out-talked by smarter subordinates. What is necessary is to influence others sufficiently to accept new ideas and efforts.
- Taking the high moral ground and eschewing 'politics' in organizations is short-sighted, and is likely to drive free discussion underground.
- Ignoring or not sensing the political moves afoot within organizations is dangerous, both for individuals and for the organization at large. Do everything in your power to promote a healthy attitude to politics.
- If senior executives are to be held personally responsible for the veracity and accuracy of records of corporate performance, political behaviour must also be ethical and intended to support corporate as well as personal goals.
- Political behaviour, such as the identification of key movers and shakers and their subsequent engagement in discussion, is a key aspect of the discussion or discourse phase in the *Leadership Unplugged* continuum.

- Political behaviour can be open and honest, and must be sustained in this style if organizations are to sustain the momentum of change.

QuestionBank

Take time out to answer these questions.

1. To what extent do you believe organizational politics is a necessary part of business life? Why do you take this position? What sort of political practices do you or have you engaged in, and what has been their outcome? How often do you plan your political activities, as opposed to engage in informal or *ad hoc* activities such as water cooler discussions?

2. How do others – for instance, peers, subordinates and other stakeholders – regard politics? What is your relationship with these other parties like? (Generally constructive, or generally unhelpful?) Why?

3. How quickly do you hear about a political problem within the organization? To what extent do you expect people around you to solve their own political problems? Why would you intervene in a political deadlock within the organization? How would you set about intervening?

4. How can you tell if senior executives within the organization are engaged in unhelpful political behaviour? What gives you a clue about when executives are eschewing political behaviour? How do you know when executives are blind to organizational politics? What would you do, if anything, if you recognized any of these situations within your organization?

Notes

1. From Machiavelli's *The Prince*, a classic work on politics (London: Penguin).
2. Quoted in Janner, Greville, 1994. *Complete Speechmaker*. London: Century Business.
3. Buchanan, David and Badham, Richard, 1999. *Power, Politics and Organizational Change: Winning The Turf Game*. London: Sage, p. 22.
4. In a speech to shareholders. Lowe, Janet, 1998. *Jack Welch Speaks*. New York: John Wiley & Sons, p. 99.

5. Lazarus, Ralph, 1963. The case of the oriental rug. *Michigan Business Review* 15(3), November 1963.

6. Rockwell, Willard F., 1971. *The Twelve Hats of a Company President.* London: Prentice Hall.

7. Semler, Ricardo, 1993. *Maverick!* London: Arrow, p. 314.

8. Buchanan and Badham, op. cit., p. 46.

9. Pfeffer, Jeffrey, 1992. *Managing with Power.* Boston: HBS Press, p. 495.

10. ibid., p. 497.

11. ibid., p. 498.

12. Scott-Morgan, Peter, 1994. *The Unwritten Rules of the Game.* Maidenhead: McGraw-Hill. This practical guide captures these issues at length.

13. Herkströter, Cor, 1998. Royal Dutch/Shell: rewriting the contracts. In Dauphinais, William, and Price, Colin (eds), *Straight from the CEO.* London: Nicholas Brealey, pp. 86–93.

14. ibid.

15. Buchan, David. Big projects to keep Shell upstream, *Financial Times*, April 2002.

16. Farkas, Charles, de Backer, Philippe and Sheppard, Allen, 1995. *Maximum Leadership 2000: 'Add value or get out!'* London: Orion Business, p. 52.

17. ibid., p. 148.

18. Dyer, Geoff. Latest whys and wherefores of the maverick. *Financial Times*, Inside Track section, 18 October 2001.

19. From Buchanan and Badham, op. cit.

20. After Enron: Reforms to restore confidence in business. *Financial Times*, leader page, 19 October 2001.

CHAPTER 6

Discussion: The Complexity of Change

What most managers think of as scientific management is based on a conception of science that few current scientists would defend. [W]hile traditional science focused on analysis, prediction and control, the new science emphasizes chaos and complexity

David Freedman[1]

Once we think of the economy and society as a complex, living system, the frequent failures of policy can be readily understood. These systems are inherently difficult to predict and control. This is not merely a point of intellectual interest, but of great practical import. For it implies that much of the control which governments believe they exercise over the economy and society is illusory.

Paul Ormerod[2]

Leadership lies in large part in generating a point of reference, against which a feeling of organization and direction can emerge.

Linda Smircich and Gareth Morgan[3]

Headlines

Organizations are complex systems comprised of a medium sized number of intelligent individuals who act on the basis of local knowledge. None of these individuals can know the whole picture of what's going on in and for the organization.

If you accept that the context of business life is too complex for any one individual to grasp, the key questions for senior executives are 'what do I do?' and 'how do I do it?'

Organizations can perform above expectations if they are at 'the edge of chaos'.

Complex organizations tend to evolve towards order, not disorder.

The emergence of new organizational forms takes place through the self-organization of the individuals in the firm.

> The task of senior executives in complex organizations is to nurture self-organization and emergence. They must do this by facilitating, guiding and setting the boundary conditions under which individuals operate.
>
> There is no role for directive, coercive management in complex organizations. It doesn't work.

The Complexity of Change

Let's get a few things straight. Today, business life is far too complicated to be understood by any one individual. We believe this to be as true for small entrepreneurial family firms as for global Fortune 500 corporations. Also, the business environment today is far more complex than it has ever been. A cliché, but it's true. The trend towards global firms and 24/7 trading has made that a certainty. The inevitable conclusion to be drawn from this is that leaders ought to be guided by their experience, to do what they know, to remain risk averse. The alternative – to try new things, to innovate, to deviate from their personal experience of business – is commercial suicide. But today many business executives preach the mantra of change. And this is a mantra not only of change, but of constant change. Why? Because as soon as an organization introduces change into the equation it magnifies the complexity of business life infinitely. Organizations are even less likely to be able to predict the outcomes of their behaviour, and their future performance.

What is even more perverse is that we usually praise to the skies those business executives who drive for change – until the project fails, at least. Why is that? Is it for their drive and enthusiasm or (more likely) their 'clarity of vision'? This chapter may prove the most difficult for some readers to accept, in that we take the position that no executive can have clarity of vision. No executive can see his or her way through the complexity of business life. Strategic visions, compelling visions, audacious goals – they are all just one form or another of sophisticated guess, hunch or gut feeling. Yes, we can and do teach people to become better strategic thinkers, but on the whole we collude with the executives themselves to support the fantasy that they will, over time, reach some strategic nirvana – a complete and perfect picture of the organization, of the industry in which it competes and of the global environment.

'But what about the gurus?', you may ask. Well, we can and do devour the airport books of every business hero – from Iacocca to Welch – who has taken on the might of corporate America. But in our view the retrospective histories of 60-year-old white men, no matter how well their recipes for success might be articulated, can't be taken seriously as a guide for all firms in all industries in all parts of the globe to conduct businesses. What about the scenario planners, you may ask, who steep themselves in data and paint different potential scenarios, all of them equally plausible? While these techniques, too, have their place, we fear that they oversimplify the extreme complexity of the business world and contribute to stereotyping, reinforcing the tired view of senior executive as superhero leader, as 'born and not made'.

Instead of supporting the fantasy industry by producing further simplistic prescriptions for success, this chapter poses an alternative and increasingly compelling view. While no satisfactory theory of complex systems has yet been defined, we believe that the implications of complexity science for senior managers and leaders have not been addressed adequately as a series of research questions. This chapter therefore suggests that there is a place for a theory of strategic leadership that encompasses the behaviour of senior executives in complex organizations. Much evidence from management research supports our view, and at the chapter's end we offer a health warning in case you want to explore the evidence further.

Our view, in short, is this. We believe that the context of business life today is so inescapably complex that there is almost no point trying to get to grips with it at all. So leadership is all about taking your best guess and making a punt. We make no apologies for such an overtly pessimistic view. But we are firmly of the opinion that the complexity of business life is of so great a magnitude that none of us can control or manage it. And as soon as you too adopt this view, as you surely must, your inevitable next question will be 'So what is the role for senior executives?'

Do Leaders Make a Difference?

There is a significant body of research showing that senior executives do nothing for the performance of the firm. Many researchers can find no link between senior executive behaviour and organizational performance (Table 6.1). These researchers are sceptical that the individual statements and actions of the managerial elite can have any serious impact on the behaviour of the rest of the organization. Not surprisingly, those of us who teach and consult to senior executives, either through business schools or in private practice, rarely highlight this material. Perhaps this is because we think our clients don't want to hear the message; perhaps we feel uncomfortable that our work as executive coaches or workshop leaders might actually be meaningless.

Table 6.1 Do leaders matter? Some management researchers think not

Groups of management researchers arguing that managers do not matter	Main argument	Some authors who have adopted this view, and classic examples of their work
Population ecologists	Organizations are largely driven by inertia and hemmed in by environmental and organizational constraints (e.g. fixed investment in specialized assets, internal political constraints; legal and fiscal barriers to entry)	Hannan and Freeman, 1977
Institutional theorists	Under pressure to appear normal and rational, firms adopt conventions that make them conform with external expectations. In the face of uncertainty managers behave as their predecessors did, leading to widespread homogeneity within firms and across industries.	DiMaggio and Powell, 1983
Homogeneous managerial elite	Managers are a homogeneous group. Fortune 500 CEOs are largely 50–65-year-old white men with college degrees and significant experience in other large organizations.	March and March, 1977
Variance in financial performance	Taking account of factors such as the year, the industry and specific company, organization or institution, researchers can attribute only 5–15% of the variance in performance to senior executive behaviour	Lieberson and O'Connor, 1972; Salancik and Pfeffer, 1977

This work is supported in large measure by the efforts of management researchers exploring complexity theory. Over the past ten years increasing attention has been given to the complexity sciences and to what they can tell us, for instance, about the way economies and markets work, and how small changes can sometimes lead to a large impact. Table 6.2 summarizes some of the specific insights that are regarded as scientifically well established (primarily in the biological sciences). However, the new vocabulary of complexity sciences has been taken by some researchers and applied wholesale to the management and strategic behaviour of our organizations. This chapter considers why this might be worth doing.

The key issues in complexity science that seem to have generated interest and support among management thinkers are:

- complex adaptive systems theory
- the 'edge of chaos' concept
- the ideas of emergence and conditioned emergence
- and self-organization.

Organizations as Complex Adaptive Systems

So much has been written about chaos theory and complex systems generally that, apart from some brief excursions, we propose not to delve too broadly here.[4] As far as *Leadership Unplugged* is concerned, we believe it is worth focusing on the question of what a complex system is. Ultimately, what does it mean for senior executives if we define organizations as complex systems?

John Casti is a member of the Santa Fe Institute, a world-leading collection of complexity specialists. He has worked towards a viable theory of complex adaptive systems over a long period, and he defines the likely components of the theory as:[5]

1. a medium-sized number
2. of intelligent agents
3. who act on the basis of local information.

Let's deal with Casti's components of complex systems theory in turn.

1. Complex systems contain, or are comprised of, a medium-sized number of agents. By comparison with relatively simple systems such as superpower conflicts (which tend to involve a small number of interacting agents), or large systems such as galaxies or containers of gas (which have a large enough collection of agents that we can use statistical methods to

Table 6.2 Can insights from complexity science be applied to management?

Insight from complexity science	Possible implication for management science and leaders
1. Many dynamic systems do not stabilize or reach a cyclical equilibrium.	Firms and industries are constantly changing and will never reach a steady state or a predictable equilibrium; leaders must appreciate change programmes will never reach a conclusion. *Leadership Unplugged* argues that the leadership task must be more associated with developing change or innovation capability within organizations than with implementing policies once, or attaining particular structures as an end state.
2. Processes that appear to be random may in fact be 'chaotic'. Specifically, this means that they revolve around identifiable types of attractor and seldom, if ever, return to the same state.	No clear view on attractors has developed in the management research literature, though much opinion has been expressed about what might constitute attractors. An implicit aspect of this insight would seem to be the supporting view that change is constant and that a complex system, having identified and used an an attractor, then moves on. It's a cliché to suggest that change is constant, but here at least complexity research offers proof that this is so. A greater appreciation of this may lead senior executives to focus more on the processes of change and innovation than on short-term outcomes and returns (ROI).
3. The behaviour of complex processes can be sensitive to small differences in initial conditions, so that two apparently similar entities can follow radically divergent paths over time.	No two people, groups or organizations are alike and strategic decisions must be taken with explicit attention to the context of each entity. We cannot rely on our own experience as recipes of behaviour drawn from the past or from our knowledge of other groups are as likely to fail as to work. *Leadership Unplugged* argues for one-to-one attention to the ideas and thoughts of individuals, teams and organizations – they are just as likely to be valid as our own views.

Table 6.2 (continued)

Insight from complexity science	Possible implication for management science and leaders
4. Complex systems resist simple analysis, because interconnections and feedback loops prevent us from holding some subsystems constant while studying others in isolation.	The behaviour of groups and organizations is tacit and intangible and cannot be identified and replicated elsewhere. We do not and cannot know why some groups are successful and why some fail. This is a disappointing message for many senior executives.
5. Complex patterns can arise from the interaction of agents that follow relatively simple rules.	Establishing simple rules or strategies to guide our strategic behaviour can nevertheless result in extremely complex behaviours or outcomes. Some researchers say we may be able to use this insight to guide our teams and organizations.
6. Complex systems tend to exhibit self-organizing behaviour; starting from a random state they usually evolve towards order instead of disorder.	If organizations are complex systems, the individuals and teams within them identify priorities and develop actions without intervention from managers or leaders.

study them), complex systems contain a number of agents that interact to create an interesting pattern of behaviour. When we pushed him, he wouldn't be drawn on what 'a medium number' was, beyond saying that 'medium' is 'more than two agents and fewer than 10^{26}'.

2. Agents in the system are intelligent and adaptive. Agents such as molecules or people make decisions on the basis of rules, but can modify the rules if new information becomes available. Interestingly, the agents can generate new rules if these better suit the information they have available. This means that an ecology of rules emerges and continues to evolve during the existence of the system. (This may help explain the evolution and existence of the unwritten rules of behaviour that we discussed in Chapter 5.)

3. Agents can only have local information. In complex systems, no agent has access to information describing what all the other agents are doing. Each agent may only get data from a small subset of local agents, and must process this information to decide how he or she will act.

Putting the components together, then, a complex adaptive system contains a medium-sized number of intelligent, adaptive agents. None of them knows everything that's going on in the system, and they interact only on the basis of local information. For the purposes of *Leadership Unplugged*, this conveys a realistic and valuable description of how organizations are structured, and one that we can use and explore for the time being. Freely translated, organizations (as complex systems) contain a medium-sized number of intelligent, adaptive people, who interact with one another only on the basis of local knowledge.

Building on this definition of organizations as complex systems, then, we can suggest that the characteristics of complex systems are also the characteristics of organizations. That being so, the fact that organizations as complex systems tend to evolve towards a state that has been described memorably as 'the edge of chaos' seems worth exploring, not least because extraordinary performance gains appear to be possible under these circumstances.

Organizations at the Edge of Chaos

One of the most fascinating aspects of complexity theory is the argument that all complex adaptive systems evolve to what has been called the edge of chaos – a point at which small as well as unusually large performance changes occur, but where the system hasn't descended into total chaos. This property of complex systems is in sharp contrast with a chemical equilibrium, where small changes in the presence of an acid, say, are self-correcting and the system quickly readjusts to steady state neutral by changing the amount of alkali present. In a complex system, small changes in behaviour can have a small, medium sized or large impact on system performance. No one really knows why, and the transitions are unpredictable. Furthermore predicting how, when or whether an organization is at or near the edge of chaos seems impossible. Many mathematicians have made great strides towards documenting the edge of chaos in theoretical terms, but this research is not yet available to us in a practical form and so remains outside the scope of this book. The fundamental practical point to grasp, however, is that this edge of chaos state appears to give systems some performance advantage, and also some advantage in terms of their ability to survive. Following our line of argument and applying it to organizations, perhaps these would survive longer – or perform more effectively for a time – if they operated at the edge of chaos (Figure 6.1).

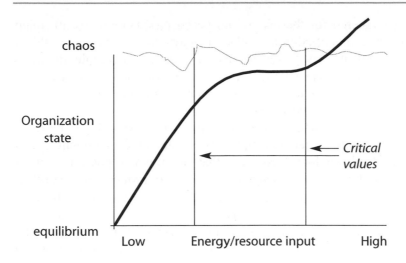

Figure 6.1 At the edge of chaos

So how does this edge of chaos state come about in practice? And can it be influenced? Well, complex adaptive systems theory suggests that organizations adapt to their environment through the efforts of the individuals who make up the organization attempting to improve their own payoffs. This is individualistic behaviour, suggests the theory, because individual agents are not able to forecast the organization-wide consequences of their local choices. In other words, individuals better their own positions (or, in the jargon, 'optimize their own fitness') to increase their own value over time. But as every individual within the firm is constantly adjusting and shifting, the payoffs they receive (both financial and non-financial) depend on the choices that other people or agents make. The organization's performance over time is therefore a combination of the frequent small improvisations and changes everyone makes in an ad hoc manner. Occasionally these accumulate into radical strategic innovations, changing the terms of competition fundamentally.

One example of the manner in which organizations evolve towards the edge of chaos concerns the evolutionary processes that alter the weakest agent in a system. Practical examples of this behaviour might be seen where organizations replace their least efficient members, for instance, or where the least effective firms in an industry tend to go into receivership. Usually a new member of staff, or a new entrant to an industry, drawn at random will conform with the prevailing environment of the time more closely than a failed predecessor, setting off a cascade of new adaptations and interconnections within the firm and the industry. The so-called fitness landscape is altered for the better, and performance improves all round. Sadly, however, this usually takes place in ways that no one seems able to measure or replicate. And this is the dispiriting aspect of complexity theory taken to its logical conclusion. It offers a very reasonable explanation of what happens in organizations but it cannot, in all honesty, be used in a predictive or a prescriptive sense.

How can we nurture or influence something as inextricably complex as a non-linear system of relationships between adaptive intelligent agents, riddled with feedback loops? Not only that, but how is it possible to influence a system that evolves when new agents are introduced, some of them perhaps drawn from a pool outside the current system? Can the most successful agents in a system be spliced together into a new agent, as we learn more about the 'genetic engineering' of organizations? How can that new system be influenced in turn? These approaches, although rooted in the hard scientific world of modern biological and quantum theory, seem far too demanding of us as everyday business leaders. No immediate return from the application of complexity theory seems likely.

So what is the point? Where is the value of the knowledge that organizations tend to operate as complex adaptive systems, and to evolve towards the edge of chaos?

The value, in terms of *Leadership Unplugged*, is buried in the remaining two aspects of complex system behaviour: *emergence* and *self-organizing behaviour.*

Case 12. The UK's National Health Service – the complexity of leadership

Early in 2003, the NHS Leadership Centre in the UK issued the findings from an in-depth study of 150 chief executive officers across the country. The Hay Group, a human resources consultancy recognized for its work in profiling executives, was chosen to conduct the study, which was intended to identify the qualities associated with both successful and outstanding performance at the senior level. The results were published in the form of a series of leadership qualities. A series of briefings and documents was then prepared to help NHS Trusts across the United Kingdom pilot the application of the resulting standards, and to try to make them 'live' development tools for raising standards of leadership across the United Kingdom. The qualities were captured in a graphic lovingly referred to as 'the doughnut' (Figure 6.2).

The findings were derived from a variety of data sources, including records of on-the-job performance and interviews with Hay consultants. The research was rigorous and thorough – an essential aspect of any public

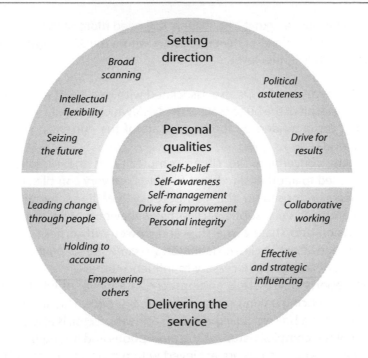

Figure 6.2 The NHS's leadership qualities capture the imagination of trust CEOs. Reproduced by kind permission, NHS Leadership Centre.

sector project at this time – and what the NHS learned about its leaders was provocative. The research found that all leaders were capable of engaging in complex behaviours. Among the outstanding leaders were individuals who, rather than using different competencies seen in other successful or effective leaders, were able to adopt the more complex behaviours more often or with more sophistication.

There was some concern that the 'leadership qualities' model might simply replicate the behaviours of the past, without necessarily capturing the specific qualities that people needed to develop or exhibit in the future. 'The information gathering phase of the research was deliberately structured to elicit information about the leadership demands of the future', says Hay, 'and data were gathered from many sources to support this'. Nevertheless, the qualities benchmark was stretched in one significant arena where the qualities of NHS leaders were found wanting:

The only area where NHS leaders most commonly appeared to be operating at a level below their private sector counterparts was in a quality called 'drive for results' (a competency concerned with explicit and ambitious goal setting). It is our view that NHS leaders will need more of this in the future and we have therefore set the benchmark within the 360-degree feedback tool at a slightly higher level.

The 'missing' level, says Hay, is also associated with calculated risk taking. This is probably a result of the huge scale of the NHS, which – frankly – discourages risk taking, compounded by the huge scale of the current government's change agenda.

This issue, concerning the sheer complexity of the National Health Service, has led to another significant finding. 'The very complex leadership behaviours categorised in the competency "Leading change through people" combines very subtle facilitative behaviours with the ability to create a vision and share ownership and power with others, rather than leading from the front.' A classic definition, in *Leadership Unplugged* terms, of the qualities of leadership necessary to influence others.

In fact, reports Hay, there is an unprecedented level of what they term 'strategic influencing' taking place across the service. This level, which is much higher than Hay would expect in the private sector, is also probably a reflection of the complex nature of the amorphous and intangible NHS, and the manner in which things are achieved within it only through subtle use of influence and calculated persuasion.

Questions:
1. How likely is it that the structure and size of this public sector service acts as the driver for leadership behaviour? How important is the demographic profile of the management cohort, and their background as risk averse financial managers, likely to be?
2. How might creativity and innovation be introduced into future leadership qualities within this traditionally hierarchical, cost-driven service?
3. What role might people development play in breaking the culture of control, and in introducing a culture of outstanding leadership qualities across the service?

Emergence and Conditioned Emergence

In the new biological sciences of the last 20 to 30 years, scientists have focused their attentions on processes of adaptation and the conditions under which new order emerges. It's important to note, too, that emergence deals with system or organization level effects, and doesn't address what each of the agents in a system does. And while the exact form of these emergent structures cannot be predicted by scientists, the range of broad possibilities is to some extent contained within the set of simple rules that the system applies to generate the new order.[6] Applied to organizations, we believe that senior executives could interpret a new structural arrangement resulting from a financial crisis, for example, as an example of emergence. And here's the crux of the matter – what does complexity theory tell us about the new emergent form, or about the process behind its emergence? If it doesn't tell us anything, or give us any new levers to use to manage organizations, then the application of complexity science to organizations will not be that helpful for practitioners.

During a crisis, or some period of organizational transition, a critical moment arrives when things change (Figure 6.3). Either the organization pulls through the critical moment and is successful, adopting the upper trajectory, or performance continues to decline and the organization follows the lower trajectory. But what exactly takes place at this critical moment?

Before the critical moment (or bifurcation point) the organization is in tune with its environment and reasonably well adapted to its role there. As

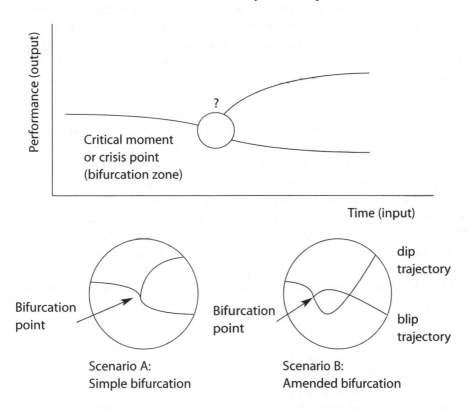

Figure 6.3 What happens at the critical moment? (Adapted from Leifer, 1989)

it approaches the crisis zone, however, it comes under increasing pressure from the complex interrelations of external and internal forces. This will involve some mix of (for example) new legislative pressures, competitive forces from industry, employee dissatisfaction with the status quo or senior executive powerlessness. The organization soon becomes unstable and a brief period of uncertainty and ambiguity arises – this may even amount to chaos, both figuratively and literally.

Taking Scenario A in Figure 6.3 and considering the case of a critical moment that has been successfully managed, the organization has quickly identified and settled into a new way of working and performance has picked up immediately. If the critical moment had been handled badly, however, performance would have continued to decline as shown on the lower trajectory.

We believe that Scenario B, however, offers a more realistic description of events at a critical moment, and that applying complexity theory as a lens to view the critical moment helps us see what appears to be happening in rather more detail. We can see, for instance, that the organization is moving away from equilibrium to a position that is far from equilibrium, and that the individuals within the organization are all trying to figure out how to maximize their payoffs. Perhaps new ideas are being generated in some quarters, for example, while restraints are being established in others at the same time. Elsewhere inside the organization, small actions and experiments may be being tried – sometimes with success, sometimes without.

All of this will have been for nothing, however, if managers respond as they typically do in a crisis – by treating what they see as nothing more than a temporary performance problem. In our experience we usually see managers at this critical moment crank up control levels, step in to cut costs and set tougher targets. In other words, managers' usual response is to push the old system harder. Interestingly, often this does improve performance in the short run – we see an initial 'blip' on the performance line following the bifurcation point in Scenario B. But this short-term response is unlikely to address the underlying issues facing the organization – that it is no longer adjusted to the environment in which it operates – and in the longer term performance will decline. Another way of looking at this is to consider that, while the tougher controls got the organization through the critical moment, the organization that existed before the critical moment hasn't changed fundamentally. Some kind of mismatch with the environment remains.

The alternative path for the organization – pursuit of long-term success – invariably begins with a fall in performance as individuals within it learn how to adopt new ways of working, engage in new relationships or structures and experiment with the new conditions. Unfortunately, however, most executives across the organization tend to fall back on the prospect of immediate short-term gains. They usually drive it towards the 'blip' trajectory. There's pressure, too, on the firms that adopt the 'dip' trajectory to switch back to old ways of working as short-term performance gets worse instead of better.

Assuming, for a moment, that long-term success is a better target to aim for than short-term gain, how can we encourage organizations and their executives to adopt this route? Exactly this question – how to help organizations and executives embrace emergence – has been studied by Robert Macintosh and Donald Maclean in the Department of Management at the University of Glasgow for the last five years or so. And their *conditioned emergence* framework, they believe, represents a step in the right direction.[7]

Conditioned emergence encapsulates three steps:

1. conditioning
2. creating or anticipating far-from-equilibrium conditions
3. and managing the feedback processes.

STAGE 1: CONDITIONING
A central feature of complexity theory is the emergence of order through the repeated application of simple rules. Prior to flipping from one organizational form to another, then, the organization must consider exactly what the present structure is, what it means and what rules underpin the current form. What Macintosh and Maclean call the 'deep structure' of the organization and its rules are the barely articulated views on what the organization represents and how it operates. Through facilitated discussions, Maclean and Macintosh propose that firms engage in dialogues about what needs to be done and how, and which of the old rules, if any, need to be rejected. They suggest adopting facilitation tactics drawn from organization learning specialists and from business process re-engineering advocates, but without necessarily adopting the philosophies of either system. (Many texts and recipe books exist to explain the tactics of facilitation, which we do not consider in our discussion here.)

STAGE 2: CREATING OR ANTICIPATING FAR-FROM-EQUILIBRIUM CONDITIONS
The onset of some crisis, or another compelling reason for change, creates the opportunity for beneficial change to take place and for the emergence of new structural forms. A typical mechanism used here by managers is the major restructuring exercise, which must be more than just a paper exercise to have any impact. To demonstrate how futile restructuring can sometimes be, consider the global telecommunications player with whom we worked

which had recently merged its information systems and engineering divisions to create a new combined division. But no jobs were lost, no central functions were curtailed or taken over by another department and no central buildings or services were closed as a result. In other words, the only place the merger occurred was on the organization chart.

During any period of uncertainty a new order, based on the new interrelations between people and departments, attempts to assert itself. This new order, suggest Macintosh and Maclean, reflects both the content and the process of the new organization as defined by the new relationships between the individuals within it.

STAGE 3: MANAGING THE FEEDBACK PROCESSES

As the new organizational form emerges, feedback needs to be given as appropriate. Traces of the old structure and the old ways of working will inevitably resurface, and there will be pressure to back-pedal and resume them. During this phase, the key managerial task is to listen and watch for small signals that indicate that new structural forms are emerging. Positive feedback welcoming and encouraging these early signals provides a multiplier effect, accelerating the development of new systems and procedures still further. This is a tricky time for the organization, as the two potential trajectories – up and down – are competing with one another. It would still be relatively easy to fall back into old ways of working, especially if the pressure to realize the short-term gains remains obvious and in the forefront of people's minds.

In essence, Macintosh and Maclean suggest that it may be possible to nurture organizational change, and to create the initial context and conditions for change by conditioning the organization to allow for emergence.[8]

> We believe that the key difference in applying complexity theory ... to organizations is that organizations have the capacity to bring about [change] ... through consciously creating the conditions in which successful transformations can occur.

There is a proviso. Organizations, and therefore the senior executives sponsoring change, must promote experimentation, allow errors to be made and nurture reflective managers. This is hard to do while simultaneously being in the unstable, ambiguous zone we've called the critical moment. And while power and political struggles may hinder the emergence of new organizational forms, the conditioned emergence framework does attempt to deal with this explicitly through the use of facilitation techniques including theory sessions, seminars, workshops and simulations.

Self-Organization

The single most important characteristic of complex systems, in our view, is what is known as *self-organization*. Complexity theory as applied to organizations begins to explain why collections of individuals in a densely interconnected network appear to self-organize spontaneously into new arrangements, many of which significantly outperform previous configurations. There's no doubt that *self-organization* exists in scientific terms. Observing the molecules of a gas as energy is pumped in, we can witness abrupt change as the molecules spontaneously point in the same direction, creating a laser beam that casts for miles. When considered with regard to humans in organizations, however, questions remain. How can we recognize self-organization in corporations? What are its implications? And how can we initiate and control it, if at all?

This is one of the trickiest aspects of complexity theory for senior executives to accept, because we believe it means senior executives giving up the control that they have striven for throughout most of their working careers. If leadership in a complex organization is about the creation of high-performing, self-organizing teams, then what role is there for leaders? This new concept seems to involve nothing more than creating an environment in which people can do their jobs effectively and without undue interference. Our task as senior executives then becomes straightforward. The simple rules of *Leadership Unplugged*, if you will, become nothing more than:

- recruit the best people
- train them well
- and constantly tell them how they're doing, so they can get even better.

This is much more than a cosmetic change to the way we lead. It doesn't necessarily destroy the traditional leader–follower power balance, but (for instance) it puts decision-making responsibility in organizations into the hands of the people who need it: the workforce. It casts serious doubt on the idea that planning, controlling, organizing and coordinating is really the senior executive's role – this doesn't make sense. Instead, we believe it is the job of senior executives to create the conditions that allow their people to plan, control, organize and coordinate their own work. After all, in a complex organizational system there is no hierarchy. Senior executives are just another handful of agents in the system, and the truth of the old chestnut that 'leadership is getting things done through other people' becomes extremely clear.

In the context of the relationships between people within organizations, and in their relationships with their key contacts outside them, it is clear that we should be talking in detail here about the local interactions between individual agents trying to improve their local payoffs. That being so, we believe that the self-organization of individuals taking place within an organizational context provides a perfect illustration of the political behaviours that we introduced in Chapter 5. In other words, organizations are complex systems in which the emergence of new ways of working occurs through the self-organization of individuals that make up the collective. From the other direction, self-organization is a description of the interpersonal political processes that individuals engage in to maximize their own payoffs and their own value to the organization.

As we've watched executives leading their firms over the years – with varying degrees of success, it has to be said, in generating self-organizing teams – we have come to realize that the concepts of complex organizations and of complex political processes are inextricably intertwined, and that they work together very effectively. But (and here's another tough call for paranoid senior executives) it only seems to work where there is an underlying honesty about the organization's situation and the context of, and the processes to be involved in, any proposed change. In some respects this is about conditioning or preparing the organization for the critical moment to come, and explaining in advance the process that the organization will adopt for managing the critical moment.

Fundamentally, we believe that the mechanism individuals use both to engage politically and to engage in self-organization are one and the same – conversation. Controlling the future strategy of the organization is as simple as engaging in conversation with the person next to you. Who are they? What do they stand for? Why? What do they make of the situation? Where do they think the organization should be heading? All these, and more, help you to clarify your own position and explore the positions of others. Along the way both of you are influenced by each other, and both of you and the organization evolve, one micro-step at a time. The evolution of organizations in this way has been described as their 'animation' – the organization moving into the future frame by frame but with all the appearance of free and fluid motion.[9] Is this, then, what leadership in complex organizations is about? Is a manager a director of animation who creates the atmosphere and sets the tone for the movie, but lets the artists get on with completing each frame?

So What is Leadership in Complex Organizations?

Let's take stock. Perhaps the most significant elements of complexity theory for *Leadership Unplugged* – in terms of explaining unanticipated yet significant organizational change – appear to be the related concepts of self-organization and emergence that we've just looked at. What is described as self-organizing behaviour arises in complex systems when, starting from some random state, they usually evolve towards order instead of disorder. This significant and observable phenomenon is a defining feature of complex systems. Building on these ideas, various researchers have suggested that the most effective complex organizations evolve strategies that lie neither in a zone of complete stability nor in a complete state of flux. Instead, they lie 'at the edge of chaos'.

This suggests to us that it is important for leaders to:

- rethink what they mean by organization, especially their concepts of hierarchy and control
- learn the art of managing and changing contexts, but learn to leave personnel free to plan, organize and co-ordinate their own work
- live with continuous transformation and emergent order as natural states of affairs, even at times of apparent crisis, and learn to coach peers and subordinates to live with the anxiety too
- and be open to new processes that can facilitate the processes of self-organization.

In short, we believe that leadership behaviour supportive of highly responsive, innovative, self-organizing teams can help build high-performing organizations. We believe that complexity theory offers a strong business case for empowerment and a facilitative, participative management style. We think it behoves managers and leaders not to consider the details of what the organization must do at a micro-level, but to consider instead what the organization stands for – *who* it is. In our experience, organizations with a clear sense of their own identity can have a clearer course of action. Faced with difficult decisions about direction, strategy and tactics, a clear understanding and expectation of who we are and what we stand for makes choices much simpler.

The key leadership questions then centre on how leaders facilitate or influence self-organization in complex organizations. How does this translate into an exploration of our own, and our organization's, identity? And what does this mean in terms of the *Leadership Unplugged* philosophy? Some of these questions can be answered by looking at how organizations have successfully engaged in change in the past, but through the lens of complexity science. Of course Brabantia, in the next case study, did not explicitly use complexity science to structure and plan the changes it undertook. Looking at the changes through the lens of complex systems theory reinforces how successful the organization was, however, and begins to explain why the changes were so successful.

Case 13. Brabantia – less control, more leadership

Founded in 1919 and based in the Netherlands, Brabantia is one of Europe's leading manufacturers of household utensils, making products such as bread bins, storage containers, trays, ironing boards, kitchen gadgets and letterboxes. With an annual turnover of circa 80 million, the company employs some 850 staff in the Netherlands, Belgium, Germany, Great Britain and Italy.

During the 1980s and 1990s, Brabantia experienced major increases in competition. Imports increased, while demand petered out as population growth slowed and the buyer power of new hypermarkets and specialist DIY superstores increased. In response, Brabantia decided to focus on its reputation for quality, durability and value. To achieve this, however, competitiveness needed to be improved dramatically. Its major problem was that the traditional life cycle for most of its products was 15 years and its innovation cycle (from initial idea to product launch) was too slow. Furthermore, Brabantia needed simultaneously to match or improve on leading standards of cost, quality and flexibility.

First, Brabantia restructured its organization. This created the critical moments it needed to explore its complexity and identity, and a new corporate culture emerged based on devolved accountability and a quality focus. The revised culture was supported by the introduction of revised staff assessment and remuneration systems.

Following the restructuring, the organization reported an organizational philosophy now based on involving staff in the development of the mission of the company, giving staff greater control over their work, developing individuals and encouraging creativity. The firm understood for itself the need to engineer a clear split in responsibilities between senior management and other staff. Top management now agree the final strategy and policies of the company and are also responsible for designing the overall organizational structure. Operational control and improvement of business processes, on the other hand, is clearly devolved to the staff responsible for carrying out those processes. Operational staff also influence the evolution of overall corporate policy. Earlier organizational structures lacked such clarity concerning responsibilities, and excluded operational staff from policy development.

Another example of what Brabantia did to lead this complex organization was to support the development and emergence of a new organizational structure based on semi-autonomous work teams, as opposed to the previous traditional hierarchies and rigid division of labour. Each team has considerable responsibility and freedom. Within limits, each team is able to make decisions about ordering raw materials and machinery parts, scheduling production, and organizing time, holidays, and the recruitment of temporary staff during busy periods. Teams replaced a more traditional organization of work activity based on formal hierarchies, task specialization and a functional structure. Additionally, the teams now had a process focus – ensuring high quality – as opposed to a fixed target such as output or cost. In part, this has been reinforced by all of the semi-autonomous teams adopting continuous improvement programmes based on advanced problem identification and resolution techniques.

Of course, a significant investment in training was needed to equip team members with the skills to work in groups, and the knowledge needed to apply quality management and continuous improvement techniques. In the past, training had been focused on the development of functional skills.

Change has been evolutionary and participative, reports the organization, though initially there were problems. Many staff rejected the early initiatives, some of which were perceived to be too 'top down' and directive in nature. In response, however, the company developed an approach to managing organizational change which placed greater emphasis on staff involvement. This proved successful and began to create the cultural and structural foundations on which the current organization is based.

Senior executives at Brabantia are engaged in developing and maintaining the current processes by:

- Using formal policy statements (opening the debate) to explain the organizational philosophy of the business to all staff members. Two key policy statements are of particular importance. One makes explicit the company's respect for employees, and its authorization of employees to manage their own work. The other explains the company's training and development policy. Brabantia aims to achieve optimal development and utilization of people's qualities by educating them for lifetime employability.
- Engaging the organization through a combination of 'top down' and 'bottom up' initiatives (discussion) to evolve key corporate policies, including those covering organization development.
- A step-by-step approach to managing organizational change, including consultation with teams (dialogue) prior to the introduction of new ideas.

The changes have helped Brabantia enhance its competitiveness, protect jobs and enrich the work experience of its staff, the company claims. There has been a major reduction in the innovation cycle, and the time needed to develop new products has been reduced by 20 per cent.

Case included by permission of European Commission DG Social Affairs, the European Union.

Leadership as the Exploration of Identity

Organizational identity has been characterized as the core facets of an organization that are enduring and distinctive.[10] They feed into an organization's brand and reputation, but are more closely allied with the values and beliefs of the individuals that make up the organization. These core, enduring and distinctive characteristics relate to or describe an organization's deep structure, which we touched on earlier, and it is these characteristics that will change in an emergent fashion. They are deep rooted and cannot simply be imposed by edict in a company's annual report.

There are three key reasons for regarding the exploration of leadership in complex organizations as an exploration of identity. First, it's valuable because researchers increasingly believe the answers to organizational success lie in the tacit, intangible processes of what dynamic organizations do, rather than the static resources they own or develop. Second, we seriously question what formal leadership role there can be for senior executives in complex organizations. Directive, coercive, controlling action just doesn't seem to work. And this leads to the third reason – when senior executives feel powerless in organizations they tend to focus on instituting controls and performance measures, while forgetting to address processes and identity issues. This has been shown to contribute significantly to what researchers call 'identity drift' in complex organizations. This is a situation where different people or groups across an organization have different views about what it stands for, and therefore act differently in support of those ideas.

Taken together, these points lead to the logical conclusion that a dynamic theory of identity-based leadership provides a useful and real basis for what leaders in complex organizations must do.

More Process Research is Necessary

Many researchers have contributed over the last ten years to the growing literature of complexity science as applied to the study of organizations. As with all new approaches, though, many scholars continue to warn of the risks of bandwagon science. 'Caveat emptor', one paper warns.[11] 'Complexity is nothing more than a fad', says another.[12] We believe, however, that more research into complex systems is needed, specifically into how they work and whether they can be influenced in any meaningful way. Already there is real value in a complexity approach to leadership, we suggest, because it challenges the way we must think about social processes and therefore about how we should engage in leadership. Because complexity sciences are concerned with explaining behaviour in a dynamic, and not a static or simplistic, way they hold much promise for a better understanding of organizational processes than scholars have yet achieved.

Directive, Coercive Leadership does Not Work: the Paradox of Control

The second reason for exploring leadership as the management of identity in complex organizations is that directive, coercive patterns of leadership do not work in these contexts. There can be no command-and-control leaders in complex organizations. The related concepts of self-organization and emergence mean that organization occurs of its own volition. This leads to some leaders seeing emergence and self-organization – and therefore the complexity of their organization – as a challenge to their positional authority and power.

So what forms of leadership are required in turbulent times, and how can leaders manage the nature of organizational boundaries more effectively? What are the implications for leadership when complexity theory suggests they cannot choose, plan or intend the long-term outcomes of their interventions? The question can be posed even more bluntly – how do you have a leader direct an emergent system? Because if the leader really leads, according to the 'directive, coercive' conception, he or she shuts down emergent structures.

This paradox of control – leaders believe they have control, but apparently cannot exercise it – often raises anxiety amongst senior executives, who respond by tightening their controlling grip.[13] We believe that the logic of *Leadership Unplugged* – involving debate, discussion and dialogue among organizational stakeholders – helps senior executives to moderate this dysfunctional tension and to forestall the emergence of chaos. The leadership task becomes that of leading the corporate brain without shutting it down. And leaders can do that, we believe, by facilitating, guiding and setting the boundary conditions within which successful self-organization can take place.

The key implication of this paradox of leadership control is that there is a clear need for a theory explaining the nature of leadership underpinning complex organizations. Existing leadership theories tend to focus on fixed formal structures, variants of command-and-control styles or combinations of both, none of which effectively address the paradox of control faced by leaders in complex organizations.

These insights from complexity science suggest it is important to rethink what we mean by organization, and especially the nature of hierarchy and control (see Case 14: Fasson France). In summary, therefore, it appears to be the issue of diminished managerial control, and the feelings of power-lessness it creates, that have the most frightening implications for managers used to the props of planning, structure, hierarchy and other traditional modes of control.

Executive Powerlessness Contributes to Identity Drift

Rather than being so heavily engaged with controlling organizations, then, managers should focus on nurturing self-organization among the people in their firms. If managers adopt this view they should then see the corporate strategic mind as a form of distributed intelligence, driven in effect by conversation. Taking this view of organization as conversation, then, the role for managers should be focusing on creating debate, discussion and dialogue. Managers should be immersed in creating coherent institutional leadership through conversation.

This very immersion, though, can create problems. Complexity science suggests that many individuals in firms may become overloaded with conversations at times, and that this overload causes disorientation and, in time, identity drift. Questions such as 'Who are we?' and 'What are we meant to do?' would be symptomatic of this state. And this highlights the importance of a leader's constant involvement in influencing organizational identity through conversation and positioning.

Case 14. Fasson France – complexity coaches

Fasson France produces and distributes pressure-sensitive adhesive mate-rials and coated papers for use in a wide variety of industrial, commercial and consumer applications, including wine bottle labels. With annual sales of more than　98 million, the company employs 250 people. Fasson France is a wholly owned subsidiary of Avery Dennison, a US-owned multina-tional and one of the world's leading producers of self-adhesive base materials and self-adhesive consumer and office products. With annual sales in excess of　3 billion, Avery Dennison employs 15,800 people in more than 40 countries.

Fasson France operates in a challenging business-to-business market. Competition is strong. Customers are powerful, well informed, and under pressure from final product manufacturers to cut costs and develop new labelling ideas. At the same time, printing technologies are changing rapidly, particularly with the emergence of digital and non-impact technologies such as laser printing. For Fasson France, this leads to demands for continuous improvements in adhesive and coating applications, and for improvements in customer service.

In the past, Fasson responded to these competitive challenges by focusing on technological leadership (Avery Dennison invented self-adhesive labels) and advanced process technologies. A supplementary focus on 'quality' was added during the 1980s, with Fasson France winning a French quality prize in 1985. ISO 9002 status followed in 1988.

During the early 1990s Fasson's global management team recognised that this approach was no longer adequate. The problem was how to respond to pressures from customers for better service and lower prices, whilst at the same time sustaining technological leadership, manufacturing excellence and a focus on quality. Fasson's managers quickly recognized that the problem could not be solved through additional investment in equipment or product innovation. The solution lay in reforming the organization of work and changing the values and attitudes of the workforce.

The principal changes in work organization included a new organizational structure designed around workflow, with fewer functions, and decentralized decision making. For many activities, such as control, production planning, safety, quality, procurement and stock control, decision making was decentralized to new, flexible teams. At the same time, groups of functional specialists were replaced by individual coordinators.

The new, flexible teams were based on groups of multi-skilled operators, and replaced the previous functional division of activities. Each team was to be self-managed and to contain the skills needed to carry out defined business processes. Teams are responsible for meeting a series of agreed objectives covering safety, quality, delivery time and cost. To achieve these goals, they are empowered to make decisions and are given continuous access to relevant production information. Teams are also responsible for carrying out many tasks, such as safety, quality and production planning, previously undertaken by functional groups.

Perhaps the most critical change Fasson made, and one intended to sustain the development of the flexible teams, was that line managers adopted new roles and responsibilities. Supervisors and foremen were removed as part of the reduction in layers of management, and those managers that remained redefined their roles. Managers were no longer to be 'controllers' or 'regulators' – they become facilitators, coaches and guides. Teams worked towards clear objectives, while managers provided advice and support. This change has been reinforced by a realignment of pay and appraisal systems for managers. The pay of managers is now linked, in part, to their effectiveness in carrying out these new roles.

Making these changes was no trivial exercise and Fasson France invested in a four-year training programme, with more than two-thirds of the workforce receiving a minimum of 60 hours training each year. Each participant has an individual training and learning plan, based on their specific needs. In addition to technical and professional development, the training has addressed communication, problem solving and group working. The annual training budget of Fasson France was increased from 0.15 million in 1990 to 0.53 million in 1995.

An intensive programme of communication was set up to sustain these changes over time. All teams, for example, meet weekly to discuss performance and to identify opportunities for improvement. And throughout the period of change, employees were consulted and involved in setting goals and drawing up policies. They have also been involved in revising the programme to improve its effectiveness in the future.

Case included by permission of European Commission DG Social Affairs, the European Union.

New Directions in Leadership

Perhaps the most significant issue for leaders today is how, through their behaviour, they can create continuously adaptive organizations. This emerges as a central theme from much of the research that has been conducted into strategic change. Many commentators are still exploring whether change can be directed strategically, planned and logically executed, or whether it is emergent, brought about by the interplay of competing interest groups. All of this suggests a role for leadership far from the command-and-control style of a general. *Leadership Unplugged* supports the view that strategic leadership behaviour must shift the locus of responsibility for the formation of adaptive solutions from senior executives to the employees in the wider organization.

Although this is an argument for empowerment and workforce participation in the management of the organization, the task of charting the firm's direction through the complexity rests squarely on the shoulders of its senior executives. Don't think that this is a recipe for abdication of responsibility or accountability – the top management team will remain accountable for the entire firm's performance. It's only that performance will be delivered in a different way. We believe that the exploration of identity constitutes a fundamental and strategic responsibility for top-level managers. We believe it is vital for an organization's long-term success and survival.

There is no doubt in our minds, after observing senior executives in their day-to-day business lives, that the theory and implications of complex adaptive systems are full of insights into the strategic leadership of organizations. Complexity theory describes perfectly how leaders today face such a bewildering array of interactions within and outside the organization, and why they are involved in creating, nurturing or breaking thousands of non-linear relationships each day. Predictably, this constant creation and recreation of relationships leads to unpredictable behaviour and a rapid rate of change. And because these changes can result in small, medium or large cascades of adjustments, the organizational imperative is to evolve temporary advantages faster than anyone else can. The critical word here is 'evolve'. Adaptation must evolve – it can't be planned. And this is the real role for the senior executive elite, captured well in a seminal 1999 paper by Phil Anderson at Amos Tuck School, Dartmouth, New Hampshire:[14]

> Adaptation is the passage of an organization through an endless series of organizational microstates that emerge from local interactions among agents trying to improve their local payoffs. The task of those responsible for the strategic direction of an organization is not to foresee the future or to implement enterprise-wide adaptation programs, because non-linear systems react to direction in ways that are difficult to predict or control. Rather such managers establish and modify the direction and boundaries within which effective, improvised, self-organized solutions can evolve ... In his or her role as an organizational architect, the strategist influences the extent of improvisation, the nature of collaboration, the characteristics rhythm of innovation and the number and nature of experimental probes by changing structure and [employee diversity].

Conclusion

The key points we want to emphasize at the end of this chapter are:

- There is no role for the command-and-control leader in complex organizations. Directive, coercive behaviour does not work over time.
- Senior executives who nurture self-organization and emergence will achieve better performance in the medium to long term, and will ensure the organization survives.
- Leading complex organizations is challenging, and fraught with uncertainty and anxiety. Part of the leadership role is not necessarily to overcome the uncertainty but to learn to live with it.

- Leadership in complex organizations is about exploring identity. Knowing 'who we are' and 'what we stand for' helps individuals in organizations make decisions and choices for the good of the organization, as well as to improve their own payoffs.
- Exploring identity can be undertaken by engaging in debate, discussion and dialogue with individuals in the organization.

QuestionBank

Take time out to answer these questions.

1. What is the purpose of this chapter? Why was it written in the way it was? What impact, if any, did it have on you? Why did you respond in this way? How will you approach the subsequent chapters now?

2. To what extent do you believe you can change an organization one person at a time? To what extent do you support the idea that an organization is animated through an endless series of microstates, and that your role is perhaps that of director of animation?

3. How many organizations, in your view, are 'complex' as we've defined it in this chapter? What are their characteristics? How do they behave? What does a complex organization look and feel like? What differences are there, if any, between your conception of organizations having read this chapter and your previous view of organizations? What views of organizations do the people around you hold, and what challenges might this raise for you?

4. What does the definition of a complex system mean for managers and leaders? How does it change, if at all, the way you might need to manage?

Notes

1. Freedman, David, 1992. Is management still a science? *Harvard Business Review* 70(6), p. 26.
2. Ormerod, Paul, 1998. *Butterfly Economics*. London: Faber & Faber, p. xi. A beautiful account of economics and complexity theory, from one of the few clear writers on economics.

3. Smircich, Linda and Morgan, Gareth, 1982. Leadership as the management of meaning. *Journal of Applied Behavioural Sciences* 18, pp. 257–73.
4. Gleick, James, 1987. *Chaos: The Amazing Science of the Unpredictable.* London: Vintage. Waldrop, M. Mitchell, 1992. *Complexity: The Emerging Science at the Edge of Order and Chaos.* London: Penguin.
5. Casti, John, 1997. *Would-Be Worlds.* New York: John Wiley & Sons, p. 213. Casti is a rare example of an academic researcher able to write clearly and well for a non-specialist audience. Here he makes this claim for a definition of complex adaptive systems.
6. Eisenhardt, Kathleen and Sull, Donald, 2001. Strategy as simple rules. *Harvard Business Review* 79(1), pp. 106–16. This is a fascinating account of how we might use the simple rules idea.
7. MacIntosh, Robert and Maclean, Donald, 1999. Conditioned emergence: a dissipative structures approach to transformation. *Strategic Management Journal* 20, pp. 297–316.
8. ibid.
9. Lewin, A. and Koza, M., 2000. How to manage in times of disorder. In Dickson, T. (ed.), *Mastering Strategy.* London: Financial Times Ltd, pp. 115–18.
10. Albert, S. and Whetten, D. A., 1985. Organizational identity. In Cummings, L. L. and Staw, B. M. (eds), *Research in Organizational Behaviour*, Vol. 7. Greenwich, CT: JAI Press, pp. 263–95.
11. Johnson, J. L. and Burton, B. K., 1994. Chaos and complexity theory for management: caveat emptor. *Journal of Management Inquiry* 3, pp. 320–8.
12. Goldberg, Jeff and Markoczy, Livia, 1998. Complex rhetoric and simple games. *Emergence* 2(1), pp. 72–100.
13. Sonsino, 2000; 2002a.
14. Anderson, 1999.

CHAPTER 7

Discussion: Leading Opinions

What is above all needed is to let the meaning choose the word, and not the other way about.

George Orwell[1]

If new strategy is needed, it must be communicated to a variety of stakeholders: employees, stockholders, the financial community, and even competitors. Most stakeholders have a more distant and simplified view of past strategy than the central executive group and are less aware of the stress and strain that preceded the need for strategic change. Stakeholders must be apprised of the company's new direction and shown the inadequacies of the old strategy can be overcome by the capabilities of the new.

Karen Fletcher and Anne Sigismund Huff[2]

Most models of organization are based on argumentation rather than narration ... yet most organizational realities are based on narration. ... This means that people are often handicapped when they try to make sense of organizational life, because their skills at using narratives for interpretation are not tapped by structures designed for argumentation.

Karl Weick[3]

Headlines

In discourse or discussion, the increasing number of people and groups to deal with makes it difficult to control the agenda and the content of strategic conversations.

Executives should focus on the arguments raised by participants in discussions (not on raising their own arguments); they should engage in checking the evidence supporting those arguments and in challenging them.

The discussion phase, though characterized by argument, is primarily a learning phase, where parties explore the positions others hold through logic and rational challenge.

> Executives should appreciate that they cannot hope to understand every issue in every discussion taking place around the organization – no one individual can know everything about what's going on.

The Language of Leadership

In this middle part of the *Leadership Unplugged* book, as well as in the middle phase of the unplugged leadership process, we are dealing with the topic of arguing the business vision. Earlier in the book, in the *Unplugged Framework* (Figure 2.2), we painted a picture of this phase as having twin purposes: argument and learning. The elements of this twin phase, we said, included:

- identifying your cynics and your supporters
- kick-starting mini-debates with these different stakeholding groups
- scaling the debates to the different speakers
- lobbying, listening and learning from both cynics and supporters
- and, finally, listening for the vision echo – the signal that it's time to move forward into the dialogue phase.

In this chapter we cover some of the key language tools we've seen that can help senior executives kick-start those mini-debates. We explore the idea of scaling the debate and choosing media appropriate for different stakeholding groups; we consider public speaking versus publication. And we talk about structuring the language of leadership – about argumentation and the communication of opinion. As well as being helpful to you in conveying your leadership messages, this will also clarify what to listen for in the discussions you are engaged in. Additionally, these structuring techniques will help you to recognize early signs of the vision echo – that echo back to you of your original vision, albeit distorted, which is a key sign that some people are moving ahead in the *Leadership Unplugged* process and can be nudged into the next phase, dialogue.

The Message Not the Medium

If you are going to engage both the cynics and your supporters in the change process you had better be sure of what it is you're going to say. Too many executives get far too absorbed with choosing the best format for the message, leaving the content until the last minute. Deciding how you're going to convey your message is the next step. Worse still are those executives who are governed by a media timetable or a pre-determined format. For these executives, the question 'What are we going to put on the video this week/month/year?' becomes the driving force behind the message. This is a great mistake and contributes to the cynicism that often surrounds the pronouncements of senior executives.

George Orwell, author of *1984* and *Animal Farm*, was a writer who was most of all concerned with precision, and with the accuracy of the message he wanted to convey. In his essays on writing he shared this thinking, providing helpful guidelines for all of us engaged in communication:[4]

A scrupulous writer, in every sentence that he writes, will ask himself at least four questions, thus: What am I trying to say? What words will express it? What image or idiom will make it clearer? Is this image fresh enough to have an effect? And he will probably ask himself two more: Could I put it more shortly? Have I said anything that is avoidably ugly?

Orwell's thoughts on clarity build on the formal works of classical authors such as Cicero, who defined rhetoric as 'the art of speaking well – which is to say, with knowledge, skill and elegance'.[5] Cicero's view was that ideas and language should be capable of being used to produce eloquent discourse in any given situation, and this was a skill to be accorded high status. The Greek philosopher and scientist Aristotle took the slightly different view that rhetoric was 'an ability, in each particular case, to see the available means of persuasion'.[6] In other words he saw rhetoric as persuasion, and persuasion as argumentation. In fact Aristotle identified three specific types of argumentation, and it is useful to reflect on these:

- *ethos*, a speaker's ability to establish a positive image of himself with the audience
- *pathos*, a speaker's ability to affect the emotions of the audience
- *logos*, a speaker's ability to reveal the inner logic of the subject.

Aristotle favoured *logos* – rational argumentation – as perhaps the most important way of persuading the audience of a particular point of view, though he understood well that the character of the speaker and the emotional state of the audience contributed significantly to the speech's effectiveness. This was indeed a complex activity to engage in.

Persuasion and argument were such important aspects of day-to-day life for the ancient Greeks that they conferred on rhetoric the status of *techne* – a productive knowledge, or the skill of being able to produce something. In fact *techne rhetorike*, the knowledge of how to produce and deliver an eloquent speech, had for them the same status as architecture, the skill of designing beautiful and functional buildings. This chapter, then, seeks to recapture that sense that speaking and writing – the language of leadership – is a technical skill that can be learned.

This is a significant issue. If classical rhetoric is dealing with the question of how to develop effective arguments, then not only is it concerned with argument in the linguistic sense, but it could also be used to shape the thinking of executives on how to present a case or justify a position. In other words, the most valuable contribution of rhetoric to the skills of business leadership can be seen in the development of persuasive arguments for what the corporation should do. And to serve this purpose really well, leadership development programmes for all executives should include the logic of argumentation, so that leaders at every level can incorporate the formal logic of argumentation into the very fabric of managerial decision making. Unsound managerial decisions made without consideration of how they will be justified to different stakeholder groups have little chance of being communicated well. It is the issue of stakeholder groups, perhaps, that could be said to demand the development of persuasive argumentation in organizations. When any organization is faced with an attentive and active stakeholding group, there is always the possibility of confrontation. Even in friendly discussion among cooperating partners, *Leadership Unplugged* argues that professional communicators need to ground their claims and justify their positions on every issue they represent.

Beyond this brief overview, we will not consider classical rhetoric further; there are many readable works on this topic that would repay direct study. Instead we propose to draw on our combined experience of journalism and the media as a source for guidance on argumentation and communication. The skills and tactics of journalism as taught today – to guide the communication of complex messages in a manner that is simple and time-constrained yet memorable – offer powerful tools of real value to executives.

At this point some readers may be thinking they should reject the persuasive aspects of leadership strongly, because they see persuasion as nothing more than manipulation. The latter is persuasion in the sense of an individual or organization trying to impose its interests or views on its stakeholders. Of course, language can be used in this way – indeed, the debate phase is where this attempt at imposition mostly occurs, although our perspective is that this is a necessary positioning of the vision as a platform for later discussion. But here, in the discussion phase, we should see more of a transition towards a discourse aimed at discovering and refining the ends, purposes and values of different stakeholders. This distinction is well recognised in formal theories of argumentation and is captured as the distinction between 'argumentation as advocacy' and 'argumentation as inquiry'. The first of these strives to prove certain claims, while the second is intended to discover solutions to problems and to develop common ground between parties. This is akin to our conception of dialogue, and will precede fuller dialogue in the *Unplugged Continuum* (Figure 2.2).

What is Truth?

At this point, some executives might find themselves trying to hide from engaging in argument behind a naïve belief in truth, objectivity and impartiality as valid criteria for judging its outcome. But in the context of day-to-day leadership of an organization, where almost every decision is a best guess about the way forward, truth is a hard concept to define. Of course no one should be allowed to manipulate the public or to lie on a controversial – or indeed on any – issue, but we must remind executives that in strategy the 'truth' is not an absolute. It can only be reached through a discussion that reveals which of the parties to the discussion has better arguments. That being so, you'd better be certain of how to argue, and of how to assess, judge or weigh up arguments.

This question of judging arguments highlights the possibility of learning here from how justice systems and the law operate. In brief, courts tend to use a sequence of four basic questions in their enquiries; we can use them to illustrate where disagreements can arise, and they form the point at which active participants should start to argue their case:

- What are the relevant facts of an issue?
- How is the issue defined?
- How should we evaluate the relevance of circumstances?
- What kind of discursive and institutional procedures have been used to resolve the three earlier questions?

The questions are posed in sequence to help us define where to start the argument. If there is disagreement on the facts of the issue, then an argument about the facts starts. If there is agreement on the facts, there might then be a disagreement about defining the issue. So an argument about definition starts. If there is agreement on definitions, however, there might be a disagreement about the circumstances, and so on. Legal proceedings in a court represent one example of an argument about a complex situation, and on most continents are regarded as the highest means of arbitrating disagreements between two parties. Indeed the answer to the fourth question is that most situations can be clarified through the formalized argument process between prosecution and defence.

In practical terms, then, this sequence of questions can be used to help executives identify areas of agreement and disagreement between parties with precision. For example, when assessing someone's strategic vision you could use it to establish whether everyone is agreed on the facts. Or are there actually disagreements over the interpretation of the facts? The framework provides a structure for rigorous analysis of the situation, which – if conducted thoughtfully and openly – comes across more in the form of a discussion between professionals than of an all-out disagreement.

The Science of Arguments

Stephen Toulmin suggested a way of thinking about disagreements that provides a well regarded (in academic circles), but little known (in executive circles) framework for explaining the structure of arguments.[7] It provides a mechanism for teaching people how to argue, as well as a reasonable framework for analysing arguments presented by others.

Toulmin suggested that arguments could be broken down into a series of elements:

- *the claim* – a statement the speaker wants us to consider
- *grounds or data* – the evidence to support the claim
- *qualifications* – suggesting the limitations of the claim, the strength with which the claim can be made, or the degree of certainty the proposer is prepared to give the claim
- *warrants and backing* – general linking statements that justify a logical connection between claim and grounds.

Consider an executive's bald assertion or claim: it's a proposition we can only accept as valid if we ask further questions. The more convincing the supporting answers are, the more rational and acceptable the claim is likely to be. It is also a fundamental element of argument, suggests Toulmin, for proposers to incorporate possible rebuttals or reservations into their statements. These would contain details of extraordinary or exceptional circumstances that might undermine the force of the argument, and explain why they should be excluded from the claim.

Here is a fictional example of how the different elements of the framework might be used to analyse an argument.

Initial claim or assertion	The Xbrand Consultancy (Xbrand) contributes to the reputation of major organizations in the United States.

Ground	Xbrand is a private organization responsible for promoting technological innovations across the United States.
Warrant	Public awareness of spreading US technology is an indispensable contribution to firms' reputations.
Backing	As leading market research firms have shown, the reputations of US firms depend in large part on the innovation they demonstrate.
Reservation	If we exclude states where innovation is regarded as detrimental to the environment by local media and pressure groups ...
Qualification	... we can infer with great certainty ...
Confirmed claim	... that Xbrand contributes to the reputation of technology firms across the United States.

At the beginning of an argument, the executive making an assertion presents a claim that he or she wants to be accepted. At a meeting, an opponent rises and questions the soundness of the proposed claim: 'Why should we believe this?' The claimant must demonstrate that the claim is well founded; otherwise the claim will appear to represent either a personal opinion or a decision to be imposed on others in an authoritarian manner. Therefore the proponent must reveal the grounds on which the claim is based. The grounds may not immediately confirm the claim's reliability, because other parties to the argument don't immediately see the relevance of the grounds to the initial claim, so warrants are used to authorize or legitimate the step from the grounds to the claim. In a way, the warrants are rules that confirm the association between the various grounds and the claim. Since the reliability and acceptability of warrants is also open to question, however, additional backing from authoritative sources can also be supplied in their support.

Despite all this heavy artillery in favour of the main assertion or claim, there is still some unfinished business to attend to. First, just how strong is the proposed argument? And second, what if something extraordinary happened that destroyed the claim? As regards strength, it's helpful to use a set of qualifiers such as 'certainly', 'so far as the evidence goes' and 'very likely' to qualify the strength with which you might support a claim. And finally, by using rebuttals and reservations you can acknowledge that your reasoning may not be valid under certain exceptional circumstances. Both of these tactics help to show how precise you're trying to be, and demonstrate a degree of humility. Importantly, too, you are giving your opponent in an argument the opportunity to make up his or her own mind. We'll return to the importance of this later.

In practical terms, Toulmin's argumentation framework can be used to help prepare your arguments before you go into print or engage in public discussions. But the framework can also help you analyse the gaps in someone else's argument. Typical questions you might use to help unpick someone's argument include:

- Where is your evidence for this?
- How does this support your claim?
- What other data do you have that confirms this?
- Under what conditions might this approach not work?

The Arguments of Science

In the study of literature there has long been an acceptance that language has two uses. This was captured simply but evocatively by Ivor Richards, one of the most significant 20th-century English teachers at the University of Cambridge. He suggested that a statement may be made for the sake of a simple reference – true or false – that it triggers in the receiver's mind. This is what he described as the scientific use of language:[8]

> In the scientific use of language not only must the references [in people's minds] be correct for success but the connections and relations of references to one another must be of the kind which we call logical. They must not get in one another's way, and must be so organized as not to impede further reference.

This underpins Toulmin's ideas of warrants and backing for claims that we dealt with in the last section. But language may also be used for the sake of its effects on the recipient's emotions and attitude, says Richards:[9]

> For emotive purposes logical arrangement is not necessary. It may be and often is an obstacle. For what matters is the series of attitudes due to the references should have their own proper organization, their own emotional interconnection, and this often has no dependence upon the logical relations of such references as may be concerned in bringing the attitudes into being.

We'll address this 'emotive purpose' of language in much more detail in Chapter 10, 'Leading with Emotion', but considering these dual applications of language acts as a useful introduction to a very special style of argument that the business world can learn from: that conducted by scientists.

If you're planning to wager the future – if not the very existence of the firm – against some future strategy, business executives should adopt the rigour of scientists when analysing proposals from their colleagues and peers. In a sense this is due diligence as applied to strategy.

Our *Due Diligence of Strategy Analysis* has been adapted from a framework used to assess management research, and highlights strengths, weaknesses and gaps in strategic thinking extremely well.[10] Why should you use a rigorous approach such as this? Well, in assessing someone's proposed strategy for the organization you need to know they've done some basic research, and that they can back up their thinking with data. So share the Due Diligence of Strategy Analysis with your colleagues and have them construct their proposals along these lines (Table 7.1). If they don't have data available to back up the proposal, it can be gathered shortly afterwards.

First of all the proposed strategy must be logical, given the overall environment in which your firm operates. The proposal should explain this clearly. A sample strategy statement might describe a new departure for the organization – for example, 'to be the leading mobile phone licence operator in Western Europe'.

The proposal should include some testable propositions, indicating how the organization could achieve the vision. These are short statements or objectives, each of which can be articulated, assessed and measured independently. For example, a vision proposition might indicate how re-branding the organization might be carried out, and how the results of this exercise could be evaluated at various stages before, during and after a marketing campaign. Each of these should be assessed logically, and a decision taken as to whether they support the strategy. If these propositions support the proposed strategy, the strategy is said to have *internal theoretical validity*.

Finally, you should be able to generate some *internal empirical validity* if you have the capacity to engage in market research. You should be able to show that undertaking a re-branding exercise, for instance, will result in a certain increase in brand awareness or reputation improvement. In a sense, rooting your strategy in research at this early stage begins to link the marketing and strategy functions within the organization.

Assessing the strategies of organizations is the major task of our next book, *Strategy Unplugged*, and we'll revisit the Due Diligence of Strategy Analysis in that publication.

It's important to realize that this Due Diligence of Strategy Analysis isn't assessing the strategy itself, or the data, though these do enter your discussions. Its purpose is to assess the relationships between the data and the strategy proposals. Its value lies in assessing the argument that you and your team have put together to get the strategy through your

Table 7.1 How to assess strategy proposals:
the Due Diligence of Strategy Analysis

Concern	Explanation	Type of validity
Vision of environment (e.g. current/future industry concerns)	Relationship of the proposed vision to the actual performance or behaviour of other organizations and external data	External validity, or how the proposed vision sits within the broader industry the firm operates within
Proposed strategy	Explanatory statement about where the organization ought to be headed	Internal theoretical validity; how the specific testable propositions support the proposed strategy
Strategy propositions	Specific testable propositions about what the organization ought to be doing to deliver the strategy	
Research planning	Decisions about research methods: how do you propose to research, what data collection techniques, do you propose, how to engage in sampling, what variables to use and what units of analysis	Internal empirical validity; to what extent is the research planning supported by data? How do the results justify the planning and fieldwork methods, and how they inform or alter the strategy?
Research fieldwork	Collating data, problems of implementing research plan	
Results	Data analysis leading to findings, interpretations feeding back to strategy, strategy propositions and research planning	

internal decision-making process. It's also about giving you the confidence to engage in discussions and arguments about what to do next, and why. The sole purpose of the Due Diligence of Strategy Analysis is to help you persuade others more effectively.

Disproof Positive

Most people try to build a business case by identifying all the evidence that supports their view and by incorporating this into some report, presentation or other form of communication. In doing so, we tend naturally to ignore or trivialize evidence that doesn't support our case. This is false logic. One of the most useful things that scientists usually do is to *disprove* things, and this may be a useful lesson for us in our own construction of arguments. We said earlier, when considering argumentation, that it was useful to mention situations where restrictions or reservations applied. We take that view further here – it is only by trying to disprove something that you can begin to think something might be valid.

In a famous series of experiments, people were presented with the three-number sequence 2–4–6.[11] Their task was to divine the numeric rule which determined the selection of the numbers. The people taking part in the test were allowed to generate other sets of three numbers that would be confirmed as adhering to the rule or otherwise, and they could stop at any point when they thought they had succeeded. Before reading ahead, think how you might approach this problem.

The rule governing the selection was, in fact, 'any three ascending numbers', which required participants in the experiment to generate evidence disproving, rather than confirming, their hypotheses. Trying the sequences 1–2–3, 10–15–20 or 122–124–126 will only lead you into the confirmation trap. Only six of the original 29 subjects taking part had found the correct rule the first time they thought they knew the answer. That we prefer to test for confirmation of our ideas, rather than seeking to disprove them, has been confirmed many times since.

The easy lesson for a *Leadership Unplugged* approach to argumentation is that we should seek, and take care to address, evidence that refutes the very case we are trying to make in presenting our argument. By the same token, challenge the arguments of others if all they provide is confirmation of their arguments. Ask them to show how they have sought to refute or disprove their own argument. If there is no sign that they have sought contrary evidence, at least ask them to try.

Remember that refutation need not necessarily be numeric, either. In the past much attention has been given to merely *quantitative* analysis – the counting, coding and measuring of events, of how many people hold certain views, or of variations in statistical measurements of corporate performance. Of course, the old cliché 'what gets measured gets done' favoured by 'hard numbers' executives is important, but not (we believe) to the exclusion of other data. Compared with a quantitative approach to argumentation, a *qualitative* approach can help us explore the nature and origins of people's viewpoints – or the reasons for and consequences of the choice of certain performance criteria – in more depth. Managerial decision making bereft of these data will be poor indeed. Make sure you have the data relating to your arguments, and challenge others whose arguments ignore the qualitative aspect of data collection and presentation.

Case 15. Nigel Berridge, Orange – 'What's on Channel Orange?'

After completing a project in Switzerland Nigel Berridge was posted to the United Kingdom as a troubleshooter with a fairly open brief. 'I don't have any formal role and the job titles round here often don't mean much in a traditional sense.' Orange was known for having people called Ambassadors of Strategy, for instance, and a group of people from a department known as MIB (Managing Integrated Business) who were inevitably renamed the *Men in Black*, after the film starring Tommy Lee Jones and Will Smith.

But despite the general uncertainty about strategy in the telecommunications business at the time of this case study (the battle for 3G licences was just getting under way in the UK) Berridge was clear about what his role was. 'I have to ask some questions around the place. I feel there is a good deal of complacency. We've been doing well and things are taking off. But I'm beginning to wonder if we're missing something.' Berridge reports reflecting long on the process of teaching and coaching as aspects of leadership. 'When I started to address the process of meetings with questions (rather than providing solutions), my communication and relationships improved.'

So he enticed a number of colleagues into a discussion and issued a question to a cross-functional task force of movers and shakers from around the business. The question was enticing, and about 20 people set aside a couple of days at a neutral venue to address it. The question was: 'What's on Channel Orange?'

For Berridge, the question captured the idea that Orange might be seen as a broadcaster of content as opposed to 'just a mobile phone company' or 'just a brand'. This begged the question what sort of content might Orange carry, and how? And how would it compete in this different marketplace? He knew that no one individual could answer all these points and make anything happen.

The use of the question to kick-start the event was astute. It captured Berridge's actual intent – to signal the beginning of a new debate in the business – but it was not framed as a debate since this might have been perceived as a confrontational. Instead, the question captured the idea that this was intended to be a thought-provoking discussion, and that everyone's ideas were valid.

As it transpired, the ideas behind the question were not new to everyone in the workshop – indeed, a small number of people had been involved in similar meetings in other parts of the business. They appreciated being involved, however, as this helped them see that the issue was more significant than they had thought previously. On the other hand, the fact that similar meetings had taken place across different parts of the group meant that some participants felt frustrated. The debates seemed real enough, they said, but nothing ever came of them.

This, of course, was the classic Catch-22 of organizational change. Senior executives in a lively, innovative culture, such as Orange had in the late 1990s, didn't want to be prescriptive of what its people should be doing. But the movers and shakers in the (now much larger) organization felt frustrated that they didn't perceive much overt direction in its published high-level strategy. So no one was as active as they might have been in simply experimenting, or in launching small projects or creating new ways forward. The thing that had made Orange different and 'special' in the past had apparently been suspended, and no one at any level took responsibility for progressing anything of their own accord.

The group concluded that while the discussions were critical for Orange's future – 'We need a wake up call', said one participant – there was a strong perception that internal education was vital, especially regarding who Orange's competitors actually were and what business the firm was really in. Interestingly, the group felt that the meeting had been valuable and that there was a greater need for interaction and communication between departments.

After the meeting, questions were asked about Orange's strategy creation process and what could be done to improve it. In the words of a strategic planning manager:

As you would expect, we have all of the normal debates such as how to make the strategy process flexible enough to reflect the realities of a turbulent market whilst providing appropriate focus and structure; how to balance bottom up and top down input and how to put enough management emphasis on constantly evolving the strategy without taking our eyes off the day to day operations of the company. But I hope that we are going to find time to step back and review the process that we have been through. If we do carry out a review I think that it might be very beneficial to have some outside facilitation and input.

The concerns were highly appropriate. How were the strategic and operational planning processes supposed to work in theory, and how did they work in practice? Why plan at all? And what changes should Orange make to strengthen the planning process? So there was no danger that Orange did not understand the debates and discussions it needed to undertake. It was asking all the right questions and doing everything in its power to engage with its people in a participative way. But what else could be done?

Questions:
1. From the evidence of the case study, what does Orange do particularly well? How could Orange better have moved the discussions along?
2. Who else could be involved in future discussions to address the underlying difficulty – not peculiar to Orange – of creating momentum around possible new directions?
3. Whose task is it to take the next step in the implementation (and why), and how should they begin?

By this stage we've covered the structure of argumentation and the importance of having accurate quantitative and qualitative data at your fingertips. Knowing what you want to say is half the battle. This is intended to give you confidence to engage in argument both with cynics and with your supporters. This second half of the chapter is about how to structure arguments for your various audiences. It should help you to define the medium and the style of the debate, discussion or dialogue you want to engage in.

Our approach to the language of leadership has grown from our experience of writing, editing and teaching journalism over the past 20 years, and our transition to working with managers and executives on this material over the past decade. We firmly believe that the skills taught every day to journalists have real value in the executive boardroom. These techniques have been distilled from our work with thousands of journalists and hundreds of executives – the crossover works.

The rest of this chapter, then, is our attempt to capture these tools and techniques in a practical, non-theoretical way, as a 'language of leadership toolkit'. Our intention is to help you articulate your opinion successfully, both in print and in person. It's only knowing what you want to say, and knowing how to say it, that can help you begin to lead the opinions of others – not in a manipulative and sinister way, but with the logic and

Table 7.2 The communicator's writing style

What you wish to convey to whom	*Appropriate* Leadership Unplugged style
Information, data or the latest news for powerful stakeholders	News reporting style, ostensibly objective, though your choice of what to include and what to leave out will invariably be biased
Explanation, problem solving or background for interested shareholders	Feature or article writing style enabling you to discuss and address important issues at greater length; more room for opinion, but caution needed
Opinion and/or emotion for powerful and interested stakeholders	Opinion or leader writing style, also known as comment (though this can be different); enabling you to address sensitive issues in writing (but maintain a personal format) or in public (through speeches to powerful and interested stakeholders)

cohesion of your arguments twinned with the openness and sincerity of your style (Table 7.2).

The section begins with an assessment of a simple information-giving style derived from news reporting and then follows with mechanisms for structuring more complex discussions, derived from feature-writing standards. The chapter concludes with guidance on that most difficult of tasks – capturing your opinions and emotions in print and in person.

Speed, Simplicity and Sense: Communicating Information

The most important aspects of communicating information to people inside and outside the organization are *speed*, *simplicity* and *sense*. Get your news out quickly. Too much control by an all-too-busy individual at the top is dangerous. Often, promoting simple news about what the organization is doing isn't a high priority for a senior executive – it's just that the senior executive basically doesn't trust the people around him or her to do a good job. Maybe the senior executive has been 'burned' before, and so sits on material for days, weeks or months instead of discussing the process and letting people get on with their task. Beware the symbolism of late news – if people say 'I knew that months ago', it's almost as if the organization is saying 'We hid this because we didn't want you to know'. Too many organizational newsletters and bulletin boards start with a flourish and end up a flop. Most never make it past their first year of existence. Communicating simple information need not involve a massive communications infrastructure. It's simply a case of having everyone understand how to communicate simply and sensibly. First of all, this involves recognizing what organizational news is. Over the years many overlapping ideas have developed about what news is – here are the five ideas that we find most useful when talking with executives.

What is News?

1. *News is an event.* News is new information on a recent event, hence the desire for speed. Daily newspapers turn round the most complex stories within 24 hours. Television news transmits instantaneously. It is no wonder that employees often come to rely on the media for their news of what's going on inside organizations. It's important to appreciate that news is usually something that has actually happened – at a definite time and date. It isn't possible for a CEO to get a profile of an ageing product range onto the front page of the *Wall Street Journal*, no matter how much they might spend there on advertising. So news is more about a change of policy, the launch of a new product or the latest opinion of a relevant person on something else that's newsworthy. The president of the day may talk rot, but people listen to what he or she says on the issues of the day because of who they are. Not many executives are accorded this position.

2. *News is out of the ordinary*, and preferably unexpected. News is the discovery or announcement of the first or last, the biggest or smallest, the fastest or slowest, the richest or poorest in the world. And if it is an unexpected winner (or loser), so much the better. The chances are people won't have heard the news. This issue of unexpected news often helps answer the question 'Why doesn't the media publish good news?' Well, the fact of the matter is you expect organizations to trade legally and profitably. What's 'new' about that? You expect them to behave well. It's usually only when there is insider dealing, improper accounting practices or executives going to jail that the front pages are emblazoned with pictures of CEOs and senior executives.

    There is an important lesson here for all executives – don't withhold publication of information that you consider might be detrimental.

Better to be the first with the news than be accused of withholding news. We don't agree with the individuals who suggest it's better to wait: 'what if no one knows?' Someone always knows.

3. *News is something the reader doesn't know* – it's surprising. The US media magnate William Randolph Hearst is supposed to have said that 'News is something that someone somewhere wants to suppress – all the rest is advertising'. This ties together our first two ideas, of speed and the unexpected nature of news. There was a famous poster on the walls of Rupert Murdoch's *Sun* newspaper in the United Kingdom saying that news should make people say 'Gee whizz!' It's clear that news should be dramatic and large scale. This explains the media coverage of massive golden handshakes, senior executives being bribed or widespread corporate corruption.

4. *News is money.* News is what it costs to do business, or how much cheaper or more expensive it will be tomorrow. What other people earn, win or lose is also news. (There, but for the grace of God, go I.) This also applies to what other organizations earn, win or lose – whether they are our alliance partners or our dreaded competitors.

5. *News is people.* One of the things that seems most difficult to communicate to senior executives is that news is about people and what affects people – particularly their employees – and this effect can be either emotional or financial. The biggest news is what affects the largest number of people. So early news through appropriate channels of plant closures, or redundancies, is essential.

Because 'news' is fundamental information that an organization must divulge, it's important to be sure you do in fact have some real news to communicate. Here are five simple tests, or questions to ask yourself, to help you make sure you do in fact have something newsworthy to say.

1. *The pub (or bar) test.* If you went into a public bar filled with your employees, or your shareholders or suppliers, and shouted your 'news' at the top of your voice, what would they say? Would they yawn, or would they say 'Wow'? This 'thought experiment' is salutary and can save you from many errors of judgement.

2. *The pocket test.* News, especially for business executives, should pass one simple test – how does this affect the stakeholder's pocket? This applies whether the stakeholder is an employee, a supplier, a customer or a shareholder.

3. *The time test.* Can you say exactly when your news event happened? Can you say at what time, and on what date, it happened? If it

happens regularly, the chances are that what you have in mind isn't news.

4. *The 'so what?' test.* Reflect on what you think the news you want to promote is, and reflect on your different stakeholder groups. If you can't answer the question 'so what?', then there is no story. It has no implications for anyone. Don't bother to publish or promote it. Not everything you do, or everything the company does, is necessarily news.

5. *The first five words test.* Do the first five words of what you're thinking of telling someone grab your attention? Do they make you want to know more?

At this point you may be beginning to get a sense that what you have to say is actually newsworthy. Now the task is to couch it in a way that's easy to take in. The first five words are extremely important, much like an 'elevator pitch' for venture capitalists or an executive summary in a full-report. But the whole of the introductory paragraph or intro is crucial when it comes to communicating the story.

News Intros

What makes a good introductory paragraph for a news story? In an ideal world, the opening paragraph should:

- sum up the story
- have the most important facts first
- be short and punchy, and contain only essential facts
- use emotive words early on
- possibly contain an appropriate quote
- appeal to the reader in his or her area, in his or her business or because it affects his or her pocket or way of life.

The easiest thing for an intro to do is answer all the questions a reader may have.

who?	former senior executives at X Corp
what?	were arrested
how?	by FBI agents
where?	in New York
when?	today
why?	on suspicion of tax evasion.

There isn't the space here to deal fully with the art of writing news intros, though we'll address the use of questions again in Chapter 11. Two points that are worth emphasizing, though. The first is the importance of not venturing your opinion or commenting in what is intended to be the dissemination of information. We'll move on in a moment to how you can and should deliver comment or opinion, but if the fundamental purpose of news is to inform then it's crucial to allow your readers to make up their own minds on the basis of the information you provide. Do not try to sell your own opinion as fact. The second key point is that the most important information should appear first. We'll explore that now when we look at the structure of news stories.

The Structure of News Stories

Research tells us that people only skim-read news – they don't have much time for it. Relatively few people get past the sixth paragraph in a news story, for instance. Business executives are among the busiest people on the planet (or so they tell us), so we must package the news to provide the most important information quickly. The techniques we use to structure news, then, must deliver the hit as quickly as possible. Here are three we have found very effective in corporate circles.

1. THE HARD NEWS FORMULA: W.H.A.T.
- What's the story?
- How did it happen?
- Amplify the main points, in order.
- Tie up the loose ends.

This simple structure gets straight to the main point of the story you wish to communicate, explains briefly how it came to pass and then deals with loose ends. If space is short it is always possible to cut the story from the end, so never write or develop a news story with the main point at the end – a 'to the barricades' conclusion.

2. ORDER OF IMPORTANCE
- First most important point
- Second most important point
- …
- Least important point.

This kind of structure, listing items in order of importance, is useful for complex stories such as budget announcements, or when you have rafts of statistics. You may need to discuss with colleagues which aspect is the most important, but you can always refer to the tests for 'what makes news' to help here.

3. TELL IT BACKWARDS (REVERSE CHRONOLOGY)

In a complex story, such as the Enron saga, that will run and run for days or weeks at a time, newspapers often use the technique of 'telling it backwards', or reverse chronology. This means that every day the latest developments can be cited and placed on top of yesterday's story, which is revised in the light of the new happenings. To do this, you need to plan the story chronologically but write it backwards. Using this technique you can begin to predict what might happen next, and make informed guesses that put your story even further ahead than today's news.

> Scientists of the future will be able to ... following the discovery this week of the XYZ gene. ... Researchers have been looking for XYZ since 1989 when ...

So what makes news? Well, change makes news – and if the very purpose of senior executives is to lead change then everything senior executives do, potentially, is news. What's new today or what will be different tomorrow is news. The arrival of the biggest, fastest or last is news. The unusual or unexpected is news, especially if we benefit (or lose) from this. There's a significant human dimension to news ('It could have been me ...') so think of news as anything that affects any or all of your stakeholder groups. And the biggest news is the news that affects the most people.

In short, the news agenda for your organization is a communications agenda. Discussing and distributing responsibility for news publishing around and across your organization is, in essence, the development of a coherent communications strategy. As we intimated in Chapter 4, this is essential to the well-being of the organization and isn't something that senior executives should abdicate responsibility for. Having established effective processes, however, do let it happen. The symbolic significance to others of halting the publication or distribution of news amounts in itself to news. And what does that tell your workforce, or the shareholders at large?

Explanation, Problem Solving and Background: Feature-Length Discussion

In newspapers and magazines the world over, the majority of space is given over to feature-length explanations, case studies and 'backgrounders'. In far more space than that allocated to a news story, writers communicate their ideas, experiences and emotions very effectively, yet still in a compact format. Of course, fewer people will read such lengthy articles unless they really catch and hold their attention, and deliver the goods in terms of information or insight.

For business executives, the feature writing style is appropriate if you wish to articulate a strategy, explore a case study success or discuss an issue with key personnel in an interview style. This is where the argumentation structure can be used to good effect as preparation for writing the feature, but don't feel the need to follow it slavishly. Only use the argumentation framework to gather the necessary data you need. Feature writing is an art in itself – it is a discussion in print.

How Features Differ from News

Whereas news writing is praised for its short, tight style, feature writing is more individual and the use of language can be varied according to your purpose. In features, too, the conclusion to the piece is much more important than in news, where the conclusion is (literally) the least important piece of information. The other distinction is that the feature writer has to work extremely hard at sustaining the momentum of the piece, and at linking each theme or item in the piece to the next. As with news, the feature writer must be clear why he or she is writing – and because the piece often amounts to a discussion with him or herself, it can be quite complex to design and deliver well. We'll deal with each of these points in turn.

Feature Intro Styles

A news intro has to grab the reader's attention instantly. So, too, the writer of features must stop readers in their tracks and make them want to read on. But the news writer knows that the reader won't have to take in that much to get a complete picture of the story, and has a relatively slim armoury of news intros. Feature writers, in comparison, have at their disposal an almost infinite number of intro styles and must hold the reader's attention over a sustained period – maybe 20 minutes or more. So in addition to grabbing attention, a features intro has to create a sense of a story or narrative – of suspense or promise, if you will – that will sustain the reader through the entire piece. Here are five well-used styles that seem to work.

1. A narrative intro tells a story in the third person singular. This tends to work as long as the story is riveting enough and has a good deal of

detail that is likely to be interesting, valuable or newsworthy to the reader.

> When Michelle Smith first became CEO she never anticipated X ...

2. A descriptive intro intrigues the reader by setting a scene vividly. This is difficult to do well, and often has the ring of cliché about it.

> In the most windswept mountains of northern Canada, hundreds of feet above sea-level, stands a small, one-storey log cabin. From the balcony the smell is of pine oil, which drips like rain in slow motion from four-inch gashes in the firs that surround the cabin.

3. A strong quote from a key protagonist, or a question, are similar attention-grabbing devices and often signal an open discussion between the parties and the author. These are simple and effective, depending on the quote or question, but they can be typographically ugly depending on how they finally appear in print.

> "Extortion – yes. M-murder – no." It was the hesitation that gave the game away.

> 'What would you do with $2 million?' [Generally prefer an open question, which is more engaging than a closed 'yes/no' question.]

4. A striking statement of fact will often have the reader wanting to know more, but the choice of which fact to lead with is often difficult.

> The graphics technologies of gaming computers are more powerful today than the graphics systems on most nuclear submarines.

5. An outrageous opinion that annoys and infuriates can often be used to stimulate discussion. Exercise caution here in corporate settings.

> 'TV chefs should be boiled in their own juices.'

How to Structure Features

Most people faced with the task of writing a lengthy article simply panic. The writers' block caused by the blank screen or sheet of paper is a common malady among people not used to putting their thoughts on paper. The solution? To give detailed thought to the length of written materials and how much – or rather how little – can actually be covered. As a rule of thumb we suggest that no more than five or six points be covered in a feature of 1000–2000 words. This equates to about 150–300 words a point, allowing a little extra for the intro, the conclusion and any link phrases that might be needed to ease the transition between points. Now, 150–300 words per point isn't much, in our view, and makes it much easier to write a feature. The problem then becomes not so much where to start, but making the hard choices about what to include and what to leave out. There's also the question of how to structure each of the points you want to make. On this issue, we have found that the best writing almost always treats each point as a separate essay, with its own beginning, middle and end (Table 7.3).

Of course, these guidelines can be ignored – they are only basic ideas intended to help you structure ideas and to get started. With this in mind as a basic building block for a point, you can then move on to begin to structure entire features.

There are many ways of structuring features – in effect, of marshalling your argument – but there are two simple methods many people find useful. Your choice depends largely on the way you prefer to work. If you are clear what point you wish to make, and if you work in a natural or intuitive way by moving from point to point, then the 'river technique' (style 1 below) captures well how you might structure features. The 'building blocks' technique (style 2 below) may be more appropriate if you feel uncertain at the outset of the key message you want to report. Perhaps you are developing the argument as you write, or you are researching the material over a period of time. Let's look in a little more detail at these two styles.

THE RIVER TECHNIQUE

This is so called because it has an origin or source in the intro and then flows logically from one point to the next. Though the piece may meander a little between the first and the sixth, or final, point the links between the points are strong and effortless. To write in this way you need a good grip on the material, as it is in a sense a form of structured 'brain dump'.

Adopting the river technique, then, you might write a working intro that captures roughly what you want to say or where you see the feature going; then you might draft a working conclusion related to the introduction. The idea of writing a working intro is simply to get you under way. The working conclusion is intended to give you an end point, something to work

Table 7.3 Making your point: a typical structure for the building blocks of features

Element	Rough length	Example
Opening sentence(s) of the point (a mini-intro)	50–80 words	Another reason that the leaders of tomorrow cannot be found inside our organizations is that they are buried inside by the very senior executives who are placed in charge of their business units. There is much evidence to suggest that this is directly the fault of those senior executives, acting – on false logic – in the 'best interests of the organization' (60 words)
Up to three pieces of evidence or observations surrounding the main point.	Each of 50–80 words; minimum 50–60, but no more than say 200 words in total.	The day-to-day pressures senior executives themselves face ensure they pass on the pressure to their teams. (1) Many senior executives, for example, have their high potential executives exclusively focused on the delivery of short-term results – nothing they accomplish, therefore, has an impact on the long term and the high potentials invest nothing of themselves and feel nothing for the future of the organization. (2) In addition, because high potential executives often prove so valuable in their operational roles, the argument is made that they 'cannot be spared' for in-house or third party leadership development programmes, which would help them step into more responsible posts as they arise elsewhere in the organization. So they are not personally prepared for the future and even less likely to be identified.

Table 7.3 (continued)

Element	Rough length	Example
		(3) There is evidence, too, that high potentials are excluded from both formal and ad hoc job rotation schemes, which would broaden their experience of the organization, again adding to their value as the leaders of tomorrow.
		(147 words)
Conclusion of the point of the paragraph, reiterating the mini-intro point more strongly; ideally suggesting or containing a link to the next idea or point	60–80 words	So for various reasons associated with the current leaders and managers of organizations, tomorrow's leaders simply cannot be seen outside their immediate teams. Not only this, but their future development is impeded, albeit for 'good' reasons. Unless more senior executives change how they think about their responsibilities to the future of the organization, this situation is unlikely to change in the short term.
		(63 words)
Overall point	*150–350 words*	*This example, 270 words*

towards. You may revise both later in the light of what you write, or if better ideas come to you as you write. The idea of referring or looping back in the conclusion to the ideas in the intro is an extremely important mechanism – it reminds people of the key point the feature makes and gives a sense of closure.

If the intro is one of the structural devices we looked at earlier, you will then need to write the main point, theme or thesis of the feature in a straightforward or relatively blunt style. Then, reflecting on the material you want to cover, the next point you want to cover should become obvious. It should be the point that, to you, follows most naturally in the sequence. The link is almost implicit in the structure of the piece.

This same procedure – write the point, reflect on what it says, then identify the next most obvious point – should carry you through the material relatively effortlessly. Of course it is possible to plan the five or six ideas you most want to include and then write the paragraphs, but we often find that this type of author needs to write the paragraphs to create a sense of direction and purpose.

Soon the final point is made and the conclusion reached. Your original working conclusion can be reworked, revised and edited or it can be jettisoned in favour of a new, more appropriate ending. Do loop back to the intro, though, wherever possible.

THE BUILDING BLOCKS TECHNIQUE

This is more appropriate for writers who prefer to plan more thoroughly, but also for writers who (for whatever reason) are less certain of what they want to say.

- Here the writer explicitly uses (say) the argumentation framework we discussed earlier to identify six things he or she wants to say (points he/she wants to make), and lists them.
- The writer may be able to identify a possible intro, and a possible conclusion, from these points but that isn't necessary at this time.
- The six points should then be listed in some logical order – perhaps their order of importance. (News structuring techniques can be used here.)
- Text on each of these points may then be written independently, using the paragraph structure we explained earlier. Writers often do not appreciate the importance of what they want to say until they actually write their material.
- Then, with a word processor, it's easy to reorder paragraphs until there is a logical flow and the material reads fluently and well. Here you are judging the links between the paragraphs automatically, ensuring the points run fluently from one to another and that there are no jarring *non sequiturs*.
- The intro may naturally be the first point you identified, or you may need to write an intro to sit in front of the points you've identified.
- The final point you identified may well make a possible conclusion, but the intro you decided on may suggest a more apt one.
- A final review to check the links are as strong as they can be, and the piece is complete.

More ideas for structuring features – and for using persuasion in print – are incorporated into Chapter 9, when we consider the stakeholding audience in more detail. There we outline our thinking that writing, done well and with an intimate knowledge of an intended audience, can be a performance of ideas. Not just a living argument or discussion as we have tried to outline here, but a true dialogue. This won't necessarily be a dialogue in the writer's mind, but it can be a dialogue in the mind of the reader or recipient who engages with the words of the text and – occasionally – is changed by them.

From Point to Point: Linking Ideas

Because of the length of features, it's imperative that you work hard to give readers a smooth and logical read. A complete change of direction, a *non sequitur*, or indeed any uncertainty about what a particular point or sentence means and the reader gives up. So the most dangerous spots you must be aware of – and these are recurring ones – are the links between your different points. This is especially true if you've used the 'building blocks' technique, where the blocks may sit together slightly less naturally than if you had used the 'river' technique.

Fortunately there are many ways of linking points, and with practice it becomes a straightforward matter to search for the most appropriate link (Table 7.4).

Table 7.4 From point to point: links of person, place, time and concept

Form of link	Links of similarity	Links of contrast
Person	Francesca Jones went on to explain…	Ricardo Montane, however, felt very differently…
Place	Mike Smith also located his business in Atlanta…	In Madrid, however, things are not conducted in the same way…
Time	Next year the company intends to keep the same portfolio…	In the future, though, the company intends to try…
Concept	The second most important aspect of astrophysics for the biologist…	Actually, the evidence suggests that venture capital firms are interested in short-term returns, despite what they might say about being in business for the long haul…

The significance and importance of making links is considered in Chapter 9, when we look at the effect of the audience on what you communicate and its impact.

Concluding Features

The endings of features are extremely important. Unlike news stories they must have a definite ending, and some form of call to action is quite common. The 'to-the-barricades' ending, though, is better saved for out-and-out opinion pieces, often called 'comment columns' or simply 'leaders'. It's better to reserve the feature style for in-depth discussion of issues, for problem solving or for case studies. We'll address this special kind of feature writing in Chapter 9.

Conclusions must loop back, however, and refer to the idea or point of the introduction. In part this is just a signal that the feature is ending, but the repetition of a key theme or symbol also helps people remember your key point. And even though the reader has just spent maybe 20–30 minutes absorbing your one-sided discussion, it's very likely that they will only retain one or two key points. So the intro and conclusion together, if they both deal with the key theme, are likely to form a powerful *aide-memoire*. And this is the key point here. Your feature, despite the effort you've put in to gathering information and marshalling your argument, will probably only live in the mind of your readers as a single key theme. There is a symbolism, too, to the written arguments of plans, reports and business proposals. This is why we say 'don't patronize' and 'don't be pompous', and why we urge you to be simple, accurate and direct in your language. It reflects on you as an individual, so you do not want people to remember you as pompous or inaccurate. The use of overblown language like this is a good signal that you may be trying to deliver too much opinion and comment in a feature article, which in our view is usually too long a format for this purpose.

A special warning must also be given about moralizing. Conclusions can, fable-like, contain the moral of the story, but many readers find this especially patronizing. Worse still is trying to make people's minds up for them. If you're trying to lead someone's opinion, it's always wiser simply to lay out the facts and give them a choice. So, in the context of writing for business executives it's worth simply suggesting which one or two courses of action, if any, you feel are appropriate. Then let the readers make up their own minds. If you've done a good job discussing the issue, giving as much information as you can in support of each of the points you make, people will often reach decisions surprisingly close to your own.

An important tool you can use in a conclusion is urging people to engage you and others in discussion. In a sense you're giving people permission to talk about things, to challenge the status quo. The cultures in some organizations are not used to having the doors to discussion thrown open. 'The way we do things round here is to agree in public, but disagree violently behind closed doors' – therefore one of the simplest, most powerful things you can do is to tell people the door is open. Give them an e-mail address. Point them in the direction of an intranet web discussion platform (but make sure you scan it regularly and respond). Most of all, offer to talk about things in person.

Most newspapers and magazines set great store by the involvement they have with their readers. But most readers of a paper are reluctant to waste their time writing in if they feel they won't be heard, or if they feel the editor and publisher just do not care. As an indication of how highly the *Economist* regards its readers' letters, look at where they appear in the magazine. To save you the trouble, we'll tell you now that they usually appear on the editorial page immediately following the contents. This is before any material by any of the *Economist*'s world-renowned writers. On the *Economist* the opinions of its readers matter more than the opinions of its journalists. Ask yourself why.

Living the Discussion

This chapter has largely dealt with the issue of creating a living discussion, a living argument. It will help you create an effective business case for your issues and concerns, but will also help you absorb the messages communicated by others. If others don't communicate as well as you do, you can use these frameworks to help ask questions. Use them to plug the gaps in the arguments and discussions of your counterparts. This must be an exercise not in political point scoring, but in helping people how to think clearly and well.

While the chapter has concentrated on articulating that discussion in print, it is also true that the effort and thought put into drafting what you want to say gives you greater confidence to articulate your arguments in person. This issue of confidence in your arguments becomes even more important when you must deal with people who disagree with you, either in print or face-to-face. You must be able to handle:

- the challenge to your own interpretation of the facts
- your emotional response to that challenge
- and the emotional response your own arguments arouse in others.

You should be able to handle challenges to your own facts by detailed preparation of your argument, as described in this chapter. The emotional response to being involved in discussion and argument – handling both your own responses and the reactions of your counterparts – is dealt with in Chapter 9, when we consider the stakeholder response to discussion and dialogue. Chapter 10, when we look at the emotional response to discussion and dialogue, will also be useful.

Our main message is that you must be deeply concerned with arguments, at a factual and emotional level, and you must know how to get into and out of discussions easily and well. If, as we suggest, discussion and argument are your main forms of communication with the majority of people at this phase in a change programme, you must be sure you're comfortable with the mechanisms. And as you move more and more towards the emotive crux of discussions and find out about people's real causes for concern, you must start listening extremely hard to what people are feeling as well as what they are saying. The highly charged discussions in the later stages of change processes are important signals that you're moving into the third phase of change, dialogue.

Conclusion

The key points we want to reinforce at the end of this chapter are:

- The prime purpose of using argumentation frameworks is to help you build the best business case for the change you'd like to see in an organization.
- The purposes of writing down your views are (a) to reach different stakeholder groups as part of a broad communications strategy, and (b) to build your own self-confidence through planning and analysis so that your arguments are deep and strong.
- You must know your readers, know the different audiences you must address, and know what they want and need in information terms. More on this in Chapter 9.
- One of your fundamental tasks is to lead people to develop their own opinions. Your articulation of your own arguments will help them in the process of making sense of the situation from their own perspectives.
- Your task is to help people to make sense of the situation and to articulate their own vision, so that you can hear and know what they think. Because you believe your own views to be correct you may see the articulation of counter-arguments as a threat. It is not. You should

appreciate how healthy the situation is if people feel able to disagree with you.

- A powerful way forward for the organization will emerge from the healthy cut-and-thrust of argument. But for this to happen you must be prepared to listen to alternative points of view, and to listen to what makes sense for others. A deeper exploration of sensemaking is the subject of Chapter 8.

- To summarise, the *Leadership Unplugged* approach suggests that your leadership task is to create a number of living discussions with different stakeholder groups. These discussions will explore your and your discussants' views as openly and honestly as possible. The more emotionally charged the discussions, the nearer you are coming to the issues of real concern to people, though this may never be articulated directly. Your sensemaking and listening skills are crucial to revealing, and then addressing, the real obstacles to progress.

QuestionBank

Take time out to answer these questions.

1. How effective are you at arguing and discussing issues of real importance to you and your organization? How much do you use your positional authority to override people's views and opinions? What impact do you think freedom of speech has within the organization, if any?

2. To what extent are your executives taught how to research, plan and present arguments and discussions? How helpful would it be if the people you worked with knew how to articulate their views? How would it help you personally if you knew why people agreed or disagreed with you, and on what grounds?

3. How much do you use writing – e-mail, memos, budgets, plans, reports, proposals, letters – to persuade? How successful are you, in your own view, as a writer? Why?

4. How easy do you find it to manage your emotions during arguments? How good are you at noticing emotions in others? How could you become even better at this? Why is it important to understand, and to some extent manage, emotions during discussions and arguments?

Notes

1.　In George Orwell's brilliant essay 'Politics and the English language' (1946) he reminds us of the importance of writing simply and also of how all writing is in effect political, involving the author in taking a stand and making a statement, regardless of the author's apparent explicit intention. The essay is included in *The Penguin Essays of George Orwell* (1984: London: Penguin, pp. 354–65).
2.　Fletcher, Karen E. and Huff, Anne S. 1990. Strategic argument mapping: a study of strategy reformulation at AT&T. In Huff, Anne S. (ed.), *Mapping Strategic Thought*. Chichester: John Wiley & Sons, p. 166.
3.　Weick, 1995.
4.　Orwell, op. cit., p. 361.
5.　Cicero. *De Oratore*, Books I and II (Sutton, E.W. and Rackham, H. trans., 1988), London: Harvard University Press, p. 201.
6.　Aristotle. *On Rhetoric* (Kennedy, G. trans., 1991). Oxford: Oxford University Press, p. 36.
7.　Toulmin, S., 1958. *The Uses of Argument*. London: Cambridge University Press.
8.　Richards, I. A., 1926. *Principles of Literary Criticism*, 2nd edn. London: Routledge Classics, p. 251.
9.　ibid.
10.　Rose, G., 1982. *Deciphering Sociological Research*. London: Macmillan.
11.　Wason, P. C., 1960. On the failure to eliminate the hypotheses in a conceptual task. *Quarterly Journal of Experimental Psychology* 12, pp. 129–40.

CHAPTER 8

Discussion:
Making Sense in Senseless Times

Sensemaking is clearly about an activity or a process, whereas interpretation can be a process but is just as likely to describe a product. It is common to hear that someone 'made an interpretation'. But we seldom hear that someone made 'a sensemaking'. We hear, instead, that people make sense of something, but even then, the activity rather than the outcome is in the foreground. A focus on sensemaking induces a mindset to focus on process, whereas this is less true with interpretation.

Karl Weick, 1995[1]

Discourse is the articulation of intelligibility.

Martin Heidegger, 1927[2]

Headlines

Leadership Unplugged sees senior executive behaviour as a mixture of sensegiving and sensemaking. Sense*giving* in that senior executives should articulate their view of the future as best they can. Sense*making* in that the aim of senior executives is to help colleagues, subordinates and other stakeholders to make sense in their own way.

Sensemaking as a process is rooted in the constant construction and reconstruction of a sense of identity for individuals and organizations.

The leadership literature of the past hundred years offers no support or advice for senior executives in turbulent or complex organizations. We build on the concept of leadership as the management of meaning, and suggest that leadership in complex organizations is actually the dynamic management, or rather influence, of identity.

The long-standing and most influential conception of organizational identity suggests that it comprises the essential values or characteristics

---

of an organization that are core, enduring and distinctive. Our research supports the idea that organizational identity, rather than being enduring, is fundamentally dynamic and unstable.

The implications of organizational identity being adaptive and flexible are that firms in which senior executives heedfully develop and maintain value-based organization identities are more likely to avoid crises, weather crises and rebound after crises.

Leadership Unplugged suggests that the mechanisms and tactics of influence in an organization are the verbal behaviours and skills of its senior executives.

How Do Senior Executives Make Sense of It All?

For us as authors, in our day-to-day roles as international newspaper journalist and international leadership development specialist, the multiple and complex realities of everyday organizational life far exceed the stereotypical challenges endlessly debated in the mainstream leadership literature. The turbulence of increasing competition, the growing demands of multiple stakeholders and the unsettling uncertainty of life at the top drive us to ask: how do senior executives make sense of it all? How do leaders unplug all the complexity? This chapter explores some of the thinking we undertook as we tried to make sense of the question and to develop our own views as to what the answer, or answers, might be, as well as what the questions were.

Our views – developed over the past decade in the merging of our teaching and consulting practice with our academic scholarship – build on definitions of leadership as the management of meaning.[3] Although we began our work some years ago thinking that it was straightforward to 'manage' meaning, and to create alignment between the visions of senior executives and the actions of their subordinates, now we're not so sure. Now we hold a view that leadership is more accurately described simply as sensegiving and sensemaking (Table 8.1). We're moving to a conclusion that leadership is how you might influence, guide or teach the people to whom you relate to see the world in their own way, not in yours. We'll try to explain what we think we mean in this chapter. (If you have a different take on what we think we mean that's fine. But please let us know.)

When we began to explore the concepts of sensemaking and, at the same time, the new concepts of complexity science (Chapter 6) we realised they

Table 8.1 The properties of sensemaking (after Weick, 1995)

Properties	Description
Grounded in identity	Sensemaking begins with a sensemaker, some one or some organization trying to establish who they are and what they stand for; it's important to remember that identities are constructed out of the process of interaction. To shift among interactions is to shift among definitions of the self.
Retrospective	Sensemaking is gleaned from meaningful lived experience – note the past tense. Weick maintains that people can know what they are doing only *after* they have done it, and even then only when they are reflexive enough to capture or make sense of it. That experience exists in the form of distinct events, but the only way to get this impression of it is to step outside the stream of experience and direct attention to it.
Enactive of sensible environments	Weick uses the word 'enactment' to preserve the fact that in organizational life people often produce part of the environment in which they live. He describes an air traffic controller who puts five aircraft in a holding pattern over an airport one morning and then has to deal with ten near-collisions in the subsequent six minutes. People are very much a part of their environments. 'They act', he says, 'and in doing so create the materials that become the constraints and opportunities they face'.
Social	The word 'sensemaking' and the consideration of individual sensemakers creates a blindspot. We forget that human thinking and social relationships are essential aspects of one another. Sensemaking is a social process in which the conduct of one is dependent on the conduct of the few or the many. In organizations, says Weick, decisions are made in the presence of others, or with the knowledge that they will have to be implemented, understood or approved by others. And this influences our sensemaking and our subsequent decisions.

Table 8.1 (continued)

Properties	Description
Ongoing	Weick cleverly reminds us that 'sensemaking never starts'. It never starts because it is ongoing, and has never stopped. There are no absolute starting points because we always find ourselves in the middle of complex situations that we try to untangle by making, then re-making, a continuous series of provisional assumptions.
Focused on and by	Sensemaking is a rapid process, prompted by what Weick calls cues, the seeds from which people develop a larger sense of what may be occurring. Which cues people notice depends in part on context but often include unpleasant items or events, deviations from the norm, extreme, intense or sudden cues, predictions of best and worst outcomes.
Driven by plausibility rather than accuracy	Weick points out that the word 'sense' in sensemaking is misleading. To help people act or decide it is enough that 'enough sense' is made. People's reasoning need not be correct for them to make sense, suggests Weick, but as long as their current version of sense fits the facts they are usually satisfied. In a trade-off of speed versus accuracy, executives tend to prefer speed. Acting promptly often shapes events before they have crystallized anyhow (see enactment above). The ability to use minimal cues quickly is what gives an organization its advantage in complex, risky environments.

were both pointing, albeit obliquely, to the same leadership gap. It was a gap we had been trying to address in our research and teaching: what was the role for senior executives in turbulent or complex organizations? Our conclusion, building on the concept of leadership as the management of meaning, is that leadership in complex organizations is actually the dynamic management of identity. In other words, who are we as individuals, who are we as a team and who are we as an organization? We are not suggesting here that identity can be managed directly or manipulated according to some marketing formula, but – we think – it can at least be influenced.

Introducing a Sense of Identity

Organizational identity is a concept influentially defined as the characteristics that are core, enduring and distinctive in an organization.[4] By organizational identity we don't mean the concept of 'brand' or 'corporate identity' (which relates to image, and is more often associated with marketing or reputation management). We refer broadly to what members perceive, feel and think about their organizations. More recent definitions of organizational identity, though, are more interesting to us because of our interest in complex and turbulent organizations. Recently identity has been described as having *adaptive instability*.[5] It was worth exploring exactly what that meant, we thought, as it supported the idea that organizations were much more like complex systems than scholars had imagined before. But it is also worth exploring in terms of our conception of *Leadership Unplugged* because it begs an important leadership question: if identity is so unstable, how can it be managed or even influenced? Is language the key?

When we started to explore the research that existed on how senior executives in complex organizations used language and persuasion, we were surprised by what we found. There were two distinct but overlapping gaps in the knowledge here. First, no one had much idea about how senior executives engaged in sensegiving. The father of the sensemaking movement Karl Weick, for instance, suggests sensemaking is a retrospective process – how did executives make sense of the unexperienced future for their organizations? Second, no one had much idea of how language influenced organizational identity. So we concluded that no appropriate description or theory of what leadership looked like in a complex or boundaryless organization had yet been developed, but that the concept of identity could be a pivotal element. In large measure this was because of the idea that identity reconciled a strong emphasis on continuity (core, enduring and distinctive) with a strong emphasis on change (adaptive instability). Organizations appeared to need both of these if they were to flourish in complex and turbulent environments.

It also became clear to us that a theory of identity-based leadership would be based on the language skills of senior executives. How else could deep-rooted concepts and ideas about who we were, who we are and who we might become be explored? Weick also suggested language was an answer, and that the rich vocabulary of executives engaged in sensemaking might be a critical tool.[6] We seemed to be moving towards a view that organizational life was a series of conversations between different stakeholders and that language might be a mechanism for influencing identity, if not managing it. Maybe we were beginning to develop a theory of identity-based leadership, and we've written about this in depth elsewhere.[7]

Table 8.2 A sensemaking agenda for senior executives who want to explore identity (adapted from Bouchikhi *et al.*, 1998)

Agenda issues	Key issues and questions
The central problem for senior executives	How do senior executives create, jointly construct or influence identity in their complex organizations?
Definition of executive focus	What are the continuously renegotiated and updated set of meanings about identity in organizations? (How do senior executives engage in linguistic positioning?)
Key assumptions	1. Humans have a need for some stability of meaning 2. Emergent identity is a socially constructed phenomenon 3. Social groups strive toward some level of convergence around meanings of identity.
Purpose of executive inquiry	To discover or disclose the meanings and the meaning structures that are negotiated among organizational members by the linguistic positioning of senior executives.
Data	1. Data important to senior executives; variety of symbols, language 2. Data important to researcher: a) language, symbols b) how senior executive make sense of identity (interpretive schemes) c) interpretive schemes of researcher.
Implications	1. Core characteristics: emergence of identity is related to meanings that senior executives agree are central 2. Enduring characteristics: only to the extent that social context affirms the projected emergent identity 3. Distinctiveness: identity derives both from similarity with and differences from other organizations 4. Adaptive instability: identity is fluid and malleable.

Such a theory – that leadership in essence involved the influence of an adaptive unstable identity – would clearly support our view that organizations were complex systems (Chapter 6). But could leadership really be described as the influence of organizational identity? We had to look further.

Organizational Identity: From Enduring to Unstable

We've already highlighted the fact that organizational identity has long been thought to comprise the essential values or characteristics of an organization that are core, enduring and distinctive. This idea suggests that the work of leaders is to maintain the identity of their organizations (the idea of who they are and always have been) in the minds of stakeholders. But we also highlighted the news that some research suggests that organizational identity is fundamentally dynamic and unstable, rather than enduring. Dennis Gioia, long an explorer of identity in organizations, said, for example, that organizational identity was 'a potentially precarious and unstable notion, frequently up for redefinition and revision by organization members'.[8] Other researchers take a similar line, describing organizational identity as emergent, fluid or fractured.

Interestingly, Gioia suggests that it is this very instability of identity that facilitates organizational change. Through the conception of 'adaptive instability', Gioia offers an alternative reading of change in modern organizations. The logical conclusion is that senior executives, by influencing or nudging elements of the unstable identities of our organizations, can have a significant influence over what or who we are, which may therefore change what we do and where we are headed as a firm. The other logical conclusion, however, is that this cannot be directly controlled or planned. So although there is a strong prevailing notion that organizational identity does adapt as changes occur in our industries, this change is not at all predictable and is very difficult to manage or influence. But if that's the only thing that senior executives can influence, they certainly will want to know how to try. So how can you influence organizational identity?

Initial Tactics for Influencing Identity

A very useful way of looking at organizational identity is to assume not that organizations have one identity at all, but that they are schizophrenic – that they have multiple organizational identities. Very few researchers have examined how organizations control or cope with multiple identities, involving as they do a myriad set of ideas about who we are, each of them held by a different stakeholder group. It may be that holding multiple identities in parallel might give firms an advantage over organizations with a clear and singular identity, when faced with a complex organizational environment to which they need to adapt or respond. It also suggests ways in which identity can more easily be influenced, or indeed managed.

There are at least four tactical approaches to managing multiple identities:[9]

- *Compartmentalization*, when the organization and its members want to keep all the different identities but don't want to try to obtain any kind of synergy from them. They want to keep the identities separate. A multinational company built by the acquisition of very different constituent organizations might want to keep its different local identities, despite fundamentally operating as a global concern. This also saves the effort and expense of trying to integrate or co-ordinate the different parts of the firm. Compartmentalized identities often give rise to political infighting, however, usually for resources, people and status within the organization.

- *Deletion*, when managers actually get rid of one or more of the identities within the organization. This can happen quickly and consciously, or by unconsciously allowing identities to atrophy over time. Business units that are new or peripheral to the mainstream, for instance, can be divested relatively easily. A key risk in deleting a part of an organization's identity portfolio is that key stakeholder groups who have supported the entity privately may become alienated. In addition, managers who see only the poor economic performance of a unit may not see its symbolic importance to the organization or its stakeholders. Pruning the portfolio can be light, leaving a smaller number of identities to manage, or can be drastic, leaving just one umbrella identity.

- *Integration*, when managers attempt to merge or blend all peripheral identities into a distinct new whole. The fusion of partners in a merger, for instance, would be described as an integration to create or take advantage of synergies between the different elements. Occasionally integration leads to ambivalence, or even paralysis, as stakeholders become unsure of who or what the organization stands for. On the plus side, more effective and efficient organizational responses should be possible. Although integration is widely thought too difficult for many organizations, mergers and acquisitions still occur at a blistering pace.

- *Aggregation*, where managers try to retain the portfolio of identities but to forge an increasing number of links between them. One effective form of link is represented by those formed from natural partners, who locate each other through their work and engage in joint-venture-style arrangements. By seeking synergy and forging links between units, managers avoid the conflicts that occasionally strike compartmentalized identities. Aggregated identities may, however, fall prey to the ambivalence or even paralysis that organizations having integrated identities may struggle with.

These tactics are all geared towards simplifying the complexity of organizational life; towards reducing the anxiety of senior executives faced with managing the complexity. No managers in their right minds should complicate matters, should they? Or shouldn't they? Well, the reason for simplifying and not 'complexifying' things is that to complicate identities or increase their number, surely, will raise further problems. How would managers manage the emergent or latent organizational identities that arise, for instance?

Interestingly there is real evidence, contrary to the expectations of many managers, that complicating organizational identity might be worth exploring. Basically, strategists suggest that we will increase the value of our firm if we make our organizational identity more difficult to copy, because our very identity becomes a strong source of sustainable competitive advantage. Yes, it still leaves us the problem of how to manage this, but we have some inkling how to tackle this thanks to complexity science (Chapter 6). We should leave the people in the various units to get on with their jobs. They'll sort themselves out.

Whatever we choose to do with our organizational identity or identities, the dynamics of identity need to be better understood by us as managers and leaders. We should learn as much as we can about how the identities in our organizations evolve and change, and also how our people and stakeholders actually identify with our organizations. So whether we define organizational identity as sticky or unstable, singular or multiple, these recent reconceptualizations do suggest that now is the time to think about how we should lead organizations by concentrating on our dynamic identity. In such complex and turbulent times we have nothing else left to try.

Influencing Identity Sustains Advantage

How organizations display identity has long been held to be a social phenomenon, constantly negotiated and renegotiated in the relationships of the people who make up the organization. This 'co-constructed' aspect of individual, group and organizational identity has been at the heart of most research work to date and taps into the rich stream of thought associated with sensemaking, which as we discussed earlier is grounded in identity construction. Two concepts that add real value to the strategic management debate on identity were captured and highlighted during a series of meetings in the 1990s, described as conversations about identity.[10] First came the idea that firm identity – because of its rarity and the fact that no one could imitate it – was a valuable resource for the firm that conferred sustainable competitive advantage. And, second, came the parallel consideration that the process of managing identity, because of its very complexity, also conferred sustainable competitive advantage. In other words, because no one can copy who we are but also because no one can copy how we handle who we are (as long as we do that effectively), we stand a good chance of competing extremely well in our industry.

Let's consider first the idea that identity is a valuable resource in itself. It's widely held now that for a firm's resources and capabilities to be sources of superior performance they must be:

1. valuable, enabling the firm to exploit opportunities or neutralize threats
2. rare among current and potential competitors
3. costly to imitate
4. and without close strategic substitutes.

Whether or not something can be copied is a significant concept to grasp, and there are several reasons why resources may be costly as well as difficult to imitate. Consider the following three basic sources of inimitability:

1. The firm's unique history – who can copy the history of a firm?
2. The role of causal ambiguity – in other words, it simply may not be clear how firm X manufactures product Y or performs service Z.
3. The role of socially complex resources and capabilities – when a great many people get together to do something, it is extremely difficult to tease apart who is responsible for what.

It is the third of these categories – the idea of socially complex resources – that best captures the competitive advantage that identity might bring to an organization. Examples of socially complex resources include a firm's culture, teamwork among its employees and its reputation with customers. So identity is regarded as a classic socially complex resource. It can:

- Allow the firm to do something its competitors cannot do. In the space race, NASA was for many years the only organization capable of launching payloads into outer space consistently.

- Allow the firm to do something better than competitors. The team behind Michael Schumacher has been leading the world of Formula One racing for years, and no one has been able to imitate what they do
- Prevent the firm from succumbing to fads. Firms with a history and well-enshrined culture tend to adopt new ways of working only with difficulty.

While managers might be able to describe socially complex resources, their ability to manage and change them rapidly is limited. However, this very difficulty means that the process of managing identity, provided there are mechanisms for handling it, is also likely to be a source of sustained competitive advantage, especially in complex organizations in times of uncertainty. Furthermore, when a firm grows in complexity and size one of the ways it may cope is by adopting more flexible or more abstract kinds of identities. This is easiest to see in entrepreneurial firms. Here the firm is almost an extension of the entrepreneur, and his or her identity very often transfers to the organization. The gain in moving to a more abstract identity seems to be that more activities can be subsumed under that identity. There is greater flexibility regarding which activities the organization can engage in. The downside is that organizations and their leaders risk losing the emotional buy-in. They risk losing the ability to articulate the identity easily, and therefore risk losing identity as a straightforward guide to strategy and action.

On the other hand, Weick describes as 'a recurrent thread' the idea that interpretation, sensemaking and social construction are most influential in settings of uncertainty. He suggests, for example, that the phenomena of sensemaking, such as enactment, should be most visible in young, small professional organizations that must make non-routine decisions in turbulent environments. They will be less visible in old, large, non-professional organizations that exist in stable environments.

Complex Firms, Drifting Identities

It's clear that organizations of all sizes must possess the ability to adapt quickly to increasingly turbulent business environments. In complex firms, with complex identities, it is logical to predict that you will see the organizational identity drift over time. We believe that this identity drift is not wholly out of control, but neither is it wholly controllable. It is perhaps most appropriate to describe organizational identity as a perpetual work-in-progress, a product of social interaction grounded in specific contexts at specific times so that one's sense of self-in-organization is emergent and somewhat fluid. In other words, neither the nature of organizational identity nor the extent of an individual's identification with the organization are determined by the pre-existing nature of the person or the organization. Yet another way of considering this is to suggest that individuals, groups and the organization mutually shape one another over time and become mingled – not static but dynamic; not discrete but contiguous. This joint or co-evolution of self- and organizational identity is a powerful argument for an identity-based theory of leadership in complex organizations. Indeed, the constant message we've tried to convey from the complex systems perspective is that organizations cannot be manipulated or controlled. The people within firms organize themselves and order simply emerges following their actions.

If new and emergent identities are constantly renegotiated states within the organization, then a question arises. What is the catalyst? What is it that disturbs the dynamic equilibrium? And when does the disturbance occur?

Disturbing Identity

The implications of firm identity being adaptive and flexible are that firms in which senior executives heedfully develop and maintain value-based organizational identities are more likely to avoid crises, weather crises and rebound after crises. The organization that can better manage the transformation of identity has a better chance of being successful. Thinking about this constructively and pragmatically has real value. We suggest that a real strategic concern for organizations is therefore the management of *instability* in identity, rather than the more frequently touted idea of trying to keep identity fixed. We can envisage that intentionally destabilizing an organization's identity for the sake of instigating change might be a viable recommendation for senior executives, as long as the attempt is conducted thoughtfully and with regard for the fact that the eventual outcome may not be exactly what was originally conceived.

Taking this extreme thought further, we're prompted to ask how, otherwise, we might account for virtual organizations or hollow corporations, where at present there is no clear view of how identity develops or can be managed. Organizations operating in volatile, hypercompetitive environments – Silicon Valley, for instance – that seem to incorporate changeability into their very definitions of themselves also appear to offer a challenge for leaders. Issues of identity are of special interest in many knowledge-intensive companies – in part because of the presence of multiple, competing identities, but also because employees need their own autonomous space to allow them to act on their own understanding. These examples point to ways of organizing in which impermanence is a special hallmark, perhaps even a source of pride. And because these kinds of organizations are burgeoning, it becomes imperative to develop ways of managing and leading that suit them better than the outmoded command-and-control or charismatic forms of leadership.

Let's be clear, then. We need to consider how to influence, if not to manage, identity because the pressures of globalization, for one, and the technological changes facing all businesses are hard on everyone's heels. From the perspective of an organization's leaders, then, faced with all and any competitive threats we must consider what the organization is and what it stands for, as well as what it wants to be, before we can determine any effective strategy for the future (Case 16: making sense of the new economy). We need to explore how the leadership of an organization, its employees and all its stakeholders make sense of the complex environments in which they operate. We need to identify Weick's 'phenomena of sensemaking' and ascertain whether they are effective means of influencing identity in complex organizations.

It should be fairly clear at this point that *Leadership Unplugged* takes as its underlying approach the idea that organizations are complex systems and cannot be controlled. We believe that the organizational identity of these complex organizations is the only thing left for senior executives to influence, or to disturb. And we believe that it is the constant verbal positioning of everyone within a firm that subtly refines and recreates a series of organizational identities, transient and endlessly emergent. The principle catalyst for change, then – a catalyst that evinces our own views as leaders, and simultaneously encourages others to establish their take on who we are and what we stand for – is the language of leadership.

Case 16. Microsoft – making sense of the new economy

It's common now for senior executives to post-rationalize the way they thought and felt about the new economy revolution and the dotcom boom. 'I never thought it would amount to much', one said to us, when we knew he had been actively involved in trying to promote the new economy and new economy business models within his organization. But this revisionist attitude is understandable. Some organizations had made expensive efforts to take advantage of the new economy rollercoaster and now – only shortly afterwards – have little to show for it.

We were fortunate enough to be leading a quarterly survey of senior executives that was taking place exactly while the new economy rollercoaster was running. We were able to get a glimpse of what senior executives were actually thinking as the new economy was booming, and as it slowly began to run out of steam. What we were looking for were the triggers and signals of the new economy. How did senior executives make sense of what was happening to them and how did they articulate it? The survey, known as the Cranfield School of Management/Microsoft Business Barometer, was to check the pressures facing businesses regularly as the new economy emerged and unravelled. The survey was conducted quarterly from 1999 through 2000, and in that time we were able to spot some of the things that triggered sensemaking in senior executives.

What is clear from the data is that the senior executives taking part in the survey did not feel themselves to be under much pressure at all to change the way they thought about or conducted the fundamentals of business practice. The new economy advocates were at this time cock-a-hoop about the perceived successes of Internet Initial Public Offerings and regarded the 'head-in-the-sand' attitude of senior executives with scorn. But those senior executives could definitely see the threat from their competitors overseas. That the web broke traditional trading barriers was easy for senior executives to see. In addition, suggested the executives, e-commerce was set to generate a significant amount of revenue for their firms within three years – that is, by the 2002–3 season. But despite the twin pressures of competition and the barriers suppliers, for whatever reason they appeared not to want to do anything about it.

Our research explored the strategic priorities held by more than 300 senior executives in the United Kingdom in their answers to our quarterly questionnaire. The responses stayed remarkably stable between 1999 and 2000, with executives' views toughening marginally in later months. Our conclusions give some insight into how senior executives made sense of the strategic new economy environment between 1999 and 2000, pretty much the height of the new economy boom.

There are three key results that are relevant:

- At the time of the study (1999–2000) these senior executives, at or near board level in a range of industries and sectors, were clearly not interested in e-commerce business models. Paradoxically, though, they did foresee major revenue streams from e-commerce within three years, in other words by 2002–3.
- As well as this opportunity, they foresaw major threats to UK businesses, notably from US players and from firms in the Asia-Pacific region.
- However, the study showed that executives planned no competitive response either to the threat or to the promise of the new economy. We don't know exactly why, but probably this reflected some mix of risk aversion, general caution and procrastination.

From the data, the triggers that seemed to prompt sensemaking in executives were:

a. Productivity Pressures

There was a perceived market demand to cut lead times for products, perceived demands from shareholders for increased returns, and general business pressures, specifically legislation and government policy, that in effect drove productivity at this time.

b. Competitiveness Pressures

Three strategic forces were identified by companies as being key to the future competitiveness of their businesses. These were (in order of importance) growth strategy, technology strategy and business strategy. Growth strategy appeared to be clearly defined in terms of people as a key competitive resource. The dimensions of technology strategy acknowledged the importance of information systems and e-commerce to businesses. And the business strategy – in terms of strategic alliances, mergers and acquisitions and diversification – was clearly seen as less of a focus or vehicle for future competitiveness.

All organizations clearly saw growth strategy as the key, but the sector analysis found significant differences between organizations in terms of their rating of the importance of technology and business strategy issues. Specifically, a firm in the construction industry was less likely to see a technology strategy as yielding a significant competitive advantage for them. This was the reverse for firms in telecoms/computing and in finance industries. In terms of their business strategy, companies in the retail industry were the least likely to see alliance, diversification and mergers as providing them with a competitive edge, while this was the reverse for energy, chemicals and pharmaceutical companies.

c. Technology Pressures

Technology was seen as playing two primary roles for companies: as a strategic tool and an operational tool. Interestingly, the role of technology as an operational tool was seen to be of greater significance than its role at the strategic level.

d. Future Revenues From E-Business

When we questioned executives on what they thought might happen in the months and years ahead, the story became somewhat paradoxical. Despite suggesting that they were not about to adopt e-business systems and software wholesale, the CEOs and senior executives in the study reported that about a fifth of their revenues (21 per cent) would come from e-business within three years. Furthermore, this was expected to double to 39 per cent of revenues within six years, they said – in other words, by 2005. At the time of the study, barely 10 per cent of revenues were reported to come from e-business, although over a third of respondents (34 per cent) said they did not actually know what revenues they were currently making from e-business.

On the subject of the erosion of market barriers because of web-based trading, the UK's CEOs and senior directors reported a major threat from the USA, with 38 per cent believing that North America posed the most dangerous threat. Almost a third (31 per cent) of survey respondents warned that the Asia-Pacific region would be the major threat to their customer bases. In summary, 69 per cent of respondents saw the chief threat to UK businesses as coming from outside Europe.

e. Present and Future Business Models

Despite the fact that survey respondents saw a distinct threat from the USA and the Asia-Pacific region – and the fact that they hoped for substantial revenues from e-business – the UK's CEOs and senior directors did not report at all that they would change their business models. Almost two-thirds (64 per cent) reported that they were not trading on the web. And operating solely over the internet, using e-commerce alone, was the least favoured business model for the future. Almost half of respondents (44.7 per cent) suggested that adoption of a pure e-commerce model would be most unlikely.

Interestingly, however, the senior executives in the surveys did say they would consider using e-commerce in alliance with other organizations, though about 30 per cent were still unlikely to use e-commerce even with alliance partners. This did not change between 1999 and 2000.

Overall, then, the survey painted a picture of senior UK executives as unable or unwilling to engage in unrelated diversification or innovation, either of products or of services. They did not appear to condone innovation, or indeed any change in strategy. Quite the reverse. They were much more interested in consolidation, favouring mergers with and acquisitions of firms operating in the same arena.

What we sense from the surveys is that the senior executives canvassed, despite seeing the potential threat and the potential benefits of the internet economy, did not at heart perceive themselves as managing new economy firms. In fact – and this is a major paradox at the heart of the survey – despite seeing these pressures to change, the firms in the survey made themselves even more like old economy businesses. Their talk was all of consolidation and not of diversification; of IT as operational rather than strategic. So while firms may have been moving forward in terms of their published IT strategies, they were actually consolidating and retrenching in terms of their actual business strategies. Perhaps this consolidation was even a result of the perceived internet pressures. We are left wondering whether this sensemaking paradox actually contributed in part to the speed with which the new economy rollercoaster rolled over.

The silver lining to this parable of new economy sensemaking is that senior executives were very clear about the pressures they faced. They do seem to be extremely good at sensemaking at the organizational level. Their leadership task remains, however, to drill deeper into the organization, into the informal groups and teams that comprise the organization itself. They must make even more sense about what's going on in the boardroom and in corridor conversations. Had they been able to do so a few years ago they might have saved themselves much heartache or (perhaps) have taken advantage of the rollercoaster sooner.

Case included by permission of the Strategic Management Group,
Cranfield School of Management

Language as the Phenomenon of Sensemaking

Our research on the language of leadership has focused on three significant areas: language itself, language-in-use and the production of research texts, such as this book.

Regarding language itself, it must be fairly clear to every manager today that language is not a mirror to reality. We have known for decades that language is not a transparent medium for the transportation of meaning. Language is ambiguous, metaphorical, context-dependant and symbolic. A second focus has been on language-in-use, or how it works in the real world.[11] Language is what we find in the accounts and conversations produced by people in various contexts. The productive, functional, interactive and context-dependent nature of all language use – including research interviews – is central here. Our intention is to study social practices – language use – in social contexts. A third important focus is on the research process itself, and in particular the production of texts. The main point here is that our writing of *Leadership Unplugged*, for instance, as a research report has not been a routine and dispassionate exercise. The book has been a vehicle for our own learning. It has changed our experiences of the past as we have reflected on our work in different ways and it now stands in an ambiguous relationship between us and our observations of the past. The book transcends our experiences, our work and us. This has implications for how this work will be taught, both to practitioners and to masters level students, and should also have implications for how future readers might eventually come to learn from it.

We would also like to return to an issue we raised at the start of the book – namely the idea that text, talk and narrative are forms of action and *vice versa*. This relationship elevates the significance of language as having real practical value for managerial practice.

In summary, *Leadership Unplugged* takes the view that language is a crucial issue for managers everywhere, and we propose a sensemaking agenda to help senior executives explore their own language-in-use in the context of identity management in complex organizations. This has implications for all executives, who must capture the intricacies of language use in organizational settings to better their knowledge of organizational realities.

A Sensemaking Agenda for Identity-Based Leadership

The concerns of a sensemaking agenda for identity-based leadership are the ways that different stakeholder groups organize and develop their thinking and their practices around identity. This may relate to how people use identity to facilitate or constrain their everyday conduct. This is helpful because if identity is the continuously negotiated set of meanings about who we are as an organization, then clearly it will be constructed via processes of interaction within the organization and with outsiders – with customers, media, rivals and regulatory institutions, for instance. Executives can use the agenda informally or formally to explore their own and others' conceptions of identity, and what the sensemaking mechanisms are. Driven by our experience of using the sensemaking agenda as a framework for analysing organizational conversations, it became clear to us that identity and conversation were inextricably linked. Very soon, the use of language to construct or position organizational identities emerged as a significant research area for us. In essence, we quickly identified the linguistic positioning of senior executives as a key mechanism or catalyst for the influence of identity.

The theory of positioning explicitly focuses on understanding how psychological phenomena such as identity are produced in language. It suggests that the constant flow of everyday life is fragmented, through discourse, into distinct episodes that constitute the basic elements of both our biographies and of the social world. It goes further, by developing the idea that the skills people have to talk are not only based on their abilities to produce words and sentences, but rest equally on their capacities to follow rules that shape the episodes of social life.[12] These conversational episodes, we suggest, help to constitute both self and organizational identity.

These ideas appear in another format in the inspirational work of Barbara Czarniawska at Gothenburg University, Sweden. Czarniawska suggests it is useful to treat organizational identity as a narrative, or more accurately as 'a continuous process of narration where both the narrator and audience formulate, edit, applaud and refuse various elements of the constantly produced narrative'.[13] If this works, then acquiring a new organizational identity simply becomes a matter of including those who constitute the organization in an ongoing discussion, fostering their active participation in bringing out a new consensus on identity in language.

Taking this to another level, then – and trying to bridge Chapters 5, 6, 7 and 8 – how senior executives describe or construct or make sense of the very complexity of their organisations appears to us to offer a critical role for leaders in influencing identity in complex organizations (Figure 8.1). This is in part about leaders constructing their own identity, but also about the construction of identity in their organizations.

Building on the idea that organizational identity emerges through processes of social construction leads to the question of whether the social construction of emergent identity, or of complexity generally, might be the key leadership role (or even leadership itself, the overlap between the two circles in Figure 8.1) in complex organizations. Our key proposition here is that those leaders who can position, frame or construct complexity (and

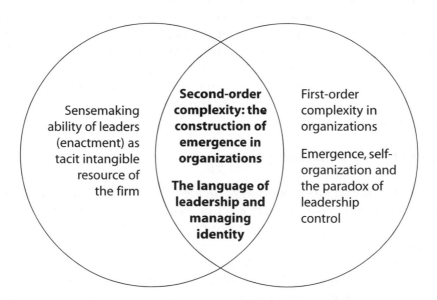

Figure 8.1 Conversation, construction and sensemaking as the role of leaders in complex organizations

specifically emergence) in their organizations are less likely to be anxious, and will probably be better able to contain their anxiety and the anxiety of others. This in turn means they are more likely to encourage than inhibit self-organization and emergence. There is much evidence to suggest that this, in turn, will lead to organizational innovation, organizational learning and sustainable competitive advantage. If that seems a tall order, consider it this way. By letting go of their hierarchical desire for control, executives who can encourage their peers and subordinates to do what they think is best for the organization, within certain guidelines, are mobilizing tens or hundreds or thousands of workers to become autonomous, relatively free agents. For the first time, perhaps, leadership really could be about motivating the workforce to give of their best.

So one way of helping executives to make sense of, or see, organizations as complex systems is to explore complex ways of thinking about them. This is, in part, what this chapter is concerned with. We contend that the puzzle of defining leadership in complex organizations leads directly to a concern with description and interpretation, and therefore to the issue of the everyday language of senior executives.

In essence, then, it appears that a critical role for leaders lies in the social construction of emergence in organizations, and that this appears to offer a more comprehensive way of explaining and influencing complex social phenomena, such as identity, in complex organisations than existing leadership theories. Indeed, what we and other researchers are beginning to find is that senior executives who are tolerant of ambiguity, experienced in adaptation and change and have strong interpersonal networking capabilities are best able to construct complexity in complex organisations. What is also of interest, through our work with the Tomorrow's Leaders Research Group at London Business School, is that this appears to be a way of identifying effective leaders of the future.

Case 17. 3M – sensemaking in action

3M, one of the world's most highly regarded organizations, has long been considered innovative. Recently a set of leadership attributes, created by chairman and CEO Jim McNerney and his direct reports, was launched to create a common language that will create the understanding the organization needs to drive performance forward over the coming years. The attributes are intended to apply to everyone in the organization – they comprise a global model based on the premise that at 3M everyone is a leader. This is regardless of whether you lead a division, a function, a group, a team or your own individual efforts.

At the heart of 3M's leadership model are what the firm calls *global competency knowledge factors*. These are corporate knowledge, business acumen, and functional expertise. Then there are the six *leadership attributes*:

- charts the course
- raises the bar
- energizes others
- resourcefully innovates
- lives 3M values
- delivers results.

In a sense there is little new here – indeed until recently the organization had identified a cluster of seven global competencies, though these had been phrased a little more stodgily in human resource jargon. So what's new and where's the value? Well, the organization recognizes that the shift to the leadership attributes is not a drastic change, but it does describe what it has done as 'a shift in clarifying and aligning how we talk'. And this acceptance of language and conversation as a key mechanism for managing these issues is crucial.

At the forefront of 'aligning how we talk in 3M' are a series of tough questions that could be ignored, but do – when taken seriously – offer a tremendous opportunity to reflect on heavyweight leadership issues. The prominence and significance of the executives behind the questions are proof that 3M, at a senior level, takes leadership as sensemaking extremely seriously. All that's left is to see what the managers actually using the model actually make of it. As a 'tick-the-box' appraisal system it is surely doomed to failure. As a challenge to constantly reflect and review your day-to-day lived experience it could prove hugely powerful.

A selection of the questions from across the model are included in Table 8.3. Read and reflect on your own contribution in your own business.

Table 8.3 A lesson in sensemaking: some questions from 3M's Leadership Attributes model

From 'Charts the course'
Has 3M's vision been clearly communicated? (To you or by you?)
How does the vision translate/relate to your own specific job function/tasks?
How does your own individual vision (objectives and action plan) align with the corporate vision?
What discussions/feedback/input have you had around the vision? (With whom?)
How often (and to whom) do you give updates on the status of your action plan?
How do you keep your focus on the vision?

Table 8.3 (continued)

From 'Raises the bar'
What have you done to raise the bar on your own performance?
What have you done to raise the bar on your development?
What have you done to raise the bar on the performance of others?
What have you done to raise the bar on the development of others?
How have you utilized Six Sigma to 'dramatically elevate' employee satisfaction?
How have you utilized Six Sigma to 'dramatically elevate' customer satisfaction?

From 'Energizes others'
Describe how you create a winning atmosphere within your group
Describe how you make sure you and /or others stretch, take risks, create, contribute and learn
What is the personal touch that you bring to the workplace?
What do you do to encourage others on the team?
How do you celebrate your successes? The successes of others? The successes of the group?
What have you done to teach others?
What have you done to inspire, influence or motivate yourself and others around goals and plans?

From 'Resourcefully innovates'
Describe examples of ambiguity and complexity that you face in your job and how you deal with them.
What is your mindset toward change and what does it add to your contributions?
How have you created and sustained an investment in processes and tools?
What do you do that earns people's trust and respect? (Daily? Monthly? Yearly?)
What do you do within your circle of influence to reward diverse styles?
Give an example of how you have constructively challenged others.
Give examples of where you have been boundaryless in your behaviour.

From 'Lives 3M values'
What do you do in your job to fulfil 3M's Corporate Vision and Values?
In your job, how do you demonstrate the HR Principles?

From 'Delivers results'
How consistently do you deliver results? (Day-to-day and month-to-month?)
Give an example of a recent shortfall in your results and describe how you corrected the situation.
Give an example of when you recently confronted an important issue with someone.

Towards Linguistic Positioning as a Sensegiving Catalyst

So can organizational identity be controlled and managed? Ultimately we think not, but we believe it can be influenced, and that verbal behaviours or conversations between organizational actors have a major role to play as influencing mechanisms. In recent research among organization scientists, many researchers have synthesized a view that talk, or more accurately dialogue, is the primary medium and method of the social construction processes behind identity. From the complexity literature, we have seen that conversations are themselves seen as complex adaptive systems, with self-organizing elements, co-creating an emergent narrative. The only way to grasp the socially constructed element of our identities effectively is through discourse. Talk matters, in essence, because it creates a context for the emergence of new senses of identity.

Even from the world of mainstream leadership research, Boas Shamir at the Hebrew University in Jerusalem, a long-time supporter of traditional leadership theories, believes that senior executives harness conceptions of individual and organizational identity by their verbal and symbolic behaviours.

Perhaps the most helpful linguistic concept in the context of managing identity is *positioning*, the discursive process whereby people are located in conversations as participants in jointly produced storylines. The elements of positioning theory are contained in the triad of position/speech-act/storyline (Figure 8.2).

The act of positioning is a dynamic conversational practice and is the means by which the display of identity is accomplished. It is usually undertaken by several individuals at a time and the constant flow of their everyday organizational life is fragmented, through discourse, into distinct positioning episodes. These episodes constitute both self- and organizational identity, and can be analysed. The position/speech-act/storyline triad in

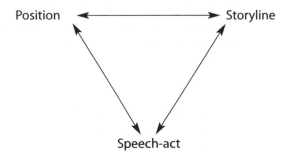

Figure 8.2 The positioning triad

Figure 8.2 is an effective framework to use to analyse positioning episodes as it highlights the intercourse between the conversation, the story someone is telling and the position it construes on events. Take the following simple example:[14]

Finance Director: 'Why didn't I see you at the meeting yesterday?'

Chief Executive: 'What a ridiculous question – because I wasn't there.'

Strategically, the Finance Director takes the position that the chief executive failed in her duty (she should have been at a particular meeting in the FD's view) and asks where she was. The CEO, seeing the Finance Director's intention, refuses the positioning (morally wrong) and the storyline ('CEO fails in duty') and re-positions herself as a critic of the Finance Director's naïvety. Both participants are aware of their intentions in what actually turned out to be quite an amiable exchange.

This is one simple example of a sequence of deliberate positioning and repositioning events. Four broad kinds of positioning can be identified from the countless hundreds of everyday positioning episodes that occur (Table 8.4, Figure 8.3).

Table 8.4 Making sense of positioning

Modes of positioning	Elements
Direct versus indirect positioning (First-order versus second-order positioning)	Direct (or first-order) positioning refers to the way people locate themselves and others within a certain moral framework by using different categories and storylines. If Jane says to John 'Please type the notes from the meeting' then both Jane and John are positioned. (This is also described as *performative* positioning – the positioning involves the performance of duty according to the moral order.) In other words, Jane is someone who has the moral right to ask John to type the notes. There are three responses John can make: he can accept the position, delete the position or block the position. For instance, if John refutes the position ('No, I'm not your manservant') an indirect (or second-order) positioning occurs, in which the direct (first-order) position is blocked and must be renegotiated. This is also called *accountive* positioning as John is asking Jane to account for her reasoning behind the direct (first-order) position.

Table 8.4 (continued)

Modes of positioning	Elements
Indirect positioning (second-order) versus removed positioning (third-order)	Indirect and removed positioning can both be thought of as talking about talk. In indirect (second-order) positioning, the talk about talk occurs in the current conversation and involves one of the parties challenging or exploring the positions posed by a speaker, as in 'No, I'm not your manservant' in the example above. Later Jane may tell James about the conversation he had with John in which John is positioned as an anarchist because he wouldn't do Jane's typing. This is a removed (third-order) positioning because it takes place outside the original conversation. Note that this conversation also contains its own first-order positioning.
Moral versus personal positioning	It is often enough to say what roles people occupy in order to understand the positions they take. If Delia asks David to send the budget details from David's department, then this first-order positioning can be perfectly understood if we know that Delia is a Finance Director and David a junior executive in her department. If Delia later asks David why the details have not yet been sent, then the storyline shifts from moral to personal, as David explains why he has had to deviate from what Delia could expect of David in his role as department junior.
Self versus other positioning	In conversation, people always position others while simultaneously positioning themselves. One cannot position oneself without implicitly positioning another person.

We'll look in more detail at strategies for dealing with difficult positioning episodes, especially by Machiavellian partners, in Chapter 9.

Building on a sensemaking framework, then, it is clear that identity and conversation are inextricably linked and the positioning of organizational identities has emerged as a significant mechanism for influencing identity. For instance, positioning theory explicitly suggests that the constant flow

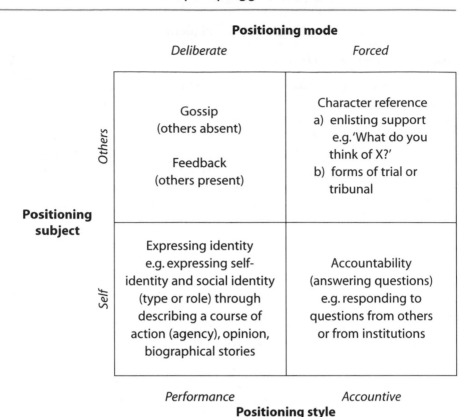

Figure 8.3 Positioning in action

of everyday life is fragmented, through discourse, into distinct episodes that constitute the basic elements both of our biographies and of the social world. It goes further, in developing the idea that the skills people have to talk are not only based on their abilities to produce words and sentences, but equally on capacities to follow rules that shape the episodes of social life. These conversational episodes, it is suggested here, help constitute both self and organizational identity (Figure 8.4).

Underpinning the conception of storyline in conversations about identity is Czarniawska's suggestion that we should treat identity as a narrative, or 'a continuous process of narration where both the narrator and audience formulate, edit, applaud and refuse various elements of the constantly produced narrative'.[15] Although many scholars have touched on narrative as a mechanism for appreciating the mental processes involved in strategy development and implementation processes (Table 8.5), it is Czarniawska who has written most extensively and eloquently on a narrative approach to organization

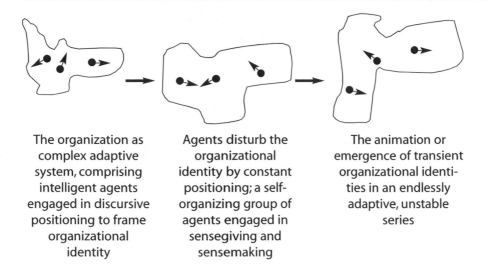

The organization as complex adaptive system, comprising intelligent agents engaged in discursive positioning to frame organizational identity	Agents disturb the organizational identity by constant positioning; a self-organizing group of agents engaged in sensegiving and sensemaking	The animation or emergence of transient organizational identities in an endlessly adaptive, unstable series

Figure 8.4a The animation of organizational identity through conversation or an endless series of positioning episodes

studies. Importantly, she considers organizational identity as a history of positioning acts.[16] The logical implication is that the construction of identity, through positioning acts, never ends. In other words, linguistic positioning by people in the organization offers a catalytic mechanism for the constant construction and reconstruction of organizational identity.

While the idea that positioning in conversation is continuous can easily be seen, we find the idea that identity is a history of positioning acts is rather a problem. Although the history idea supports Weick's take on sense-making as retrospective – and that this happens as we reassess our past experiences – it would appear more useful to us to conceptualize position-ing as being concerned with making sense for (and of) the future. In other words we shouldn't think of positioning as retrospective sensemaking at all. Instead we prefer to think of it as prospective, or future-focused, sense-giving. Furthermore, that sensegiving will invariably be focused on posi-tioning the uncertain, unstable future. Therefore we suggest a reconception of enduring (past) identity not as a narrative history of positioning acts but as a narrative fiction, an extemporization or improvisation of positioning acts (Figure 8.5). This, in summary, is how we influence identity – by our constant conversational positioning, our accounts of who we are, what we think each of us is doing and why. This can be undertaken to destabilize people's perceptions of organizational identity and to make it easier to adapt and change people's ideas. But it can also be used to paint a more compelling vision of what the future holds for us.

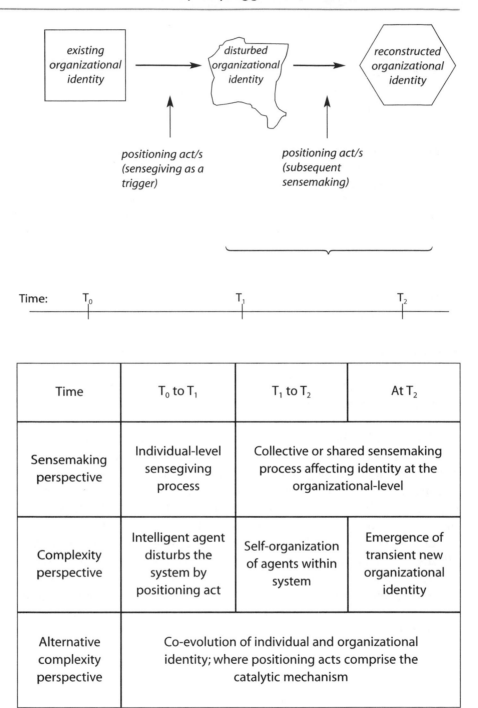

Figure 8.4b How positioning acts disturb organizational identity

Table 8.5 The storytelling continuum: from domination to expression (adapted from Gabriel, 1998: 138)

Theme	Context	Grounding
As an expression of political domination and opposition	Stories as an element of the political system	Political theory
As a vehicle for organizational communication and learning	Stories as 'cognitive depositories', memorable and able to facilitate transmission of knowledge	Communication theory
As elements of organizational culture	Like myths, rituals, ceremonies and material artefacts, stories are treated as manifestations of shared belief systems	Sensemaking (interpretivist) approach, seeking to identify the meanings and symbolism of stories for organization members
As narrative constructions	Stories as literary constructions, as texts	Narrative analysis, deconstruction
As performances	Stories in use, relations between storyteller and listener, as performance text	Dramaturgical context, dramatic and performance theory
As expressions of unconscious wishes and desires	Stories seen as manifestations of unconscious processes, stories as expression	Psychoanalytic approach

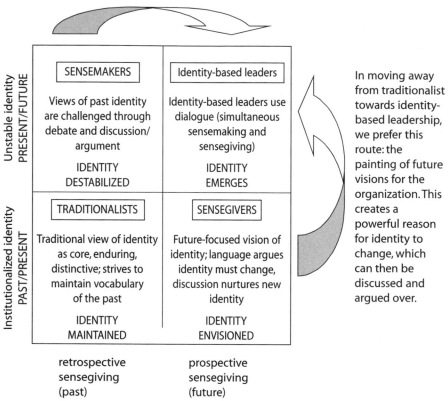

Moving from being a traditionalist to destabilizing identity often invalidates past identity of the organization, challenging the success of the past. Difficult for some to accept their part in a 'wrong' identity.

Unstable identity PRESENT/FUTURE

Institutionalized identity PAST/PRESENT

SENSEMAKERS	Identity-based leaders
Views of past identity are challenged through debate and discussion/ argument	Identity-based leaders use dialogue (simultaneous sensemaking and sensegiving)
IDENTITY DESTABILIZED	IDENTITY EMERGES
TRADITIONALISTS	SENSEGIVERS
Traditional view of identity as core, enduring, distinctive; strives to maintain vocabulary of the past	Future-focused vision of identity; language argues identity must change, discussion nurtures new identity
IDENTITY MAINTAINED	IDENTITY ENVISIONED

retrospective sensegiving (past)

prospective sensegiving (future)

In moving away from traditionalist towards identity-based leadership, we prefer this route: the painting of future visions for the organization. This creates a powerful reason for identity to change, which can then be discussed and argued over.

Figure 8.5 Sensemaking, sensegiving and identity-based leadership

Towards Dialogue

It seems appropriate to save our closing paragraphs for a summary of what sensemaking means for senior executives engaged in discussion or discourse. In our view, sensemaking is a search for identity by people in the conversations taking place in our complex organizations – our particular interest is in the search of senior executives. And it seems more appropriate, in these senseless times, to view this search for sense not as 'walking the talk' but as 'talking the walk'.[17] Walking the talk some describe as articulating something you've already decided on, with no concern for the ideas and opinions of others. Talking the walk, on the other hand, is about discussing things you've found along the way by finding out what people think, how they feel and where they walk.

Building on these ideas, and incorporating ideas from complexity science (Chapter 6), we can see that it is only when intelligent people are in discussions with one another that they articulate their sense of identity, or challenge the identities held by others. Then our collective sense of identity is disturbed and emerges renewed, thanks to our conversations with others, in often-unpredictable ways. And inexorably our organizations change – a process that sometimes is punctuated occasionally with critical incidents, sometimes affected by far-reaching avalanches of identity change. David Oliver and Johan Roos from the Imagination Lab in Switzerland have also addressed the twin themes of complexity and identity, concluding:[18]

> The only way to effectively grasp the socially constructed element of our identities is through dialogue. It is through dialogue that we can make new connections and new insights and behaviour emerges. We should take time in our communities and our organizations to talk about our co-operative and competitive co-evolutionary partners.

And that's where we're heading in the final section of *Leadership Unplugged*.

Conclusion

The key points we want to emphasize at the end of this chapter are:

- *Leadership Unplugged* is a blend of sensemaking and sensegiving behaviour by senior executives. In sensemaking it's how perceptive you are in observing people, teams and organizations – do you notice what's going on beneath the surface? In sensegiving it's how articulate you are at painting your view of the future, but also how well you can help others to articulate their views.
- Sensemaking and sensegiving are processes that occur informally in conversations between two or more people. You can become better attuned to what's going on by focusing hard, by really listening to what's taking place.
- In complex organizations, where absolute control and total planning are not possible, leadership appears to be nothing more than a constant focus on who we are and what we do – leadership is the influence of organizational identity, which is unstable and therefore malleable.

- The implications of organizational identity being adaptive and flexible are that firms in which senior executives heedfully develop and maintain value-based organization identities are more likely to avoid crises, weather crises and rebound after crises.
- *Leadership Unplugged* suggests that the mechanisms and tactics of influence in an organization are the verbal behaviours and skills of its senior executives.

QuestionBank

Take time out to answer these questions.

1. How good are you at sensing what's going on in your relationships with people? How easy do you find it to sense what's happening between the different people that make up the teams in your organization? How effectively can you sense what an organization – your own or the competition, say – is really trying to do?

2. How much do you feel in control within the organization? What do you make of the general state of play in your organization and in your industry or sector? Is everyone faced with the same level of uncertainty, for instance? How do other people – and other organizations – cope in comparison?

3. How good are you at articulating and communicating your views of the future? To what extent must you plan how you describe your desired future for the organization? How effective are you off-the-cuff in ad hoc discussions? How much formal training have you had in interpersonal communications? In written communications? How many different writing styles can you adopt? How often do you commission others to do your writing for you? Would it be possible to undertake more writing and face-to-face communication?

4. What do you personally stand for? How and in what ways do you communicate this, if at all? What, in your view, does your organization stand for? How and in what ways do you communicate this? What do other people think the organization stands for, and how do you know? How many methods do other people use to communicate their views of what the organization stands for?

Notes

1. Weick, 1995, p. 13.
2. Heidegger, Martin, 1927. *Being and Time* (Macquarrie, J. and Robinson, E. trans., 1962). Oxford: Blackwell, p. 203.
3. The philosophy of leadership as the management of meaning was captured most cogently in the 1980s and 1990s by authors such as Jay Conger, Lou Pondy, Linda Smircich and Gareth Morgan. Any literature search should bring up these authors, and all of their work is worth exploring.
4. Albert, S. and Whetten, D.A. 1985. Organizational identity. In Cummings, L.L. and Staw, B.M. (eds), *Research in Organizational Behaviour* 7. Greenwich, CT: JAI Press, pp. 263–95.
5. Gioia, D., Schultz, M. and Corley, K.G., 2000. Organizational identity, image, and adaptive instability. *Academy of Management Review* 25, pp. 63–81.
6. Weick, 1995, p. 183.
7. Sonsino, Steven, 2000. Managing identity in complex organizations: towards a dynamic theory of identity based leadership in complex organizations. In McCarthy, Ian P. and Rakotobe-Joel, Thierry (eds), *Complexity and Complex Systems in Industry*. Warwick: University of Warwick, pp. 430–45.
8. Gioia, Schultz and Corley, op. cit.
9. Pratt, Michael G. and Foreman, Peter O., 2000. Classifying managerial responses to multiple organizational identities. *Academy of Management Review* 25(1), pp. 18–42.
10. Whetten D.A. and Godfrey, P.C., 1998. *Identity in Organizations: Building Theory Through Conversations*. Thousand Oaks, CA: Sage.
11. Alvesson, M. and Kärreman, D., 2000. Taking the linguistic turn in organizational research. *Journal of Applied Behavioral Science* 36 (2), pp. 136–58.
12. Harré, R. and van Langenhove, L., 1998. The dynamics of social episodes. In Harré, R. and van Langenhove, L. (eds), *Positioning Theory*. Oxford: Blackwell, pp. 1–13.
13. Czarniawska-Joerges, B., 1996, Autobiographical acts and organizational identities. In Linstead, S., Grafton-Small, R. and Jeffcutt, P. (eds), *Understanding Management*. London: Sage, p. 160.
14. Derived from Harré, R. and van Langenhove, L., 1998. Introducing positioning theory. In Harré, R. and van Langenhove, L. (eds), *Positioning Theory*. Oxford: Blackwell, pp. 14–31.
15. Czarniawska-Joerges, op. cit.

16. Czarniawska, B. and Wolff, R., 1998. Constructing new identities in established organization fields. *International Studies of Management and Organization* 28 (3), pp. 32–56: 35.
17. Weick, 1995, p. 182.
18. Oliver, D. and Roos, J., 1999. *Striking a Balance: Complexity and Knowledge Landscapes.* London: McGraw-Hill, p. 167.

PART III

Dialogue:
Listening to the Vision

Dialogue:

A conversation between two or more persons; a colloquy (or talking together); conversation.

Conversation:

Interchange of thought and words; to convey the thoughts reciprocally in talk, spiritual or mental communion; the action of living or having one's being in or among; behaviour or manner of life.

Shorter Oxford Dictionary, 3rd edn.

CHAPTER 9

Dialogue: Listening to Audiences

Communication between actor and audience takes place at two levels, 'wave' and 'undercurrent'. ... Actors communicate to an audience on a conscious level by the words they say, the gestures they make, the movements they do, etc.; but they also communicate at the 'undercurrent' level, by means of the thoughts they 'emit'. When an actor's thoughts are not in accord with his actions – i.e. when there is a clash between wave and undercurrent – the audience/receiver experiences a phenomenon similar to interference on the radio; the audience receives two contradictory messages and it is impossible to register them both.

Augusto Boal[1]

To most of his readers he might as well have written '*it is assumed that the* blub-blub *is a* blub maximizer, blub-blub blub-blub-blub *and* blub *in perfectly* blub *and* blub-blub. *Given these limiting assumptions, the* blub blub blub blub blub blub blub. *It follows by* blub blub ...' The audience that can understand this argument is the audience of people who already understand it, leaving one to ask why the argument was necessary ... The apparent form of the passage is explanation; its actual and intended effect ... is to terrify the onlookers ...

Donald McCloskey[2]

In ordinary life we know how to listen because we are interested in or need to hear something. On the stage, in most cases, all we do is make a pretence of attentive listening.

Constantin Stanislavski[3]

Headlines

Dialogue is not discussion, nor is it argument. It's about seeking common ground, about building across groups and across diverse positions. It's about listening to your audience, not preaching to them.

Knowing your audience – both what they want and what they need from you – is the first prerequisite of communication.

The second prerequisite of communication is knowing what you want to say. The third is knowing how to say it.

The skills of public speaking closely resemble the skills of writing persuasively. So poach ideas, devices and structures from public speaking and presentation skills.

Knowing how to express opinion and emotion is more complex than communicating information and facts. In many ways it is the structure or pattern that communicates rather than the content.

When you don't know what to think, writing down your ideas and arguments can be an effective way of rehearsing your thoughts, especially for face-to-face communications.

The leadership behaviour of senior executives should be seen explicitly as a series of performances, rehearsals or improvizations. If the performances genuinely reflect the ideas, thoughts and intentions of a senior executive he or she will be perceived as believable. Performing is not pretending.

If organizational life is seen as a daily performance or drama, the leader can in effect be seen as director: recruiting, auditioning and rehearsing with key actors.

Not Discussion, But Dialogue

The physicist David Bohm, who devoted his final years to the investigation of dialogue, put it this way. Dialogue is:[4]

> ... not an exchange and it's not a discussion. Discussion means batting it back and forth like a ping-pong game. That has some value, but in dialogue we try to go deeper ... to create a situation where we suspend our opinions and judgements in order to be able to listen to each other.

We would tend to accept this view in our depiction of *Leadership Unplugged*, as we have found that people usually hold to their relatively fixed positions in a discussion and argue in favour of their own views. They simply try to convince other people to change their stance, their position, or themselves. We are not casting doubt on the discussion phase's value at all – it is an essential phase and offers great benefits in that it can, if facilitated well, help you to articulate your views when perhaps you were not able to before. ('How can I know what I think until I see what I say?') In addition, in building or developing one's argument one may realize that certain issues, ideas or concepts are untenable and so may revise them in the light of the ongoing arguments. Also, since discussion is the stage where key movers and shakers in your world are identified, this phase and the arguments that ensue cannot be ignored. However, the dialogue phase, we believe, is much more powerful at the individual level in managing or influencing organizational change – both for the people you work with and for you yourself.

In the next two chapters, then, we'll move towards a practical definition of our concept of dialogue by first exploring two other aspects of *Leadership Unplugged*: performance and authenticity. Authenticity we'll deal with in more depth in Chapter 10, on unplugging the emotions, but we'll deal with performance here in an exploration of leadership and audience.

Why leadership and audience? Well, a few moments ago we wrote the phrase 'in dialogue ... to create a situation where we suspend our opinions and judgements in order to be able to listen to each other'. This, we believe, is a truly apt description of a powerful metaphor – that organizations are theatres and what goes on inside organizations are performances. But before we explore the value of this approach in detail, we'll begin by developing some of the themes from Chapter 7, 'Leading Opinions'.

We want to start here because, in our view, much of the writing that senior executives undertake is a form of performance. You only have to think of a chair's or CEO's statement in an annual report to see this perspective in action. So we'd like to begin by making explicit the suggestion that, just as everything senior executives do can be seen as dramatic, so too their writing must be considered as drama – as performance. In addition, however, writing can also be a powerful and private way to rehearse your thinking. Don't know what you think? Try to write it down. It's a salutary experience.

Know Your Audience

We have implicitly discussed the needs of the audience throughout *Leadership Unplugged*. In discussing the debate, discussion and dialogue

Table 9.1 The roles of audiences in *Leadership Unplugged* and their needs

	Debate audience	*Discussion audience*	*Dialogue audience*
Who	Often the entire organization or entire groups of stakeholders. Unusually can be small groups in conversation.	Sub-groups within different sections of the stakeholder audience; occasionally smaller groups of 10–50 in workshop format. Occasionally can be small groups in conversation.	Small groups of individuals, from one to 25, say; either in conversation, counselling-style meetings or facilitated workshops.
Want	At times can want a sense of direction and want the senior executive team to tell them what to do. Many want to be left to get on, with the status quo left intact. Some may want to be left to get on with creating or managing change.	Want to hear the specific details about how change may affect them or their unit. Want to know the reasons behind proposed or actual change. Want to know that they and their peers will be looked after by senior executives.	Want to know and understand the ideas, thoughts and feelings of others involved in the change process. Want to get into the shoes of the other parties. Want a way forward out of argumentation, towards co-operation, usually.
Needs	Need to have the views of senior executives articulated in the form of debate to provoke further debate and the beginnings of rational argument.	Need to be engaged in argument, in part to clarify their own thinking, certainly to be involved in the process of managing change.	Need to be listened to and in turn to listen to others involved in the organization. Need to work towards constructive solutions to issues affecting all parties.

continuum we have given emphasis to defining roles for senior executives and other stakeholders in the mix (see Table 9.1 for an explicit account of this).

In building on the argument or discussion phase, we want to make a distinction between structuring arguments from our own perspective and articulating arguments and discussion that take account of an audience's position or perspective. This, in our view, is the first stage of moving into the dialogue phase. It means writing more openly and honestly about one's opinions and emotions for the benefit of others, not for our own amusement or for egotistical reasons. It is also about attempting to deal with, or understand, the opinions and emotions of others. But this is not easy. Most senior executives, for instance, when they're writing something for broad publication to stakeholders forget the first rule of persuasion, the first rule of communication and everything they were ever taught on any communications course they ever attended. The key to clear communication has to be knowledge of your audience (Table 9.2). Only then can you begin to think about what you want to say and how you want to say it. This is because what you want to say depends *entirely* on what the audience wants to hear

Table 9.2 The three keys to clear communication and the problems they solve

The three keys to clear communication	The problems of communication
1) First know your reader or audience	Being unclear of purpose Pressure of time
2) Know what you want to say	Not planning Writing not thinking
3) Know how you want to say it	Uncertainty over length Knowing what to leave out Knowing what to put in Knowing how to start Not varying style Gaining speed, saving time Knowing how to structure the piece Blind fear and panic (otherwise known as blank page or blank screen syndrome)

from you, and on what they *need* to hear from you. And there is a distinct difference.

Essentially, then, our research for *Leadership Unplugged* shows that the people you work with simply want to know what you think. They also want to know that you have listened to what they think, which appears to be even more important. We'll come on to dealing with this in face-to-face conversations shortly, but let's look first at ways of expressing opinions to your audience in print.

Structuring Your Published Opinion

In addition to the two basic structuring approaches we dealt with in Chapter 7, there are three useful additional frameworks for creating a sense of direction, of persuasion even, in your writing. These apply both to the preparation of general articles and of problem-solving case studies. We have called these structures the Tennis structure, the Everest structure and the Trench structure (Figure 9.1).

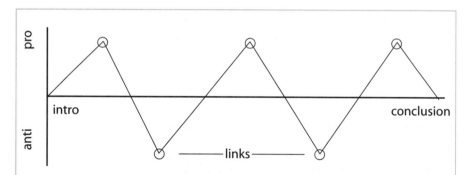

Following the intro, points are made in favour or against the main issue under discussion. The piece may start and end either in favour or against, or allow the audience members to make up their own minds. This style is difficult to write convincingly, as after each point a link has to countermand the idea and send the discussion back the other way. ('On the other hand...'; 'In Atlanta, though,...'; 'The State legislature prefers to do it another way...') It can make for an irritating read. Used sparingly, though, the structure can be powerful – so save this for occasions when you want to reflect indecision, perhaps, or the repercussive nature of a discussion.

Figure 9.1a Structuring persuasion in print: the tennis structure

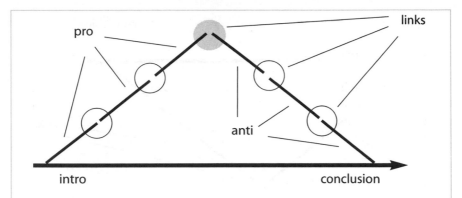

Following the intro, two or three key points (marked here 'pro') are made in favour of the main issue under discussion. Each of these is linked simply with a link of similarity. The second half combines the two or three major reasons against the issue (marked here 'anti'), also with links of similarity. The piece usually ends with the single most important or telling reason against the issue under discussion. This leaves readers in no doubt as to your views on the topic, but ensures they hear both sides of the argument. Knowing both sides, the audience members can make up their own minds. The trickiest element in the Everest structure is the key link at the heart of the piece where a U-turn in the discussion needs to be convincing enough to carry readers into the second half. A simple 'On the other hand…' probably isn't enough. The link should probably give a clue as to the severity of the compelling reasons against the key issues, and may call on significant stakeholders who disagree or key geographic regions where the key issue simply would not be upheld.

Figure 9.1b Structuring persuasion in print: the Everest structure

Of course, these simplistic structures do nothing more than give you a head start in putting your arguments down on paper. They can then be adapted and elaborated as you choose, but we caution against overmuch to-ing and fro-ing in your writing. Changing direction too often in print only serves to confuse readers. Remember it's the structure that tells the story. If readers are left with the impression that you favour (or refute) one particular approach, and if they can remember maybe one of your key points, you'll be doing well.

There is a distinct type of journalistic writing that executives can draw on to develop their communication skills with different audiences. These skills, geared entirely towards the communication of opinion, are the techniques and tactics of the opinion or comment columnist. Interestingly,

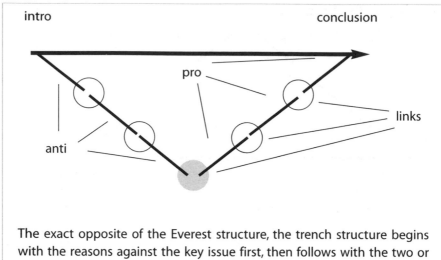

intro   conclusion

pro

links

anti

The exact opposite of the Everest structure, the trench structure begins with the reasons against the key issue first, then follows with the two or three major reasons in favour of the issue. The piece ends usually with the single most important or compelling reason the issue under discussion should be adopted. Again the trickiest element is the key link at the heart of the piece where the U-turn occurs.

Figure 9.1c Structuring persuasion in print: the trench structure

opinion columns in newspapers are sometimes known as leaders – in the sense that they are opinion leaders – and purport to be the opinions of the journal or newspaper. But the reason we have incorporated these devices here (instead of in Chapter 7, where we explored writing as a tool for argument) is that they serve writers far better when you appreciate and know the views of the audience you write for. Most newspaper leaders, for example, reiterate and magnify the known views of their readers. So while these devices are used occasionally to challenge and provoke readers, generally they are used to demonstrate understanding and solidarity. In a very real sense, then, this is writing as 'performance' to an explicit 'audience'. The publication of comment or opinion columns is a public rehearsal or rendition of an argument or discussion.

Before moving to an explicit identification between writing and performance, let us simply conclude with the view that while coaches and speechwriters can be helpful for executives, in that they save time, we believe that writing or drafting opinion pieces is too important to be contracted out wholesale to communications specialists. Not least because the very act of writing down what you want to say helps you figure out what it is that you believe.

Writing as Performance

There are four key things to be thinking of when you draft your opinion as a piece of writing for a specific sector of your stakeholder audience.

- Who are you writing for?
- Why are you writing?
- What concerns do the audience members have?
- How will you know if your piece has been effective?

Thinking about the 'who', of course you should consider explicitly who you are writing for – which section of the audience, which stakeholders? Is there a specific person you have in mind? A favourite topic of some newspapers is to write an open letter to the president, the chancellor or some other high-profile individual. 'Dear Mr President, it's time we stopped ...'

This is, of course, related to why you are writing. What are you trying to achieve? And this needs to be explicit. It is only through considering these elements that you can begin to identify what point you are trying to make for this audience. You also need to ask if what you are talking about it is important to them and, perhaps, in tune with their view? If it is not, find out what is. Don't assume you know best. Regarding the timing of your piece, you might also consider whether it occurs at the beginning of a campaign for change, or whether it is intended to resurrect interest or attention. This will colour your writing and suggest whether your piece is principally a salvo in a debate, a thrust in an argument or a call for more dialogue with the audience itself.

Do ask yourself what the concerns of the audience around this topic or theme might be. What do they think about the issue you're writing on? What concerns of your own must you elaborate upon or reveal? What will your readers think of this? The essence of dialogue is to find out what the other party is thinking. Help them to express themselves. And this links in to the idea of success criteria. Getting a response from the audience is essential, which means that watching for a response from the audience is also essential. But this means that you will know if your piece has been successful when you get a response. So do you want to receive letters, phone calls or e-mails, for instance? Or do you want some other form of response? If so, what? This idea of a specific call to action is very often the defining characteristic of an opinion column, as opposed to a general article exploring an issue in case study or problem solving format. This is exactly the place for a piece with a rousing, 'to the barricades' ending.

Of course, there are often problems in finding an effective writing style when you're dealing with the complex issues that organizations face. Working out what the single most important point you're trying to make is difficult, as always, but the most useful advice here is to be decisive and be imperative. Remember that while this style can be used in the debate phase of change, here you're using it to reinforce existing views. Remember, too, that being upbeat and positive without seeming trite or insincere is often tricky. (It's almost always easier to be cynical or sceptical in print.) And finding the facts to back an argument can be time-consuming. But these are all things we must strive to do. In addition, understanding the complexity of emotions – your own and those of the audience – doesn't come easy. But it is something you must also try to do. It is important to build on and use the emotions that drive you on important topics. That emotion communicates itself to others in many small ways. Ask yourself what makes you passionate about this subject. Can you articulate this in your writing? (More on emotions in leadership in Chapter 10.)

There is one form of opinion article that sometimes sidetracks the unwary writer. This is the comment column, in which the writer simply comments, remarks or criticizes but makes no suggestion as to what should happen next. In many instances this style of writing is twinned with sitting on the fence to create a pallid cliché of journalism: 'Nuclear power is neither a good nor a bad thing – it depends entirely on the use to which it is put.'[5] This is indecision as an art form. It does not persuade. It has no use in the armoury of business executives. The leader article, by comparison, offers comment but also guides the reader with a solution or proposition of its own.

A very simple format for leader articles, then, might be the archetypal presentation format – tell them what you're going to tell them, tell them, then tell them what you've told them – but with certain modifications:

- Tell the audience what you want them to do, or what you want to happen.
- Tell the audience why you want this to happen and offer some facts about the situation, its causes or implications.
- Tell the audience what you want them to do again, but using even stronger language and perhaps pointing out the implications of not doing what you suggest.

It's easy to see why the typical presentation structure often works in writing about opinions – because in a very real sense leader writing is a performance. It is rhetorical writing, in the classical sense, with clear links with performance and public speaking. It's very much for this reason that the media – particularly television, because of its immediacy, but also the printed media – are taken over during a coup and are always government-controlled in dictatorships. Free expression is revolution.

Rhetoric and Public Speaking

Let's begin to consider public speaking as opposed to writing, but bearing in mind that the same devices and structures can be applied in both. Every rhetorical article or speech involves four basic steps, to bring together speakers and audience:

1. The writer/speaker uses language, not force, to bring change.
2. The writer/speaker is seen as a supporter of the audience, not an exploiter or manipulator.
3. The writer/speaker must convince the audience that new choices need to be made.
4. The writer/speaker must help the audience narrow options and establish criteria for making its choices.

And while facts, evidence and proof are important sometimes we forget that it is ordinary language, used in this extraordinary way, which swings opinions. We forget that actually it is the structure that tells the story; the pattern of sense that the writer/speaker weaves that wins the day. And, in addition, we forget that if you are to persuade an audience then it is the perceptions of the ordinary people that comprise that audience that represent the acid test of your success.

In the extract by McCloskey at the head of this chapter you can see and hear a real concern for the communication of science – in McCloskey's case economics – and the key question is 'Exactly who is the audience?' But McCloskey is radical in suggesting that the way of speaking modifies the idea. The message itself is changed, he suggests, by the demands of the communication – in other words, by the presence and character of the audience. The message is also affected, says McCloskey, by the attitudes of the audience and the speaker to each other. He goes further, taking issue with the simple idea of sender and receiver. This notion oversimplifies communication, he says, making an argument sound like a job for the repairman:[6]

> Science, to put it another way, is human persuasion, not mechanical demonstration. Of course, the scientist will claim every time that what she is arguing is demonstrated – that is seen, plain shown, obvious, indubitable, exhibited wordlessly. ... If science is mostly persuasion rather than demonstration, then it is a good idea to watch the persuasive devices.

Table 9.3 Tactics for reaching the audience

Tactic or structural style	Purpose	Examples
Simple contrast	Creates a sense of irony or highlights extremes.	'The smallest companies in this sector have the highest profitability …'
Narrative	To convey a complex story; try to use a simple introduction and conclusion.	'The Enron saga is a tale of malpractice on a huge scale …'
Puzzle-solution	To create a sense of suspense or intrigue, to hook the reader; often uses rhetorical questions. Can be combined powerfully with a simple contrast, for example.	'Why are the smallest companies in this sector always the most profitable? An obvious answer lies in the way they …'
Three-part list	Creates a structure for dealing with a range of material – often the structure tells the story; lists of three are very memorable.	'Three years ago we were the newcomer in this business. Today we are in sight of the top three. And within three years we will lead this sector.' (Yesterday–today–tomorrow)
Scenarios	In an intriguing way sets a structure and style for the piece.	'The case for the prosecution rests on evidence from three key witnesses …' (courtroom, for example) 'The most difficult grilling I ever faced was when my six-year-old son asked me what I did at work. As I recall, the conversation went something like this…' (Q&A)

Table 9.3 (continued)

Tactic or structural style	Purpose	Examples
		'We are guilty of maybe five of the seven deadly sins of business strategy. ... This must change.' (list)
Combinations	Some of the structures can be combined with others to create even more powerful and memorable structures.	'It is not the end. It is not even the beginning of the end. But it is perhaps the end of the beginning.' (A puzzle with a three-part list as the answer.)

This conclusion – to watch and learn from the persuasive devices – is helpful advice indeed. For the pinnacle of persuasion has to be the face-to-face argument or disagreement that we know as public speaking. As we've said, many of the devices for writing leaders can be used equally well in public speaking. So it's no surprise to hear three-part lists, simple contrasts and rhetorical questions occurring regularly in the speeches of politicians and canny business executives.

Case 18. Max Atkinson and the case for rhetoric

We first met Max Atkinson at a conference organized by the British Association for the Advancement of Science, after which we invited him to design and deliver a public speaking element for the 'Editors' Academy', a residential development programme for senior journalists at the Anglo-Dutch publishing corporation Reed Elsevier. Atkinson was already well known as the author of *Our Masters' Voices* and highly regarded as a scholar of public speaking.[7] He had long studied the very public oratory of the British political system. Here approval and disapproval were instant and measurable – the braying and cheering of British politicians in the House of Commons, notably at Prime Minister's Question Time, gave an instant assessment of what worked, rhetorically, and what didn't.

Atkinson first came to the attention of the broader public in 1984 when, at a televised political rally for the Social Democratic Party, he coached a novice speaker in the black arts of rhetoric. 'Equipped with a script that bristled with contrasts, three-part lists and rhetorical questions Ann Bren-nan's speech … generated so much applause that she only managed to deliver about two-thirds of it before running out of time', says Atkinson.[8]

The speaker won a standing ovation, which was largely attributed to the devices and linguistic structures she had used. But there was cynicism and scepticism over the value of these techniques, which some regarded as manipulative and insincere. The Lord Mayor of London, Ken Livingstone, for instance, is reputed to have said that 'Public speakers are born not made' – at once using rhetoric (in the form of a simple contrast) to deny the existence of rhetoric. Atkinson, though, does not flinch.[9]

> However much people may complain about the evils of soundbites it is difficult to conceive of how it could ever be possible to eliminate them. Whether we call them soundbites, quotable quotes, slogans or aphorisms, lines that stand out from the vast mass of forgettable sentences have always been with us, from the Bible, through literature and politics, to tele-vision advertising.

What Atkinson finds strange is that while the rhetoric of the past clearly has served its purpose, and is revered, collected and stored in dictionaries of quotations for almost every occasion, the rhetoric of the present is hailed with suspicion and derision. His conclusion, on our ambivalence to present-day rhetoric, is that perhaps 'we are more willing to be impressed if we think that someone is a "gifted" speaker, naturally endowed with an ability to get the message across effectively, than if we think that they have been schooled, coached or otherwise assisted by speechwriters and coaches'.

But why? If the views communicated to an audience are genuinely the strongly held beliefs of the speaker, Atkinson suggests that there is no manipulation involved. Only if a script was imposed on a speaker, rather than arising from his or her own views, would he have qualms.

> To dismiss or denigrate rhetoric is to ignore the fact that its structures and devices provide an infinitely adaptable toolkit for packaging messages in a simple and striking way that audiences can grasp immediately. Without it persuasive discourse and debate become much more difficult, probably to the point of impossibility.[10]

In many respects we have found that executives coached in the devices of rhetoric can debate and argue constructively in public where they could not have done previously. Knowing that they must be direct and decisive, that they must have an opinion and communicate it, appears to liberate even the most tongue-tied executives. Some have said to us that they feel they can disagree with people in public for the first time. This, in essence, can be an important first step towards being honest in a constructive and sustainable way.

A Very Public Disagreement

Disagreeing with people is hard to do well. In cultures where saving face is important, or simply where saying 'no' is implicitly frowned upon, executives are often passive and do not reveal their true thoughts. This hamstrings the organization. It makes debate less confrontational, discussions become less argumentative, and dialogue as we are describing it simply becomes impossible. Without some mechanism for disagreement, executives can find it difficult to take an appropriate part in the conversations of the organization. Of course, some executives find it very easy to reject people's views and ideas, but because they are actually quite aggressive in the way they do this they sometimes do just as much damage to their business relationships, if not more. These executives could learn to temper their aggression.

There is a middle ground – neither overly passive, nor overly aggressive – where executives can publicly disagree with someone, or express a different opinion, and still respect or even support the individual whose views they challenge. This is the manifesto of assertiveness, based on the rights of every individual to be heard, if they wish. The language of assertiveness is simple and powerful and its mechanisms are straightforward to learn (Table 9.4).

These techniques are simple to practice, but not so simple to adopt in reality. The natural anxiety executives feel about trying new ways of working often gets in the way. So it's important to think broadly about what you are trying to achieve in adopting the techniques. Simply adopting these tactics uncritically will not work well. Executives need to be helped to consider the effects and consequences of their actions, both in the short and the long term, as the foundation for developing their skills here. They also need to think through the consequences of *not* changing the way they relate to people. And they need to be aware that not every relationship will improve, or even change at all, as a result of altering the way they relate to people. Human relationships can break down irretrievably. So it's important to realize that not every relationship can be sustained using these techniques, and that you need a sense of when to call 'time'. But you'll see from Table 9.4 that the techniques are arranged in a specific sequence, with responsive and simple assertion capable of handling the majority of the workload, so the very framework helps you identify when it's 'time to call time'. The table has been developed

Table 9.4 The language of assertiveness (after Back and Back, 1999)

Level	Description	Examples
1. Responsive assertion	Where you try to find out the other person's views, wants, needs or feelings, often by questioning. It's important to ask the questions in a way that encourages a response, not in a way that curtly demands a response. And you must genuinely want to know what the other party's views are – insincerity can easily be spotted.	'What do you think, Mikhail?' 'I'd like to hear your views on this, Ben.' 'What problems would that create for you?' 'What would you prefer to do?'
2. Simple assertion	A direct and simple statement of your own views, wants, needs or feelings. This is how you might react to someone else's question in a responsive style. Note that no excuses, justification or lengthy explanation are needed here. This is a simple assertion of your needs.	'I'd prefer to do it this way.' 'I need to leave at 10 o'clock.' 'In my view the process works well.' 'I'm pleased with the way we have resolved this.'
3. Empathetic assertion	A statement that reprises the simple assertion in level 2, while acknowledging the perspective of someone else.	'I can appreciate that you don't like the schedule for the new team, John, but until we've got this quarter's results in I'd like to keep to the plan.'
4. Discrepancy	A form of assertion that highlights the difference between what you thought would happen and what has happened, or appears might happen in the future.	'In the strategic plan we agreed that there would be room to bring the schedule forward if we needed to. I'm still keen to keep that flexibility in the plan.'

Table 9.4 (continued)

Level	Description	Examples
5. Emotive assertion	This is a framework that can be used to deliver positive or negative feedback, but is perhaps most useful to convey difficult emotions. It follows a structure that brings to someone else's attention the impact they are having on you. This usually takes the following structure: • situation • effects • emotions • preference	'When you send in your quarterly reports late it means I have to calculate the spreadsheets myself from last quarter's figures. It makes me feel frustrated that our meetings then don't have the latest information. I'd prefer to have your figures in on time in the future.' 'When you get your reports in to me ahead of time, and with the additional data you provided this month, it takes so much pressure off my schedule. I'm grateful and hope we can keep working together like this.'
6. Consequential assertion	This structure lets someone know clearly what the consequences are of their not changing the way they work. Importantly, it also gives the other person a way of saving face and of changing the way they relate to you. This helps them to save face and prevents the simple statement from sounding like an ultimatum. Because it could be interpreted as an ultimatum this form of assertion must be delivered calmly, without vindictiveness, and it should be focused on the action that is needed, not on the person.	'Martine, I'm concerned that we haven't been able to resolve our differences on how we should proceed on this project. Unless we can take the time to agree how we work together and then stick to that process I'm left with no alternative but to recommend my team withdraws from the project. I'd prefer not to.'

Table 9.4 (continued)

Level	Description	Examples
6. Consequential assertion (continued)	This usually takes the following structure:· • situation· • preferred situation· • consequences of not agreeing· • the all-important 'get out' clause.	'William, when you persistently block my requests for support it makes it difficult for me to manage my team's workload effectively. If I give you enough notice I'd like to be able to count on your support. Unless we can reach an agreement on this I'll have to involve Amy. Personally I would rather we managed this between ourselves.'

from the work of Ken and Kate Back, whom we came across in 1990, and which we explored in greater depth under the tutelage of Hilary Harrison and Sally Arthur in 1995.

As you can imagine, the dynamics of the assertive leadership behaviours interlink with the responses of your partner in the discussion. And the successful adoption of these techniques then creates an interlinked series of positive feedback loops, reinforcing the success of this respectful, 'unplugged' language. We have seen in our work that assertive language reinforces its own success and begins to change your behaviour as a leader, building confidence quickly. This in turn begins to change the behaviour of others.

Of course there will be setbacks and mistakes, but the language of assertiveness has mechanisms for dealing with this in a constructive way. The concept of moving between the different levels of assertiveness is useful here, and almost always helps to keep the relationships between you and your partners on an even keel. We have seen more relationships kept open and workable when people have adopted these ideas than when people choose not to change.

With sustained assertive behaviour comes a change of mind, and often a change of heart. This can involve adopting a new set of beliefs or values about the people one works with, and how they might behave more constructively towards one another.

So our research into the language of leadership behaviour has shown us that changing the language executives use changes their behaviour over

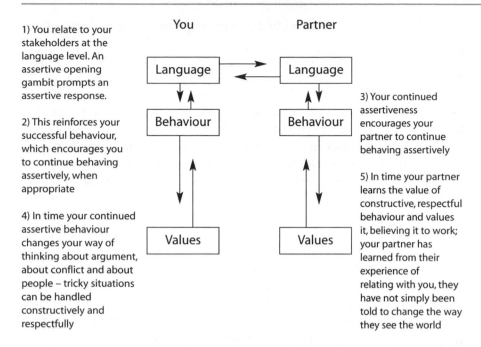

1) You relate to your stakeholders at the language level. An assertive opening gambit prompts an assertive response.

2) This reinforces your successful behaviour, which encourages you to continue behaving assertively, when appropriate

4) In time your continued assertive behaviour changes your way of thinking about argument, about conflict and about people – tricky situations can be handled constructively and respectfully

3) Your continued assertiveness encourages your partner to continue behaving assertively

5) In time your partner learns the value of constructive, respectful behaviour and values it, believing it to work; your partner has learned from their experience of relating with you, they have not simply been told to change the way they see the world

Figure 9.2 The link between language and values

time, and that this changing behaviour – learned and stilted at first, then more natural – is a precursor to changing values. And we mean here both your values and the values of others. And for this reason alone – that changing the style and structure of the very language you use can affect values in the organization – assertiveness is worth exploring (Figure 9.2). We'll return to this concept of the link between language and values in Chapter 12. Suffice it to say that it's your appreciation of the other person's position that defines how you change your behaviour. And it's this, in turn, that changes your partner's behaviour. It's a classic thread of the *Unplugged* philosophy that you can't simply tell someone to change their behaviour and expect it to stay changed.

The Leader as Actor or Director

That language is the key to effective leadership should come as no surprise by now to readers of *Leadership Unplugged*. That we propose to broaden the discussion to include the idea of leaders as actors, if not as directors of drama in our organizations, may still need some explanation, however. In other words, we suggest that leadership behaviour itself is a performance – in the dramatic sense – and that we must consider closely our relationships with all the stakeholding actors in the ongoing performance or drama of our organizations.

This idea is rooted in our proposals in Chapter 2 that the strategic objectives of debate, discussion and dialogue are related to organizational vision (Table 2.2). The purpose of the debate phase, we said, was to position the vision – to articulate a senior executive view of what the vision could be. The discussion phase, in comparison, was about arguing the vision. In this phase our participants in the organization begin to develop their own concepts of the vision, and to discuss that with us through arguments in different formats and in different venues. In the final dialogue phase, however, the strategic objective for senior executives is to listen to the vision. And we have a specific set of meanings associated with listening, which we'll come to over the next two chapters. After a period of time, the people within the organization will have a clear view of what it is they need to do to take the organization forward. They articulate the vision constantly in everything they say and in everything they do. It is the echoes of these words and actions that senior executives must be attuned to and listen for – in effect, then, the leader of the team is the director of the performance and the members of the team are the actors engaged in it.

Taking this view of leader as director prompts us to ask what is it that senior executives actually do. By analogy with the theatre world, first they hire the best people for the job, auditioning widely and strenuously. Yes, they may hire people they've worked with before, but if this doesn't work out they have no qualms about replacing them with more appropriate personnel. Second, they rehearse the team extensively. There is the read-through of a play, or the experimental development of the production, and the physical, vocal and psychological development of characters. Finally, however, the cohort of actors that make up the production and the back-stage team that allows the production to go ahead have finished their preparations. The day of performance arrives and the director (in effect) retires. The team, once it has been honed to peak performance, takes over. Yes, the director is involved in reviewing specific aspects of performance, and also in the refinement of key elements that haven't worked, but on the whole his or her task is now done.

This is very different from traditional conceptions of strategic or visionary leadership. In the traditional leadership literature, for instance, leadership is often described as a series of specific steps – beginning with the development of a compelling vision, then moving to the widespread communication and buy-in to the vision, all of this magically leading to empowerment of the workforce and superhuman performance by all concerned. This unidirectional take on leadership and vision seems to regard language much as machine-gunners regard their ammunition: something to be fired in the vague direction of the enemy and replaced as soon as possible. Taking the view of organizational life as drama prompts a more dynamic conception. In the words of Frances Westley and Henry Mintzberg:[11]

> Here action and communication occur simultaneously. Idea and emotion, actor and audience are momentarily united in a rich encounter which occurs on many symbolic levels ... It may be brief, but it is the goal of playwright, director, actor, and audience, the result of 'rehearsal', the 'performance' itself and the 'attendance' of the audience.

This conception of the 'attendance' of the audience – what theatre director Peter Brook prefers to call 'assistance', from the French – is significant here. 'When the actor goes in front of an audience he finds that the magic transformation does not work by magic', says Brook.[12] The audience may just stare at the spectacle, expecting the actor to do all the work. On what actors call a 'good night', on the other hand, they encounter an audience that by some chance brings 'an active interest and life to its watching role – this audience assists'.

Like performance, leadership behaviour involves a two-way current. The behaviour doesn't happen in isolation – it too needs assistance. The best business audience is not only inspired and motivated by its actors; the audience itself inspires in return. Translating this more into business language, there is a dual accountability that businesses need to foster. Senior executives are accountable, yes, but there is also an accountability that senior executives need to foster in their stakeholder audiences. In other words, stakeholders have a responsibility to take an active interest; to provide feedback to the leaders as actors and directors. All too often the business audience abdicates this responsibility, preferring to play the role of the cynical 'I told you so' critic. Exactly what the audience in business circles does to 'assist' senior executives is something we could usefully explore further.

The Drama of Leadership

Some people believe that actor and audience take static roles divided by an arch or curtain. The *Leadership Unplugged* view, however, is that the roles are much more fluid and dynamic than this, with the audience playing far more of an active role than you might think. Through its focus and attention, the business audience becomes an active participant, helping all business players at whatever level in the organization to construct their own versions of themselves. This is the audience helping organizational actors to create and endorse a believable sense of identity. This applies to the audience, too, as the members consciously and subconsciously think through the implications of plot and character and reflect on what this means for them personally. This constant creation and re-creation of meaning is exactly what occurs on the business stage every day, except that the involvement of the audience is even more striking. Here the audience is comprised of what the Brazilian playwright and director Augusto Boal describes as 'spect-actors', as opposed to spectators. Spect-actors, he suggests, are people who actively respond and take part in everything that takes place. And in this sense, even remaining silent and listening attentively is to take action.

We are interested in the roles of different audiences in business because we believe that the focus and attention of listening is perhaps an even more important skill for an audience than the abilities of actors to persuade us of their sincerity through words. As a reminder, let's state here that our goal in this chapter is to begin to understand the benefits and limitations to both acting and audience aspects of the performance relationship. For the rest of this section, though, we'll focus on what senior executives traditionally take away from a study of theatre and drama – a focus on physical performance. Because performance is something of a catch-all phrase, however, here we break it down into four sub-sections (Figure 9.3):

1. *framing*
    - language and sensegiving
    - sensemaking and reflexive capabilities
2. *scripting and improvization*
    - casting, auditions and the identification of cynics and supporters
    - screenplay, text and dialogue
    - leader as director
3. *staging*
4. *and performing*
    - role modelling
    - promoting the vision
    - identity work.

Framing

The essential tool of the manager of meaning is the ability to frame. To determine the meaning of a subject is to make sense of it, to judge its character and significance. To hold the frame of a subject is to choose

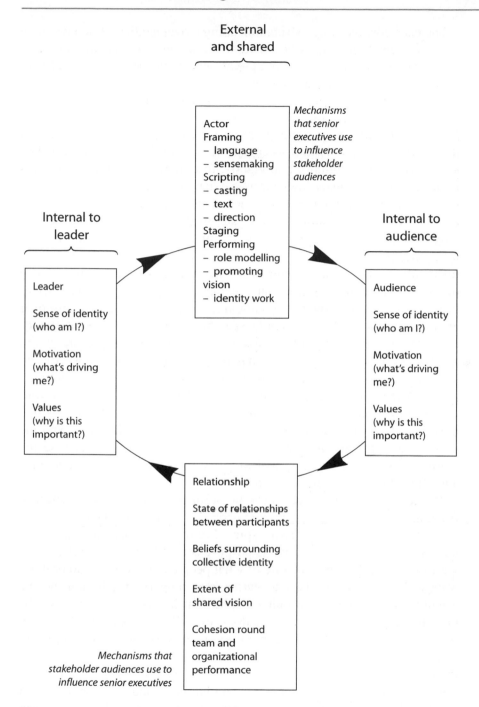

External
and shared

Actor
Framing
– language
– sensemaking
Scripting
– casting
– text
– direction
Staging
Performing
– role modelling
– promoting
vision
– identity work

*Mechanisms
that senior
executives use
to influence
stakeholder
audiences*

Internal to
leader

Internal to
audience

Leader

Sense of identity
(who am I?)

Motivation
(what's driving
me?)

Values
(why is this
important?)

Audience

Sense of identity
(who am I?)

Motivation
(what's driving
me?)

Values
(why is this
important?)

Relationship

State of relationships
between participants

Beliefs surrounding
collective identity

Extent of
shared vision

Cohesion round
team and
organizational
performance

*Mechanisms that
stakeholder audiences use to
influence senior executives*

Figure 9.3 How *Leadership Unplugged* is performed (inspired by Gardner
and Avolio 1998

one particular meaning (or set of meanings) over another. When we share our frames with others (the process of framing), we manage meaning because we assert that our interpretations should be taken as real over other possible interpretations.

Gail Fairhurst and Robert Sarr[13]

The critical elements of framing are an executive's use of language, and therefore his or her abilities to engage in sensemaking (of the past) and sensegiving (of the future). Importantly, too, framing involves executives thinking about and analysing their own experiences. How much executives can learn from reflecting on experience is also significant.

The importance of reflection for managers arises because the language we use is capable of being interpreted – or should we say misinterpreted – in many different ways. Everyone sees the world differently so knowing something about framing is useful, especially in organizations, and at times, that are particularly complex. The art of framing is knowing how to use language to highlight one meaning over another. It's about letting people see the world as you see it (hence sensegiving), but more importantly it's about letting people know you see the world in the same way that they see it (sensemaking). It's no surprise that 'framing' is derived from the phrase 'frame of reference', as the process involves being sensitive to the business context of your organization and to the contexts of the individuals within the teams that make up the organization. In short, you must know your people and the issues that motivate and drive them. This enables you to choose the words, images and symbols that amplify the values of your audience and stress how important they are.

It's important, then, to recognize the nurturing and supportive aspect of framing. Some might take the impression that framing is manipulative, in the sense of the pejorative term 'spin'. We don't go that far. Framing is interpreting a situation, yes, but its purpose is to help people to articulate a view or vision. Painting a picture of what people don't want to do or don't want to hear is hardly likely to garner real support. In addition, people usually spot exaggerated framing ('spin' that has been doctored) so the medium term loss of trust that results – even if there is some short-term success from manipulating people's early impressions – is simply not worth it.

We have already covered some techniques for framing – including the use of structure, lists and contrasts – and Fairhurst and Sarr highlight still more in their seminal work on framing.[14] Here are three that we've seen widely used in organizations:

- *Metaphors*, used to highlight a subject or situation's likeness with something else to bring new insights – for example, the use of the theatre metaphor to describe organizations helps us to explore the issues of performance and audience.
- *Jargon and catchphrases* frame a subject in familiar terms and also put the speaker in a familiar frame of reference – for example, using financial jargon with an audience of finance specialists can create credibility for the speaker.
- *Stories and narratives* can frame a subject by example – stories also make it easier to remember the frame and to pass it on to others.

Perhaps the most important aspect of framing is that, in order to engage in the framing process, you have to have been thinking about what's going on. You must have reflected on the past and given thought to the future. Many executives don't give much thought at all to what happens has happened or will happen in business. They speak in the moment, of the moment. They are severely disadvantaged.

Scripting and Improvization

Scripting relates to the often unconscious and unspoken guides that govern how actors relate to other actors. It usually helps you to define a scene (for example, 'this is an important meeting'), to identify key actors ('with the chief executive and our key customers') and to outline expected behaviours ('and we have to work hard to win this business'). Scripts in this sense are not definitive word-for-word screenplays but an emergent guide to what is taking place, or to what is about to take place. They are guides devised by the various actors involved, in conjunction with directors and stage managers advising on what is possible and what is not.

A key aspect of the scripting phase – the identification of actors and audience – is known as casting, and this relates directly to the identification of the cynics and supporters described in Chapter 5, 'The Politics of Change', casting – in organizational terms – also involves identifying the competition. A notably dramatic example is provided by the interrelated rallying cries of two earthmoving giants, Caterpillar and Komatsu. For new market entrant Komatsu, the strategic imperative was 'Maru-C', or 'encircle Caterpillar'. Caterpillar's clarion call, by contrast, was 'kill Komatsu'.

Scripting also involves planning, or at least preparing, elements of what you intend to say, especially which metaphors, analogies and stories best capture your thinking. We've explored and highlighted many of the tactics that people use elsewhere in this chapter and in Chapter 7, 'Leading Opinion', and it is worth remembering that these tactics are powerful because they are memorable. This helps senior executives to keep them in mind for an appropriate moment, and helps other actors and the audience to recall them later in passing them on to others.

As well as thinking through what they intend to, or may, say, research tells us that the most effective leaders and managers also give thought to *how* they intend to communicate. Your expressiveness as a senior executive is only partly related to the verbal impression that you make – it is also related to the unspoken impressions that you give off.[15] These radically different signs and symbols – verbal versus non-verbal, if you will – create problems for the unwary. The natural non-verbal displays our bodies 'give off' are difficult to control and audiences automatically pay close attention, giving a good deal of weight to any apparent discrepancy. 'He looks shifty', they say, or 'she doesn't believe what she just told us'.

Turning this reflection on its head for a moment, it's worth reminding ourselves that senior executives can also use these subtle evaluation techniques. By watching the small movements of their different audiences, you will soon establish if there's a discrepancy between what people are thinking and what they are saying. Even if you can't be certain what people are thinking you can always highlight that concern explicitly when you sense and reflect back people's mood. 'You seem thoughtful, Michael, what's on your mind?', or 'I'm not certain I made that point very well, what was the muddiest point for you?' In this way you are acting as the director of the audience, encouraging them to open up and reveal their thinking to you.

Because of the possible confusion between this definition of script and the idea of a hardcopy script or a screenplay we prefer to use the term *improvization*, though some might quibble. 'Improvization means being completely unplanned', we have been told. 'We could not countenance improvization in this organization', others say to us. Actually, the best improvizations *are* tightly planned. They follow extremely detailed rules of their own. In theatrical terms, for instance, improvization has many different rules that govern how to get the best out of teams and people.[16] In the engineering sense, improvizing a solution involves making something new and different out of the materials to hand. This is creativity at its best, which often teaches us something about innovation and about leadership.[17] Jazz improvization has very clear rules about what can and can't happen.[18] No, we are quite comfortable with the idea of improvization as an element of *Leadership Unplugged*.

Staging or Stage-Managing

Some readers may be uncomfortable with the idea of stage-managing a performance. But we see this as a vital planning and preparation phase. Not only must we plan for the meeting or other business event, in terms of a set of PowerPoint slides or the most up-to-date Excel spreadsheet, the concept of staging reminds us that we need to give some attention to other logistical elements – such as the venues or settings involved, and the props or physical symbols relating to our message. Our physical appearance and grooming are important symbols, too. How much effort should it take to prepare, and how conventional or unconventional are you? What about the venue or performing space you occupy – is it fit for its purpose?

Performing *Leadership Unplugged*

When watching senior executives in their roles it is usually quite straightforward for peers, employees and other stakeholders to assess and decide what the senior executive is doing, intentionally or unintentionally. It's important for senior executives to realize that they cannot pull the wool over the eyes of their different audiences. This is worth remembering because we have found that the performance of senior executives can be described in terms of four substantive categories:

1. role modelling or exemplary behaviour (where executives are trying to be an example on their own terms, not necessarily that the behaviour is exemplary according to some notional high standard)
2. promotion – of the organization's cause, of their own vision for the organization or of themselves
3. intimidation – where executives attempt to use their positional authority to assert their will
4. or ingratiation – where executives attempt to gain the favour of others in exchange for some benefit to themselves.

In our experience, as soon as stakeholders have found that executives are using the classic stick or carrot techniques – intimidation or ingratiation – they tend to withdraw their respect and trust. In fact, because today's stakeholder audiences are well used to seeing executives 'perform', they are attuned to insincerity and tend to discount blatant self-promotion. These forms of leadership are very focused on the short term and are intended to deliver rapid results, but neither builds long-term loyalty. Instead, audiences seem to prefer the less selfish approach of executives who genuinely put the organization first, and whose behaviour is credible and involves an element of self-sacrifice.

Promoting the vision of the organization can involve articulating one's own view of the future, but it appears to have much greater impact with both internal and external stakeholders when executives promote the vision of the company as devised and described by the organization itself. This supports the theme of opinion reflection, which we explored earlier in discussing the preparation of opinion columns by writers who are actually articulating the opinions of their audiences.

In a way, this reflects the distance that senior executives have travelled – away from peddling their own vision or view of the organization's strategy towards a point where they are able to support and articulate the vision of the organization as defined by the organization itself. This is reaching the point where the senior executive has internalized and adopted the organization's sense of itself and its own identity. This contradicts much of the leadership research that focuses on the communication of vision by senior executives. We believe that, unlike the leader or senior executive persuading the organization of the validity of his or her vision, the more successful communicators of vision are able to identify with and encapsulate *their organization's* view of strategy and direction. This reversal of the direction of vision communication is significant. Senior executives may well be articulating a sense of shared vision, but the vision is the vision defined and derived by the organization itself. We'll look at this in more detail in Chapter 12.

Case 19. The Actor's Institute – rehearsing for leadership

Taking time out from the Actor's Institute just off New York's Broadway one of the directors, Gifford Booth, prepares for another session with a corporate client. In recent years the trend for business executives to call on the Institute for help in rehearsing for leadership has accelerated. Why? And what can executives possibly get from the Institute, which started life putting people on the stage?

Business executives, says Booth, are no different from actors. They are people with a vision and an audience they need to relate to. The problem arises when business executives do not realize that they need to build and nurture that fragile relationship. He relates the increasingly familiar story of a PowerPoint presentation. 'One client had been giving hour-long presentations with 60 or 70 slides. They were basically just reading the text that appeared on the screen. No relationship was formed with the audience. What we've done with them is take away the slides.'

Taking away the crutch provided by the computer means executives are forced to face the reality that it's people they face in an audience, not just a projection screen. The message is plain. 'You have to talk to them.' And to be truly effective you have to be a real person, says Booth, talking sincerely about issues that matter. But what does it mean, to be a real person?

'Even if you have an audience of one, in a face-to-face meeting you are not looking forward to, for example, the person you're facing needs to feel and to hear that you yourself are really there. That the meeting isn't a farce, that you're not pretending.' For Booth, being real is about believing what you're saying and how that affects the rest of your performance. 'Most everything about the performance of leadership is below the neck', he says.

There's a problem here, though, isn't there? Some executives think 'performance' and 'acting' are nothing but pretending. Pretending to be something else or someone they're not. 'Absolutely, and that's why we spend so much time with people talking about their material, what they want to communicate.' Without being involved in the material,' says Booth, 'no communication can follow and no relationship with an audience can develop. Most people get the idea of a relationship with the audience intellectually, but they don't understand it, they don't get it until they try it over and over.'

It's a question of logic versus emotion, initially, as the Actor's Institute team help people appreciate that sincerity comes from being human, fallible and – sometimes – vulnerable. 'Until I as a member of the audience sense that your personal platform, what you're talking about, means something to you, then I don't buy it. You only get my attention when I feel that you are authentic. And this is uncomfortable for many executives.'

Imagine a hostile room, where you have to deliver harsh news. Most executives see the situation as one requiring a monologue, to be delivered as quickly as possible. A sequence of words, delivered without meaning. Some executives see the situation as a scene where the presence of different actors must be acknowledged, but still with the sense that it will soon be over. Still other executives begin to appreciate the scale of what's talking place. That the scene is only part of a larger play, and that everyone in the room has a character that will live on after the scene in close or distant relationships with them.

So we help people by asking them what is it they are trying to cause or achieve? Is it acceptance of a message? Is there an agreement to be struck? And we remind them again and again to strike up a relationship with the audience. And sometimes this is not at all comfortable.

So how do you build a relationship with an audience, even an audience of one? What are the skills you need? 'First it's about listening to people – what they say and what they don't say. Then there are physical cues. The eyes. Physical traits. More widely there is an energy, a quality in the room that you can begin to sense when you've experienced enough of life and can learn from that experience.' It's only in part about the words you use. 'People get too hung up on the script, sometimes. We also help them to let go of the script and of the control they generally like to have. It's a comfort thing', he says.

Perhaps letting go of the need for control represents the biggest hurdle to overcome.

It feels like surrendering, but acceptance of the reality of the situation, that it's your audience that has control, actually brings a huge sense of relief. In a strange way you become more confident in yourself and that's when the authenticity comes back. You've got nothing left, but yourself. This is learnable, but because it's a set of new experiences we have to learn from it takes time.

Booth describes the process as rehearsing for leadership. Instead of pretending we're fully fledged, fully formed and perfect leaders, he says, we should rehearse more, think it through, try it out. And the idea of continuous rehearsal, continuous improvement, is nowhere captured better than in the words of the playwright Samuel Beckett. To one poorly performing actor Beckett said: 'No matter. Try again. Fail again. Fail better.'

Questions:
1.   What do you think it means to perform leadership? How can you ensure peak performance? Is it possible always to perform at or beyond peak levels? (If so, how? If not, why not?)
2.   What do you think are the most important signals your audiences give to you? Can you classify or describe them? What are the signals indicating that an audience wants something different from you?
3.   How can you learn more about how you perform leadership? Who can you learn from in the organization about performing or rehearsing? What do you think it means to improvise, and when might it be useful for you as an executive to engage in this process?

Performing Leadership: Who is the Audience?

In closing this section on the performance of leadership, it's worth attempting to settle a key concept that has great meaning for us. Unless and until senior executives have a clear sense of who they are and what they stand for, their attempts to lead through communication are doomed to failure. Executives must be authentic and sincere in what they are trying to achieve. Some people might suggest that thinking about leadership as performing – as acting – is at odds with this view, and that because acting is about pretence and deceit it cannot help senior executives to be authentic and sincere. We disagree, but it's taken us many years to figure out how to explain this. Most recently, working with the Actor's Institute has helped us to see that acting is not simply about learning the lines and using the tricks of the trade to lie convincingly, or to manipulate the minds and emotions of our various audiences. Acting is about being oneself in another role.

> Never lose yourself on stage. Always act in your own person, as an artist. You can never get away from yourself. The moment you lose yourself on the stage marks the departure from truly living your part and the beginning of exaggerated false acting. … Always and forever, when you are on the stage, you must play yourself. But it will be an infinite variety of combinations of objectives, and given circumstances which you have prepared for your part.
>
> Constantin Stanislavski[19]

We believe that by approaching leadership or the performance of our daily business as drama or theatre, we can gain useful insights into the level of detail we need to go into to make leadership behaviour work for us. Performing or acting is a way of being ourselves – a philosophy of self, if you will – that can help us on a broader stage. And we want to close this chapter with a reminder that although we've been discussing performance we are very much concerned with performing, with performance as a verb. This is because it is the process of performing that is most valuable, not the outcome of the performance itself. In the words of Augusto Boal:[20]

> I believe it is more important to achieve a good debate than a good solution. Because in my view, the thing which incites the spect-actors into entering into the game is the discussion and not the solution which may or may not be found. … Debate, the conflict of ideas, dialectics, argument and counterargument – all this stimulates, arouses, enriches, prepares the spect-actors for action in real-life.

And does performing ever end? No, says Boal. Never. Not if its purpose is change. The objective of the theatre of change is *not* to close a cycle, generate a catharsis or end development. 'On the contrary, its objective is to encourage autonomous activity, to set a process in motion, to stimulate trans-formative creativity, to change spectators into protagonists.'[21] And this is where we believe the real leap of faith has to happen. For senior executives are not the actors on the stage of our organizations – they are the audience.

Senior executives start programmes of change by telling a story, but must end their performance by performing as an audience themselves. By listening and handing over responsibility for the performance of the action to the organizational spect-actors. Purged of all preconceptions, senior executives must play, must *be*, involved members of the audience. Through involved listening they must assist others, and prompt others to articulate their views and perform their thoughts and actions. If executives are to lead through others they need to learn how to behave like an assisting audience. Because if everyone were an actor and there were no audience, no performance would take place. After all, actors on their own are just rehearsing.

Finally, acquiring the tools and techniques of performance represents an important stage to go through in learning how to become a powerful audience. But there is a dangerous moment on the journey when you begin to think that the tools are all you need. Raymond Chandler, the American author of detective fiction, was also an articulate critic of the genre and he spotted this threat for writers of crime fiction:[22]

> Everything a writer learns about the art of craft of fiction takes just a little away from his need or desire to write at all. In the end he knows all the tricks and has nothing to say.

To be truly powerful in performance you must know what it is you want to say and – in time – to realize that the best performance is actually that where you play the role of audience. Patricia Hodgins, a colleague from London Business School, tells of the time she met Bob Galvin, charismatic director of US chipmaker Motorola. She had so much to ask him about his experience of leadership and of building the Motorola empire, but he was not interested. 'Tell me about you', he said.

Conclusion

The key points we want to remind you of at the end of this chapter are:

- Knowing what the audience needs and wants is the first pre-requisite of *Leadership Unplugged*.
- It is the structure or pattern that communicates and is memorable, rather than the detail of what you say.

- Promoting the organization's vision of itself has more impact than peddling one's own vision, no matter how much support you think your vision has.
- Writing and speaking are forms of performance – be authentic and sincere in both.
- Assertive forms of language allow you to disagree constructively in public.
- Leadership behaviour is a series of performances, rehearsals or improvisations – it is not pretence, manipulation or deception.
- The goal of senior executives is to become an involved audience, helping others to articulate their point of view and coaching others to high levels of performance.

QuestionBank

Take time out to answer these questions.

1. How much do you appreciate that every word you say, and every action, is in fact a performance and that everyone around you is the audience? How comfortable are you with the fact that you live your business life almost entirely on stage, in full view of your stakeholders? Are you conscious that different stakeholder groups require different performances, or do you prefer to play your leadership role the same way for every group?

2. How much do you appreciate the issue of authenticity – that people believe you if you sincerely believe what it is you're saying and doing? What does authenticity mean for you? Are there moments when you do not believe what you are doing? How do you personally cope with this situation? How do you think your stakeholder audiences react to you when you are, literally, insincere?

3. How do you coach those around you in the performance of their leadership duties? How capable are your peers of delivering their messages sincerely, believably? What else can you do, or how else might you learn, to perform even more effectively as leaders on stage?

4. How can you encourage more active listening on the part of your different stakeholder audiences? How can you engineer audience participation in the day-to-day realities of your organization?

Notes

1. Boal, Augusto, 1992. *Games for Actors and Non-Actors*. London: Routledge, p. 211.
2. McCloskey, Donald, 1994. How economists persuade. *Journal of Economic Methodology* 1 (1), pp.15–32.
3. Stanislavski, Constantin, 1950. *Building a Character*. London: Methuen, p. 111.
4. Quoted in Briggs, John and Peat, David, 1999. *Seven Life Lessons of Chaos – Spiritual Wisdom from the Science of Change*. New York: Harper Perennial.
5. The loose writing of journalistic leader articles that make indecision an art form was lampooned gloriously in Howard Brenton and David Hare's 1986 play *Pravda*, in which Anthony Hopkins played a tyrannical newspaper proprietor (London: Methuen Books).
6. McCloskey, op. cit.
7. Atkinson, Max, 1984. *Our Masters' Voices*. London: Routledge.
8. Atkinson, Max, 2001. Mere rhetoric? In Brack, D. and Little, T. (eds), *Great Liberal Speeches*. London: Politico, pp. xxx–xxxv.
9. Ibid.
10. Ibid.
11. Westley, Frances and Mintzberg, Henry, 1989. Visionary leadership and strategic management. *Strategic Management Journal* 10, pp. 17–32. A seminal paper on leadership and strategic management as drama, this is still widely quoted by scholars today and has yet to be bettered.
12. Brooke, Peter, 1968. *The Empty Space*. London: Penguin Books, p. 156. Brooke's superb exploration of theatre applies equally well to organizations and their audiences as to audiences and the theatre.
13. Fairhurst, Gail T. and Sarr, Robert A., 1996. *The Art of Framing*. San Francisco: Jossey Bass.
14. Ibid.
15. If you want to explore these issues further, read Erving Goffman's 1959 classic *The Presentation of the Self in Everyday Life* (New York: Doubleday).
16. There are hundreds of techniques and games for creating situations for improvization, for example, in Keith Johnstone's 1999 collection *Impro for Storytellers* (London: Faber & Faber).
17. The improvization that NASA engineers engaged in to create an airtight hose to keep the astronauts of the stricken Apollo 13 spacecraft alive, using only the materials in the lunar module and command module, is a case in point. Cooper, Henry S.F. Jr., 1972. *Moonwreck*. St Albans: Panther Books, pp. 88–9.

18. Hatch, Mary Jo, 2002. Exploring the empty spaces of organizing: How improvizational jazz helps redescribe organizational structure. In Kamoche, Ken, Cunha, Miguel Pina E. and Vieira Da Cunha, Jãoa (eds.), *Organizational Improvization*. London: Routledge. In a number of papers, including this recent one, Hatch has memorably explored jazz improvization as a metaphor for organizational improvization.

19. Stanislavski, Constantin, 1936. *The Actor Performs*. London: Methuen, p. 177.

20. Boal, op. cit., p. 230.

21. ibid, p. 245.

22. Chandler, Raymond, 1950. *Pearls Are A Nuisance*. London: Penguin, p. 9.

CHAPTER 10

Dialogue: Leading With Emotion

As emotional arenas, organizations bond and divide their members. Workaday frustrations and passions – boredom, envy, fear, love, anger, guilt, infatuation, embarrassment, nostalgia, anxiety – are deeply woven into the way roles are enacted and learned, power is exercised, trust is held, commitment formed and decisions made. Emotions are not simply excisable from these, and many other, organizational processes; they both characterize and inform them.

Stephen Fineman[1]

Psychologists think of motives in terms of what individuals want, and of social motives as responses wanted from others. This is part of the story of affiliative or intimacy motivation – people want to be liked. But it is more than this, especially for those ... who are seeking a close relationship. Much of the behaviour associated with the affiliative drive requires co-operation: that is, it takes two (or more) to do it – as in dancing, tennis, sex and conversation.

Michael Argyle[2]

Our artistic emotions are, at first, as shy as wild animals and they hide in the depths of our souls. If they do not come out spontaneously you cannot go in after them. All you can do is to concentrate your attention on the most effective kind of lure for them.

Constantin Stanislavski[3]

Headlines

While people can and do make rational, logical arguments about their actions and intentions, we are fundamentally driven by our emotions.

Emotions or emotional responses are triggered by events or interruptions that change the direction in which we were moving. For most people, managers are the cause of these interruptions.

Emotions are a state of mind caused by someone or something and they change the way we see that thing or person, often permanently.

Emotions such as anger, fear and joy are very real for the person experiencing them and it is extremely hard, if not impossible, to make them dissipate – they simply seem to fade over time.

Each of us is living in a stone-age body, wired and motivated largely by instinct – understanding how we react to the opportunities and threats of modern business life can therefore be extremely helpful for managers at every level.

It is possible to assess and evaluate our own emotions and the emotions of others. Different people have different abilities in this field, which is known broadly as emotional intelligence.

When someone experiences an emotion it means something – skilfully engaging them in conversation can help them identify what it means, and what the implications of this are.

Conversations that Matter

There are two myths that are detrimental to leadership development in almost all of our organizations today. The first is that most successful executives became successful because of their success in their job function, with their concentration on The Task, and in their focus on the bottom line. For the task-focused manager, the increasing short-term focus of the post-internet economy is a boon as the markets and other stakeholders seek to minimize risk and keep the phrase 'return on investment' uppermost in everyone's minds. In this worldview no successful executives care about people for any reason. Why should they? The important thing, always, is to maximize return.

On the other hand – goes the second myth – the managers of the first myth have forgotten how to deal with the fact that their people are people, and that their behaviour is fundamentally governed by their emotions. The implications of myth number two are that if a leader or manager understands better how emotions matter to people in different contexts, and the implications of the way humans are wired for emotions, the better he or she will be able to understand, work with and even manage those people. The important thing to remember here, suggests this view, is not the task itself but the fact that returns will come as a result of more people being motivated to meet more of the organization's targets.

Unfortunately leadership development has tried to steer a course between these two extremes – at one moment favouring a task focus, at another favouring humanistic development ideals. Occasionally some liberal organization promotes a compromise or balance between the two poles, but this doesn't seem to work either. We don't know how to tread the path between the myths because it's a compromise too far. We don't know how to value both the outcome *and* the people involved equally highly. Across many organizations, many people pay lip service to the mantra of a shared task–people focus but, in all honesty, firms can't seem to do it at all well. And it's nigh impossible to teach. Our view is that in striving for the compromise people are trying to do the two things – to focus on task and person – simultaneously.

Instead, we propose the *Leadership Unplugged* approach, which is about doing one thing only. And the one thing we believe senior executives should be doing to get the organization moving and keep it moving is listening. For some this seems simplistic, but the whole philosophy and practical content of this book is about listening, in one way or another. It certainly is not simple. No, the implication of what it means to listen has not yet been explored or accepted by enough managers in business. In our view, for leaders to listen means they must be involved in a wide range of conversations. Further, it means they must listen not only to the actual words people are using, but also to the emotions they are experiencing. Ross Rynehard of Change Australia described this to us as 'listening to what people are feeling'. And if we begin to articulate a view of leadership behaviour as listening, we must once and for all quash the myths of task- versus people-focused leadership. Leadership is neither about an exclusive task focus, nor is it behaviour geared exclusively to the understanding of people's feelings. Leadership behaviour, instead, is about engaging in different forms of conversation at different times and with different goals in mind.

If we begin to accept that leadership behaviour is about listening, then dealing with the motivations of different people and with their emotional states becomes a relatively straightforward task, whatever the context. That task – leadership itself, if you will – becomes that of engaging people in conversations that matter to them. Engaging in meaningful conversations may be difficult and – sadly – far too few executives are willing or able to engage in perhaps the most difficult conversations of all, those related to people's concepts of themselves and their innermost thoughts and beliefs. But we must. Senior executives must be able to deal with the raw emotions and feelings of people, whether their superiors, subordinates or external stakeholders. And they must be strong enough to disclose some of their own hopes and fears. Disclosure breeds trust. Also, a degree of believable vulnerability is essential. If you're asking followers to engage in dialogue with you on issues that matter to them, you must be willing and able to listen deeply

to what they say and to how they say it. You must be willing to reveal some
of your own doubts, fears and uncertainties, too. It's in this final phase of
Leadership Unplugged that we call dialogue when conversational partners
are most likely to change their stance and beliefs, as they find out what it is
they actually think and what they are prepared to say. And sometimes you
may change your mind, too. If the conversation matters.

The rest of this chapter explores emotions in organizations, and the
recent arguments over the existence of emotional intelligence as a key indicator of success in leadership. When you're through we hope to have
convinced you that it is no wonder that so many executives shy away from
the emotional aspects of leadership: it is personal, powerful and unpredictable. We also hope to convince you that this doesn't mean you can
ignore it. Conversations about emotion matter.

The Myth of the Task-Focused Manager

Most executives reach the top of the tree because they are successful at carrying out tasks and at meeting financial targets. They may well have good
people skills – they may be good at involving staff in discussions, seeking
their opinions, handling the organizational politics. As they climb their way
up through the branches, however, the tasks become more complex. The
ultimate goal is still to improve the bottom line, but the ways of achieving
this can seem indistinct or hidden. Other executives and members of staff
don't seem as committed to the goal, make too many mistakes or don't
behave as we expect them to. And we cannot easily figure out why.

All too often, business leaders have forgotten – or maybe they never
knew – how to handle one of people's most significant motivators, sources
of inspiration and inhibitors. Their feelings and emotions.

You may believe that it's up to individuals to cope with their own
emotions, and that you have more important things to deal with. However,
you are taking a great risk if you ignore the emotional side of business. You
are turning your back on something that has a fundamental impact on your
bottom line – not through a one-off cost-cutting exercise or a one-off
increase in the marketing budget, but on all aspects of your business.

Emotions tend to surface in the most difficult conversations of all – those
related to people's innermost thoughts and beliefs. You must be able to
listen to what other people say and how they are saying it. As we shall show
in this chapter and the next, it is during these uncomfortable dialogues that
people are most likely to change – change their views, attitudes, and
beliefs. You must therefore be able to deal with the emotions of those you
are talking to, whether they are your superiors, peers or subordinates. This

is where the potential of your business will be unleashed. And it is worth reiterating that since engaging in dialogue is the best way of helping others to change, you are likely to be changed by it too.

Emotion as a Smokescreen

Most businesspeople recognize that workers have emotions. The anger of a workforce at a smaller-than-expected pay rise can provoke industrial action. Their pride in their work can be used to improve productivity or innovation. At Dana Corporation, the auto parts manufacturer based in Ohio, the workforce was encouraged to submit ideas – two ideas were sought each month from each employee. The firm had 48,000 employees worldwide in the late 1990s. Southwood J. Morcott, who was CEO until 1999, believed – somewhat unusually for a leader in the 1990s – that people were not necessarily motivated by financial reward.[4]

> Suggesting ways in which the company can continuously improve gives people a powerful sense of contributing to Dana's success and enhances their personal growth, pride in their work, and the feeling of truly making a difference.

This emphasis on 'sense', 'pride' and 'feeling' shows the 'positive' emotions that can be encouraged in the workforce.

It is also generally recognized that 'negative' emotions that can be engendered among employees. For example, W. R. Grace, the industrial conglomerate, apparently set out to upset staff with a new incentive plan introduced in the 1990s. J. P. Bolduc, then chief executive, wanted to end the tradition of regular salary increases and predictable bonuses:[5]

> We told people we wanted to differentiate between the performers and non-performers. We wanted to reward and motivate the performers. We also wanted to be fair to the non-performers by assuring constructive feedback and adequate training opportunities were available. But, in the final analysis, we wanted the non-performers to understand the new value system. We wanted them to salivate to get what the performers were getting, and after all that, if they couldn't or wouldn't perform and accept the new culture, then they ought to leave, because this was not the culture they were going to be happy with.

Bolduc's emphasis appeared to be on improving, or weeding out, what he called the 'non-performers'. He set out to do this by exploiting the workers' fear ('Will they think I'm a non-performer?'), envy (at the bonuses of others) and, ultimately, misery (making it clear they would no longer be 'happy' at Grace). Workers were construed as emotional beings and the levers of emotion were used at Grace to effect change.

However, it's perhaps not surprising to note that emotions are not seen as the driving force when it comes to the leaders of organizations, as opposed to the employees. Not by leaders, at any rate. Instead senior executives are often depicted as entirely rational – after all, managers clarify objectives, specify problems, and seek and implement solutions. 'This is a comforting picture of the controlling, thinking, manager – able, dispassionately, to sort and prioritize information to the best of ends', says Stephen Fineman, long an articulate advocate of the detailed study of emotions in organizations.[6]

Fineman goes further by pointing out that many theorists still insist that rationality is the supreme human accomplishment, a feat achieved by taming our emotions. But, he adds, what we call rationality in organizations 'is a remarkable facility to present – to ourselves and to others – emotionalized processes in forms that meet "acceptable", "rational" images of objectives and purposes'.[7]

In other words, most of us employ tactics of emotional suppression – keeping our true emotions in check. In Vincent Waldron's words:[8]

Fear. Enthusiasm. Pride, Sympathy. Anger. Delight. Envy. These and other emotions must be detected, manufactured, elicited and controlled as ordinary working relationships are enacted. Just as importantly, leaders and members who are more attuned to the emotional consequences of their actions might be better prepared to participate in ethical and humane relationships.

This picture may be comforting, but it does not depict the nitty-gritty reality of everyday organizational life at all. Such rational acts that there are – those of 'mere' employees as well as senior executives – are invariably influenced, guided or derailed by emotions and cannot, in truth, be separated from them. In the words of Stephen Fineman (author's emphasis and parenthesis):[9]

Sorting priorities and making sense of events are often fraught with anxieties, self-doubt and emotional preferences; our understandings are often (always?) emotionalized. We have 'gut feelings' – what feels intuitively right, good, uncomfortable or uneasy. Our calculative decisions are sometimes at odds with our own, and others' intuitions. We can be emotionally swayed in our choices because of moral pressure – such as the outrage or hurt of others, or fear of reprisal.

Executives we work with regularly tell us that they find the picture of the dispassionate leader making rational decisions a comforting one, and these leaders often pretend that emotions do not exist or do not matter. 'I leave my feelings at the door when I come to work', one senior finance officer told us. But what actually happens, of course, is that people bottle up their emotions. Hidden emotions, however, still have an effect on the person hiding them – possibly an even greater effect as the emotions, and the effect they might have on their thinking and their behaviour, simply become less easy to manage.

The hidden emotions of senior executives also influence colleagues, customers and subordinates around them, exacerbating the problem caused by not having the honesty or courage to face whatever the emotion might be telling them. And this is the crux of the problem – senior executives fear that expressing their emotions, no matter how carefully or constructively, will be seen as a sign of weakness. Compare this with how publicly most managers discuss their ulcers and heart attacks – these are seen as war wounds or badges of office. These opinions must change. And to make that change executives first need to explore in more depth, and in a rational and logical way, what emotion is, where it comes from and how it arises.

What Motivates Emotions?

Before we begin to look in detail at what emotion is and how it is expressed in organizations, we ought to look first at social interaction and the reasons why we participate in it. What motivates us to relate to other people? Most of us spend a good deal of our time in organizations engaging in some kind of social interaction. Why? The main reason seems to be that we get some fundamental personal benefit – for example, to be approved of by or to help others, to dominate them or to depend on them. Research tells us that there are at least seven different drives of this kind, a drive being defined here as a persistent tendency to seek certain goals. Drives are usually the result of previous experience, often from childhood, and some may derive from our own innate tendencies. It is also clear that, in animals at least, the social behaviour that results from these drives is important for the survival of species.

The significant point to make for us as executives today is that, apart from the essential biological drives, all the other drives (Table 10.1) identify either responses from or types of relationships with people. And if this is what truly motivates us in our social interactions in organizations, it is in the expression of these drives that the strongest emotions will be expressed as we achieve our goals or are frustrated in the search.

The effects of and interrelationships between the different drives are complex – the same person can behave in very different ways on different occasions, and we still don't really know why. But while motivation is a huge topic, well beyond the scope of this volume, it is worth exploring in a little more detail. In the interests of brevity we have summarised the key drives in Table 10.1.

Table 10.1 Drives and social motivations

Type	Drive	Description	Comment and observations
VALUES-LED	Other motivations	Including the need for achievement or money, for example, interests and values.	These higher level motivations depend in large part on the interaction between our own values and sense of identity (e.g. 'I believe in ethical investments') and the values and identity espoused by other individuals and organizations (e.g. 'We believe in ethical trading'); uncomfortable conversations at this level affect our sense of who we are as individuals and may be perceived as personal attacks.
	Esteem & identity	The need to have approval from others who should accept our self-image as valid.	
COMPETITIVE	Aggression	The need to harm other people physically or verbally.	Sarcasm and apparently mild banter can be intended and perceived as acts of aggression.
	Domination	The need to be accepted as task leader, to take decisions and be acknowledged as leader by a group.	Senior executives having this drive often find it difficult to cede control to other managers and subordinates.

Table 10.1 (continued)

Type	Drive	Description	Comment and observations
COLLABORATIVE	Sex	The need for physical closeness and sexual intimacy.	For many people work is a place to find short- or long-term life partners; inappropriate or unwanted attention can be difficult to deal with.
	Affiliation	The need for warm responses and acceptance.	Usually from peers, but also with senior executives around the organization; unless managed well this can create the impression of a 'crawling' executive.
	Dependency	The need for protection, support, guidance or help.	From parents, siblings, friends and life partners, but also from people in positions of power or authority at work; unless the dependency is appropriate in the eyes of all parties this can create difficult relations.
BASIC	Biological needs	Eating, drinking and bodily comfort.	For some, the overwhelming time pressures of work can affect eating and voiding patterns leading to stress-related illnesses and poor health; in addition to the illness itself, this may lead to resentment in a wider pool of people.

The key point worth bearing in mind in this brief exploration of drives and motivation is the earlier point about how significant these drives are for us. It is no surprise, then, that when we meet someone who is driven in a different way from us, first of all we simply cannot understand him or her. Second, it is also very confusing when what our colleague needs or wants appears totally at odds with our own needs and wants. This can take place when we both ostensibly have the organization's best interests at heart – we're both on the same side, as it were. The outcome inevitably is conflict, and the conversations around the issue are invariably two one-sided conversations that rarely take account of the other person's perspective.

It's worth noting that these drives, as well as motivating us towards certain goals, act as a source of energy which sustains us on the journey. In other words, the drives are self-sustaining and it is extremely difficult to let them go. It's also worth pointing out that it is usually the process of seeking the goal that motivates us – actually achieving the goal may remove the motivation, or in fact may not satisfy us. One interviewee mentioned her firm's regular acquisition of smaller competitors – once they had been acquired the senior executive driving the purchase lost interest, and moved on to the next acquisition. The motivation, clearly, was the thrill of the chase. So bear in mind that things change over time. What motivated a colleague last week may not be the same today, but it might return next week.

Sometimes, on the other hand, as we get closer to our goal, a greater motivation may surface actually to prevent the goal from being realized. A child seeing a dog for the first time, for example, may want to pat the dog, but as the dog gets closer a fear of the animal sets in and at some point the child halts in its tracks. An individual we interviewed in one institution described his feelings of awe towards an authority figure who had inspired him to join the organization. But that awe kept our interviewee from speaking with his contact on anything but the most mundane and trivial matters, even though there was the possibility of almost daily contact. The fear of rejection had become greater than the need for closeness.

This brief description of the approach-avoidance conflict (Figure 10.1) is one example of the complexity involved in getting to grips with motivation,

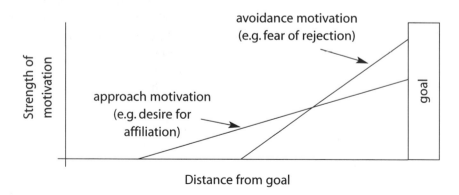

Figure 10.1 The approach–avoidance conflict and why you can't always get what you want

and illustrates well the dangers involved in outlining these ideas in this brief format. The field is huge and we do not intend everyone to become pop-psychologists. The point we hope to emphasise once again, as we continue to develop the central *Leadership Unplugged* theme, is that people are all different and are driven by different things. We can't hope to know exactly what lies behind someone's behaviour but perhaps now, when faced with what appear to be the peculiar actions or statements of a colleague, you may be less afraid of or less concerned about talking with that colleague. Because it is only in exploring the true goals that people hide behind their emotional smokescreen – consciously or unconsciously – that we can move beyond uncomfortable conversations and towards constructive change for the future.

What are Emotions?

Now we can begin to look at exactly what emotions are. We know that many managers dismiss them – and their effects on us – simply because of their intangible and ephemeral nature. 'It's just fancy and whim; an excuse not to get on with the job', one manager told us. 'They can't exist, not really. And spending time trying to understand "emotional people" is point-less.' We can't agree. If the intangible and ephemeral nature of sub-atomic particles hasn't kept nuclear physicists from investing time in practical research, then the scientific research into emotions is equally worthy – if not more so – for practical everyday reasons.

First, emotions should be seen as a state of mind, and they have real meaning for the people experiencing them. Extreme emotions such as fear, joy, anger and love, but also subtle emotions such as suspicion and disquiet, are all accompanied by bodily responses – flushes, increased heart rate and sweating, for example. And science can measure these physiological differences. One interesting question, though, is the matter of which comes first. Is it the emotional response or the physiological? Do feelings of fear trigger the release of adrenaline in the muscles ready for fight or flight? Or are our emotions a response to the physiological changes? Is our emotional response nothing more than a signal to the brain that something's changed and that we've noticed it?

Early research on emotion suggested that this second idea was correct, that emotion was the consciousness of some bodily disturbance. In other words, our emotions were perceived as just another form of behaviour. When, at the end of our tether, we can think of no other way of getting what we want, frustration boils over into anger, and we shout and stamp and throw things. This actually reduces our own stress level, because it's far easier than staying in the conversation and trying to reason a way out of the frustration – a new way that we've never thought of before. You could describe this kind of emotional response as a behaviour of defeat, a defensive reflex.

Other research suggests that emotion is much more complex than a primitive reflexive behaviour. It doesn't appear to explain, for example, why we may react to sudden aggression with anger or fear. And there's a thread of research that suggests that emotions are a more or less conscious behaviour. The conscious mind chooses to have us burst into tears precisely because it cannot or will not pursue a conversation that has become distasteful. In other words, anger with a subordinate – for example – is neither an instinct or a habit, nor a calculated action. It is an abrupt solution to an internal conflict. Being unable, in a state of stress, to find a delicate and precise answer to a problem, anger reduces the tension for some of us. Of course, that anger then may trigger another reaction in the audience.

While this view has merits in explaining why we can have subtle emotions, it largely fails to satisfy us as an effective explanation for why we have emotions at all.

There is a third approach to emotion that blends well with the *Leadership Unplugged* philosophy and approach. This is the conception of emotion as a state of mind triggered by an interruption. Initially we are aware that we are frightened, for example, and it's important to realize that we are frightened of something. Indeed, the emotion is triggered by and becomes fixated on that 'something'. Or someone – a manager, a subordinate or an important shareholder, for instance. The emotion feeds on the fixation and is either heightened, as the relationship becomes even more tense, or lessens over time as the immediate significance of the relationship fades.

Let's turn for a moment to this relationship we have with the object of the emotional response. Figure 10.2 shows two forms of emotional response. In the first or primary emotional response, the state of mind of the subject experiencing the emotion is intimately involved in the relation-ship with the object of the emotion: 'I hate you' (Table 10.2). The locus of emotion is internal; it is inside 'me', the person experiencing the emotion. The emotion in this instance reflects our attitude – an intensely personal one – to the object.

In the other form, the secondary emotional response – 'the world is beautiful' – the locus of emotion is external. It is out there, in the world. We appreciate the things that make the world beautiful, but our relationship is a symbolic relationship with the whole of the beautiful world. The emotion we feel here still reflects our attitude but it is a slightly impersonal one, hence we call it a secondary emotional response: 'I am touched [primary

Primary emotional response: the locus of emotion is internal, personal and discrete

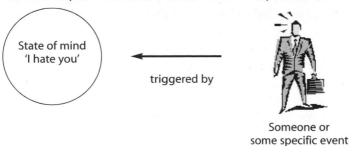

Secondary emotional response: the locus of emotion is external, impersonal and holistic

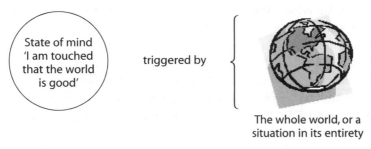

Figure 10.2 The locus of emotion

Table 10.2 Analysing emotional grammar

Traditional grammar	Subject	+ Verb	+ Object	= sentence
Emotional expression	'I ...	... hate...	...you'	
Emotional grammar	emotional subject	+ expressed emotion	+ emotional object	= emotional relationship
	(indicating where the emotion is located or harboured)		(indicating what triggers the emotion	(in this instance indicating the emotion is harboured internally – an internal locus of emotion)

response] that the world is so beautiful [secondary response].' Of course, we may not always be reflecting on the whole world, but we may be reflecting on a complete situation.

In summary, then, the locus of emotion can be either internal (my perception of something or someone) or external (my perception of the world out there – a symbolic perception that the world is good, bad, hateful).

In the next section we'll look at some examples to clarify how this affects leadership on a day-to-day basis.

The Practical Implications of Understanding Emotion

Imagine an individual bringing a case of constructive dismissal against your organization. The individual is experiencing intense emotions, often including anger against an individual or a specific event that prompted their action for constructive dismissal. He or she feels every twist and turn of the case personally – after all it is their job, their profession, their career, their security, which hangs in the balance. The emotional rollercoaster followed by the individual in this situation involves intense and very personal primary emotional responses.

But what of the other employees in the organization? They may not know the full details of the situation but can see their colleague – formerly respected – on garden leave, or coming to work but suspended from daily duty. They see the situation as a whole and feel perturbed, uncomfortable. This is what happens when we hear people say 'the morale around here is low' – they are reflecting on the general situation and are describing a kind of collective secondary emotional response.

If people's emotions are unleashed when things get interrupted, we as managers need to take account of the implications. Will the conversation we're about to engage in become the event that triggers an emotional response? Will we become the ones our stakeholders or employees fixate on? If you take away one thing from this chapter, make it the question 'what interruptions do I as a manager create and what are their implications?' For in every case the problem will be different and the behaviour you need to adopt to minimize fallout, if you wish to, may be different.

Thinking about situations over a period of time you can see a dynamic of planned sequences of activities, interruptions and emotional responses begin to emerge (Figure 10.3). Our people are carrying on their daily lives as normal (at point ①) when we interrupt them (at ②) with news of a plant closure or layoffs. The release or emergence of emotions (point ③) takes place in everyone's autonomic nervous system between the time the interruption is first made and the time when it is removed, or something is

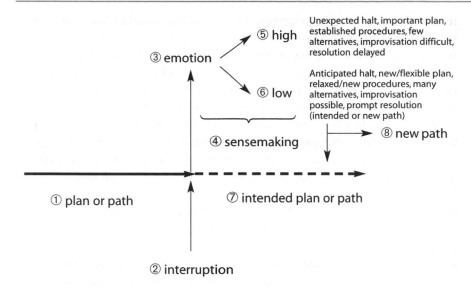

Figure 10.3 Sensemaking interrupted

done in its place that allows the original sequence to be completed. Until the interruption is removed or something else is done the emotion continues to intensify (point ⑤).

If people can tackle or solve the problem in a variety of different ways, then the emotional intensity of the situation is not likely to build much. It may even lessen over time. This suggests that generalists, as well as people who are able to improvize, should be better able to handle the stress of a turbulent daily life. People who are less skilled at improvizing or at problem solving are likely to experience higher levels of anxiety and anguish.

Thinking more broadly about organizations, you might ask where the interruptions and therefore where (and when) the emotional outbursts are most likely to occur. Clearly this is wherever there are managers who have the power (or inclination) to change things or to stir things up. If in practical terms, then, you can describe the dynamics of your organization in terms of interruptions and emotional responses, you can begin to predict where making sense of what's going on will be especially influential as a skillset. Then you can ensure the deployment of emotionally experienced managers at the right places in the organization.

Looking even more deeply at the dynamics of emotional responses, you can expect positive responses (gratitude and enthusiasm, for instance) to occur when someone enables you to clear things up more quickly than you expected. Or when there is the sudden and unexpected removal of an interruption – when a poorly performing superior or subordinate is transferred, for example, or when a two-day offsite meeting few people want is unexpectedly cancelled.

In organizational settings there are many opportunities to trigger negative emotions – by holding things up, or by introducing new hurdles or restrictions, for instance – but there are far fewer opportunities to generate positive emotions. How can you improve the lot of every employee and do it in unexpected ways? Isn't the job of a manager to smooth the path? Sustaining positive emotions in a work group is a task involving prodigious effort. It might be accurate to think it impossible to sustain over any length of time, and to conclude that people always become disillusioned with their managers and leaders.

At a big-picture level, then, it's clear that the emotions we experience transform the way we see our world. When we experience emotions our relationships with colleagues, customers and friends are changed. Most of us change the way we behave or speak in those relationships. Most importantly, we believe implicitly in the new situation, from our own viewpoint. We are not acting or playing a game. And this is why more managers must take emotion and its implications seriously. If the state of mind of our colleagues, peers, superiors or customers reflects the way they see the world then we, as managers, must become more sensitive to emotions in people. At the very least, the fact that someone is behaving 'strangely' should be a big signal that all may not be well. And this is where the concept of emotional intelligence arises. Just how good are we at sensing whether all is well with someone? And what do we, or can we, do about it?

What is Emotional Intelligence?

There has been much debate, over the past decade, over the concept of emotional intelligence. Originally academics developed the concept as a simple, single construct associated with how well we interpret and make sense of emotional information. In this way, it is believed that emotional intelligence is an element of intelligence, in much the same as spatial intelligence or verbal intelligence. Furthermore, as elements of intelligence, they are also associated with learning and growing.

By 1999, the formative definition of emotional intelligence had developed to encompass two elements: the appreciation and understanding of emotions – our own and others – and their appropriate expression or use.[10]

Emotional intelligence refers to an ability to recognize the meanings of emotions and their relationships, and to reason and problem solve on the basis of them. Emotional intelligence is involved in the capacity to perceive emotions, assimilate emotion-related feelings, understand the information of these emotions and manage them.

However, Daniel Goleman and other researchers who have popularized the concept over the last decade describe emotional intelligence as a wide-ranging portfolio of interpersonal skills. In articulating their thoughts on emotions they have also helped many practitioners, as well as researchers, begin to deal more effectively with the issues surrounding emotions in organizations. Sadly, the popularity of this approach, and the apparent ease with which Goleman and colleagues have promoted their

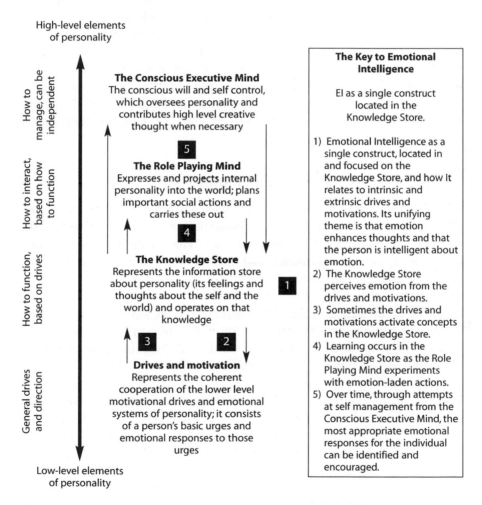

Figure 10.4 What is emotional intelligence, and where is it in our personality?

views and claims, appears to have annoyed many academics. There is, it must be said, limited research data supporting the portfolio view of emotional intelligence – outside, that is, of a host of anecdotal reports and numerous questionnaires that claim to measure it in people. Probably the biggest issue for the academic researchers are the unfocused claims in the press that emotional intelligence is far more significant an indicator of future success than traditional measures, such as intelligence. How can it be an indicator, the research argument goes, if we can't even be sure what is being measured?

Our view is that while the narrow band definition of emotional intelligence, which researchers appear to be able to measure reliably, is perhaps the more accurate and rigorous definition we also welcome the broadband view of Goleman and others. It puts a wider agenda of people-related issues up for discussion. At a time when corporations are cutting back on people development because they don't see an immediate return on their investment, Goleman's popularization of the portfolio view of emotional intelligence is useful and welcome. Yes, it means caution is needed on what exactly is being discussed and assessed, but Goleman and colleagues would certainly welcome that clarity.

Emotions and Organizational Change

It's clear to many researchers that business leaders must strive for emotional awareness – awareness of both their own and others' emotions. Goleman defines emotional awareness as: 'The recognition of how our emotions affect our performance, and the ability to use our values to guide decision making.'[11] He adds:

> Emotional awareness starts with attunement to the stream of feeling that is a constant presence in all of us and with a recognition of how these emotions shape what we perceive, think, and do. From that awareness comes another: that our feelings affect those we deal with.

He goes on to describe the way we influence each other's emotions as being like a 'social virus' that we catch from each other.[12] This idea that we transmit emotions – that emotions are contagious – is worth thinking about. It taps into a stream of research on body language and non-verbal communication skills that has no place here, but that is well worth exploring by the interested reader.

One business leader who recognized the value of emotional awareness was Andy Grove, chairman, co-founder and former CEO of Intel. He suggests that executives' emotions determine whether a company can successfully get through a crisis or not.[13]

> How a company handles the process of getting through a strategic inflection point [a point at which the old strategic picture dissolves and gives way to the new, allowing the business the ascend to new heights] depends predominantly on a very 'soft', almost touchy-feely issue: how management reacts emotionally to the crisis.

This is not so strange. Businesspeople are not just managers; they are also human. They have emotions, and a lot of their emotions are tied up in the identity and well-being of their business. Grove continues:[14]

> If you are a senior manager, you probably got to where you are because you have devoted a large portion of your life to your trade, to your industry and to your company. In many instances, your personal identity is inseparable from your lifework. So, when your business gets into serious difficulties, in spite of the best attempts of business schools and management training courses to make you a rational analyser of data, objective analysis will take second seat to personal and emotional reactions almost every time.

Grove believes the leader of a company going through a crisis experiences emotions more usually associated with personal loss and grieving. Any manager undergoing such stress in a business is likely to experience the fairly well-known stages of what individuals go through when dealing with a serious loss, including denial, anger, frustration, depression and ultimately acceptance. This should not be surprising because the early stages of change are fraught with loss, says Grove:

> ... loss of your company's pre-eminence in the industry, of its identity, of a sense of control of your company's destiny, of job security and, perhaps the most wrenching, the loss of being affiliated with a winner.

An example of an entire nation undergoing such an emotional transition in recent years is provided by the whole Japanese business culture. The weakness of the world economy has forced Japanese companies reluctantly to end their deeply entrenched tradition of jobs for life. Toshiba, NEC, Matsushita Electric Industrial, Sony, Fujitsu and Hitachi between them had to pay billions of dollars in severance payments in the year ending March 2002.[15]

Pride in the Japanese way of doing business is apparent in the words of the founder of electronics company Sony. Writing before those rounds of job cuts, Akio Morita's language is gentler than Grove's – he uses words such as 'close', 'cordial', 'morale' and 'affinity' – but nevertheless places emotions at the centre of a successful business. He sees a contrast between the western way of doing business and the Japanese way.[16]

> Americans pride themselves on being rational in their business judgments: the total logic of the American business schools seems to be cold, de-emphasizing the human element. We in Japan see the bases for success in business and industry differently. We believe that if you want high efficiency and productivity, a close cordial relationship with your employees, which leads to high morale, is necessary. Sometimes it is more important to generate a sense of affinity than anything else, and sometimes you must make decisions that are, technically, irrational. You can be totally rational with a machine. But if you work with people, sometimes logic often has to take a backseat to understanding.

What Morita describes simply as 'working with people' is, of course, extremely difficult and necessarily entails dealing with their emotions as well as with your own. It is strange to reflect that this idea so close to Morita's heart derives from a national culture that prefers to save face and to protect the egos of other parties. But, as we have already suggested, one of the most successful ways of coping with emotions is through dialogue, the respectful two-way exchange driven not by talking but by listening. And it is this two-way respect, a dual accountability, that needs to be instilled in firms if the *Leadership Unplugged* philosophy is to take hold.

How Do Firms Prepare Executives for Dealing with Emotion?

Business leaders are all too often unaware of the effect their behaviour can have on their employees, and therefore on corporate performance. People's emotional reactions to particular behaviours in the CEO, for example, can have a serious effect on the company's potential. Keith McCambridge of Whitehead Mann, the consultancy firm that specializes in executive assessment and development, explains how this can happen:[17]

> There are some people [CEOs] who say: 'This lot are awful. I need you to give me some data so I can go to them and say they're awful, because at the moment it's just intuition. So just assess them, will you?' And then we have to do some education, to say: 'Well, we can do that, but we need

to make sure that the individuals know why you're doing this. Would you be prepared to say what you've just said to me to them?' They say 'no' or 'yes' and that's when we start to design the communication process. Where we can, we make sure that people participate in it [the assessment process] rather than being subject to it.

An important point for business leaders to recognize is that even those processes introduced to help executives with their own personal development can be traumatic for those involved. As McCambridge points out: 'It's a stressful process being assessed – even if it's for a development purpose, or with the intent of making you better. It's a hard process for some people to go through – though an exciting process for others.' Sadly this vulnerability is one that some managers are frightened to expose themselves to, for fear of being found wanting in some way. And so the organizations that succeed in developing themselves in terms of emotional character will have a distinctive advantage over those organizations that exclude interpersonal and emotional development of their workforce. Thankfully, there are mechanisms for beginning to develop this aspect of leadership and management and make it less overtly threatening.

Emotional Capability Within Organizations

A researcher at the French business school Insead suggests that in the same way as individuals may have emotional intelligence, organizations may well have something similar. He calls it 'emotional capability'. But this is more akin to a set of organizational routines and doesn't suggest there is some form of collective organizational brain, says Quy Nguyen Huy:[18]

> Unlike emotional intelligence, emotional capability is not innate ... it can be developed over time and doesn't necessarily require a large number of emotionally intelligent individuals in influential positions to make it work.

This concept of emotional capability sits well within the *Leadership Unplugged* philosophy, and it's worth exploring here. Emotional capability is thought, overall, to be driven by three critical processes:

- receptivity – how receptive the organization is on the whole to exploring emotions
- mobilization – how capable it is of mobilizing and using that emotional information

- and finally learning – how quickly and how well the organization can learn about its emotions.

First, the concept of emotional receptivity is related to how willing a person or an organization is to even consider change. It also relates to the continuous sensemaking and sensegiving activities that take place between people in firms. It's a valuable concept because the processes that are needed to trigger radical changes in a firm's fundamental identity or purpose, for instance, often trigger strong emotional responses among people within it. How receptive a firm might be to the change affects not only how the change is seen – positive or negative – but also affects what follow-up actions people take. We know that people act on the basis of their perceptions. Receptivity poses the questions 'How ready are we, as an organization, to deal with whatever business throws at us?' and 'What are we prepared or able to do about the emotional kickback inside the organization that will inevitably arise?'

The flip side of the receptivity coin is, of course, resistance to change. This can be expressed in a range of ways, from moral outrage – leading even to vandalism and sabotage – to quiet cynicism and an unspoken withdrawal of support. These more discreet responses, as everyone knows, can be equally debilitating to the organization, widely affecting morale and performance.

In contrast, the concept of mobilization refers to the concrete actions an organization can take to bring about change. It could also be described as a kind of 'change efficiency' or 'change effectiveness'. It's linked as a concept with receptivity, because the more receptive a firm is the more likely it is to be able to mobilize a greater number of people and resources to bring about change. It has its downsides, too, but more on that in a moment.

The third element – learning – is perhaps the most important, and research suggests that the open expression of emotions in organizations is one of the primary feedback mechanisms that exists. It alerts us to the fact that targets and objectives are not being achieved – or perhaps that they are. In other words, expressed emotions signal that there is a mismatch between the current state of affairs and what we might have expected before. This mismatch in effect stimulates learning and change, even at an organizational level. Like individuals, the organization 'learns' when its repertoire of routines and behaviours has evolved.

Emotional Capability as Debate, Discussion and Dialogue

In a sense, when radical change to the core beliefs and values of the organization are exposed and challenged by us or by others we are operating at the debate level of the *Leadership Unplugged* continuum. In the central discussion phase, mobilization – or the act of getting resources together – may help us streamline what we're doing, but because we've decided what to do it may also stop us looking for more or better solutions. It may also bring an unwarranted optimism that evolves into complacency. All of which escalates the commitment of managers to the status quo. This is why learning, the next element, is so critical. Effective learning processes help us spot mistakes early on and to rectify them before they become insurmountable. Importantly, when we're engaged in learning we're involved at the dialogue end of the spectrum. This is critical for the unplugged manager or leader because being open to possibilities helps us to address, and eventually to deal with, the perceived uncertainties of the future. A potential problem for those of us who want to engineer learning at the organization level is that many managers tend to see learning and reflecting as a waste of time, a drain on resources and as fundamentally opposed to efficiency. This may explain why many managers, on a daily basis, prefer not to develop their people because it takes their eye off the current task, which will always remain bringing in the business today.

Challenging Our Sense of Self: Uncomfortable Conversations

Understanding emotions and the impact they have on day-to-day business life is fundamental to understanding the basic challenges that change can pose to a firm's core purpose and its very identity. If identity is defined as those characteristics of a firm that are core, enduring and distinctive, then a deep change in core identity potentially requires simultaneous changes in all of an organization's structures, systems and personnel. Furthermore, this almost always results in a major and pervasive redistribution of resources and power. In fact, the upheaval engineered by senior managers and leaders often subsequently unseats them. This can be highly disturbing for an organization already beset with problems.

But think about this as a management problem, not as a problem about managers. If people in your organization have emotionally invested in non-negotiable assumptions that shape their thinking about the organization, challenging this source of stability is likely to make them feel attacked personally. And it is this feeling of being attacked personally that triggers powerful emotional defence mechanisms such as anxiety and defensiveness. In other words, we suggest, almost any suggestion of change will inevitably trigger feelings of anger or fear that must be dealt with in some way. An added complication is that if there is no perceived threat, then the people challenging the core identity are considered as outsiders who don't understand the organization. They may be ignored or excommunicated. This creates a tangible atmosphere of discomfort in almost all conversations taking place in an organization.

Now while many managers regard uncomfortable conversations as conversations to be avoided at all costs, because they feel awkward and raise things we would rather not deal with, our suggestion is that it is only when we are engaged in an uncomfortable conversation that real learning and real change can occur. This applies for individuals as well as, more broadly, for organizations. Change never occurs when we're comfortable – change only occurs when our core assumptions about whom we are as individuals or who we are as an organization are shaken. In other words, being engaged in a sequence of comfortable conversations where nothing untoward or unexpected crops up is unlikely to shake you, or make you consider new ways of looking at things or new ways of working. An uncomfortable conversation, on the other hand, can challenge you to reflect on things you would rather not consider, but that are critical to moving forward.

The real skill in handling the emotions of the organization, then, lies in how well and how safely you as managers or leaders can get into or engage in uncomfortable conversations, and how well or safely you can get out again. This also applies to managers in countries such as France, where being blunt is seen as a virtue. It is a long-standing cliché that managers in certain continental European countries prefer not to engage in participative forms of management, and that many are dictatorial and aggressive. Our view is that being blunt and honest is all very well as a starting position or posture, but that it is hardly an effective long-term strategy if it does not build influence for you as a leader. In fact, attacking individuals in an attempt to get them out of the way or to clamber over them because they are weak is not a helpful short-, medium- or long-term strategy. We can be assertive and stand up for our rights, but we must be equally concerned with how we get into and out of uncomfortable conversations. This is a face-saving strategy that builds a degree of trust and signals to managers that it will be all right to support you and to work with you again in the future. The well known but ill-understood tactics of offering constructive feedback are essential here, as are the tactics of disclosure and vulnerability. We'll deal with these issues again briefly in Chapter 11.

Tomorrow's Emotional Research Agenda

There is still much work to be done in the area of emotions in organizations. Far too few management texts, and only very few leadership development programmes, deal explicitly with emotion and its impact on how we manage and lead. Tomorrow's leaders are likely to be exposed to an emotionally sanitized picture of the world of work unless we change the way we view emotions and feelings in the workplace. We could do far worse than simply making appreciation and awareness of emotions in our business relationships a legitimate concern, instead of treating it as inappropriate for the world of work. (See Table 10.3 for some instances of how to increase emotional awareness within organizations.) If we could then begin to help people develop a greater emotional awareness we may be able to come to new emotional interpretations and a new understanding of many traditional organizational and management processes – decision making, layoffs and organizational control, for instance. How do feelings and emotions shape creativity and change management, leadership and communication?

Daniel Goleman argues that emotions are themselves a form of communication – one we can spread between us without words:[19]

> Our emotions tell us what to focus on, when to be ready to act. Emotions are attention grabbers, operating as warnings, invitations, alarms, and the like. These are powerful messages, conveying crucial information without necessarily putting that data into words. Emotions are a hyperefficient mode of communication.

In other words executives who try to keep emotions fenced off, regarding most of them as irrelevant to business life, are missing the tremendous advantages that emotions, properly managed, can bring an organization. Emotional competence requires being able to tack safely through the emotional undercurrents that are always in play, rather than being pulled onto the rocks by them. Engaging in dialogue is one way of piloting through those undercurrents. Not only does an atmosphere of openness make it easier for communication to take place. This two-way channel encourages people at all levels to keep everyone informed, in the difficult times as well as in the easy times. So being more open to the emotional undercurrents in your business is not simply a question of keeping yourself well informed; nor is it a concession to fluffy, feelings-driven leadership. It is a strong business case for strong leadership. Dealing with people is immensely difficult, but without their emotional support and commitment

Table 10.3 Actions that can facilitate emotional expression in organizations

Experience more emotions: The introduction of experiential learning through coaching or training	Creating greater understanding by coaching all members and especially change agents to experience the same or other appropriate emotions in response to others' feelings; then to help them communicate or act on this internal experience
Develop interpersonal awareness: Development of interpersonal awareness or skills training	To improve people's ability to read accurately the subtle social cues and signals we give each other; this can help people to determine what emotions are genuinely being expressed
Find out about human nature: Understanding personality differences	Understanding the perspective of other individuals and why they behave the way they do is a necessary precursor to being able to relate to others
Find out how caring for people counts: Understanding commercial reasons why we need to care for others	Demonstrating a 'caring concern' for other people constitutes a basis for building and sustaining trust and is found to lead a better performance owing to better co-ordination between people and more trust
Offer appropriate counselling: Availability of counselling and other 'listening' interventions	Emotional support structures such as counselling services, self-help groups, team groups helps people in organizations come to terms with new realities
Introduce reflection: Introducing the opportunity for greater personal reflection and regular reviews of learning from projects or daily work	Introducing the opportunity to review projects and to reflect on things that helped and things that hindered (what Chris Argyris calls double-loop learning – learning from the process of what we did as well as from what we actually did) is valuable
Support informal communications: Introducing informal as well as formal communications systems or structures	Firms can establish informal communication structures to foster dialogue and sensemaking during this threatening period; this helps reduce anxiety among stakeholders
Have fun at work: Building a lively work atmosphere	Emotional tension can be released through displacement of aggression; by using the tactics of displacement – for instance, by insulting the objects of anger in safe places or by joking

to the courses of action necessary for keeping a business alive and kicking we may as well leave the steering of our business to fate and the wind.

Conclusion

The key points we want to emphasize at the end of this chapter are:

- Despite what we might suppose intellectually, most people are driven in large part by their emotions and feelings – we need to understand how people tick in order to understand better the impact of their actions and ours.
- Senior executives trigger many emotional problems in organizations as they are often involved in initiating change. We can, however, minimize the aftershocks by understanding the dynamics of emotions in organizations.
- It is impossible for us to 'park our emotions and feelings at the door' when we come to work. Therefore as leaders we need to understand the whole person.
- We can build organizational routines to develop emotional capability in our organizations, by making our organizations more receptive to emotional change and by introducing more organizational-level learning processes. The inevitable conclusion is a more effective mobilization of organizational resources in support of organizational change.
- Exhorting executives to understand the emotions of key stakeholders better does not mean anyone can abdicate responsibility for how they behave. It does mean that we can become better leaders by understanding more about human nature and the impact that we can have upon people.

QuestionBank

Take time out to answer these questions.

1.   How good are you at sensing the emotions behind your relationships with people? How easy do you find it to assess what people are feeling in the teams that make up your organization? How can you become even better at becoming more emotionally aware of what's taking place in your organization? Do you want to do this? Why?

2. How much do you think that understanding people's emotions will affect the way you can manage the organization? How would you characterize leadership in your organization – heavily task focused or heavily people focused? What are the implications of this if you wish to become even better at understanding people's emotions? What do you make of the general state of play as regards understanding people's feelings in your organization, and in your industry or sector? Does everyone behave the same way, for instance? How might this be changed? (Should it be changed?)

3. How do other people in your organization – or in other organizations – manage the emotions of their workforces, in comparison? What can you learn from watching and working with others? Do you want to learn from others? Why?

4. How effective are your management development or internal consulting processes at revealing the emotions of the organization? How receptive would you say your organization is to change? How much could that be improved by your being more open as an organization towards the emotions people are feeling?

5. How good are you at articulating and communicating the emotions of the organization to outside stakeholders? And how much do you know about the feelings of your external stakeholders? Why might this be important?

Notes

1. Fineman, Stephen (ed.), 2000. *Emotion in Organizations*. London: Sage. From the introduction to this volume, which includes contributions from some of the finest current thinkers on the topic.
2. Argyle, Michael, 1994. *The Psychology of Interpersonal Behaviour*, 5th edn. London: Penguin. A classic work on motivation and interpersonal skills, this is well worth re-reading.
3. Stanislavski, Constantin, 1936. *An Actor Prepares*. London: Methuen, p. 191.
4. Interview in Dauphinais, William and Price, Colin (eds) 1998. *Straight From The CEO*. London: Nicholas Brealey, p. 247.
5. Farkas, C., de Backer, P. and Sheppard A., 1995. *Maximum Leadership 2000: 'Add value or get out!'* London: Orion Business, p. 150.
6, Fineman, op. cit., p. 10.
7. ibid., p. 12.

8. Writing in Fineman, op. cit., p. 75.

9. ibid., p. 10.

10. Mayer, J. D., Caruso, D. and Salovey, P. 1999. Emotional intelligence meets traditional standards for an intelligence. *Intelligence* 13, pp. 119–33.

11. Goleman, Daniel, 1998. *Working with Emotional Intelligence*. London: Bloomsbury, p. 54. This articulates a portfolio approach to emotional intelligence, at odds with the single-construct view originally put forward by academics.

12. ibid., p. 164.

13. Grove, Andrew S., 1996. *Only the Paranoid Survive*. London: HarperCollins Business, p. 123.

14. ibid.

15. Suzuki, Hiroshi. Japan's electronics makers may shed more jobs to boost earnings. *Bloomberg News*, 20 December 2001.

16. Morita, Akio, with Reingold, Edwin M., and Shimomura, Mitsuko, 1986. *Made in Japan*. London: Collins.

17. Interviewed for this book.

18. Huy, Quy Nguyen, 1999. Emotional capability, emotional intelligence and radical change. *Academy of Management Review* 24 (2), pp. 325–45.

19. Goleman, op. cit., p. 165.

CHAPTER 11

Dialogue: Listening Furiously

In dialogue people are no longer primarily in opposition [debate], nor can they be said to be interacting [discourse], rather they are participating in this pool of common meaning which is capable of constant development and change.

David Bohm[1]

All human relations should be dialogues: men and women, blacks and whites, one class and another, between countries. But we know that these dialogues, if not carefully nurtured or energetically demanded, can very rapidly turn into monologues, in which only one of the interlocutors has the right to speak: one sex, one class, one race, one group of countries. And the other parties are reduced to silence, to obedience; they are the oppressed. And this is the Paulo-Freirian concept of the oppressed: dialogue which turns into monologue.

Augusto Boal[2]

Listening is only powerful and effective if it is authentic. Authenticity means that you are listening because you are curious and because you care, not just because you are supposed to. The issue then is this: Are you curious? Do you care?

Douglas Stone, Bruce Patton and Sheila Heen[3]

Headlines

All conversations fall into one of three types: debate, discussion (or discourse) and dialogue. The most significant, but the rarest, form of *Leadership Unplugged* is dialogue.

The defining element of dialogue is listening, listening furiously, or listening intently. Listening is the key to understanding and interpretation. The Greek roots of the word *dialogue – dia* and *logos* – suggest 'through meaning'.

> The most uncomfortable conversations are about people's perceptions, their emotions or their sense of identity.
>
> Questions are the key tool to help us engage in tricky conversations in a constructive and challenging way and to help us explore people's assumptions.
>
> Many managers find listening or trying to listen frustrating, but beneath the chaos of frustration it is possible to see order evolving.
>
> In dialogue, senior executives must risk being influenced and must risk changing their minds, too. Senior executives who do not listen, who do not change their minds, hinder the free exchange of ideas and experience.

Introduction

The most significant style or type of strategic conversation is dialogue, and it is dialogue that is at the heart of *Leadership Unplugged*. Sadly, so few managers and leaders ever engage in true dialogue that they never experience what it can achieve, and never experience its power. Some senior executives disagree with us. ('Nonsense, I engage in dialogue with my people all the time.') In our estimation, however, they are often only in the debate phase, exchanging hand grenades that outline fixed and non-negotiable positions. No, our working definition of dialogue is different and we'll come to it in a moment. What we want to do at the start of this chapter, though, is emphasize to you that we ourselves are still learning about dialogue. With every client or research project there is something else to learn about what dialogue is, or how people engage in it. And that's why we offer this chapter as a work in progress, a beta version[4] if you will, on what is possibly the most misunderstood form of conversation. Please tell us what you think.

Revisiting the *Leadership Unplugged* Continuum

To set the context for a closer look at dialogue, let's review how far we've come by looking again at the *Leadership Unplugged* continuum from Chapter 2 (Table 11.1). Remember that conversations fall largely into one of three types: conversation as debate, conversation as discussion (or discourse) and conversation as dialogue. Each has different characteristics and different dynamics. In debate, for instance, participants articulate their positions as being different from, and opposed to, one another. Debate is therefore a strategy of conversational confrontation. The parties do see

Table 11.1 Analysing debate, discussion and dialogue

Phase	Conversational dynamic	Strategic objective
Debate	Telling	Positioning the vision
Discussion	Exchanging	Arguing the vision
Dialogue	Listening	Listening to the vision

diverse opinions, which is to be applauded, but they focus exclusively on the differences between the positions rather than the similarities. Notably, each party regards their own position as superior. Debate, therefore, is a tool for crystallizing opinion, so that people can decide for themselves which version of events is preferable. It is also the catalyst for change, sparking or signalling the fact that change is about to begin.

In the dynamics of discourse or discussion, on the other hand, we break up the agenda of a larger debate and begin to rebuild a different framework around a system of ideas or discussions. We begin to deconstruct a debate and then to integrate different parts of the conversation with different people in the audience. These become sub-debates or discussions. We build links between certain ideas from the debate and we exclude other parts. We start to build links between different ideas or parts of the different debates that make sense to us, and we begin to build links and – importantly – relationships between the ideas and the people whose ideas they were. Some relationships are positive and constructive, others less so. What we also find is that instead of simply discussing our own position we begin to introduce and discuss ourselves, and our feelings, as an integral part of the discussion at this point. This explains why discussions around change and moving away from the status quo are usually such sensitive matters.

The most difficult of our three conversational phases to define, and yet the most important, is dialogue. Our working definition of dialogue, derived from our work with a range of executives from the private and public sectors, is that it is the search for common ground where both parties, often from different sides of a fence, build meaning through conversation. Here we begin to integrate our own self and the ideas we hold with the ideas held by others. Our intention in dialogue is to pursue unity, or the potential for unifying our different ideas.

Perhaps the defining element of dialogue, though, is actually not to do with talking at all, but with listening – listening furiously, or listening as an activity and not as a passive state. The Greek roots of the word *dialogue* – *dia* and *logos* – suggest 'through meaning' or 'stream of meaning'. For us, then, dialogue is a dynamic process intended to help two parties jointly capture or create shared meaning. And this forms the very basis for understanding each other.

There's a further point we need to remember when we're engaged in dialogue, which concerns the timing of dialogue in the sequence of organizational conversations. By the time dialogue becomes possible and necessary we should already have been involved in debate and in discussion with people. This can sometimes help the situation – we know the person we're talking with and have some common, if not shared, ground with him or her – but mostly we believe that the previous conversational contact we have had with him or her has been a hindrance. We have become set in our views of the other party and so are far less likely to engage in tricky conversations, especially if we think the person we are talking with holds opposing views. We are also unlikely to engage in difficult conversations if we know the person – for fear of challenging the relationship and of losing an ally. This combination of fear and risk probably explains why so few of us engage in difficult conversations. This being so, we need clear guidelines and tactics for getting into and out of uncomfortable conversations safely.

The rest of this chapter highlights some of the reasoning behind our belief in the power of dialogue, points to some the necessary skills and explains how they work (Table 11.2). We'll also explore some of the theoretical perspectives behind dialogue and what it means for the *Leadership Unplugged* approach. We hope that this chapter, and the book as a whole, begins to build an argument for a sustained approach to dialogue in our daily business lives.

From Talking to Listening

'Very well', replied M. Danglars, who had listened to all this preamble with imperturbable coolness, but without understanding a word, engaged as he was, like every man burdened with the past, in seeking the thread of his own ideas in those of the speaker.

Alexandre Dumas[5]

We've said a number of times through this book that dialogue is more about listening than about talking. 'Is that all it's about?' you might say. 'Listening? But I do listen. I do all the listening things they talk about in books and on courses.' And often this is the problem. We know and are told endlessly about active listening, using silence, asking questions – so much so that we think listening itself is the solution. That after 'active listening'

Table 11.2 Exploring the key elements of dialogue

Theme	Questions to consider
Listening We need practical tips on listening and to reflect on the outcomes of listening	What are the skills of listening? How do we listen to emotions? (What are the dynamics of emotions and how do they change over time?)
Understanding We need to appreciate the importance of listening for understanding others and ourselves – often understanding someone else helps us understand our own position more fully	What role do disclosure and feedback have in dialogue? How can we learn from conflict and uncomfortable conversations? What role does coaching or mentoring play for senior executives?
Dialogue in organizations Unless there is a clear return to the organization, few managers will set aside time for dialogue	What is the value of dialogue for the organization? Where are the risks to the organization?
Dialogue and questions The role of questions in sustaining dialogue and conversation generally	How can we use questions to sustain listening? How can we use questions to sustain dialogue? When do we get answers?
Dialogue as teaching Teaching as leadership – the idea of the 'teachable point of view'	How far is it possible to teach someone without guiding their learning, without predetermining or manipulating the outcomes they take from the process?
Dialogue and *Leadership Unplugged* How significant is dialogue for *Leadership Unplugged?*	What is the philosophy behind dialogue and what does this mean for the practice of *Leadership Unplugged?*
Renaissance of the values proposition The concept of values – underpinning authentic dialogue and strategic conversation generally	How do people's values underpin dialogue and *Leadership Unplugged?*

– offering perhaps slightly more attention to people than we might have given previously – we can then ignore what we've learned, if we've learned anything at all, and say 'OK, I've listened to you, now it's my turn and I want you to do THIS …'.

The first step towards listening effectively – listening *furiously* – is to stop *not* hearing. This is not as trivial as it might sound. If dialogue is, as we believe, a liberating form of communication in which everybody respects everyone else and their ideas, why aren't more of us doing it? Of course the answer is far from simple, but there is much to be said for unlearning what we do already. When people say to us '… but I do listen to people', our usual reply is that this is not what we have seen them doing. Most people tend to believe that they already are listening to other people in an effective way. It seems to them that the main trouble is with the other people, who are prejudiced and not listening. We can all point to how other people are 'blocked' on certain issues or questions, and usually – without being aware of it – that they are avoiding confrontation over ideas that may be extremely dear to them. Our main contention here, and it's a difficult one for most of us to take, is that we rarely see this in ourselves.

It is essential, then, that we learn to become extremely sensitive to our own blockages and to the issues that are non-negotiable to us. How can we do this? Well, the symptoms to look for are those fleeting sensations of fear that stop you thinking about certain questions. Or – more insidiously – the questions that elicit pleasant thoughts that stop you from dwelling on other, less comfortable issues. While thinking on these issues and subtly defending our own ideas, we are forgetting to listen to or – worse still – we are immediately discounting what other people might have to say. In the words of David Bohm:[6]

> When we come together to talk, or otherwise to act in common, can each one of us be aware of the subtle fear and pleasure sensations that 'block' his [sic] ability to listen freely? Without this awareness, the injunction to listen to the whole of what is said will have little meaning.

For us, though, listening is not an end in itself. Listening is an important tool that acts as a precursor to reflection and interpretation – for both parties in the conversation. Listening allows more serious reflection on the issues that matter to people. This can lead us to a greater understanding of what is happening to people, what facts mean for others, or what their perception of a situation is. Also, listening leads to a deeper understanding of what things mean to people emotionally. This often leads us to reflect on what things might mean for us at an emotional level, too, which is some-thing senior executives usually don't give much credence to. Listening is also essential to help us to understand what these thoughts and feelings – in combination – mean for a person's self-esteem and for their sense of self. And this in turn might cause us to reflect on our own sense of self – both who we are and what we stand for.

With careful questioning then, and by listening furiously, we can begin to hear what is happening at three distinct levels:

- at the surface level of what's happening to the people we talk with, but importantly from their perspective, not from our own
- at the emotional level of how people feel about what's happening to them
- and at the core level of how people feel about themselves – what this all means for their sense of self, or their identity.

Furthermore, these three levels can be explored across three time periods:

- what happened in the past, to bring us to the situation we face now
- what's happening now at each of the three levels
- and what the person thinks will happen in the future at each of the three levels.

And a further, or different, exploration can take place after assessing options for the future:

- What are the most important things going on right now at each of the three levels?
- What are the implications of these things for us, what options do they leave us with or what options do they create for us?
- And what are we going to do now, if anything, as a result of these reflections?

These nine themes are captured diagrammatically in Table 11.3 and to some extent explain why listening furiously, or listening intently, is so difficult – in effect, there are nine conversations going on at the same time. Abraham Maslow captured the difficulty well:[7]

> To be able to listen – really, wholly, passively, self-effacingly listen – without pre-supposing, classifying, improving, controverting, evaluat-ing, approving, or disapproving, without duelling with what is being

said, without rehearsing the rebuttal in advance, without free-associating to portions of what is being said so that succeeding portions are not heard at all – such listening is rare.

If we can do it, though, and begin to attend more fully to what people are saying to us, we can perhaps achieve what dialogue means to do – to build and sustain the relationships that really matter to us. And maybe this is why managers who 'tried listening once' never see an immediate return on their investment. It may be that listening never immediately affects any task or project – because dialogue and listening are not about tasks and projects. They are about relationships. Only with the relationships in place can a return become possible. A word of warning, though. Should a return on the investment of the relationship be forthcoming it will probably be an unlooked-for one. We'll explore this in the next section.

Table 11.3 Nine conversations at once: why listening is so difficult

	Past (What happened to bring you or us to today?)	Present (So what? What are the implications for you or us?)	Future (What now? What could your or our plans be?)
What's going on at a perception level? (What are the facts as you see them?)	Perception conversations		
What's going on at an emotional level? (How do you feel about this?)	Emotion conversations		
Who am I in this? (What does this mean for your sense of self?)	Identity conversations		

Four Conversations about Dialogue

There are many practical descriptions and definitions of dialogue that executives can use as a basis for building or convening their own 'conversations that matter' (Table 11.4). We propose not to delve too far into the logistics and practicalities of organizing 'dialogue events' as there are many books that can allocate more space to this. But there are four theoretical perspectives that we need to unpack, albeit briefly, as we lean on them particularly in framing our own approach. In a sense, none of these perspectives completely captures the pragmatic, down-to-earth nature of what we call *Leadership Unplugged*. Indeed, some readers will mistrust and feel deeply resentful of the blue-sky liberal optimism of some of what follows. But as a set of underpinning values it makes good sense.

David Bohm on Clear Thinking

The British quantum physicist David Bohm spent the last years of his life exploring the process of creating dialogue, which he saw as a way of slowing down our all-too-hasty thought processes. He used the word 'thought' to include what we consciously consider, but also to include the subtle and conditioned non-verbal thought processes derived sub-consciously from our past learning and experience. Interestingly, he says:[8]

> ... with the aid of a little close attention, even that which we call rational thinking can be seen to consist largely of responses conditioned and biased by previous thought. If we look carefully at what we generally take to be reality, we begin to see that it includes a collection of concepts,

Table 11.4 The dialogue continuum

Approximate number of participants	one-to-one	3–12	13–100	> 100
Form of dialogue	conversation	roundtable	workshops	search conference
Practice exemplar	counselling or therapy (Rogers, 1961)	facilitation (Heron, 1999)	facilitation (Heron, 1999) or dialogue (Bohm, 1991)	real-time strategic change (Jacobs, 1994)

memories and reflexes coloured by our personal needs, fears, and desires, all of which are limited and distorted by the boundaries of language and the habits of our history, sex and culture.

It is extremely difficult if not impossible, he suggests, to disassemble this mixture or ever to be certain whether what we are perceiving – or what we may think about those perceptions – is at all accurate. Dialogue, he suggests, is a way of slowing down our thinking and challenging our assumptions in a constructive way.

Carl Rogers on Unconditional Positive Regard

This theme of being constructive is significant for us in our interpretation of dialogue. Carl Rogers, an American psychologist famous for his development of the non-directive or person-centred approach to therapy, many times explored the characteristics of what he called a 'helping relationship'.[9]

> By this term I mean a relationship in which at least one of the parties has the intent of promoting the growth, development, maturity, improved functioning, improved coping with life of the other. The other in this sense may be an individual or a group. To put it in another way, a helping relationship might be defined as one in which one of the participants intends that there should come about in one or both parties more appreciation of, more expression of, more functional use of the latent inner resources of the individual.

Besides this idea of the 'helping relationship', the other aspect of Rogers' work worth highlighting is his view that how people develop and grow in very large measure depends on their own self-concept, their opinion of themselves, and on the way they are treated by others. Positive regard in organizations is today very often conditional. Senior executives approve of their people when they perform above and beyond the call of duty, for example. Miss a big contract, though, or don't do what you're expected to do and soon the positive regard evaporates. On the other hand, according to Rogers, unconditional positive regard is acceptance 'with no strings'. Rogers believed that in unstructured interviews, where clients led the discussion, they would eventually reveal their true self, as well as their ideal self – the kind of person they would like to become. Rogers believed it was his goal as a therapist to facilitate the client becoming that ideal self. Now, we've said before that we are certainly not suggesting every one should immediately become a psychologist. But we are suggesting that the underlying philosophy – of helping others – is one that can inform the way executives engage in dialogue with people everyday. Looking at business from another perspective, if we as senior executives are not helping people, are we not oppressing them?

Chris Argyris on Organizational Learning and Skilled Incompetence

For the last 40 years Chris Argyris has systematically explored what stops people from learning. The problem, in essence, is that we are all unaware of the difference between our espoused theory (or the way we think we act) and our theories in use (the way we actually behave). We are programmed early in life by these unwritten rules and so usually don't spot them. More problematic, however, are the mechanisms we've learned that keep us unaware of the discrepancy. Our dysfunctional theories-in-use, for instance, invariably rely on impromptu evaluations, abstractions and inferences that are several logical steps away from directly observable data. However, once these are formulated we also treat them as facts, acting on them as facts and remaining unaware of our inferential leap. There is no way to detect our error.

Many of us in business share what Argyris[10] called a 'Model I' theory-in-use, characterized by a desire to:

- control situations
- win at all costs
- suppress emotions
- and appear rational.

The conversational strategies we adopt to sustain these positions include attributing motives to others without testing them, and then making evaluations and advocating positions without offering illustrations or examples. There is a story of Argyris at a meeting of the Harvard University Interfaculty Initiative on Mind, Brain, and Behavior which illustrates the point. An eminent professor of neurobiology was talking about the anatomy and physiology of the brain when Argyris said: 'If I wanted to use this knowledge to help some human being be more competent, it seems to me it ain't going to help.'[11] The provocative comment triggered a lively discussion of the links between neuroscience and social behaviour. The story illustrates Argyris' adamant belief that knowledge should be usable, so that people can become more competent. He wants us to make explicit and to question the assumptions with which we maintain the status quo.

This is very much the purpose of what Argyris calls the 'Model II' way of behaving, where we need a high degree of interpersonal skill to help us understand how our own actions inhibit learning (Table 11.5). We need to become less defensive, to inquire of others what is taking place for them, and we constantly need to test our understanding. The reduced misunderstanding that results is worth striving for – it reduces the errors we make in our interpersonal interactions and, importantly, it increases our personal learning dramatically.

Argyris makes the interesting observation that senior executives are actually extremely skilled in many of the forms of communication that we need as executives. We are on the whole skilled at automatic, spontaneous and responsive statements in business meetings. It becomes second nature to us to thrust and parry. And this skilled behaviour makes us incompetent when it comes to challenging our assumptions:[12]

> The unintended by-products are what cause trouble. Because the executives don't say what they really mean or test the assumptions they really hold, their skills inhibit a resolution of the important intellectual issues embedded in delivering [a] strategy. Thus the meetings end only with lists and no decisions.

Table 11.5 The Model II way: thinking and talking more provocatively

	Model I	*Model II*
Underpinning values	To control the situation, to win, to suppress emotions and to appear rational	Directly observable data, profound attentiveness, vigilant monitoring of implementation to detect and correct errors
Conversation strategies	Making untested attributions about others, making unshared evaluations; advocating positions without offering illustrations or examples	Advocacy supported by illustration, testing and inquiry into others' views
Consequences	Miscommunication and escalating error, defensiveness, self-fulfilling prophecy, self-fuelling processes, mistrust	Reduced defensiveness, reduced misunderstanding , reduced self-fulfilling prophecies, reduced error, increased learning

Martin Heidegger on Being-As-Care

In understanding there lurks the possibility of interpretation.

Martin Heidegger[13]

What do we do with our lives and what is our purpose in life? With the aid of a gross simplification let us suggest that for Martin Heidegger, writing in the Germany of the mid-1920s, what we do with our lives is simple – we talk with people and we try to understand them and to unpack the ambiguity of our relationships. Only when we begin to understand people and the relationships we have with them can we begin to make effective interpretations of our own place in the scheme of things. But in the first place is talk. And not only talk itself.

'In the first instance', says Heidegger,[14] 'the issue is one of working out the structure of discourse as such'. If, as we said in Chapter 7, it is the structure of what we say that communicates, then Heidegger makes perfect sense here. Not only do our words communicate ideas or information but the talking is talk *about* something. And this is the more important issue. What do we really mean by our conversation? A statement by a senior executive may be seen as a command, a wish or a demand. Or it may simply be intended to reinforce a hierarchical relationship between the speaker and the person spoken to. 'You must do this because I am more powerful than you.' In general, suggests Heidegger, we create, state and build our relationships with people in our communication. (The memo or e-mail we send to cover our backs, for instance, is a classic instance. It is not what we say that counts but the very fact that we sent it.)

More than the transmission of information, however, Heidegger was concerned with receiving information, and with meaning and interpretation. He was deeply concerned with how understanding is rooted in hearing and the special kind of hearing we need to give to reach understanding:[15]

If we have not heard 'aright', it is not by accident that we say we have not 'understood' … [L]istening to one another … can be done in several possible ways: following, going along with and the … modes of not-hearing, resisting, defying and turning-away. It is on the basis of this potentiality for hearing … that anything like *hearkening* becomes possible. (author's emphasis)

Hearkening, says Heidegger, is that special kind of hearing that understands. And the conditions for hearkening – and therefore understanding – arise neither through talking at length nor through busily hearing something:[16]

Speaking at length about something does not offer the slightest guarantee that thereby understanding is advanced. On the contrary, talking extensively about something covers it up and brings what is understood to a sham clarity – the unintelligibility of the trivial.

If talking at length covers things up, keeping silent can actually reveal things, he says:[17]

In talking with one another, the person who keeps silent can 'make one understand' (that is, he can develop an understanding), and he can do so more authentically than the person who is never short of words.

To be able to keep silent, though, you must have something to say and be known for having things to say. 'In that case one's reticence makes something manifest and does away with idle talk', says Heidegger, distinguishing between the thoughtful silence and the silence of the person who never says anything of importance.

The purpose of Heidegger's work is to establish whether or not there is an understanding 'state of mind', which could – he suggests – be considered as a central purpose or role for us in our lives. He believes that there is such a state of mind, and that there is such a role for us. That role, he believes, is 'to care'. He acknowledges that this may seem far-fetched and theoretical, but argues that care, concern and solicitude for others are what make us uniquely human. Though care is far from a simple concept – it is not a one-off event, for instance – the examples and properties of care constantly emerge. Heidegger argues that if we are ready-to-hand and present-at-hand to listen to and understand others then we are, in essence, caring for them. These are authentic human attributes, he says, and he contrasts them with wishing for things, with willing things to happen and with urges to have things happen, which he describes as inauthentic.

Interestingly, care cannot be selfish, says Heidegger. What we might call caring for the self, Heidegger describes as a kind of conscience. And this conscience he regards as a call to the self to be the best person we can be – to set aside the inauthentic, uncaring things we are or have been doing and to take up the role of caring for others again.

Case 20. Listening in Organizations – the role of the executive coach

Among all the industry sectors that have been in a state of flux in the early part of the 21st century, telecommunications has been one of the most volatile. During the internet boom of the late 1990s to early 2000, telecoms companies were among investors' most popular stocks. When market sentiment turned, however, they were among the hardest hit. For example, in January 2002 Global Crossing became the fourth largest bankruptcy in US history. In April that same year WorldCom, the US long-distance carrier, was beset by growing fears of financial crisis. This led to the departure of chief executive Bernie Ebbers, once 'the most feared man in the global telecommunications industry'.[18] By that time, the company's share price had fallen to $2.35, down more than 95 per cent from its high nearly three years previously.

So how do business leaders cope in such a dramatic environment? The human resources director of one global telecoms company said that you couldn't expect people to be able to cope unaided. Top executives needed a 'fitness trainer' to help them cope with their emotions, he said – someone to whom they could say anything and feel safe in saying it. His solution was to introduce an external coaching scheme.

> People don't wake up one morning and say: 'I'm confident with ambiguity and uncertainty.' You've got to coach them and help them. And I think coaching is a very under-utilized tool. I've got quite a number of people now being externally coached. I think one of the greatest services I can give from HR is not so much to send people away on [development] programmes necessarily ... but it's to have a minder – like a fitness trainer. Because in an ambiguous world you need some reference point that isn't your partner, your line executive, the HR person; somebody whom you feel safe in actually talking to ... you need to look at different coping mechanisms and different development programmes to help people in this new environment.

He went on to explain how the idea of hiring external coaches came to him, and that the idea itself had been born of dialogue with one senior executive when the HR director had helped him get a big job in Europe.

> Executive: 'You know, I'm really grateful to you for helping me [make the move from London to Brussels].'
> HR director: 'How do you feel about it then?'
> Executive: 'Actually I'm apprehensive about it ... but you're just like all the others. I can't even talk to you.'
> HR director: 'What do you mean?'
> Executive: 'Well, look, I can't go home to my wife and say: "Look, I'm a bit apprehensive about this." Because she'll say: "Why are you moving me and

the kids, then, all that way? I mean, are you happy about this job or not?" I can't, obviously, tell my boss I'm apprehensive because he'll say: "Well, do you want the job or not?" And I can't even talk to you, because although you're independent you still orchestrate the [corporate] succession plan, so if a job comes up in America in three years' time and my name crops up on the list, you'll say: "Hmmm. Yeah, maybe – but I remember that last time he was apprehensive."

The HR director reports his decision that 'The greatest value I could give certain people was to bring an outside coach in, so that they could talk to them'.

Of course, such a scheme needs the trust of the participants and has to be confidential, or it won't work. The HR director explained:

The only feedback I would get was if somebody was really ill. We had one person who was so distraught he was heading for a breakdown, so obviously a coach would tell me in that person's interest. The only feedback that I get from the individual is: is the service any use to them? And is the person I've chosen as the coach good at it?

The scheme eventually gained acceptance within the company but this took time, he said, as it was far more unstructured than most other schemes in the company.

People would say: 'What's the process?' And I'd say: 'Well, there is no process. You sit in a room with this person and talk about whatever you want. You can talk about sex, you can talk about sport, you can talk about your family, you can talk about how you're trying to reorganize your work. … They all ask me: 'Where's the paperwork?' And I say: 'Well, there is no paperwork. The only paperwork is, by agreement with you, your CV is sent out to your coach, and I'll sit down with you and the coach and be open and say: this is what the company currently thinks about you.'

The HR director wondered if the value of external coaches in the end was, in effect, addressing loneliness:

I think the more senior you get the lonelier you are, and therefore if you want to be a modern leader and try and develop, it's very often helpful to go to an expert coach outside, who obviously coaches people from other organizations as well.

So What are We Listening For?

Please don't imagine that becoming an unplugged leader, or simply listening more actively – listening furiously – is easy. It isn't. And don't assume it is a change that can take place overnight. If you don't already engage in a great deal of listening, then changing your own behaviour – the way *you* do things round here – *is* powerful, but through those changes we hope that *other* people will change the way they behave and think. But remember that it takes time to change the way people think. Interestingly, one group of professionals that is explicitly taught some of these ideas is teachers. At the Derek Bok Center for Teaching and Learning at Harvard University, faculty members are taught to identify where students are in their thinking by listening to the kind of questions they ask and the kind of statements they make.[19] The aim is to help faculty to teach or coach their students in an appropriate way.

What Harvard reports, after many years of watching, listening to and surveying its students, is that early on in courses students expect their teachers to have the 'one right answer', and they expect this to be given to them as painlessly as possible so they can regurgitate it efficiently in exams. As the students develop their thinking they become better able to cope with a little uncertainty from professors, and can begin to make tentative interpretations of their own when no one right answer is possible.

So key questions for us as unplugged leaders include 'What are we listening for?' Is it the same as what the Harvard professors are listening for in their students? And, equally, when do we know how and when we've heard it?

Fortunately there are helpful guidelines to assist us answering these questions. The intense training undertaken, for instance, by qualitative researchers – analysts more interested in words, images and sounds than in numbers and counting things – suggests a range of things that we can 'listen for'.[20] They suggest we listen for stories and the way people tell them. This isn't easy, as people rarely signpost their remarks with helpful phrases such as 'this is an important story'. No, we must analyse stories and conversations we're involved in for underlying themes, as well as for what the storytellers don't tell us. We must look at the actual vivid words people use and the numbers people choose to focus on – these are all extremely significant and symbolic. They mean something to us, and we use them to try to communicate meaning to others. All this being so, the astute leader needs to listen extremely closely to what people are saying (or not saying) and to reflect on it; to test out different interpretations of what he or she thinks someone is saying.

There are other things to listen for, too, to help us evaluate whether our messages are getting across. Almost 50 years ago Bloom developed a taxonomy of knowledge to help educators assess how effective their teaching and student learning was.[21] The taxonomy can be applied equally well to managers, however, because what we are listening for today is exactly the same. We want to know what people's knowledge, skills and experience tell us. We can also use the taxonomy to help us assess where people are situated along the spectrum and how far they have progressed along it – are they useful knowledge stores, helpful implementers or valuable evaluators? Knowing how far people have progressed along the spectrum (Figure 11.1) tells us how much we should be able to rely on their judgement and leadership skills.

	Level I: Knowledge	Level II: Comprehension	Level III: Application	Level IV: Analysis	Level V: Synthesis	Level VI: Evaluation
What people do	Remember facts, definitions and theories; lowest level of cognitive learning	Translate written material from one form into another, for instance; the lowest level of understanding	Use learned material in new situations using rules, laws and theories	Show creative ability in critical analysis; breaking it down to identify implied meanings, for example	Creatively combine ideas, concepts and rules to produce a unique or original process or output	Judge the value of a process or project using distinct external or internal criteria; the highest level of cognitive learning
What people say	State, describe, list	Select, paraphrase, identify	Solve, predict, modify, process	Discriminate, illustrate, differentiate	Create, design, compose	Justify, criticize, adjudicate

Figure 11.1 Unplugged listening – what to listen for in conversations with people (after Bloom, 1956)

In Search of Uncomfortable Conversations

Why listen? It's a serious point that's worth revisiting. Some clients suggest to us that listening is all very well, but why bother? People invariably hide what they really think and rarely, if ever, change their minds. Better surely just to tell them exactly what we want them to do, though maybe we should give them the best reasons we can for doing it. The problem with this philosophy is that, in our experience, people rarely do exactly what we 'tell them to do'. Furthermore they don't accept our 'best reasons for doing it'. But – and here is the important point – they are not prepared to say why or to give us what might be useful information that might affect our thinking because, clearly, in telling them what to do we're not prepared to listen.

If we were genuinely listening we would begin to hear the areas where conversation ran dry, where people didn't want to talk to us. We'd hear – from the language they used – which issues raised the hackles of our conversation partners. In short, we'd begin to reveal the uncomfortable conversations that prevent us working together effectively. Listening is the first step in drawing up an agenda of uncomfortable conversations that we sorely need to address to move forward. And the ability to zero in on the critical conversations that need to take place is desperately needed in business today. Listening is only the first step. The second step, and perhaps the more important of the two, is to challenge constructively.

Interestingly, the single most useful tool to begin both of these processes – listening and challenging constructively – is the question. Of course the question should vary depending on the circumstances and the context, but the fundamental questions facing executives rarely change. What business are we in? How much change or innovation do we need? And how much control do managers need to have? These and other questions we'll explore in the next and final chapter on the practice of strategy.

Sadly some of these have become clichés, in that the way they are used gives the illusion of listening while being in truth an excuse to air senior management's already-decided 'vision' for the future. Used properly, though, questions are a powerful way to surface, listen to and discuss the assumptions of a broad variety of stakeholders. And the bigger, the more complex the issue is, the more likely it is to involve a wide array of stakeholders. It is not until critical assumptions have been surfaced through one or more uncomfortable conversations that we can identify which are more critical or important to the success or viability of an idea.

In a powerful case study Ian Mitroff and Harold Linstone explore the question of whether to raise or lower the price of a key drug made by one pharmaceutical company.[22] Board-level factions quickly developed in support of both sides, and there was also a faction saying 'Keep the price the same'. The assumptions made by the factions were very different although none of them was actually wrong, and this is the key point, say Mitroff and Linstone:[23]

> There is no way to avoid making assumptions of some kind. Therefore they must be displayed and examined in such a way that they can be debated. *Far better to debate a question without necessarily answering it than to answer a question without debating it.* While we understand and empathize with the need for executives to take decisive action, it is better to delay than to take the wrong actions for the sake of expediency.

Mitroff and Linstone argue that new methods must be developed for systematically revealing stakeholders and the assumptions that they hold:[24]

> Many organizations pretend to do what we have advocated ... but, on deeper examination, they really don't. They certainly don't follow the thorough and systematic job of monitoring stakeholders as we do here. Little wonder why their policies stagnate and atrophy as the world changes.

The Role of Questions in Dialogue

Mitroff and Linstone's new methods, frankly, can be reduced to one single method – the use of questions. Questions are the only real tool that can help us explore people's assumptions and break them down without simply telling people to change their views or just to listen to us.

The way we can use questions to engage in tricky conversations in a constructive and challenging way is worth spending some time over. Our research shows that many people don't pave the way for offering constructive feedback, for instance, but simply barge straight in, giving feedback that the recipient isn't ready for or doesn't want in the way in which it's being offered. Better to use questions to assess whether we might engage in a constructive feedback process – to ask permission. As an expression of goodwill, a simple question such as 'Might I offer some feedback or make some suggestions at this point?' is surprisingly effective, and it is still surprising that so few managers use it. Of course, it can only be effective if the feedback is expressed sincerely, for the benefit of the person receiving the feedback (not for the giver) and not merely as the opening gambit in a point-scoring exercise. Enough has been written about the giving and receiving of feedback elsewhere so we won't dwell any further on it here. A second skill – disclosure – is very closely related to feedback in that it also involves the transfer of new information to your conversational partner. Unlike feedback, of course, it's information about your own thoughts, feelings and motivations rather than about the other party's behaviour. One way to engage in disclosure is to use the same invitation technique to open up the dialogue. 'May I share my thoughts on how I see things, which might explain my position?'

Research tells us that senior executives greatly prefer the didactic, or telling, mode of communication. It also tells us that feedback and disclosure are perhaps the two most critical interpersonal skills that a senior executive can develop. They are memorably combined in the Johari window, a two-by-two matrix devised by Joe Luft and Harry Ingram.[25] The tool plots what we know and don't know about ourselves, and what we know and don't know about other people, on the two axes of the matrix. One use of the tool is to show how, through both inviting feedback on our performance from others and disclosing information about ourselves, we can learn more about our potential and the possibilities that lie before us. Though the Johari window simply and easily helps to explain the value or power of feedback and disclosure, the tool is sadly not as well known or as effectively used as it could be.

As well as trying to detect uncomfortable issues worth exploring in conversations, it is also worth listening for the changing emotions and feelings that people can only partly hide. Using the tools in this book can help us, as managers and leaders, to see that the thoughts and emotions we express instinctively as humans are natural and dynamic – they ebb and flow over time. Furthermore, by sharing these tools subtly with our conversation partners, we can model new behaviours and establish effective emotional dynamics promptly. In a surprisingly short time these can become the norm, 'the way we do things round here'. If, as we believe, it is the unique or distinctive aspects of the way we do things round here that creates and confers sustainable competitive advantage, then very soon we are likely to benefit from a newfound sense of honesty and trust. One managing director of a Hong Kong business unit said to us:

> Since arriving back in Hong Kong I have used the methods in a one-to-one discussion which was always going to be difficult for each of us. I followed the techniques and am convinced the result of the discussion was much better as a result.

The Dynamics of Dialogue

One of the first steps towards achieving a full dialogic reconciliation between people who had previously been at odds with one another is to enable or allow adequate time for people to grieve for the ideas and events of the past. The most common mistake in launching change programmes, for instance, is to start with a new beginning. Actually it should be *endings* that come first, followed by a semi-neutral transition period and then finally the new beginning. The progress of change is most critical, we've found, in the middle transition phase, when individuals feel disconnected from the people and things of the past and yet are still emotionally unconnected with the present. This second phase is marked by a distinct disorientation, where the past is no longer appropriate but the future direction is not at all clear either. Actually it can be seen as a frightening disintegration where everything is collapsing, or perceived to be collapsing. For some people, letting go of what the organization used to be or stand for is equivalent to death and nothingness.

This key transition between the ending phase and the transition phase is important as organization members need enough time to reflect on the past and to develop new perspectives for the future. They also have to come to terms with such issues as what went wrong and why it needed changing before they can begin to think about new beginnings. 'Why can't they just come to their senses and see the reality of today?' one operating officer asked. It is still necessary to explain that people are different in that they see the world in different ways and make decisions in different ways (see Figure 3.4: the *Unplugged Matrix*).

And this is where senior executive listening comes in. First because listening – keeping an ear to the ground – gives you an early warning that there is an issue. Many executives describe issues and people that they didn't hear about or see, problems that blind-sided them one idle Tuesday afternoon. Second, listening to people with an issue or a grievance helps people come to terms with it more quickly, and the fact that business life continues. By listening to what people think of the past and to their thoughts and concerns for the future we give them confidence that their issues, and they themselves, are important.

Bypassing this listening phase and rushing into the next phase of organizational change ignores the mourning and catharsis stages that are so essential for us as humans, and often leads to organizations being paralysed by what's widely known as 'survivor syndrome'. In essence, people are likely to cause us problems when they perceive change in terms of the deletion of things or systems they value, rather than as the addition or development of valuable things.

To benefit widely from the greater sense of trust and openness that increased emotional freedom brings to organizations, there are two things we need to do. First, we must create the ability to express existing emotions freely within organizations, and second, we must gain from colleagues the permission we need to help them explore new emotions. We also must consider our ability, realistically, to achieve this. In short, we need to help people (both inside and outside the organization) to reconcile conflicting views, and to identify with both the new and the passing organization.

To help our people experience new emotions we need to encourage them. Frankly, a number of individuals in our research programme have told us that managers ignore or never see their broad effectiveness, or what they do remarkably well, but that they 'harp on about small details and errors'. In our experience it's much more effective to catch people doing something right and support that – this support then makes it easier to criticize lapses in performance, because there is a sense of balance and scale in the mind of the person being criticized. Even the criticism comes across as encouragement, which helps people to feel free enough to be themselves and to display authentic feelings.

For unplugged leaders, helping organizations to experience emotions is one way to develop greater emotional capability. We need to help members of the firm – both internal and external – to identify the variety of emotions that are aroused during a change programme. Much research shows that as emotions are aired, individuals begin to accept and internalize the issues and to act on a deeper level of understanding.

Many things can be done to help organizations experience different levels of emotions. These need to be handled in a professional and mature manner, however, with a clear sense of commercial purpose. Many people find the very idea of expressing their emotions distasteful, and this will be exacerbated in a tense situation. But it can be done. One participant in an off-site strategy review for a technology venturing organization wrote to us after the workshop to describe her feelings:

> Thank you very much for two days of very interesting discussion and debate that you organized for us last week. I have to admit that I went into the two days with quite a lot of cynicism and, although I hate to admit this, quite a closed mind to the whole event. I must say that I was pleasantly surprised by the whole experience and feel that I gained an awful lot from the two days. I felt that you handled what could have been a tricky and potentially very explosive situation in an engaging and enlightening way. I do hope that this has set us all on the path to change within the business (or at least thinking more positively).

Four months after the workshop this participant described, we wrote to the head of the business unit asking how things were. The response from the business unit head was:

All is fine – not quite stable, but getting there as much as you ever do in times of change. I believe that morale is now vastly recovered and the turning point was quite clearly the strategy workshop. The stem of resignations ceased and, thank goodness, I've got a far more workable structure, with single heads of each unit and a super-capable Operations Manager/COO starting in January. A few hard decisions on the way (rejecting internal candidates), but so be it. I would like to think in terms of another retreat early next summer.

Attending to the emotions people feel – especially during times of change – is crucial. For while change can be exhilarating when it is done *by* us, it is profoundly disturbing when it is done *to* us. Building emotional capability within organizations through interventions such as those described in Table 10.3 is important, then, because emotional pain can become extremely harmful if it is denied or treated as insignificant. And if these programmes are varied – to deal with people's different needs – and if they are made widely available in the organization, the more likely it will be that the intensity of emotional pain will be attenuated.

One of the most dangerous things leaders and managers can do is to dismiss people's emotions as irrational or illegitimate. This almost always drives the bad feeling underground. Keeping emotions above ground helps build mutual respect and sets in train the sharing of hopes and fears among organization members, who become more likely to open themselves up and to listen more constructively to proposed change.

So, in conclusion, what does it mean to listen out for people's emotions and to build emotional experience through listening? It implies attending to many small details and projecting a sense of honesty, fairness, justice and respect for those affected by change. It means truly valuing people's opinions, fears, doubts and uncertainties. It means listening to them and trying to understand them. And – here's the rub – without trying to change them by diktat.

Case 21. Philippa Morrison, London Business School – 'be yourself with skill'

The need to be understood is one of the greatest human needs, says Philippa Morrison, director of the Professional Development Initiative at London Business School. As well as working with academics at London Business School and at business schools around the world as part of the International Teachers Programme, Morrison is also counsellor to an array of senior executives in business. It is this broad experience of listening to and counselling executives working at the edge that prompted us to explore with her what it means to listen professionally.

Listening – or what Morrison describes as 'listening like mad' – is the key to unlocking understanding, she says. But despite how trivial it might sound, listening is no easy task. To be able to listen means investing all one's training and experience in trying to find and feel the dilemmas facing executives in their daily lives.' And sometimes the daily lives of executives can be quite noisy.' There is a good deal going on, in other words, and through careful, non-judgmental questioning she uncovers a lot of information about what's on the minds of senior executives.

'Sometimes this volume of information can itself pose difficulties because you have to weigh all the information. You sometimes don't know what is important and what isn't.' Even the welcome she receives, the social niceties, can reveal to her what we're thinking about – for instance, what is uppermost in our minds. But her task is to listen well and not to dismiss what she hears, whatever the source of that information. Listening gives us data, is her message.

Critics of listening as a management tool sometimes suggest that it is naïve and passive, but Morrison disagrees. 'Listening is an activity – it's about engaging with the real dilemmas that people face', she says, 'and that means facing the whole of human experience. There can be no parameters restricting the dialogue'. This leads Morrison to take issue with managers who describe themselves as being different people at work from the people they are at home – she is adamant that they are not. All of us, however, behave differently in certain circumstances. And the interesting question for Morrison is 'why?'

An intriguing and forgotten aspect of listening is what Morrison describes as 'the impossibility of being a blank screen' when you listen to others.' No one can listen impassively', she says 'and it's better to acknowledge your own intentions, judgements and agendas.' This view explains why Morrison also tackles head-on the executives who suggest we should leave our emotions and personal lives at the office door. 'Don't park your personal lives at the door', she urges.' We are 100 per cent ourselves so we must acknowledge our agendas. We must acknowledge what our concerns are.'

Morrison has a serious warning for executives who might think that they already listen to their people:

Don't think you can change another person by listening to them. Listening to someone is about getting more knowledge out into the open. It's about helping people to realize what is important for them. And what's important above all is to be yourself with skill.

Morrison expands on this idea by suggesting that listening to executives helps them to explore who they are, their values and what they stand for. Part of this listening helps them to clarify their conceptions of what management or leadership means to them and to others. The search is for greater self-awareness through reflection, she says – we should learn from daily experience, by reflecting on it and talking about it.

Morrison believes that those who think that leadership is about telling people what to do have a long journey ahead of them. 'These people have a huge amount of work to do to get people to be heard in their organizations.' But her message is that listening to people, instead of dictating to them, may actually speed up the very things that managers are trying to achieve using dictatorial methods. 'In listening to executives across organizations I find that many finally appreciate what it is they should be doing and take responsibility for addressing those changes. Others decide they may be in the wrong post or in the organization and so they leave.' Listening helps people to be honest with themselves about what they think and what they need to do.

Listening is one of the murkiest and misunderstood skills in the interpersonal arena, she concludes. Not only is it not easy, she says. 'It can be brutal.'

Questions:
1. What do you think about listening to people? How easy is it? What does it achieve?
2. What are your biases and prejudices about listening to others? How well can you relax your preconceptions?
3. Why do you think listening to people might help you as well as the other person?

Balancing the Value of Listening with the Risks

Many managers find listening, or trying to listen, frustrating. 'Why don't they understand?' or 'why don't they just take my word for it?' are common phrases we hear. But beneath the chaos of frustration it is usually possible to see order evolving. Describing what it was like to be involved in listening intently, one participant in a dialogue said:[26]

> I saw that even though I felt I was never changing anybody's mind about anything, I actually was and my mind was getting changed too. It was very subtle. If you followed the conversation around, on one level it looked chaotic, but you could also see how people would pick up each other's words and ideas. … It was pretty clear that we were all influencing each other.

Sometimes in arguing with someone you begin to see you don't really understand what they are saying, said one participant:[27]

I also saw that I didn't really understand what I meant until people brought things out in what I said. ... Toward the end of the session, even though we'd talked about a hundred different things, most of the people in the group would seem to come to something. It was like we had created or discovered something in common but it was different for each of us. It was very peculiar.

So open dialogue can allow a subtle and sincere influence to take place, without people being pressured or steamrollered in any direction. We say 'in any direction' because to achieve this value to the organization, we as senior executives must risk being influenced and changing our minds.

One of the subjects that senior executives frequently raise with us is whether what is happening in dialogue has any practical application. Again, this raises the question of what's the purpose of, and what's the return from, listening? Our research shows that this depends to a very large extent on the sincerity and the authenticity with which dialogue in organizations is facilitated. When a dialogue gets under way and people describe their thoughts, ideas and emotions about an issue of importance, ideally the facilitator withdraws and dissolves into the background, emerging merely as one of the participants. Their structural role has ended.

But many senior executives do not, or cannot, let go of the facilitation role and fail to let groups discuss things freely. Then participants in the dialogue report they are disturbed by having a senior executive as facilitator and will simply wait for 'the Decision', like tablets of stone handed down from the mountain top after some appropriate time has passed. 'Having a senior executive lead the discussion and then make the decisions without taking account of our views has the effect on me of not taking the same amount of responsibility', one participant said. 'I think there are good reasons for not having a facilitator in the room. It makes us ordinary participants more responsible for what is happening and it gives us a feeling that this is our dialogue. A responsible participant is not a guest.'

Making the assumption for a moment that senior executives might change their minds in the dialogue process, then this is perhaps the major perceived risk – a threat, even – to organizations. The old conception of leadership as firm, top-down control by powerful individuals cannot hold in the unplugged world of dialogue, discussion and debate. No senior executive in all honesty wants their organization subverted by increased participation by the workforce, or by customers, in dialogue and decision making. Not if senior executives think that everybody else's view is 'wrong'. But the economic climate of the past five years has shown us – if we didn't believe it before – that senior executives have no crystal ball to view the future and no miracle cure for turning their organizations around. Indeed, the raft of cost-cutting and downsizing activities of the early 2000s, ostensibly undertaken to protect the balance sheet, hasn't really worked. CEOs are still getting sacked. Household name firms are still closing or being bought by their rivals. Isn't it time to try listening to our people? Isn't it time to sustain the dialogue with our people, our customers and suppliers?

So is there value in attempting and sustaining an open and honest dialogue with your stakeholders? Our reply is yes, it can be sustained and yes, it has value. First, dialogue needs to be sustained over a period of time, because there is never any clear idea where it is heading. There is much repetition and iteration, much frustration. But the process of dialogue is as much about the process of leading thought as about the products or services of the organization. And it is here that the return on investment occurs. If people are truly the key assets in our businesses – and these assets don't appear to be products or patents or services – then helping our people to think more clearly, to learn what we as senior executives are thinking and to have access to the insights of board-level strategizing, develops those assets more effectively for the future. Our people, our stakeholders stay with us – are more motivated to stay with us – because we listen to them, we value their ideas and (occasionally) we change our minds. This is the biggest compliment senior executives can pay them.

Conclusion

In this chapter we have explored the issues around dialogue as listening, pointing out that our critics and cynics pose the question 'Is that it?' But where listening leads to interpretation, reflection and clear thinking, then listening is the key to understanding. What we quickly see is that the sensemaking that listening kick-starts in us becomes sensegiving as we engage in uncomfortable conversations with others. Sensemaking and sensegiving then occur simultaneously as we discuss the implications for the future of what has already taken place in the past. And all of this is taking place in the 'sensible' present. In other words, what we're seeing is that sensemaking and sensegiving are not separate operations – they are the same thing – and that they are driven by listening and understanding as their logical precursor.

What this means is that attempting to understand other people – for its own sake, the sake of understanding – is the key that unlocks change and movement in people and in our organizations. Put another way, listening is the key that unlocks a synthesis of ideas from all stakeholders in the game. Listening sincerely frees up the future, and generates high performance and high motivation from our teams and workgroups.

This, of course, is not new. Among native American Indians – the Iroquois, for example – the council of chiefs required complete agreement from all its members on any decision. They did not believe in majority rule and the council sat for as long as it needed to find a solution that everyone could agree on. Conversation – whether in the form of debate, discussion or dialogue – was often full of age-old conflict. So much so that sometimes the council sat for days, or even weeks, and occasionally decisions were not made at all because no unanimous agreement could be reached. But when a decision was taken, it was one that everybody felt committed to. It was their decision, both collectively and individually.

We are not arguing for a form of consensus leadership here. It's only that in our increasingly complex and problem-ridden organizations, we need to develop radically new understandings about collective communication and action. That radical understanding may, however, be better appreciated by looking to interpersonal values that we might have forgotten. The basis for *Leadership Unplugged* as dialogue, for instance, needs to be less selfish than leadership has been in the past. What seems certain, amidst the uncertainty, is that no one leader or system can ever resolve all the problems and challenges facing an organization. No one can have all the answers. In fact, attempts to find unilateral, top-down solutions usually lead to further complications. The presence of so many different people, all stakeholders in our corporate lives, guarantees that nobody can get their way, not even the powerful senior executives leading our organizations. But the power of senior executives can be used to ensure that the recognition of all stakeholders, through involvement in dialogue, does lead to understanding and therefore to a return for the organization. Sadly, some executives, in our experience, use their tacit power to unseat dialogue and to protect their positions of authority.

If we are honest, we have to admit that the subversive character of dialogue is also a threat to senior executives personally. What do the leaders and managers we work with make of this? Are they willing to give up their apparent authority? To what extent are they themselves willing to apply the tenets of *Leadership Unplugged*? This leads directly to the fundamental question of the identity of leaders and of leadership in practice, which we'll deal with in the final chapter. Viewed in an optimistic light, *Leadership Unplugged* could herald the ending of the top-down, autocratic leader – and this could be a change initiated by top-down and autocratic leaders themselves. This, we believe, requires passion and commitment, both from senior executives themselves and from the people who work with them as they try to listen to each other.

QuestionBank

Take time out to answer these questions.

1.   What are the skills of listening? How do we listen to or sense emotions? How is it different from listening to speech? What are the dynamics of emotions and how do they change over time? What implications does this have for how we change the way we listen?
2.   What role do disclosure and feedback have in dialogue? How can we learn from conflict and uncomfortable conversations? How can we get into and out of uncomfortable conversations safely, protecting the people we're dealing with and our relationships with them?
3.   What is the value of dialogue to the organization, in your view? What are the risks? How can we use questions to sustain listening and dialogue? When do we get answers and a return on dialogue and conversation?

Notes

1.   Bohm, David, 1987. *Unfolding Meaning*. London: Routledge, p. 175.
2.   Boal, Augusto, 1998. *Legislative Theatre*. London: Routledge, p. 128.
3.   Stone, Douglas, Patton, Bruce, and Heen, Sheila, 1999. *Difficult Conversations*. London: Penguin. Possibly the best book to come out of the Harvard Negotiation Project, which also has the multi-million selling *Getting to Yes* to its credit: its description of the three conversations taking place at any one time is powerful, yet simple to grasp and use.
4.   In developing computer software, beta versions are released at an experimental stage. Their purpose is to collect opinions, comments, observations and suggestions from experienced and interested practitioners with a view to preparing a definitive release in the future. We would like this chapter especially to be seen not as a salvo in a debate, but as a virtual question in a dialogue. How does it sound to you?

5. Dumas, Alexandre, 1884. *The Count of Monte Cristo* (1955 edition, reprinted 1976). London: Collins.

6. Bohm, David (ed. Nichol, Lee), 1990. *On Dialogue*. London: Routledge, p. 4.

7. Maslow, Abraham H., 1969. *The Psychology of Science: A Reconnaissance,* Gateway Edition. New York: Henry Regnery, p. 96.

8. Bohm et al., 1991.

9. Rogers, Carl R., 1958/1961. Characteristics of a helping relationship. In *On Becoming a Person*. London: Constable & Co, p. 39.

10. Argyris, Chris and Schön, Donald, 1974. *Theory in Practice*. San Francisco: Jossey Bass.

11. Putnam, Robert, 1995. A biography of Chris Argyris. *Journal of Applied Behavioural Sciences* 31(3), p. 253.

12. Argyris, Chris, 1996. Skilled incompetence. In Starkey, Ken (ed.) *How Organizations Learn*. London: Thomson Business Press, p. 83.

13. Heidegger, Martin, 1927/1962. *Being and Time*. Oxford: Blackwell, p. 161.

14. Ibid., p. 162.

15. Ibid., p. 206.

16. Ibid., p. 208.

17. Ibid.

18. Waters, Richard, and Kirchgaessner, Stephanie. Death of bull market leaves Ebbers in the dust. *Financial Times*, 24 April 2002.

19. Visitors to the Harvard University website can access some open materials made available for faculty at http://bokcenter.harvard.edu. Of special interest, in our view, are the documents relating to managing diversity, and one on handling 'hot moments' in the classroom.

20. Those who believe we can only rely on numbers to clinch an argument would be well advised to explore Norman Denzin and Yvonne Lincoln's (2000) *Handbook of Qualitative Research* (London: Sage). To explore more about talking with people and the art of structuring conversations also see Herbert and Irene Rubin's (1995) *Qualitative Interviewing: The Art of Hearing Data* (Thousand Oaks, CA: Sage).

21. Bloom, 1956.

22. Mitroff, I. I. and Linstone, H. A., 1993. *The Unbounded Mind*. New York: Oxford, p. 145.

23. Ibid., p. 146.

24. Ibid, p. 148.

25. Luft, Joseph, 1969. *Of Human Interaction*. Palo Alto, CA: National Press.

26. Briggs, John and Peat, David, 1999. *Seven Life Lessons of Chaos – Spiritual Wisdom from the Science of Change*. New York: Harper Perennial.

27. Ibid.

CHAPTER 12

Leadership Unplugged: The Organization as a Nexus of Conversations

Conversation, understood widely enough, is the form of human transactions in general.

Alasdair MacIntyre[1]

Linguistic exchange – a relation of communication between a sender and a receiver, based on enciphering and deciphering ... – is also an economic exchange which is established within a particular symbolic relation of power between a producer, endowed with a certain linguistic capital, and a consumer (or a market) and which is capable of procuring a certain material or symbolic profit. In other words, utterances are not only ... signs to be understood and deciphered; they are also signs of wealth, intended to be evaluated and appreciated, and signs of authority, intended to be believed and obeyed. Quite apart from the literary (and especially poetic) uses of language, it is rare in everyday life for language to function as a pure instrument of communication.

Pierre Bourdieu[2]

Organizations are created, sustained and changed through talk.

Iain Mangham[3]

All human relationships evolve round some form of conversation.

Edgar Schein[4]

Headlines
Senior executives cannot control organizations, but can only influence them and their identities through conversation with stakeholders.

> Organizations are composed of a network or nexus of conversations in which senior executives are just one of the conversation partners.
>
> *Leadership Unplugged* supports a view of leadership that is focused on the promotion and protection of values in the organization.
>
> *Leadership Unplugged* suggests that senior executives achieve more by trying to understand others than by trying to tell them what to do and how.
>
> The ultimate risk involved in *Leadership Unplugged* is that by involving ourselves in the process of listening to and trying to understand others we may change our own views, and even our own selves

Throughout *Leadership Unplugged* we have argued that personal and organizational identity are constantly co-created in today's complex organizations. We have suggested that our identities are influenced or disturbed by the conversations of senior executives and other stakeholders. We have argued that identity and organizations themselves cannot be controlled, by conversations or indeed by anything else. And we have argued that the conversations that make up the everyday reality of organizations are endless. In other words, our identities – who we are and what our organizations are – never settle completely. Although a number of research projects border on this issue, there are no substantive research studies or theoretical explorations of this phenomenon in complex organizations, and so some years ago we set out to explore how senior executives used language to influence identity in today's complex organizations.[5]

The journey has taken us in surprising directions, and we've looked at the world of leadership and the question of whether leaders are born or made.[6] We have explored the world of strategic management and how firms actually engage in or 'do' strategy.[7] And we've looked at the traditional, hard world of economics and what makes firms behave the way they do. This book in a sense encompasses elements from all these arenas. This chapter is our attempt to underpin our thinking on *Leadership Unplugged* and to explain why we think the ideas here are so important.

Language and *Leadership Unplugged*

We believe that conversations between people in organizations are the major, if not the only, influencing tool available to senior executives. Conversation is the main process we use to create our own and our organization's identities. It is the principal function of management. And – we argue here – conversation in effect *is* our organizations. This is especially true because our organizations today are so intrinsically complex that no one individual can know everything there is to know about what goes in inside them. We construct or agree what goes on through conversation with the people around us. The issue, therefore, is just how important is conversation? How important is it that we, as senior executives, have above-average ability to listen to stakeholders and to engage in the uncomfortable conversations we need to have to get business done?

In short, we believe that our ability to engage in constructive conversations with multiple stakeholders at the same time is crucial. We believe that without being well-above-average listeners, with all the interpersonal skills that this demands, we may as well hang up our spurs as board level directors of note. This is because we believe that organizations fundamentally are nothing more than networks of conversations – ephemeral, intangible and intractably complex. The rest of this chapter explores this view and articulates a wholly new way of looking at organizations today.

The Organization as a Nexus of Contracts

Economists have long described firms as a bundle or nexus of contracts. In a now-classic paper Ronald Coase suggested, almost 70 years ago, that: 'A firm ... consists of the system of relationships which comes into existence when the direction of resources is dependent on an entrepreneur.'[8]

Coase was trying to explain why firms – collections of individuals working together for an entrepreneur, or manager, to supply goods or services – should exist. Why were there not simply open and free markets with individuals trading between themselves? Since Coase, the question of how firms come about and are managed or co-ordinated has remained at the very heart of economic analysis. Although Coase did not himself coin the phrase 'nexus of contracts', he did say that firms were effectively a contractual arrangement:[9]

> A firm becomes larger as additional transactions (which could be exchange transactions co-ordinated through the price mechanism) are organized by the entrepreneur and becomes smaller as he (*sic*) abandons the organization of such transactions.

The phrase 'nexus of contracts' was actually developed and used decades after Coase by various writers who linked the management of organizations with its different stakeholders.[10] These included workers, unions, customers, suppliers and the state, among others. They replaced the conception of the firm as a production function with a theory of the firm as 'a nexus or set of contracting relationships amongst individuals'. The role for managers and senior executives in a firm was generally defined as having to enter into a series of bilateral contracts with the firm's various interest groups. Leadership behaviour became simply the design of contracts with incentives that would reduce the need for controlling many employees.

Many economists since Coase have built on this nexus of contracts framework, linking the firm and its different stakeholders.[11] In the 1990s Oliver Williamson, perhaps the key proponent of transaction cost economics, gave a new focus to the nexus of contracts view in an anthology explicitly dealing with the firm 'as a nexus of treaties' instead of as a nexus of contracts.[12] This revised view of the firm had notable benefits, said the editors, not least in dispelling unwanted legal connotations of the term 'contract'. Furthermore, and importantly for the purposes of this chapter, the term 'treaty' was meant to emphasise that the relationships between parties to the coalition were primarily self-enforcing, a hint that the treaties (as outcomes of negotiations between different parties) were concluded through discussions between the various agents.

Economic theories, however, are relatively rigid and can't cope with the issue of adapting to unforeseen contingencies. This contrasts with much of current organization theory, where seeking out and processing information about the organization's key uncertainties is considered the prime directive of organizations. In the world of organization theory, people in firms spend time communicating with one another in a never-ending sequence of negotiated exchanges of information.

Researchers Casson and Wadeson picked up exactly this issue and modelled communication costs within firms.[13] They proposed that conversations were a rational response to the communication costs involved in managing firms. In practice firms often engage their suppliers, for instance, in a dialogue or conversation. Casson and Wadeson extended this idea to model all the forms of dialogue involved in the process of co-ordination, both within and between firms. One of the most interesting aspects of their work highlighted some curious facts about who or what happens at the boundaries of a firm. What information is communicated between different stakeholders, and how that communication is structured, gives very clear signals about where the boundaries lie, they suggested. Although the boundary of the firm is something organization theory has always been exploring, it is the conception of conversation as the mechanism for reducing ambiguity and for negotiating contracts at the boundary that is most significant for this chapter.

Probably, though, we must remain at odds with economists who adhere to this contractual view of organizations, and find ourselves siding with one of the major commentators on organizations of all kinds, Charles Perrow:[14]

What advantage could there be reducing the complex, baffling things that we have been considering ... to such simple abstractions as contracts when we know that so much else, such as trust, norms, traditions and accommodation, exists?

This brief review of the economic view of organizations as a nexus of contracts sets the scene for an exploration of the stakeholder view of organizations. Following this is an outline of what is perhaps the key theoretical contribution of *Leadership Unplugged*, that a better way to describe organizations is not as a nexus of contracts, but as a nexus of conversations.

The Conversation with Stakeholders

The vast array of organization theories have been summarised comprehensively and well elsewhere, so this section highlights why a theory of the organization as a nexus of conversations makes a valuable contribution for managers and leaders.[15] In effect the theory suggests that there is a single coordination mechanism – conversation – that acts both internally and at the boundaries of the organization. Indeed, it explains why defining a clearcut boundary of the organization has proved so difficult.

When beginning to think about stakeholders, then, it is worth remembering that an organization is defined in large part by its membership – who 'belongs' to the organization – and by who lies at the boundary. Pfeffer explores the activities of formal boundary-spanning units 'such as marketing and public relations [who] seek to develop external support and demand for what the organization does'.[16] In some senses, stakeholder theory actually spells out who is involved in the various conversations of the firm and what they want. In other words it tells us what the corporate agendas for those conversations might be.

Building on the theme of stakeholder conversations, then, the next section turns to the handful of researchers who have already captured elements of this chapter's key contribution – that the organization is best theorized as a nexus of conversations.

Organizations as Conversations

Organizations have been described before as conversations or conversation-like, and conversation for most researchers is a mechanism for the management of organizational change (Table 12.1).

One of the most important researchers who has explicitly described organizations as conversations is Jeffrey Ford, who has actually defined

Table 12.1 A review of key contributions defining organizations as conversations

Author(s)	Organizations conceived as …	Theme(s)	Philosophical underpinning	Call for further research
Benson, 1977	Dialectical	'Dialectical view of organizations committed to the centrality of process'	Critical Marxist	General call
Boje, 1991	Storytelling networks	The organization as a story-telling system in which stories are the medium of exchange between storytelling actors	Critical postmodern	General call
Broekstra, 1998	Conversation	'Conversational practices appear to be the keys to transformations of social practices'; complexity theory; change management	Complexity theory	No call
Ford, 1998	A network of conversations	Change management	Constructivist tradition	No call
Hatch, 1997	Narratives (or conversations)	Conversations and their influence	Narrative theory, positioning theory	General call

Table 12.1 (continued)

Author(s)	Organizations conceived as …	Theme(s)	Philosophical underpinning	Call for further research
Hatch and Ehrlich, in press	Dialogic; a multivoiced narrative; also dialogue as novels	'Talk as vehicle for communicating between organizational constituents'; change management	Narrative theory (Bakhtin, 1981)	General call for further study
Roth, 2000	Conversations as a mechanism for diffusing innovation	Learning from experience; change management	Constructivist tradition	Methods to help organizations develop conversations
Sonsino, 2000 and 2002b	A nexus or bundle of conversations	Conversations as sensemaking and sensegiving processes in complex stakeholder networks	Social construction of reality	To develop greater awareness of links with identity (2000) and to develop greater self awareness in managers (2002b)
Stacey, 2000 and 2001	Complex responsive processes (conversations as complex adaptive systems)	Conversations as complex adaptive systems (complex responsive processes)	Complexity theory	Methods to develop greater reflexivity in managers (2000) and researchers (2001)

four different types of conversations – initiative (conversations that kick-start things), understanding, performance and closure.[17] Fundamentally, Ford believes that it is conversations that produce and manage organizational change. He concludes that change management is, in effect, 'a recursive process of generating, maintaining, modifying and deleting conversations'.[18]

This somewhat overt take on conversation management is also supported by Roth, who suggests that 'conversations, and more carefully defined and facilitated conversational practices such as "dialogue", are processes for organizational change'.[19] He explores and builds on Ford's conception of conversation as a way of effecting change and suggests that conversations can be used actively to diffuse practices of managerial innovation within organizations.

Perhaps the most obvious example of a researcher couching the organization explicitly as conversation is Broekstra, who suggests that 'alterations in conversational practices (sharing, dialogue and discussion) appear to be the keys to transformations of social practices'.[20] Broekstra uses concepts from complexity science (notably complex adaptive systems theory) to underpin what he calls his organizational renewal methodology, and this relies extensively on the idea of the organization as a conversation:

> It assumes that organizing occurs in processes of sharing, dialogue and discussion of ideas, whether tacit or explicit, and that these create reality and meaning. The conversations are not about the social relationships; they *are* the relationships.

Broekstra also suggests that people in most companies at the local level are immersed in conversation – to the point of saturation – with the organization's outside environment. In other words, more conversations occur at the boundaries than might be expected from a classical definition of an organization, which attenuates and thins out at the edges. This conversation overload blurs the boundaries between the organization and its environment and threatens to cause internal disorientation and, over time, an identity drift. The question of where the boundaries of the organization lie is raised to a new level when we add in the thinking from complexity science, though we can see that this blurring at the boundaries is entirely to be expected and is something that cannot be 'resolved' or 'decided'.

Where this chapter's conception of the organization as a nexus of conversations differs from the theories of most of the researchers cited in this section is in the degree of managerial control that we believe can be exerted. Our research shows that conversation can only be used to influence or to 'disturb' the status quo and that there is no guarantee of a successful, predicted outcome. This makes it very difficult for us to support overly prescriptive change theories, for instance. But it does help us create a way of thinking about organizations that justifies exploring practical language use and conversation in organizations.

Case 22. HSBC – unlocking the ideas in people's heads

In spring 2002 a small group of seven HSBC executives met in the United Kingdom to discuss the question of how an organization 164,000-strong could unlock the ideas in its members' heads. The people in the group all worked for HSBC but came from different levels within the organization. The meeting was set up explicitly as a 'no hierarchy' discussion forum, and everyone was encouraged to speak his or her mind.

What they discussed during the course of the meeting was the amazing passion that existed to make the firm truly great: 'from a very good organization to work for, to a great organization to work for', said one participant. This raised a number of issues around culture, leadership and accountability. Specifically, these were:

1. That the culture at HSBC did not encourage change. There was no perceived pressure to change, the group felt, and no consequences followed from not changing.
2. That the culture at HSBC was more about good stewardship, protecting the business for stakeholders and passing it on to future generations, than it was about entrepreneurship. 'We reward cost cutting more than we do wealth creation', one group member said. 'We unlock wealth by hammering down costs.'

Now this behaviour was admired in HSBC managers, as elsewhere. It created good managers, but not necessarily – the group felt – the visionary leaders that the organization needed for the future.

Despite holding such openly critical and honest views of the organization, the people attending the meeting were unanimous in their view that the culture could be developed, and that more could be done to empower its people and to unleash their potential to innovate. And the critical moment in the meeting was when someone said: 'In particular we could do more to stimulate conversation.'

The concept of workshops or meetings to explore new thinking is not at all new. It already exists as part of many organizations, and represents a mode of behaviour that all executives must be familiar with. But it doesn't happen all the time and usually it is sporadic. In the 12 months since the first meeting, HSBC has been grappling with how – in a low-key, low-cost way – to formalize these informal workshops as a better way of sharing and managing knowledge within the institution. They called the project Group-think, though this name was later changed, and it was seen as an experiment in real-time knowledge management.

The ideal goal for the group was that everyone present at the meeting should simply host another Groupthink meeting with another set of executives who hadn't been a part of the first workshop. The topic was to be the same: how do we unlock the ideas in people's heads? In addition, the participants were to enlist the group HR department to share a key organizational problem amongst (say) eight executives from around the globe, and to ask them to come up with possible solutions and ideas as to how that issue could be tackled. To enlist support for the project, the Chairman of the bank Sir John Bond was told of the idea and he gave it his blessing. So Groupthink – an outward rippling series of workshops – was born.

The Groupthink objectives were initially very clear: this was about communication, knowledge-sharing and dialogue. The project was certainly not intended explicitly to change the values of the organization. Honesty, integrity and respect for other people's ideas were very much a part of the project, but Groupthink was intended to change the way people within the firm worked at the local level. It was fundamentally about continuous improvement and renewal and was intended to achieve a number of things – not least a powerful impetus to change HSBC for the better, but among the grassroots members who attended the meetings as well as at a senior level.

Importantly, Groupthink events were always envisaged as low-cost, small and local events. Commitment for a broad, sweeping set of search conferences would never have been ratified.

'This small-scale project illustrated the importance of leadership and individual accountability as a force for change', says Guy Millar of HSBC in the UK. 'It could help us to build a learning organization that in turn will win competitive advantage.'

As a mechanism to help people build on the accepted mantra of 'think Group', it was also intended to further institutionalize the new ways of thinking and acting within the organisation. Above all, however, the goal was to create a new way of communicating, says Millar – a new team spirit that transcended business and geographical boundaries to promote organizational change. All of this sounded worthwhile, but it was difficult for some to understand just how these targets would be achieved. Building grassroots support for a low-profile project has proved difficult in a tough economic climate.

Millar pointed to the idea of teaching people how to fish, rather than giving them fish. 'Groupthink extols the virtues of self-reliance and autonomy. It reduces the need and possible dependence on external solution providers such as consultants and helps us to create an internal capability to learn and solve our own problems. We must continually seek and deliver positive change', he said, but emphasized that it was up to HSBC personnel to implement this.

The opportunity to connect to new networks of people across the organization was intended to support collaboration across the group, especially with peers outside people's normal base of contacts. It was designed to give people the space and time to connect, and to invite what Millar called genuine participation and not mere presence. 'This will build the value of HSBC's social capital', he said, 'something institutional investors increasingly recognize as a significant business performance indicator.'

Importantly, the project was intended to help translate individuals' learning on the job into organizational learning and improvement. Often organizations undertake personal development for its own sake without making an explicit link to organizational needs and outcomes.

As a mechanism for generating and sustaining conversations in the organization, Groupthink is simple enough. Attend one meeting, host another with new participants. This is the only expected outcome from each meeting. And although the overarching goals are high-level and aspirational, the practical day-to-day outcomes should subtly change 'what the organization does round here'. As long as the momentum and energy of the participants can be sustained, and as long as the upper echelons of the organization don't interfere too much in managing the process, then HSBC has every chance of achieving the process goals it has set itself.

Questions:
1. How can HSBC continue to develop and grow the Groputhink concept? What are the benefits of keeping mechanisms like HSBC's Groupthink small? What are the problems? What kind of objectives and outcomes are most suitable for participants in such events?
2. What effect would it have if the process was formalized and proceduralized too much? (What would 'too much' look or feel like?) How might participants feel if the hand of the organization was seen too much in the process?
3. What course of action might senior management within HSBC take to support and nurture the dialogue process without choking it? What would it take to kill the process?

Organizational Discourse and the Language Turn

Despite the increasing interest in research into language use in organizations, conventional organization theorists have largely tended to ignore its importance. But the so-called 'language turn' has been described as one of the most profound contemporary trends within the social sciences.[21] In the words of Mats Alvesson and Dan Kärreman: 'Most actual data generated during fieldwork is linguistic in one way or another and language should therefore be seen as the central object of study in all social sciences.'[22] They argue that this is true even though much current empirical work still treats language 'in a simplistic, uncritical and misleading way'.[23]

So strong are Alvesson and Kärreman in their view that they also argue that it should now be clear that how we use language bears little relation to any objective truth 'out there'. Language cannot mirror social reality, they conclude. This is the most profound challenge that the study of language in organizations offers to prevailing management theory, even though the field is still in its early stages of development.

We have no space here to rehearse in full Alvesson and Kärreman's eloquent survey, but it is worth summarizing the key implications they raise over what they call 'language-in-use', or how language works in the real world. Because when researchers question whether language can indeed represent objective reality, all that is left (as something worth studying) is how language is used in practice. Discourse science can do this by allowing us to identify the key processes by which ideas are formulated or articulated, and by allowing us to study the social contexts in which these processes are situated.

The contextual nature of the language sciences is one of the strengths of this emerging field. In this new field, 'communication is a conversation in that it focuses on both process and structure, on collective action as joint accomplishment, on dialogue among partners, on features of the context, and on micro and macro processes'.[24] Importantly, Linda Putnam, Nelson Phillips and Pamela Chapman spell out exactly why conversation is such a critical element of discourse. For them, it is a simile for organizations as sequential interactions among people. In many ways, they suggest, it lays the groundwork for the very fabric and community of organizing. In their words:[25]

Conversation is immediate in its claim on attention, instantaneous in its moment to moment occurrence, and fleeting or ephemeral in its form, yet it relies on patterns that become culturally sanctioned, frames that presuppose prior knowledge, and macro processes in which individuals speak as representatives for others. Conversations embody many of the elements that characterise communication as symbols, performance and voice; however, *discourse foregrounds language as the nexus for untangling relationships, among meaning, context, and praxis* (emphasis added).

This suggests that all social phenomena are generated in and through conversation. Harré and van Langenhove capture well this concept of conversation as the social construction of everyday life:[26]

> The constant flow of everyday life in which we all take part is fragmented through discourse into distinct episodes that constitute the basic elements of both our biographies and of the social world.

The Organization as a Nexus of Conversations

Considering the question of what an organization as a nexus of conversations might look or sound like, we have so far described an organization generating, maintaining, modifying and deleting conversations or parts of conversations (Figure 12.1 and Sonsino 2000b).[27] This builds on the idea of sensemaking developed in Chapter 8 as social, ongoing and principally verbal. A sensemaking perspective for the organization as a nexus of conversations begins to explain how conversations are related within organizations and over time. In other words, it suggests that sensemaking is the fundamental phenomenon occurring within the nexus and at its boundaries. Also, this explains why it has not been possible to define organizational boundaries very clearly. In essence, this is because

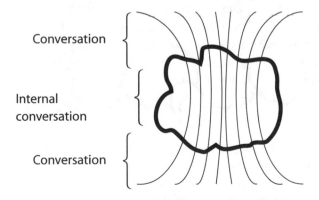

Conversation

Internal conversation

Conversation

Figure 12.1 2D schematic of the organization as a nexus of conversations

the boundaries of organizations are so inescapably complex, involving the conversations of many stakeholder groups. It would be impossible for the boundaries to be fixed and recognizable because they are fashioned from ephemeral, intangible conversations (Figure 12.2).

Importantly, the sensemaking perspective also explains the dynamic aspects of an organization that, as a nexus of conversations, changes over time as participants move into and out of the various conversations that make it up. The idea is that the conversations ebb and flow as the actors in the exchanges migrate from one conversation to another, modifying, adding and deleting conversations as they go. If you want to study the dynamics of how to organize things watch how conversations start in organizations, then see how they spread and how they influence organizational action through the interrelations between different stakeholder groups.

Considering, next, the question of who is in the nexus of conversations – well, all the different organizational stakeholders are constantly engaged in conversation with each other (Figure 12.3). In essence, then, the distinctions between inside and outside disappear. The purpose of conversations – whether formal meetings and presentations or informal gossip and small talk – is immaterial. There are only conversations. Indeed over time the conversations, and therefore the nexus, girdle the globe as business continues. The

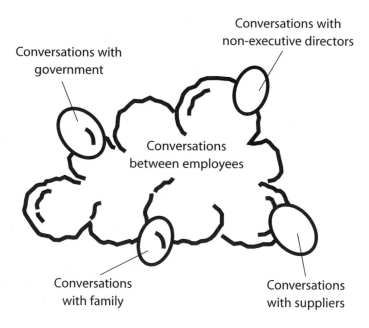

Figure 12.2 3D 'molecular' view of the organization as a nexus of conversations

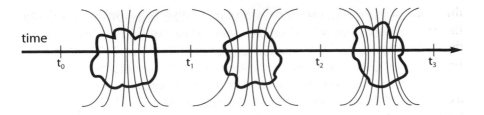

The organization as ephemeral and intangible, constantly constructing and enacting itself through time 'in an endless series of microstates' (Anderson, 1999)

Figure 12.3 The organization as a nexus of conversations over time

organization never sleeps as long as someone somewhere is talking about it. Who has control over the organization then?

This raises two difficult questions: first, how many nexuses can any individual be a part of, and second, how broad does the organization as a nexus of conversations go? Do we need separate words, for instance, for the firm or 'employer' that is legally accountable (in an institutional sense) as distinct from the organization in a 'nexus of conversations' sense? Dealing with the query on the scale of the organization first, we are reminded of Chester Barnard's thoughts when he considered the question of who belongs to a firm. For him, all kinds of individuals with only tenuous formal links may be a part of the nexus, if only for a time:[28]

> ... many persons [are] not commonly considered 'members', for example, customers; or those ... persons that are only treated as members in special senses, for example, stockholders, who in one legal sense are the organization. ... The connection of any member with an 'organization' is necessarily intermittent and there is frequent substitution of persons. ... It is almost impossible to discover a person who does not 'belong' ... at the same time to many organizations.

So as long ago as the 1930s, Barnard sensed the intangible nature of organizational membership and it caused him to think about how organizing takes place over time. On intangibility, he said: 'The sense of being "nowhere" is commonly felt. With the great extension of the means of electrical communication this vagueness has increased.'[29] However, in addressing the temporal nature of organizing he missed a logical next step. He asked himself whether an organization should be regarded as 'continuous when all co-operative action ceases to be resumed again at a later time'. No, was his conclusion. 'I have found it more convenient to regard these organizations as continuous but "dormant".'[30] The value of the constantly constructed nexus of conversations idea, then, is that issues such as Barnard's 'Where does the organization go at night?' simply dissolve. The organization 'goes' where the conversation 'goes' – around the globe. It is the conversations themselves – wherever and whenever they occur, and whoever is involved – that comprise the organization.

The Value of the Nexus of Conversations View

We are concerned in this closing chapter with two issues. First, why is a theory of the organization as a nexus of conversations a valuable contribution to knowledge? And second, why is it important to senior executives as effective leaders? Dealing with the theoretical aspects firsts, we believe it explains what is widely held to be the principal activity of organizations. It also explains both the formal and informal activity of stakeholders. And it helps us to explain how we might be able to manage change, which has proved a notoriously difficult process to define.[31] A theory of change based on a nexus of conversations view would suggest that what changes is the conversations that are taking place (Figure 12.3). We can suggest, then, that the kinds of conversations we have – especially in times of crisis or change – matter significantly, and that this choice will influence the improvement of corporate performance.

Staying for a moment with corporate performance, the question of why firms differ has long been held a fundamental question in the field of strategic management.[32] The nexus of conversations view, simply put, suggests that firms differ because they are having different conversations. Furthermore, the same organization may have different conversations over time, which would explain how we can sustain high performance – by ensuring multiple conversations between stakeholders continue to take place.

Let's move on to look at the reasons why our theory of the organization as a nexus of conversations matters for senior executives.

Renaissance of Value Propositions

It's time we, as the leaders of tomorrow's organizations, saw a return to the leadership values of another age. In a classic, but little-known leadership text from almost 50 years ago, Philip Selznick penned this:[33]

Truly accepted values must infuse the organization at many levels, affecting the perspectives and attitudes of personnel, the relative importance of staff activities, the distribution of authority, relations with outside groups, and many other matters. Thus if a large corporation exerts a wish to change its role in the community from a narrow emphasis on profit making to a larger social responsibility (even though the ultimate goal remains some combination of survival and profit-making ability), it must explore the implications of such change for decision making in a wide variety of organizational activities.

And the task of building and enshrining those special values in the corporation is still the unique and fundamental task of leadership. Without the leader's guiding hand the process will occur haphazardly, if at all. But we appear to have forgotten this in the search for short-term shareholder returns. So senior executives cannot do exactly as they wish. There are environmental circumstances, stakeholder demands and industry history that dictate how the organization ought to behave, although this is only to an extent. Nevertheless we believe that the principal role of leaders in our organizations is still as Philip Selznick had it: as experts in the promotion and protection of values. And because values cannot, in our view, be dictated by any single individual, the main objectives leaders must hold for their organizations are those that will create the conditions in which an organization's values will be developed and sustained.

Why? We believe that organizations that exhibit distinctive values become highly prized – not as a collection of assets engaged solely in the generation of a short-term return for shareholders, but as a source of personal gratification for a broad range of stakeholders, notably employees and customers. ('To make a profit' is, anyway, too abstract and literally meaningless an objective for any institution to set itself or achieve.) This infusion of values develops a distinctive identity for the organization and acts as a force for social integration, both at the centre and in the field. As Selznick says:[34]

> Even in business where self-definition may seem less important than in political and other community enterprises, there is a need to build a self-conscious group that fully understands 'the kind of company this is'.

This sense of identity means that the organization's leaders can move away from adopting traditional command-and-control styles. In the past command-and-control managers were often people whose logic told them that managers had the right to manage just because of their place in the hierarchy. But there are two things that have happened over the years to discredit the hierarchical managers 'right' to manage. Many notable researchers have revealed findings showing that hierarchical management structures and hierarchical managers, relying on power and coercive direction, have failed to prove effective.[35] There is a big difference between the way organizations are experienced at the bottom, for instance, and the way it feels at the top. A brief summary of the effects of being managed in a hierarchical organization exhibiting transactional forms of leadership includes the following:[36]

- inability to express oneself
- inability to influence anyone
- feelings of being shut out
- increasing cynicism
- feelings that one has to dominate or be dominated
- feeling that to conform is the best thing
- feeling that intolerance is acceptable
- feeling that new ideas must come from the top
- feeling that there is no way to communicate with those at the top.

Figure 12.4 offers a comparison of the purposes and styles of transactional, transformational and identity-based leadership forms that may help summarize some of the differences between the traditional or hierarchical leadership style and identity-based leadership.

Taking the description a stage further, we suggest that task- or goal-oriented leadership activity (as highlighted in Figure 12.5) relates either to the personal performance of the technical or functional role, or to traditional transactional forms of leadership. Transactional leadership in this sense uses rules of rational choice to influence a rational opponent. The purpose is successfully to bring about a goal required by the senior executive. Understanding-oriented leadership activity, on the other hand, is rooted in the self-aware or reflexive activities of an executive striving for understanding *for its own sake* among a group of people. In *Leadership Unplugged*, executives are not making egocentric calculations of personal success. They just want to understand. In *Leadership Unplugged*, individuals are not primarily motivated by their own success, although this may well be a valuable side effect. They pursue goals under the condition that they can harmonize or synthesize their plans of action with those of other stakeholders. The fundamental goal, then, of *Leadership Unplugged* is to reach understanding with as many people as possible. This does not necessarily mean reaching full-fledged agreement, or even consensus. The goal here is a situation where the overall context of the current conversation, and therefore for subsequent organizational action, is accepted as valid by all participants in the discussion. And this is difficult to achieve honestly and authentically.

Figure 12.4 Transactional, transformational and identity-based leadership

For instance, many managers charged with achieving certain ends pave the way by using apparently open meetings to talk through the way forward. The manager's real aim, however, is to manipulate the playing field, or stack the odds, so that the outcome is a course of action that he or she has already chosen. This is not management, nor even motivation, but is manipulation of the crudest kind, though few managers will openly

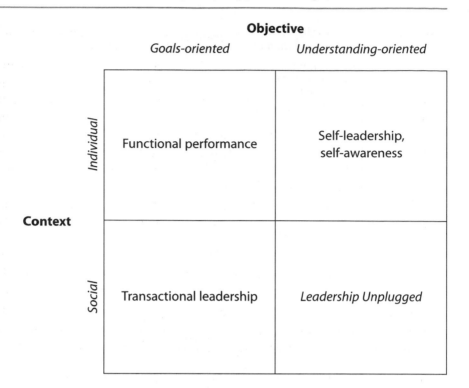

Figure 12.5 *Leadership Unplugged* as the search for understanding

accept that they intend to manipulate others. One senior manager with whom we discussed the question of leadership and influence described just such a scenario, but became most upset – antagonistic, even – at the charge of 'manipulation'. 'It's not manipulation', was his theme. 'It's getting people involved in the decision making.' We must disagree.

Most people see through this kind of event and harbour a grudge forever after. 'Why involve us when you know what needs to be done and how you want it done?' they say. Strange as it may seem to managers who adopt the manipulative style, most people would be quite comfortable with being told: 'This is what we have to do and this is the way I want it done.' They may not like it, but almost all will accept it. Perhaps the worst outcome for leaders in this situation is that every subsequent effort that the manipulative manager makes to engage in conversation – whether well meaning or not – is hampered. The trust of others, once lost, is rarely regained.

In organizations where identity is considered explicitly, on the other hand, leaders appear to take a more values-based approach, focused on whom we are as an organization and what that means for all stakeholding individuals.

'Who am I as an employee of this corporation?' becomes a legitimate and valuable conversation to engage in, as does 'What do I stand for?'

The question of whether identity and an organization's values can actually be managed at all is a moot point, though we adhere to the view that values can be influenced by our behaviour, as we've described throughout this book. We believe that as an individual can 'choose' to adhere to certain values, so too can organizations. The question then becomes whether there is a sincere and authentic desire on the part of a firm's leaders to uphold the values espoused, and therefore whether they are a believable set of values to promote to others in the organization.

This network or nexus of values in the organization then becomes the subject of, and the context for, many conversations affecting all functions within it, at every level. The values become in effect a filter or backbone for assessing strategy and policy. Interestingly, if the values are sufficiently embedded in the constant conversations of organizations, then the organizations' strategies and tactics will be spontaneously protected and promoted. As we've said many times, it just isn't possible formally to assign roles to every individual for dealing with every contingency an organization might face in the current climate. The ultimate assumption of the rational manager is that every member of an organization, and each constituent team or unit, can be made to adhere faithfully to an assigned engineered role. These roles are generalized and parallel roles that we see in other organizations. We cannot support this view. Everyone and every team and every organization is unique. But far too often we forget this. So we propose the renaissance of value propositions as the only leadership strategy that makes any sense given the complexity of corporate life today.

Another reason we've chosen to use the word 'renaissance' in our subtitle is that when it comes to the practical tools of influence *Leadership Unplugged* has again preferred to return to classical roots. For the Greek philosopher Aristotle the key tools of leadership influence did not just include rational argument or *logos*, but *pathos*, also: the understanding of people's feelings. And to these he added a third thing, not a skill, but a human characteristic, that he suggested was immensely persuasive – *ethos*, your ethical stance. Logic and rigour alone can be extremely persuasive, certainly, in terms of helping people to understand your point of view from a rational standpoint. But can you touch people's emotions and feelings, too? And, perhaps most important of all, does your own ethical stance, your actual personal values, uphold your espoused intellectual stance? Are you a sincere and authentic leader? Taken together, this triumvirate of logos, pathos and ethos are more persuasive than any Draconian, coercive directive you can issue. Use them wisely.

So What Is *Leadership Unplugged*?

At its heart, *Leadership Unplugged* is about charity and the search to understand people. But what does it really mean 'to understand'? Unless we dig deeper into the idea of understanding others, and to the tools we have for engaging in this, we run the risk of leaving the impression that the concept is trivial. The personal perception we each have is that our starting point, and our personal experience and beliefs, dictate whether we see the world as an objective external reality (that we can stand outside of) or as a subjective reality (something we are fundamentally a part of).

'Objective' leaders believe that they can remain as value-neutral observers who can study the real essence of a situation or a firm. These people believe that what can be seen – even regarding people and their relationships with one another – may be captured as in a photograph, or a mirror held up to reality. What they see actually exists, and if they could simply freeze it they could bring out its one true meaning. 'Objective' leaders engage in three tasks – observing, describing and verifying – to build an accurate picture of the world about them. Furthermore they believe that they are capable, with adequate training, of overcoming their own subjectivity by simply switching it off; by drawing a dotted line around what they want to think about and detaching themselves from it. If enough people look for long enough at market research data, they say, the one true answer to what the strategy should be will eventually emerge.

'Subjective' leaders believe that they are products of, and active participants in, the organizational community. They believe that they themselves are participants in a conversation about how to succeed in the long run. They see themselves as just one voice in a much larger conversation in which various points of view are being expressed, highlighting various personal interests and positions. They understand the futility of trying to divorce their personal feelings and values from the conversation at hand.

It should be clear to anyone reading this book that our perspective favours the subjective view of organizational life. That we are engaged in a negotiation with you, the reader, to explore and explain our theories and practical tools that can help people operate in this world. You may make sense of the book as a tool to help organize your thoughts on how to manage ambiguity and uncertainty in organizational life, or you may see it as an insight into the way people different from you might see the world. Do not make the error of labelling this latter perspective 'wrong'. Instead, suggest to us that our view of the world is, possibly, incomplete.

Or that you have doubts over how we have interpreted commercial life. Whatever you do, we hope that you trust us to a certain extent. We hope you trust that we have given our best shot to articulating our views to you. We trust that you will take our word that there is some rigour attached to our work. Your act of trust is possibly better described as an act of charity. And this book is in a sense all about acts of charity. The principle of charity should always come into play when you encounter an argument inconsistent with your own views. It's charity that keeps you in the conversation, making an effort to translate the ideas of the speaker into your own language and to incorporate the ideas into your own world-view. Walking away and concluding the other person is confused or dumb is not effective leadership behaviour. Instead, try challenging yourself – which one of your own taken-for-granted assumptions would you need to alter to align your views with those of the speaker?

So we believe that leaders must have faith – to make a leap of faith, even – in the intelligence and good intentions of their stakeholders. If equally rational people have completely different ideas about how the organization should function, what do you do? Fire them? Or listen to them? An act of charity at this point would tell you that the other person is as rational as you. So use questions. Ask why they hold their view? On what grounds? Questions are the key tool for understanding people and the issues that drive them.

At issue here is the relationship between issues of understanding and issues of dogmatic statement. Do you believe that rational people looking at the same events with complete information will reach the same conclusions? Or do you believe that the conclusions they reach will be different, or biased in some way? Our take is that while we may all reach biased conclusions, those conclusions must always be up for reconsideration.

The subjective frame of reference, in other words, emphasizes the importance of the quality of communicative acts of leadership. And to ensure debates, discussions and dialogues are of reasonable quality the language of leadership needs to:

- relate easily and well to the experiences of people, to be anchored in the present, to relate to issues we need to make sense of now and today
- liberate ideas and issues and not choke the conversation, using questions to keep open the lines of communication
- and finally, to relate to ideas and actions that are practicable to implement.

This brings us to the final lesson of this book: what it means to practice *Leadership Unplugged*? In other words, what does it mean to be a charitable leader? First, let us ask you how you interpret this book. Do we want to convince you that the study of how senior executives talk and listen can be mimicked for greater personal influence? Or are we trying to persuade you to develop a more sophisticated understanding of the processes that may lead you to a more effective interpretation and understanding of the day-to-day issues in organizations? Stated differently, do you think that our minds are closed to different ways of thinking about leadership? Are yours? Or are we just in the process of figuring out what leadership is? And whether it can really have an impact on the organization? Or maybe we are just out for a quick buck?

Which interpretation you choose depends on your frame of reference and how you apply the principle of charity. If you believe that people are generally selfish, you are more likely to believe that directive, coercive forms of leadership work best and that we are barking up the wrong tree. If you choose to dismiss personal values as an important tool in your leadership armoury, feel free to do so. It is easy. You could conclude that *Leadership Unplugged* deals with the minor niceties of leadership behaviour that tough-minded business leaders do not need to concern themselves with, and which certainly do not concern you. Maybe our excitement about the renaissance of value propositions is exaggerated – misguided, even. Or are we simply re-engaging in a debate with you in order to provoke further discussion and dialogue?

One final proposition comes from Thomas Kuhn, the historian of modern management science:[37]

> When reading the words of an important thinker, look first for the apparent absurdities in the text and ask yourself how a sensible person could have written them. When you find an answer, I continue, when those passages make sense to you, then you may find that more central passages, ones you previously thought you understood, have changed their meaning.

And this is the ultimate risk of *Leadership Unplugged*. By involving ourselves in the process of listening to others, of trying to understand others, the risk is that we will change our own views and even our own selves. Just over 50 years ago, the US counsellor and therapist Carl Rogers suggested that real communication only occurs when we listen with understanding. What does that mean, he asked? It means that we need to see the expressed idea and attitude from another person's point of view, to sense how it feels for them, to achieve their frame of reference in regard to the things they are talking about. However, he warns:[38]

> '[O]nce you have been able to see the other's point of view your own comments will have to be drastically revised. You will also find the emotion going out of the discussion, the differences being reduced, and those differences that remain being of a rational and understandable sort .... If you really understand another person in this way, if you are willing to enter his private world and see the way life appears to him, without any attempt to make evaluative judgements, you run the risk of being changed yourself. You might see it his way; you might find yourself influenced in your attitudes and your personality. ... This risk of being changed is one of the most frightening prospects that many of us can face.

So adding the tools of debate, discourse and dialogue to our leadership toolkit gives us all a real chance of developing a better understanding of who we are and what we stand for. Regularly using questions and listening furiously, and giving them as much attention as we give to the statistical and mathematical techniques of managerial operations, means we will begin to understand the people around us. Probably they will better understand us. This is because we all relate to people differently. We come from different backgrounds, we do things differently and we each have different levels of ignorance. A better understanding of charity and the selfless values of human nature may help us to cope more effectively with that ignorance. It may lead to more effective relationships between executives across the organization, and to a more efficient process of delivering a high impact corporate strategy in the future.

Conclusion

Some of the messages we have tried to convey in this concluding chapter are:

- That *Leadership Unplugged* is concerned with the promotion and protection of values in the organization by senior executives.
- That your ability to influence depends on a combination of your skills in rational logic (*logos*), your interpersonal abilities to empathize with others (*pathos*) and your ethical stance (*ethos*).
- That organizations are led and influenced by nothing more than conversations between stakeholders.
- That senior executives have a far better chance of influencing someone by trying to understand them than by trying to overrule them.

QuestionBank

Take time out to answer these questions.

1. How can you distinguish an organization from a family or a government? How transient is an organization? What happens when an office closes at the end of the day?

2. How can you distinguish between the nexuses of different organizations, if at all? How do conversation participants know which nexus they are in? Is any group in conversation an organization? What does it look or sound like?

3. How far does an organization extend temporally and spatially if it is a nexus of conversations? Where and when might you see or find a nexus? How does a nexus of conversations form, develop and cease? How transient is a nexus?

4. What impact does the topic or focus of conversations have on an organization as a nexus of conversations? What impact does a mix of physical (or virtual) locations have on a nexus? How can a nexus move, if at all?

5. How can you tell whether a nexus is concentrated or diluted? Does a nexus have 'bandwidth'? How long does a nexus last? How is it sustained? How can you recognise a nexus? What are the artefacts of a nexus? How can you tell when or if a conversational participant has reached a 'boundary' with another nexus? How can you tell you're within a particular nexus, or if you have left a nexus?

6. What purposes do conversations serve, if any? Are they an end in themselves? Where and when do they occur? Who is involved? What are the artefacts of conversation? How do we know conversations are taking place, have taken place or will take place? What styles or forms can or do conversations take?

7. How do individuals know they are in a conversation? When can individuals not be talking and still be in a conversation? How do you know you've switched conversations or left all conversations completely?

Notes

1. MacIntyre, Alasdair, 1981. *After Virtue*. London: Duckworth, p. 196.
2. Bourdieu, Pierre, 1991. *Language and Symbolic Power* (trans. Raymond,

Gino and Adamson, Matthew). Boston, MA: Harvard University Press, p. 66.
3. Mangham, Iain L., 1986. *Power and Performance in Organizations*. Oxford: Blackwell, p. 82.
4. Schein, Edgar H., 1999. *Process Consultation Revisited: Building the Helping Relationship*. Massachusetts: Addison Wesley, p. 201.
5. Sonsino, 2000.
6. Sonsino, 2001.
7. Sonsino, 2002a.
8. Coase, Ronald, 1937. The nature of the firm. *Economica* 4, p. 391.
9. Ibid., p. 390.
10. Notably Alchian, A. and Demsetz, H., 1972. Production information costs and economic organization. *American Economic Review* 69, pp. 777–95. Also Jensen, Michael and Meckling, William, 1976. Theory of the firm: managerial behaviour, agency costs and ownership structure. *Journal of Financial Economics* 3(4), pp. 305–60.
11. Foss, Nicolai J., 1994. The two Coasian traditions. *Review of Political Economy* 6(1), pp. 37–61. Laffont, Jean-Jacques and Martimont, David, 1997. The firm as a multicontract organization. *Journal of Economics and Management Strategy* 6(2), pp. 201–34.
12. Aoki, Masahiko, Gustafsson, Bo and Williamson, Oliver E. (eds), 1990. *The Firm as a Nexus of Treaties*. London: Sage.
13. Casson, Mark and Wadeson, Nigel, 1998. Communication costs and the boundaries of the firm. *International Journal of the Economics of Business* 5(1), pp. 5–27.
14. Perrow, 1985, p. 223.
15. Perrow, 1985; Hatch, 1997; Pfeffer, Jeffrey, 1997. *New Directions for Organization Theory*. New York: Oxford; Scott, W. Richard, 1998. *Organizations: Rational, Natural and Open Systems*, 4th edn. New Jersey: Prentice Hall.
16. Pfeffer, op. cit., p. 9.
17. Ford, Jeffrey L. and Ford, Laurie W., 1995. The role of conversations in producing intentional change in organizations. *Academy of Management Review* 20, pp. 541–70.
18. Ford, Jeffrey L., 1998, p. C3.
19. Roth, George, 2000, p. 69.
20. Broekstra, Gerrit, 1998, p. 175.
21. Alvesson, Mats and Kärreman, Dan, 2000. Taking the linguistic turn in organizational research: challenges, responses, consequences. *Journal of Applied Behavioural Sciences* 36(2), pp. 136–58.
22. Ibid., p. 142.
23. Ibid., p. 153.

24. Putnam, Linda, Phillips, Nelson and Chapman, Pamela, 1996. Metaphors of communication and organization. In Clegg, Stewart R., Hardy, Cynthia and Nord, Walter R. (eds), 1999, *Managing Organizations: Current Issues.* London: Sage, p. 141.

25. Ibid., p. 141.

26. Harré, Rom and van Langenhove, Luk (eds), 1998. *Positioning Theory: Moral Contexts of Intentional Action.* Oxford: Blackwell, p. 4.

27. Sonsino, 2002b.

28. Barnard, Chester, 1937. *The Functions of the Executive.* Boston, MA: Harvard Business Press, p. 71.

29. Ibid., p. 80.

30. Ibid., pp. 80–1.

31. From Dexter Dunphy's excellent survey of the change theories that exist, it is clear that there is no real consensus about how to 'do' change or manage change in organizations. Dunphy, Dexter, 1996. Organizational change in corporate settings. *Human Relations* 49(5), pp. 541–52.

32. For a thorough survey of the strategic management agenda see Rumelt, Richard P., Schendel, Dan E. and Teece, David J., 1994. *Fundamental Issues in Strategy: A Research Agenda.* Boston, MA: Harvard Business Press, p. 564.

33. Selznick, Philip, 1954. *Leadership in Administration.* London: University of California Press, p. 26.

34. ibid., p. 106.

35. Among these Lawrence, P.R. and Lorsch, J.W., 1969. *Developing Organizations: Diagnosis and Action.* Reading: Addison Wesley.

36. Rowan, John, 2001. *Ordinary Ecstasy.* Hove: Brunner Routledge/Philadelphia, PA: Taylor & Francis. This offers an extraordinarily clear review of all aspects of humanistic psychology – Rowan has long been a critic of hierarchical management structures and the intolerant, directive management styles they breed.

37. Kuhn, Thomas, 1977. *The Essential Tension.* Chicago: University of Chicago Press, p. xii.

38. Rogers, Carl and Roethlisberger, Fritz, 1952. Barriers and gateways to communication. *Harvard Business Review* 30(4).

Strategy Unplugged and Organizations Unplugged

If *Leadership Unplugged* is a philosophy of the way we actually lead through conversation, then our next volume, *Strategy Unplugged*, takes a pragmatic view of how firms actually 'do' strategy. Figure 13.1 highlights our conception of how the values and skills of *Leadership Unplugged* are at the core of how we do strategy.

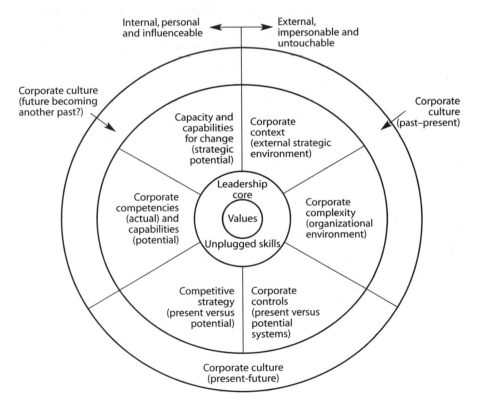

Figure 13.1 Doing strategy: how *Leadership Unplugged* facilitates *Strategy Unplugged*

Our third volume in this sequence will be *Organizations Unplugged*. This, of necessity, includes many of the aspects of leadership that we've discussed here, but focuses explicitly on leadership development and the concept of leadership as teaching. On this topic Texaco's Peter Bijur said:[1]

> It is my firm belief that more than half the task of leadership lies in teaching, learning, coaching, counselling, inspiring others – all within a framework of intellectual equality and commitment to common goals. When I look to select leaders in our organization, one of the things I focus on is that willingness to give and receive good communication deeply.

If people are truly a firm's greatest asset then leadership development is the only thing firms can do that leads inevitably to sustainable competitive advantage. And leadership development means a serious and sustained commitment to developing reflexive and self-aware leaders, high in emotional intelligence and committed to learning. Nothing more. We call this a philosophy of *Organizations Unplugged*. The combination results in sustained organizational success through people continuously learning what it takes to improve corporate performance.

Underpinning both the new volumes is our long-standing concern for the practice of strategic leadership, and how *Leadership Unplugged* can make a tangible impact on corporate performance. Of course, we believe it is the conversational aspects of leadership, and especially the use of questions, that achieve the most. We use questions to relay our most complex concerns. The more complex, abstract or sensitive the message is, the more we talk about it rather than write it down. So be reassured that we will continue our research into organizations as the nexus of conversations. Only the questions we ask will change.

The Russian writer Leo Tolstoy captured the *Unplugged* manifesto perfectly in his fable of the three questions. A king decided to reward the person who could teach him how to answer the three most important questions. He wanted to know when was the right time to do every deed, how to know who were the most essential people and how to decide what was the most important thing to do at any one time. As the fable progresses the king meets many people. Slowly, he learns that the most important time is now, the most important person is the person you happen to be with, and the most important pursuit is to somehow help the other person achieve what they want to achieve. If you take away nothing else from the new renaissance of value propositions, take away this focus on the here-and-now – a responsiveness to the people around you and a concern for others.

Also – instead of telling people what you think all the time – you could usefully ask more questions. How does that sound?

If you think you can help, or if you have a question for us, please e-mail or visit the *Leadership Unplugged* website, www.leadershipunplugged.com.

> The present moment is the only time over which we have dominion. The most important person is always the person with whom you are, who is right before you, for who knows if you will have dealings with any other person in the future. The most important pursuit is making that person, the one standing at your side, happy, for that alone is the pursuit of life.
>
> Leo Tolstoy[2]

Jacqueline Moore and Steven Sonsino
London, March 2003

Notes

1. Bijur, Peter, 2000. The energy of leadership. In Dauphinais, G. William, Means, Grady and Price, Colin, *Wisdom of the CEO*. New York: John Wiley & Sons, p. 171.
2. Tolstoy, Leo. *Three Questions*. Mankato, MN: Creative Education Incorporated.

REFERENCES

Anderson, Philip A., 1999. Complexity theory and organization science. *Organization Science* 10(3), pp. 216–32.

Back, Ken and Back, Kate, 1999. *Assertiveness at Work*, 3rd edn. New York: McGraw-Hill.

Bakhtin, Mikhail M., 1981. *The Dialogic Imagination: Four Essays*, ed. Holquist, M. and trans. Emerson, C. and Holquist, M. Austin, TX: University of Texas Press.

Benson, J. Kenneth, 1977. Organizations: a dialectical view. *Administrative Science Quarterly* 22(3), pp. 1–21.

Berger, Peter and Luckmann, Thomas, 1966. *The Social Construction of Reality: A Treatise on the Sociology of Knowledge*. London: Penguin.

Bloom, B. S., 1956. *Taxonomy of Educational Objectives: The Classification of Educational Goals. Handbook I: Cognitive Domain*. New York: David McKay.

Bohm, David, Factor, Donald and Garrett, Peter, 1991. *Dialogue*. (Working document, unpublished.)

Boje, David, 1991. Organizations as storytelling networks: a study of story performance in an office-supply firm. *Administrative Science Quarterly* 36, pp. 106–26.

Bouchikhi, H., Fiol, C. M., Gioia, D. A., Golden-Biddle, K., Hatch, M. J., Hayagreeva, H. R., Rindova, V. P., Schultz, M., Fombrun, C., Kimberley, J. R. and Thomas, J. B., 1998. The identity of organizations. In Whetten, D.A. and Godfrey, Paul C. (eds), *Identity in Organizations: Building Theory Through Conversations*. Thousand Oaks, CA: Sage, pp. 33–82.

Broekstra, Gerrit, 1998. An organization is a conversation. In Grant, David, Keenoy, Tom and Oswick, Cliff (eds), *Discourse and Organization*. London: Sage, p. 175.

Conger, J. A., 1998. The necessary art of persuasion. *Harvard Business Review*. 76(3), pp. 84–95.

Conger, J., 1991. Inspiring others: the language of leadership. *Academy of Management Executive* 5, pp. 31–45.

Conger, Jay A., 1998. *Winning 'Em Over: A New Model for Management in the Age of Persuasion*. New York: Simon & Schuster.

Conger, Jay A., and Benjamin, Beth, 1998. *Building Leaders: How Successful Companies Develop the Next Generation*. San Francisco, CA: Jossey Bass.

Conger, Jay A. and Kanungo, Rabindra N., 1998. *Charismatic Leadership In Organizations*. Thousand Oaks, CA: Sage, p. 247.

Czarniawska, Barbara, 1997. *Narrating the Organization: Dramas of Institutional Identity*. Chicago: University of Chicago Press.

DiMaggio, J. and Powell, W., 1983. The Iron Cage revisited: institutional isomorphism and collective rationality in organizations. *American Sociological Review* 48, pp. 147–69.

Eccles, Robert G. and Nohria, Nitin, 1992. *Beyond the Hype: The Essence of Management*. Boston, MA: Harvard Business Press.

Finkelstein, Sidney and Hambrick, Donald C., 1996. *Strategic Leadership: Top Executives and Their Effects on Organizations*. St Paul, MN: West.

Ford, Jeffrey, 1998. Organizational change as shifting conversations. Symposium on 'Discourse and change in organizations'. *Proceedings of the American Academy of Management*, San Diego, CA: C1–C7.

Gabriel, Y., 1998. The use of stories. In Symon, G. and Cassell, C. (eds), *Qualitative Methods and Analysis in Organizational Research*. London: Sage, pp. 135–60.

Gardner, William L. and Avolio, Bruce J., 1998. The charismatic relationship: a dramaturgical perspective. *Academy of Management Review* 23(1), pp. 32–58.

Hannan, M. T. and Freeman J., 1977. The population ecology of organizations. *American Journal of Sociology* 82, pp. 929–64.

Hatch, Mary Jo, 1997. *Organization Theory: Modern, Symbolic and Postmodern Perspectives*. Oxford: Blackwell.

Hatch, M. J. and Ehrlich, S., in press. The dialogic organization and the language of organizational change. In Roberts, Nancy (ed.), *Transformative Power of Dialogue*. Amsterdam: Elsevier.

Heron, John, 1999. *The Complete Facilitator's Handbook*. London: Kogan Page.

Jacobs, Robert W., 1994. *Real-time Strategic Change: How to Involve an Entire Organization in Fast and Far-Reaching Change*. San Francisco, CA: Berrett-Koehler.

Lieberson, S. and O'Connor, J. F., 1972. Leadership and organizational performance: a study of large corporations. *American Sociological Review* 31, pp. 117–30.

Leifer R., 1989. Understanding organizational transformation using a dissipative structures model. *Human Relations* 42(10), pp. 899–916.

Lengel, R. H. and Daft, R. L., 1988. The selection of communication media as an executive skill. *Academy of Management Executive* 2(3), pp. 225–32.

March, J. C. and March, J. G., 1977. Almost random careers – the Wisconsin superintendency, 1940–1972. *Administrative Science Quarterly* 22(3), pp. 377–409.

Perrow, Charles, 1985. *Complex Organizations: A Critical Essay*, 3rd edn. New York: McGraw-Hill.

Rogers, Carl R., 1961. *On Becoming a Person: A Therapist's View of Psychotherapy*. London: Constable.

Roth, George, 2000. Constructing conversations: lessons for learning from experience. *Organization Development Journal* 18(4), pp. 69–78.

Salancik, G. R. and Pfeffer, J., 1977. Constraints on administrative discretion: the limited influence of mayors on city budgets. *Urban Affairs Quarterly* 12, pp. 475–98.

Sonsino, Steven, 2000. Managing identity in complex organizations: towards a dynamic theory of identity based leadership in complex organizations. In McCarthy, Ian P. and Rakotobe-Joel, Thierry (eds), *Complexity and Complex Systems in Industry*. Warwick: University of Warwick, pp. 430–45.

Sonsino, Steven, 2001. The future of strategy. *Management Quarterly* 12, pp. 2–7.

Sonsino, Steven, 2002a. The leadership perspective. In Jenkins, Mark and Ambrosini, Veronique (eds), *Strategic Management: A Multiple Perspective Approach*, pp. 222–49. London: Palgrave Macmillan.

Sonsino, Steven, 2002b. Recasting Coase: a theory of the organization as a nexus of conversations. In Combes, C., Grant, D., Hardy, C., Keenoy, T., Oswick, C. and Phillips, N., *Organizational Discourse: From Micro-Utterances to Macro-Inferences*. London: KMPC.

Stacey, Ralph D., 2000. *Strategic Management and Organisational Dynamics: The Challenge of Complexity*, 3rd edn. Harlow: FT Prentice Hall.

Stacey, Ralph D., 2001. *Complex Responsive Processes in Organizations: Learning and Knowledge Creation*. London: Routledge.

Taylor, James R., 1993. *Rethinking the Theory of Organizational Communication: How to Read an Organization*. New Jersey: Ablex Publishing.

van der Heijden, Kees, 1996. *Scenarios: The Art of Strategic Conversation*. Chichester: John Wiley & Sons.

Weick, Karl E., 1995. *Sensemaking in Organizations*. Thousand Oaks, CA: Sage.

WERS, 1998. *Workplace Employee Relations Survey*. London: CEML.

THE AUTHORS

JACQUELINE MOORE

Jacqueline Moore is a senior journalist on the London *Financial Times* working on the Front-Back Newsdesk. She was launch editor and writer of the backpage FT View column and has spent 16 years on the paper, in posts from Assistant Features Editor, to Deputy Editor of the World Stock Markets page. She was launch production editor of the Business Travel Page. Before joining the *Financial Times* in 1987 she worked for technology publications including *Computer News* (IDG) and *Computer Weekly* (Reed Business Information). She was Production Editor of *Management Review* in the *Computer Weekly* portfolio.

Jacqueline co-designed and co-taught on the first Workshop & Facilitation Skills course on the MBA programme at Cranfield School of Management in 1999 and has since presented and taught on a range of workshops outside Cranfield. She was formally trained as a change consultant on a short programme at Cranfield School of Management in 1999.

Jacqueline is a former Director of the Journalism Training Centre, the only independent media communications business to win a National Training Award – 'for excellence in training' – from Michael Portillo, then Secretary of State for Education and Employment, in 1994. The business was also made Small Business of the Year in 1995 in the UK Department for Education and Employment's Enterprise Agency awards.

Her corporate clients have included Redwood Publishing, publisher of a range of magazine titles for the BBC, and Nexus Publishing, one of the UK's fastest growing media groups. She has also taught on 'Handling the media' workshops for a range of corporate clients.

Jacqueline has already started work on *Strategy Unplugged* (2004) for Palgrave Macmillan, as well as a book on corporate performance.

STEVEN SONSINO

Steven Sonsino is an award-winning tutor and writer specialising in strategic leadership and leading change. He is a Fellow of the Centre for Management Development at London Business School and is Director of the award-winning Young Professionals Programme, one of the School's flagship executive education programmes. He founded the Tomorrow's Leaders Research Group at the School in 2002.

Over the past five years Steven has taught Competitive, Corporate and International Strategy to MBA students and executives, in both the private and public sectors. He currently teaches two Masters-level programmes at Escola de Gestão do Porto in Portugal: 'Leading Negotiations' and 'Strategic Leadership'. Steven has worked extensively with Finance Directors across the UK's National Health Service, as well as with board-level executives in the private sector.

Steven's doctoral research is on the subject of leadership in complex and chaotic organisations and he is a regular speaker on the subject at conferences round the world. He is an alumnus of the International Teachers Programme 1999–2000, which was hosted at New York University.

Before joining London Business School, Steven taught leadership and strategic management at Cranfield School of Management. He was the first E-strategy Expert for the School's internet incubator. Steven undertook his MBA at Cranfield and was made Independent Student of the Year in 1998.

In addition to his teaching, consulting and research work, Steven continues to write widely; his papers have appeared recently in *Business Strategy Review* and in *People Management* among other titles. He has been a regular contributor to *Management Quarterly*, the journal of the Institute of Chartered Accountants in England and Wales, and recently completed a web-based multimedia strategy programme for the ICAEW's members as part of the *Management Quarterly* Online project. Steven writes occasionally for the London *Financial Times*.

Besides working on *Strategy Unplugged* with Jacqueline Moore, Steven is also working on *Tomorrow's Leaders* (scheduled for 2004), a book based on the work of the Tomorrow's Leaders Research Group, exploring the search for the leaders of the future. *Organizations Unplugged* (for 2005) suggests that organization development is the only sustainable competitive advantage that organizations have.